John Henry Newman

John Henry Newman

Spiritual Director 1845–1890

Peter C. Wilcox, STD

◆PICKWICK *Publications* · Eugene, Oregon

JOHN HENRY NEWMAN
Spiritual Director 1845–1890

Copyright © 2013 Peter C. Wilcox, STD. All rights reserved. Except for brief quotations in critical publications or reviews, no part of this book may be reproduced in any manner without prior written permission from the publisher. Write: Permissions, Wipf and Stock Publishers, 199 W. 8th Ave., Suite 3, Eugene, OR 97401.

Pickwick Publications
An Imprint of Wipf and Stock Publishers
199 W. 8th Ave., Suite 3
Eugene, OR 97401
www.wipfandstock.com

ISBN 13: 978-1-62032-204-8

Cataloguing-in-Publication data:

Wilcox, Peter C.

John Henry Newman : spiritual director 1845–1890 / Peter C. Wilcox, STD ; foreword by John T. Ford, CSC.

xxii + 366 pp. ; 23 cm. Includes bibliographical references.

ISBN 13: 978-1-62032-204-8

1. Newman, John Henry, 1801–1890. 2. Spiritual direction—Catholic Church. 3. Catholic Church—Doctrines. I. Ford, John T. II. Title.

BX4705 W49 2013

Manufactured in the U.S.A.

Contents

Significant Dates — viii
Foreword by John T. Ford, CSC — xi
Acknowledgments — xiii
Introduction — xv

1 A Spiritual Biography of Newman — 1
   Anglican Experiences | 3
   Roman Catholic Experiences | 14
      The Oratory Dispute | 15
      The Achilli Trial | 18
      The Catholic University | 19
      Scripture Translation | 20
      The Rambler | 21
      The Apologia | 6
      The Proposed Oxford Oratory | 28
      Vatican I | 31
      Honors | 33

2 Origins and Characteristics of Newman's Spirituality — 35
   Origins of Newman's Spirituality | 35
      Biblical | 36
      Patristics | 37
      Anglican Authors | 38
   Characteristics of Newman's Spirituality | 43
      The Unseen World | 43
      Holiness of God | 46
      Providential Guidance | 48
      Dependence on God | 49
   Relation of Theology and Spirituality | 51
      Personal Experiences as Theological Loci | 52
      Indwelling of the Holy Spirit | 54
      Centrality of Christ | 56
   Summary | 60

3   Spiritual Direction and the Providence of God   61
    The Providence of God | 64
    Achilli Trial | 68
    Submission to the Will of God | 73
    Sickness and Death | 77
    "Wounded to Heal": Trials, Trust, and Providence | 82
    Detachment and Providence: "Singleness of Mind and Purpose" | 92
    Summary | 98

4   Spiritual Direction and Faith   101
    Coming to Faith | 101
      Faith as a Gift | 102
      Faith and Certitude | 109
      Faith and Reason | 115
      Probability and Faith | 118
      Faith and Doubt | 127
      Faith and Doctrine | 131
    Growing in Faith | 135
    Summary | 138

5   Spiritual Direction and the Roman Catholic Church   142
    Newman's Conversion and the Importance of Apostolicity | 143
    Directing Others to Recognize the Church | 149
      Notes of the Church | 150
      Oracle of God and Ark of Salvation | 159
      Characteristics of Newman's Spiritual Direction | 164
    Directing Others in Particular Aspects of Church Life | 174
      Infallibility | 176
      Sacraments | 191
      Eschatology | 195
      Devotional Life and Practices | 201
    Summary | 209

6   Spiritual Direction on Vocation and Religious Life   212
    Spiritual Direction and Vocation | 214
      Nature of Oratorian Vocation | 214
      Spiritual Direction and Vocational Choice | 222
      Encouragement and Support | 227
    Spiritual Direction and Religious Life | 235
      "Santa Communita" | 235
      Building Community | 241
      Qualities of an Oratorian | 246
      Ministry of the Oratory | 250
      "Counsels" | 253
      Prayer | 260
      Penance | 266
    Summary | 268

7   Spiritual Direction and Friendship   270
       Newman's Conversion and His Friends | 271
       Friendship as Gift | 276
       Comfort of Friends | 279
       Friendship, Encouragement, and Support | 286
       "Speaking the Truth in Love" | 292
       Seeking Advice and Expressing Concern | 298
       Friendship and Trials | 302
       Sickness and Death | 308
       Fidelity and Friendship | 318
       Newman's Genius for Friendship | 327
    Summary | 330

Conclusion   333

Appendix   337
Bibliography   359

Significant Dates in Newman's life

1801	Born, February 21, Old Broad Street, London; Baptized, April 9
1808	Enrolled at Ealing School
1816	August–December: First conversion; enrolled at Trinity College, Oxford
1820	Received BA degree "under the line"
1822	April 12: Elected Fellow of Oriel College
1824	June 13: Ordained deacon of the Church of England
1825	May 29: Ordained priest of the Church of England
1828	January 5: Death of his sister, Mary; March 14: Instituted as Vicar of St. Mary's
1832	December 8: Beginning of Mediterranean voyage with Froudes
1833	July 14: Keble's Assize sermon on "National Apostasy"
1841	January 25: Published *Tract XC*
1843	September 25: Preached "The Parting of Friends" at Littlemore
1845	October 9: Received into the Roman Catholic Church by Dominic Barberi
	Finished *An Essay on the Development of Christian Doctrine*
1846	Left Littlemore for Maryvale, near Oscott
	In November, entered College of Propaganda, Rome
1847	Ordained priest on Trinity Sunday; joined Oratory of St. Philip Neri
1848	Establishes Oratory in England; admitted F. W. Faber and his companions of St. Wilfrid's to the Oratory

Significant Dates in Newman's life

1850	Newman lectured on *Certain Difficulties Felt by Anglicans in Catholic Teaching*. London Oratory established under Faber; Roman Catholic hierarchy established
1851	Newman's *Lectures on the Present Position of Catholics in England*
	Achilli sued Newman for libel; Newman invited to become rector of Catholic University in Dublin
1852	Newman lectured in Dublin on the "Scope and Nature of University Education"
	Newman found guilty in Achilli trial
1854	Newman was formally installed as Rector of the Catholic University
1857	Newman resigned as Rector of the Catholic University
1859	Newman established the Birmingham Oratory School; Newman assumed editorship of *The Rambler*; his article on "Consulting the Faithful" delated to Rome
1864	Newman published *Apologia Pro Vita Sua* issued in seven weekly installments
1865	Newman published *A Letter Addressed to the Rev. E. B. Pusey*; Manning appointed Archbishop of Westminster
1866	Newman was secretly restricted from ministering in Oxford
1867	Pope Pius IX announced the convocation of an Ecumenical Council
1869	December 8: Vatican Council I opened
1870	Newman published his *Grammar of Assent*; July 18: Vatican I approves *Pastor Aeternus* regarding papal primacy and infallibility
1874	Gladstone published *The Vatican decrees in their bearing on civil allegiance*
1875	Newman published *A Letter to the Duke of Norfolk*.
1878	Newman named the first honorary Fellow of Trinity College, Oxford;
	Pius IX died; Leo XIII elected Pope
1879	Newman made a Cardinal by Pope Leo XIII
1890	Newman died on August 11
1991	January 22: Newman declared "Venerable" by Pope John Paul II
2010	September 19: Newman beatified by Pope Benedict XVI

Foreword

JOHN HENRY NEWMAN WAS a person with extraordinary talents that resulted in an astonishing number of accomplishments in a variety of fields. Given his multifaceted interests, his writings are still highly regarded by authorities in different disciplines.[1] To people interested in Victorian literature, his *Apologia Pro Vita Sua* (1864) is a classic example of English autobiography. To educators, Newman's *The Idea of a University* (1873) is a classic statement of the importance of both a liberal education in general and theological studies in particular. To philosophers, his *An Essay in Aid of a Grammar of Assent* (1870) is a thought-provoking analysis of the nature of belief. To theologians, his *An Essay on the Development of Christian Doctrine* (1845) is the historical starting point for a reassessment of the nature of doctrine. Few authors manage to write even one classic work that has survived the test of time; Newman wrote several.

Newman's contemporaries recognized him as a commentator on current events, an historian of the early church, a translator of patristic texts, and a formidable apologist, as well as a novelist and a poet. Yet for Newman personally, all of his writings, however diverse their origin, genre, and focus, had a religious orientation; he wrote as a Christian committed to proclaiming the Gospel. At least a third of his writings—in the form of sermons, meditations, poems, prayers—were specifically written to encourage people to live a Christian life. Given the major emphasis on spirituality in both Newman's life and writings, it is nothing short of surprising that in comparison to treatments of Newman as an educator, apologist, philosopher and theologian, there has been relatively little written about Newman as a spiritual director.

Newman's spiritual advice is obviously found in his sermons, both Anglican and Roman Catholic; however, a major resource for his spiritual counsel is found in his enormous correspondence—some twenty thousand of his letters have survived and many of these letters were written in response to people

---

1. All of Newman's writings mentioned in this preface are available online at: www.newmanreader.org. Most of these writings are also available in paperback editions.

seeking his advice. While Peter Wilcox's book is primarily concerned with Newman's spiritual direction during his Roman Catholic years (1845–1890), it quickly becomes evident that Newman's spirituality as a Roman Catholic was a development of his Anglican spirituality, which was based on the Bible, the Fathers of the Church, and Anglican Divines. What also becomes evident is that people sought Newman's advice, first of all because they recognized both the seriousness of his pastoral commitment and the depth of his spiritual insight; in effect, his spiritual direction is exemplified in the choice of his cardinalatial motto—*cor ad cor loquitur*—"heart speaks to heart."

In this book, readers will meet literally dozens of people who sought Newman's spiritual direction; these people came from a wide variety of backgrounds: a few were clergy and members of religious communities; others were rich and prominent; most were middle class; a few were so obscure that the editors of Newman's *Letters and Diaries* have been unable to provide much identification. What is amazing about Newman's spiritual direction is that he was able to touch the lives of so many people from so many different strata of society. While, as readers might expect, most of Newman's correspondents were Roman Catholics, Anglicans, and Protestants, there were a few agnostics as well.

The reasons why people sought Newman's counsel were as personal as each individual. In fact, in his spiritual direction, Newman addressed the particular concerns of each person, rather than relying on a generic spirituality: his spiritual advice was tailored to each person.

Nonetheless, there are certain recurrent themes in Newman's spiritual advice—which this book has organized around five headings: Divine Providence, Faith, the Roman Catholic Church, Vocation and Religious Life, Friendship. Most readers will probably read these chapters in sequence; however, this book is written in such a way that after the introductory chapter, a reader might choose to read the chapters in order of personal interest.

Since this book includes numerous quotations of Newman's advice to particular individuals with specific questions, readers with similar concerns may have the experience of the original correspondents—that Newman was speaking personally to them. Thus, this book is not only an important academic contribution to Newman studies; this book is also a valuable contribution to the practice of spiritual direction—both for directors and directees.

John T. Ford, CSC
Professor of Theology and Religious Studies
The Catholic University of America
Washington, DC

Acknowledgments

AT THE COMPLETION OF this book, I find it difficult to adequately express my thanks to everyone who, in various ways, supported me throughout the project. I want to especially thank my mentor, John Ford, CSC, STD, for his critical observations, suggestions, guidance, and editing throughout the entire effort.

I am also most grateful to my wife, Margaret, beyond what these words can convey. Her patience, support, and encouragement were invaluable. I could never thank her enough for the countless hours she spent editing and formatting the text. And to my daughter, Colleen, thank you for your love and encouragement throughout the process.

Newman once wrote to one of his aunts: "I am quite sure it is by prayers such as yours, of those whom the world knows nothing of, that the Church is saved." I sincerely thank the many people, whom Newman would call my "thorough friends," who have supported me in the writing of this book and whose love and friendship have expressed themselves through prayer and encouragement.

Introduction

IN A SOCIETY STRONGLY influenced by science and technology, in a culture sensitive to the insights of psychology and personalist philosophy, in a Church seeking constant renewal in the spirit of the Gospel, the concern of Christians for living a spiritual life, for deepening their relationship with God and others takes on new dimensions. Spirituality is not simply an abstract area of life reserved for the elite, but rather something which touches the life of every Christian. Living a spiritual life in an active and dynamic way touches a person's fundamental attitudes and actions of life; it seeks to know how to live in order to be open to God and others.

John Henry Newman (1801–1890) was a man who sought to integrate life and holiness. He believed that the spiritual life had to be established on God's word and a strong doctrinal foundation. He did not want to separate devotion from life. From the Greek Fathers of the early church, Newman inherited a sense of the Divine Economy, and he recognized the complimentarity between the teachings of Scripture and the theological tradition of the Church. In our own times, he has rightfully been seen as a prophet of progress in various areas of theology: authority in the Church, role of the laity, ecumenism, development of doctrine, religious freedom, and Christian education.[2] During his life, he experienced misunderstanding and suspicion from his superiors for many years, but remained steadfast in his pursuit of truth and loyalty to the Church. What was the secret of his strength? By examining his life, it can be seen that his source of strength was his spiritual relationship with God.

Newman's spiritual life was fundamentally shaped as an Anglican through the Bible, by the Daily Offices and Eucharist of the Book of Common Prayer, by various English devotional writers, as well as by the personal influence of some of his contemporaries. Very early in his life, Newman was

---

2. Kelly, "Newman, Vatican I and II," 293. "Bishop Robert Dwyer described Newman as the 'absent Council Father' of Vatican II, since he was cited there more frequently than any other authority, including St. Thomas!"

Introduction

greatly impressed by Walter Mayers,[3] who continually stressed the Christian's call to holiness and the necessity of a living and genuine faith. This sense of call, coupled with his deep pastoral concern both as an Anglican and Catholic priest, led Newman to not only strive for sanctity in his own life, but constantly to encourage and direct others in their efforts.

Although Newman rejected the title of spiritual director as such, it is obvious to anyone who reads his correspondence that directing others through various facets of the Christian life is one of his dominant concerns. Surprisingly, comparatively little has been written about Newman's idea of spiritual direction. The purpose of this book is to investigate Newman's understanding of spiritual direction during his life as a Catholic (1845–1890). It examines the major areas in which Newman gave spiritual direction through an analysis of the correspondence from his Catholic years. It also explicitates those principles of Newman's own spiritual life which found expression in his direction of others. Finally, it complements previous studies on Newman's spirituality and makes available recently published materials pertaining to Newman's understanding of the spiritual life.[4]

Newman's Catholic years have been chosen for this study. It is important not only to uncover the major areas of the Christian life in which Newman gave direction, but also to trace the continuity of his direction in various areas of Christian life. Moreover, a consideration of his entire Catholic period necessarily includes the major events which affected his thinking and which could have possible implications not only for his own life, but also for his direction of others.

Newman's *Letters and Diaries* have been edited and published in a series of thirty-two volumes, embracing more than twenty thousand letters.[5] The first ten volumes deal with Newman's Anglican period; the remaining volumes, which cover his Catholic period, are the primary source for this book, and have been studied chronologically in order to determine and extract the major areas in which Newman gave spiritual direction to others, and to investigate the stages of development in his spiritual advice.

Newman himself supplied the justification for this method. Writing to his sister Jemima in 1863, he said:

---

3. There is a biographical appendix at the end of this book containing pertinent information about persons whose names appear in this book.

4. Some of the literature on Newman's spirituality is listed in the bibliography.

5. Rev. Charles Stephen Dessain of the Birmingham Oratory, who died May 31, 1976, initiated this project. With the publication of volume 32 in 2009, the twenty-two volumes of Newman's Catholic correspondence have been completed. Newman's *Letters and Diaries* will be referred to throughout this book as *LD*.

Introduction

> It has ever been a hobby of mine (unless it be a truism, not a hobby) that a man's life lies in his letters. This is why Hurrell Froude published St. Thomas A. Beckett's Letters, with nothing of his own except what was necessary for illustration or connection of parts. A much higher desideratum than interest in Biography is met by the method, (as it may be called), of Correspondence. Biographers varnish; they assign motives; they conjecture feelings; they interpret Lord Burleigh's nods; they palliate or defend. For myself, I sincerely wish to seem neither better nor worse than I am.[6]

Nine years later, after receiving a copy of John Bowden's life of Frederick Faber, Newman again stated his preference for this method: "Thank you for your copy of Fr. Faber's life. As far as I have as yet made myself acquainted with it, it seems drawn up with great skill and judgment. I am very glad you have adopted the method, which, as far as it is possible, is in my opinion the true mode of biography—I mean carrying on the course of the narrative by letters."[7]

Again, in 1872, considering the possibility of his own biography being written, he stated in a memorandum:

> I don't wish my life written—because there is so little to say. This is the case with most Lives—and in consequence the writers are forced to pad—and then readers are both disappointed at the meagerness of the composition, and angry with the padding...
>
> It may be said that, if friends do not write a life, strangers, who know nothing about me, will be sure to do it instead. I think this risk may be avoided by publishing private papers, memoranda, letters of mine, in a volume or two, with a memoir of four pages or so, to introduce them.[8]

Besides his recommendation that the use of correspondence is the best vehicle for presenting a person's life and thought, Newman provided another justification. Although he was a prolific writer, with ease and grace of expression, he noted more than once that he could only write "on call," that is to say, when some pressing question elicited his efforts. He wrote to

---

6. JHN to Mrs. John Mozley, 18 May 1863, in *LD* 20:443.

7. JHN to John Bowden, 19 June 1869, in *LD* 24:271.

8. JHN, Memorandum on Future Biography, 15 November 1872, in *LD* 26:200–201. Moreover, in considering the question of his own biography in the *Autobiographical Writings*, the editor Henry Tristram noted: "It was his settled opinion, expressed not once, but frequently, not to a single individual, but to several independently of one another, that his personal history should be narrated through the medium of his letters." Newman, *Autobiographical Writings*, 23.

Introduction

Robert Whitty in 1865 saying: "I cannot write by wishing, I can only write when power is given me to write."[9] The previous year he had explained to Canon Walker, "Then again I never can write well, without a definite *call*."[10] His letters are responses to "calls" par excellence. Various people wrote to him about many aspects of spirituality, and they elicited some of his best and clearest thinking.

Newman had a mammoth "apostolate of correspondence." When compared to his books, his opinions in a particular letter are more fragmentary, because he is responding to questions a correspondent was posing; and only rarely did he elaborate beyond it. At the same time, his range of opinions in his letters is wider than in his published works, and this fragmentary quality tends to vanish when one surveys the entire spectrum of his correspondence. A fuller vision emerges, and in the course of many years, a composite sketch of particular aspects of his spirituality emerges from his correspondence as well as the areas in which he directed others.

Today it is rather difficult to appreciate this vast quantity of correspondence in an age of computers, smart phones, and social media when so many business transactions and exchange of opinions happens almost instantaneously. The record of a person's opinions vanishes with the voice. Correspondence and memos, admittedly, continue to be useful, but people in the twenty-first century are not tied down to the written word as much as their nineteenth-century counterparts. A century ago, much more discussion and evolution of ideas unfolded through the post office; distance and separation were overcome with a stamp. People, then, were prodigious letter writers; they approached it as a literary form. Drafts and double drafts were made, copies of the autograph retained, return of letters requested. In a note to W. G. Ward, at the time of the condemnation of the *Home and Foreign Review*, Newman indicated the role of letters during a controversy. "I enclose my letter to the Bishop, and a copy of his answer, as far as it bears on my immediate subject. My letter as you will see, differs from what you saw, more by what it leaves out than by what it puts in. Do not fear I should show your letter to me to the Bishop. I wished to keep it for my own edification. However, as you seem to wish it, I have burned it."[11]

---

9. JHN to Robert Whitty, 25 September 1865, in *LD* 22:61. Newman drafted this letter but did not send it.

10. JHN to J. Walker of Scarborough, 5 August 1864, in *LD* 21:185.

11. JHN to W. G. Ward, 3 January 1863, in *LD* 20:284. In the opinion of Newman's literary executors, almost all of the Cardinal's correspondence has been tracked down. Only one instance is known of someone purposely destroying a letter of Newman's in the interest of his reputation, and even here its contents have been surmised. William Monsell, Lord Emly, burned a letter in the presence of Mr. and Mrs. Wilfrid Ward which

Introduction

Other reasons recommend the use of Newman's correspondence. Foremost is the candor one finds there. When he was writing to friends, he could afford to speak bluntly and express opinions unguardedly. When writing books, he was always conscious of writing "under the lash," knowing that antagonists would scrutinize every turn of phrase. As he wrote to Henry Wilberforce in 1868, he explained: "I know any how, that, however honest are my thoughts, and earnest my endeavours to keep rigidly within the lines of Catholic doctrine, every word I publish will be malevolently scrutinized, and every expression which can possibly be perverted sent straight to Rome,— that I shall be fighting *under the lash*, which does not tend to produce vigorous efforts in the battle or to inspire either courage or presence of mind."[12] His books, then, are carefully nuanced, and while this has great advantages certainly, there is also much to be said for the frankness of a letter written to a friend. "No one can write without making mistakes—I don't doubt I have made some, though I hope not great ones. If a man waited till he could write without any mistakes, he would not write at all. There is in every man's work matter which may be taken up for hostile criticism, if readers are so minded. But I have done my best, and have all along trusted I should be judged by my good intention and the substance of what I have written, and not by what comes of human infirmity and imperfection."[13]

Another reason why Newman's letters are important is because there is an added richness to his thought due to the diversity of persons with whom he corresponded. Newman wrote letters to leading political figures, high ecclesiastics, intellectuals, prominent Europeans. People like Faber and Manning thought he was isolating himself in a midland town. But the correspondence, to and from Birmingham, reflected all the currents of theological thought. One special group must be mentioned, the laity. After reading through thousands of his letters, one becomes acutely aware of the prominence the laity held in Newman's mind and of the influence he exercised in their lives. When he was attacked by E. R. Martin in the *Weekly Register* as being untrusted in Rome, several hundred leading laymen of England promptly signed a petition saying that every blow touching Newman inflicted a wound on the English Church.[14] Newman championed the laity, and through his correspondence he was never out of contact with them. Accordingly, Newman was constantly forced to apply his theology and spiri-

---

detailed Newman's involvement in the *Rambler* affair. This incident, and the whole task of assembling Newman's correspondence, is recounted by Dessain in the introduction to the multivolume series; See *LD* 11:xv–xxiii.

12. JHN to Henry Wilberforce, 12 August 1868, in *LD* 24:120.
13. JHN to Unknown Correspondent, 13 March 1866, in *LD* 22:181.
14. Trevor, *Newman: Light*, 39.

Introduction

tuality to the real world—to the lives of individual people. For example, the "common person" is prominent in his letters. Just after the First Vatican Council (1869–1870), letters poured in from ordinary people, confused by the recent events in Rome. With delicate pastoral understanding, Newman directed them to grasp the meaning and implications of infallibility.

Newman's letters, besides their candor and richness, also fill lacunae. Since Newman wrote his books and lectures "on call," if there was no call, he was *publicly* silent. The basis for his judging "a call," to be present rested not only on the importance of the issue; it also depended on the expedience and prudence of coming out in print. This sometimes caused great consternation to friends who wished him to speak out. For example, after a long silence following the *Rambler* incident,[15] he wrote to one close friend at the time of the *Apologia*: "As to my writing more, speaking in confidence, I do not know how to do it. One cannot speak ten words without ten objections being made to each."[16] It was during publication gaps like this, however, that the letters prove of such value. Although he might be *publicly* silent, in private correspondence he expressed himself often and eloquently. The letters offer a wide range of commentary when books and public lectures are lacking. Most of all, one comes closer to the *real* man in the letters. What Newman called the "charm of reality" was one of the reasons why he liked the early Fathers:

> Letters always have the charm of reality. I have before now given this as the reason why I like the early Fathers more than the Medieval Saints viz: because we have the letters of the former. I seem to know St. Chrysostom or St. Jerome in a way in which I never can know St. Thomas Aquinas – and St. Thomas of Canterbury (himself medieval) on account of his letters as I never

---

15. The reasons for Newman's silence from 1859 to 1864 were most serious. However, the following letter, written in a light vein to fellow Oratorian William Neville, explains in a humorous way why he is not writing: "You may send the following 'Heads of a Discourse' to Patterson.

For Patterson

Seven Reasons for not writing more books.

I do no write

Because, in matters of controversy, I am a miles emeritus, rude donatus.

Because no one serves on Parliamentary Committees after he is 60.

Because Rigaud's steam engine which was hard to start, was hard to stop.

Because Hannibal's elephants never could learn the goose step.

Because Garibaldi's chaplains in ordinary never do write.

Because books that do not sell do not pay the printing.

Because just now I am teaching little boys nonsense verses." See JHN to William Neville, 27 March 1862, in *LD* 20:178.

16. JHN to James Hope-Scott, 6 July 1864, in *LD* 21:144.

can know St. Pius Vth. There is something always to be gained by the sight of a religious man, as he is—whether he be in partial error, or on the other hand a Doctor of the Church.[17]

Newman always insisted that it is the whole person who thinks, not just an intellect. His letters show the moods in which he was thinking as well as portray his immediate reaction to issues, as contrasted with more reflective reactions which slowly evolved. While much of the profit drawn from this approach to the letters is of interest to the biographer, it is not without value for discovering Newman the theologian and spiritual director.

This last consideration suggested what is both an asset and a limitation to a "method of correspondence." The asset is that Newman's thinking is seen *within* concrete issues. In one sense, his spirituality, and therefore his spiritual direction has to be extracted from the concrete circumstances of his letters. It is not present *in modo theologico* (as a theological method). People are present. Events are present. Newman was seen looking at what was happening, and he theologized about the events. In uncovering his spiritual direction, it has been necessary to consider all his letters and extract the principles of spirituality operative behind them. There are partial views in each letter. The asset is that the correspondence makes one aware of the problem he was addressing. The concreteness of the letters brings a clarity; the problems were the problems of *people*. Each letter to Newman was "a call." Each response was from a pastor first, a theologian second.

The limitation in considering his letters is their sheer volume. The letters contain no systematic presentation of Newman's spiritual direction. However, through reading his correspondence, certain themes emerge as constant areas of the Christian life in which Newman consistently directed others.

It is the purpose of this book to delineate the spiritual direction of Newman during his Roman Catholic years as contained in his personal correspondence. Believing that one's spiritual direction is based on one's own perception of spirituality, the first two chapters are foundational in nature. There are many fine biographies of Newman, and rather than simply repeat what is contained there, the first chapter in this book hopes to build on these by exploring the various factors which contributed to the development of Newman's spiritual life. Seeing how he reacted to and was influenced by certain critical events is important because these show how he attempted to integrate his understanding of spirituality with life. Because Newman entered the Roman Catholic Church when he was forty-four years old, after serving as an Anglican priest for twenty years, his spiritual life and theological outlook had already been largely determined. Accordingly, chapter 2 will

17. JHN to Mrs. Sconce, 15 October 1865, in *LD* 22:73–74.

investigate the origins and characteristics of Newman's spirituality, along with his understanding of its relationship to theology.

The five core chapters examine the major areas of the Christian life in which Newman directed others. Because of certain experiences, Newman became rooted in the belief of the Providence of God. Chapter 3, then, investigates this unifying aspect of his own spiritual life, and the way that this belief constantly found expression in his direction of others. Faith is at the heart of spiritual direction. In fact, the way one understands faith implicitly underlies the way one would direct another; accordingly, chapter 4 explores Newman's understanding of faith and the methods he employed to help others receive this gift and to grow in their faith. Chapter 5 treats the way that Newman directed others to recognize the Catholic Church; from a theological perspective, Newman's conversion was an ecclesiological decision, and while he never wrote a systematic ecclesiology, ideas on the Church permeate his thought and were the bulwark of much of his spiritual direction. His own conversion placed him in a unique position to direct others in understanding both the nature of the Church and many facets of Church life.

It would be difficult to exaggerate the importance of Newman's vocation as an Oratorian, which provided the framework for the rest of his long life and was the source of some of his cruelest trials. Since it was through the Oratory that his understanding of religious life deepened, chapter 6 investigates Newman's thinking and direction of others concerning vocation and religious life. Finally, chapter 7 on friendship offers a unique opportunity to see the humanness of Newman. His personal correspondence portrays him not merely as a writer, a person to be admired, and a religious leader, but simply as a human being with human needs. It is from his letters that one can see the importance of friendship in Newman's spiritual development and the part that it played in his spiritual direction.

In each chapter, the focus is twofold; first, content—what did Newman believe about a particular issue; and second, method—how did he direct others? To avoid Newman's own stricture about a biographer "varnishing" one's subject, an attempt has been made to allow Newman to speak for himself as much as possible. This is important in view of the fact that this book is intended to make available to others a wealth of Newman materials on spirituality, many of which have not previously been examined. Finally, this approach provides Newman with the opportunity of implementing what he told W. G. Ward was the "motive-cause" for all his writing: "the sight of a truth and the desire to show it to others."[18]

---

18. JHN to W. G. Ward, 15 March 1862, in *LD* 20:169.

1

A Spiritual Biography of Newman

"Holiness before peace"[1]

"LET A PERSON . . . look back upon his past life, and he will find how critical were moments and acts, which at the time seemed the most indifferent; as for instance, the school he was sent to as a child, the occasion of his falling in with those persons who have most benefited him, the accidents which determined his calling or prospects whatever they were. God's hand is ever over His own, and He leads them forward by a way they know not of."[2]

From the thoughts and events of the past, an individual lives in the present and approaches the future. To understand John Henry Newman, it is important to study those people and events that helped to shape his life and affected his view of life. This chapter will explore the various factors which contributed to the development of his spiritual life in his early years. "John Henry Newman, the subject of this memoir, was born in Old Broad Street in the City of London on the 21st of February 1801, and was baptized in the Church of St. Bennet Fink on April 9th of the same year. His father was a London banker, whose family came from Cambridgeshire. His mother was of a French Protestant family, who left France for this country on the revocation of the Edict of Nantes."[3]

These are the beginning words of Newman's autobiographical memoir, which he began writing on June 13, 1874. He was the eldest of six children,

---

1 Newman, *Apologia*, 17. These sayings were attributed to Thomas Scott, who had a great influence on Newman in his early life.

2. Newman, "Christ Manifested in Remembrance," in *Parochial and Plain Sermons*, 4:261.

3. Newman, *Autobiographical Writings*, 29.

whom his parents endeavored to raise according to the Anglican piety of their day. Attendance at church services twice on Sunday, respect for the Prayer Book, daily reading from sacred Scripture, and recitation of the psalms were considered the ideal. Later in life, Newman acknowledged the benefits and limitations of his early religious upbringing: "I was brought up from a child to take delight in reading the Bible; but I had no formed religious convictions till I was fifteen. Of course I had a perfect knowledge of my Catechism."[4]

Newman was reared in the Church of England. In the first half of the nineteenth century, there were three major parties within this Church: the High Church or Orthodox party, the Liberals, and the Evangelicals. Newman's spiritual life was influenced by his association with all three parties within the Church of England. The High Church party, although in the minority and the least influential, sought to be faithful to the traditional faith. Their aim was twofold: to preserve the unity of the church along with the desire to make it a national church. Although there was very little life in this party at the beginning of the century, new life was to be given to the High Church party in the 1830s.

The Liberal party was comprised of people who regarded the Church as a kind of government department. For them, organized religion was chiefly useful for preserving morals and supporting venerable institutions; it was the cement of the entire social structure. At Oriel College resided a group of distinguished liberals headed by Edward Copleston and Richard Whately; although Newman respected these men and was initially impressed by them, he eventually found himself in basic disagreement with their principles.

The most powerful of these three schools of thought during the first three decades of the nineteenth century were the Evangelicals. Originating in the eighteenth century, the party had points of contact with the Methodist movement, but remained within the Church of England. Active in missionary work and social reform, Evangelicals emphasized personal conversion and salvation by faith, and upheld the importance of preaching and the sole authority of Scripture. By their zeal and diligence, they had much to do with the general awakening of the Church prior to the Tractarian movement. The Evangelicals emphasized the need for devotion and reinforced a hunger for holiness which greatly influenced Newman and the other leaders of the Tractarian movement. In fact, the Tractarians were in a great measure recruited from Evangelicals.

Although Newman wrote that he had been converted to a spiritual life by evangelical teaching, he never considered himself a genuine Evangelical.

---

4. Newman, *Apologia*, 14.

Yet his appreciation for the lasting contribution of Evangelicalism to his own spirituality is evident in the following reflection of 1887:

> I will not close our correspondence without testifying my simple love and adhesion to the Catholic Roman Church—not that I think you doubt this—and did I wish to give you a reason for this full and absolute devotion, what should, what can I say, but that those great and burning truths which I learned when a boy from Evangelical teaching, I have found impressed upon my heart with fresh and ever increasing force by the Holy Roman Church? That Church has added to the simple Evangelicalism of my first teachers, but it has obscured, diluted, enfeebled, nothing of it—on the contrary, I have found a power, a resource, a comfort, a consolation in our Lord's divinity and atonement, in His Real Presence, in communion in His Divine and Human Person which all good Catholics indeed have, but which Evangelical Christians have but faintly.[5]

Anglican Experiences

Insofar as faith is realized in personal experiences, it is not surprising that the evolution of Newman's spirituality can be traced through a number of critical events in his life. The first of these was his adolescent "conversion experience." As Newman recalled in a letter to John Keble in 1844, "When I was a boy of fifteen, and living a life of sin, with a very dark conscience and a very profane spirit, [God] mercifully touched my heart; and, with innumerable sins, yet I have not forsaken Him that time, nor He me."[6] In December 1859, he wrote in his journal:

> I know perfectly well, and thankfully confess to Thee, O my God, that Thy wonderful grace turned me right round when I was more like a devil than a wicked boy, at the age of fifteen, and gave me what by Thy continual aids I never lost. Thou didst change my heart and in part my whole mental complexion at that time, and I never should have had the thought of such prayers, as those which I have been speaking of above, but for that great work of Thine in my boyhood.[7]

---

5. JHN to George T. Edwards, 24 February 1887, in *LD* 31:189.

6. Newman, *Correspondence*, 314. Bracketed and parenthetical information within quotations here and throughout are in the original, unless otherwise noted.

7. Newman, *Autobiographical Writings*, 250. Similarly, in 1863 he told William Brownlow: "I should be contradicting my own individuality and personality, if I was

John Henry Newman

In March 1816, a financial crisis arose for Newman's family when his father's bank failed. Mr. Newman insisted that all the depositors were to be paid. The house on Southampton Street was sold, and by autumn Mr. Newman had settled his family at Aton in Hampshire and was trying to manage a brewery there. Due to these circumstances, John and his brothers remained at boarding school during that summer. In addition to being away from home, John was struck with a severe illness.[8] In his loneliness that summer, he was befriended by the classics tutor, Rev. Walter Mayers, who encouraged him to read Evangelical theologians; this reading undoubtedly helped to pave the way for his early conversion experience. Newman credited Mayers' conversations and sermons for being "the human means of this beginning of divine faith in me."[9] In his *Apologia*, Newman characterized this conversion experience as a "great change of thought" which occurred during the autumn of 1816.[10] He fell under the influence of a definite creed, and received into his intellect the impressions of dogma which would never subsequently be effaced or obscured.

Although Newman later denied that he had ever been a genuine Evangelical, discussion continues on whether his conversion was in the Evangelical tradition. For example, John Linnan has maintained: "Newman from his conversion till 1826 was a convinced Evangelical."[11] Louis Bouyer, on the other hand, claimed that it is "quite clear that his was no conversion after the

---

not as sure that God changed me altogether when I was a boy of fifteen, as I am of the existence of any particular creation of grace, of any actual divine working, of any given Saint, of this or that supernatural deed, in the Catholic Church. I am more sure that God gave me great opportunities of loving Him then, than that St. Ignatius was a true Martyr, or that St. Augustine is a Doctor of the Church." JHN to William Brownlow, 25 October 1863, in *LD* 20:543. In 1885, when Newman was corresponding with Anne Mozley concerning the publication of a memoir after his death, he again reflected on the importance of this conversion experience: "I am rather perplexed what to send you—whether to begin with my school time or with 1816. Of course I cannot myself be the judge of myself, but, speaking with this reserve, I should say that it is difficult to realize or imagine the identity of the boy before and after August 1816, as the memoranda, still undestroyed, describe him. I can look back at the end of 70 years as if on another person." JHN to Anne Mozley, 19 February 1885, in *LD* 31:31.

8. Many years later, in 1869, Newman mentioned the impact of this illness on his spiritual life: "The first keen, terrible one, when I was a boy of 15, and it made me a Christian—with experiences before and after, awful, and known only to God." Newman, *Autographical Writings*, 268.

9. Newman, *Apologia*, 16.

10. In his *Autobiographical Writings*, 181, Newman noted the dates of his great change of thought: "The first or last days of the half year of my conversion, August 1 and December 21, 1816."

11. Linnan, "Evangelical Background," 558.

Evangelical pattern."[12] C. S. Dessain described Newman's first conversion as "the wholehearted acceptance of the Christian Faith in the purest form then available to him."[13] Whatever its nature, this conversion gave direction to the rest of Newman's life.

Newman was more certain of his inward conversion than the fact that he had hands and feet. He temporarily (ca. 1816–1822) appropriated the doctrine of final perseverance from his reading of a work by an Evangelical theologian, William Romaine (1714–1795): "I believe that it [sense of election to eternal glory] had some influence on my opinions, in the direction of those childish imaginations which I have already mentioned, viz. in isolating me from the objects which surrounded me, in confirming me in my mistrust of the reality of material phenomena, and making me rest in the thought of two and two only absolute and luminously self-evident beings, myself and my Creator."[14]

At the time of his first conversion, Newman also became convinced that God willed him to lead a single life.[15] He called it "a deep imagination"—indicating that it was neither a mere fancy nor a rational decision, but something rising from the depth of the self beyond conscious awareness. Newman felt called to a total dedication to God's service.

In 1816, after his conversion experience, Newman matriculated at Trinity College, although he did not actually take up residence until the following June. While he was certainly aware of his intellectual abilities, he seemed particularly sensitive to the dangers of intellectual pride.[16] His first year at Oxford ended happily; he obtained a college scholarship. With the taste of academic success, he became less eager to receive Anglican Orders and more ambitious for a career as a lawyer. As he struggled to balance his vocational plans with his desire to be resigned to God's will, Newman prayed that he not be given fame or learning "if the price be transgression in consequence."[17]

12. Bouyer, *Newman*, 20.

13. Dessain, "Newman's First Conversion," 51, agreed with Newman's later statement that his conversion was not truly Evangelical.

14. Newman, *Apologia*, 16. This famous phrase provides an insight into Newman's spiritual life at the time.

15. Ibid., 19.

16. For example, after his prayer of thanksgiving to the Lord for having given him "some abilities" and having supplied him with excellent tutors, he prayed in April 1817: "If I have any abilities, if I ever did a good Action, to thee be ascribed the glory! Not unto me, O Lord! Not unto me but unto Thy Name, be the Praise." Later that same year he prayed again: "Let me attend and apply to my studies but let me have thy glory in view as the end of all my pursuits." Ivory, "Doctrine," 12.

17. Newman, *Autobiographical Writings*, 159. "I will accept of none of these, without

Three months prior to the examinations for his degree, John wrote to his brother Francis: "It is my daily and I hope heartfelt prayer, that I may not get any honours here, if they are to be the least cause of sin to me."[18] On the eve of his examination he became even more intense and introspective, as a letter to Walter Mayers indicates:

> I fear much more from failure than I hope from success. Still may I continue to pray "Give me no honours here if they are to be the slightest cause of sin to my soul." But, while saying this, I often find that I am acting the part of a very hypocrite; I am buoyed up with the secret idea that, by thus leaving the event in the hands of God, when I pray, He may be induced, as a reward for so proper a spirit, to grant me my desire. Thus my prayer is a mockery.[19]

Summoned for his examinations a day earlier than expected, Newman broke down completely and placed "below the line"; that is, he just managed to obtain his degree. On December 1, 1820, he wrote to his father: "It is all over, and I have not succeeded. The pain it gives me to be obliged to inform you and my mother of it, I cannot express."[20] Yet he accepted his situation with a certain calm: "I will not attempt to describe what I have gone through, but it is past away, and I feel quite lightened of a load."[21] In response to his mother's note of comfort, he replied: "I am sure success could not have made me happier than I am at present.... Very much I *have* gone through, but the clouds have passed away.... Since I have done my part I have gained what is good."[22]

After his failure, Newman gave up his plan to become a lawyer; he entered his decision in his diary on January 11, 1822: "My father this evening said I ought to make up my mind what I was to be ... so I chose; and determined on the Church. Thank God, this is what I have prayed for."[23]

His journal also indicates that he experienced a certain aridity in his prayer life, although he persevered in his devotional exercises, which were occasionally relieved by spiritual consolations. For example, on June 1, 1821, he recorded a dream in which a spirit came to him and discoursed so wonderfully about the other world that he instantly fell on his knees, "overcome

---

bargaining that sin is not included in the gift."

18. Ibid., 159. He asks his brother to pray for him in the same way.
19. Ward, *Young Mr. Newman*, 52.
20. Newman, *Autobiographical Writings*, 48. By this time, the Newman family was in straightened circumstances, so that his success was also financially important.
21. Ibid., 48.
22. Ibid., 49.
23. Ibid., 180.

with gratitude to God for so kind a message."[24] His journal recorded not only various confessions of sinfulness but also a paternal warning: "Have a guard. You are encouraging a nervousness and morbid sensibility, and irritability, which may be very serious."[25] Newman reflected on his father's admonition: "O God, grant me to pray earnestly against any delusive heat, or fanatic fancy, or proud imagination or fancied superiority, or uncharitable zeal. Make me and keep me humble and teachable, modest. I have sadly neglected till lately to pray against fanaticism, spiritual pride, etc. How good is God to give me the assurance of hope."[26]

Newman soon found his scholarly ambitions resurging; he decided to stand for a fellowship at Oriel College, which at that time enjoyed the highest intellectual reputation at Oxford. During the week of examinations for the Oriel Fellowship, Newman recorded on April 9, 1822: "This morning I was very, very nervous, and I prayed earnestly for strength, and God gave it to me most wonderfully."[27] On April 12 he wrote the simple entry: "I have this morning been elected Fellow of Oriel. Thank God, thank God."[28] Newman always treasured this event; many years later he wrote to Mrs. J. W. Bowden: "It is this day 27 years that I was elected Fellow of Oriel. . . . This day was quite a turning point in my life—and, humanly speaking, I should never have been a Catholic but for God's Providence to me upon it."[29] With this success, his circumstances radically changed; in a letter to his aunt, he attributed his success to Divine Providence: "A month ago, everything was uncertain and dark as to my future prospects. I seemed to have no hopes in the University. I had few friends, no reputation, no provision for the morrow. . . . Yet by that Heavenly Arm before which the most difficult things are as nothing, I was in an instant secured in comfort and tranquility. He rolled away every barrier, He dispelled every cloud."[30]

Newman's Oriel Fellowship brought him into contact with several people who greatly impacted his spiritual growth. In his *Apologia*, Newman acknowledged his debt to the Oriel Fellows for his religious development. Richard Whately (1787–1863), afterwards Archbishop of Dublin, taught him the existence of the Church "as a divine appointment, and as a substantive visible body, independent of the State, and endowed with rights,

24. Ibid., 166–67.
25. Ibid., 179.
26. Ibid., 179–80.
27. Ibid., 185.
28. Ibid., 186.
29. JHN to Mrs. J. W. Bowden, 12 April 1849, in *LD* 13:108.
30. Bouyer, *Newman*, 57.

prerogatives, and powers of its own."[31] The principle of the sacred independence of the Church was to become one of the most prominent features of the Tractarian movement. Although later disagreeing with Whately's liberal principles, Newman acknowledged: "While I was still awkward and timid in 1822, he took me by the hand, and acted towards me the part of a gentle and encouraging instructor. He, emphatically, opened my mind, and taught me to think and to use my reason."[32]

In Edward Hawkins (1789–1882), the young Newman found a kind and competent advisor during the long vacation of 1824. Newman submitted his sermons to Hawkins for critique. At this time, Newman tended to classify people sharply as either converted or unconverted; Hawkins helped him to understand that there are degrees in religious and moral excellence. Hawkins also gave Newman a copy of John B. Sumner's *Apostolical Preaching*, the book which eventually led Newman to abandon the Evangelical position and to accept the doctrine of Baptismal Regeneration. Hawkins also introduced Newman to the doctrine of Tradition.

It was also at Oriel that Newman became friends with John Keble, Edward Pusey and Richard Hurrell Froude, who became the "coleaders" of the Oxford Movement. In his *Apologia*, Newman indicated how he was influenced by Keble's religious teaching in *The Christian Year*: "The first of these was what may be called, in a large sense of the word, the Sacramental system; that is, the doctrine that material phenomena are both the types and the instruments of real things unseen,—a doctrine, which embraces in its fullness, not only what Anglicans, as well as Catholics, believe about the Sacraments properly so called; but also the article of 'the Communion of Saints'; and likewise the Mysteries of the Faith."[33] The second influence was the acceptance of Butler's teaching that "probability is the guide of life." While some considered "probability" as destructive of absolute certainty by calling every conclusion into doubt and resolving truth into an opinion, Newman "considered that Mr. Keble met this difficulty by ascribing the firmness of assent which we give to religious doctrine, not to the probabilities which introduced it, but to the living power of faith and love which accepted it."[34]

Edward Pusey (1800–1882), was elected a Fellow of Oriel the year after Newman. Although Newman's evangelical principles clashed with Pusey's High Church theology, their friendship gradually blossomed. Perhaps, the most lasting influence on Newman came through Pusey's encouragement

---

31. Newman, *Autobiographical Writings*, 69.
32. Newman, *Apologia*, 22.
33. Ibid., 27.
34. Ibid., 28.

to investigate the Fathers of the Church. Pusey's own contributions to the Tractarian Movement provided significant support and recognition to that movement because of his reputation for scholarship.

Richard Hurrell Froude (1803–1836), a pupil of Keble, became one of Newman's closest friends. Newman wrote that it was difficult to enumerate the precise additions to his theological creed which he derived from Froude. "He taught me to look with admiration towards the Church of Rome, and in the same degree to dislike the Reformation. He fixed deep in me the idea of devotion to the Blessed Virgin, and he led me gradually to believe in the Real Presence."[35] After Froude's death, when asked to choose one of Froude's books as a remembrance, Newman chose the Roman Breviary, which soon had a place in his prayer life as an Anglican.

With the approach of his ordination to the diaconate, Newman incorporated the practice of fasting into his spiritual life. He prayed to be made an instrument of God and was very conscious of having "the responsibility of souls" as the life-long task of his new office. On Sunday, June 13, 1824, he was ordained deacon by Dr. Legge, Bishop of Oxford.[36] The following year, on May 29, 1825, Newman was ordained priest in the Church of England. It was a calmer occasion than the diaconate which for him had represented his break with the secular world.

In January 1826, Newman became a college tutor, and in the autumn of 1827 he was appointed a University Examiner. Another stage in Newman's spiritual odyssey began; in his *Apologia*, he later appraised his state of mind: "The truth is, I was beginning to prefer intellectual excellence to moral; I was rudely awakened from my dream at the end of 1827 by two great blows—illness and bereavement."[37] The sudden death of his beloved sister Mary played an important role in the development of his spiritual life because it revived in him the sense of the unseen world, a world not separated from the world we see, but visible through it and beyond it.[38]

---

35. Ibid., 33.

36. Newman, *Autobiographical Writings*, 200, expressed his feelings about his ordination. "It is over. I am thine, O Lord; I seem quite dizzy, and cannot altogether believe and understand it. At first, after the hands were laid on me, my heart shuddered within me; the words 'for ever' are so terrible. It was hardly a godly feeling which made me feel melancholy at the idea of giving up all for God. At times indeed my heart burnt within me, particularly during the singing of the *Veni Creator*. Yet Lord, I ask not for comfort in comparison of sanctification. . . . I feel as a man thrown suddenly into deep water."

37. Newman, *Apologia*, 24. In 1869, Newman, *Autographical Writings*, 268, reflected about his illness: "My second, not painful, but tedious and shattering was that which I had in 1827 when I was one of the Examining Masters, and it too broke me off from an incipient liberalism."

38. See Mozley, *Letters*, 1:184, a letter written to his sister Jemima on May 10, 1828.

After Mary's death, because of a conflict with Provost Hawkins about their tutorial duties, he and Richard Froude were gradually relieved of their tutorial positions.[39] This allowed Newman more time for his sermons at St. Mary's, and for work on his first book, *The Arians of the Fourth Century*, which was ready for the publishers in July 1832.

Newman worked so unrelentingly on this book that his health suffered. He was easily persuaded to accompany Froude, who was suffering from tuberculosis, and his father on a cruise to the Mediterranean in December. When the Froudes went back to England from Rome, Newman returned to Sicily in April 1833. During this sojourn in Sicily, he fell deathly sick, but kept repeating, "I shall not die, for I have not sinned against the light." This experience had considerable impact on the development of his spiritual life. The thought of Divine Providence and surrender to the will of God characterized his reflections. He was confident that he would not die because God had some work of great importance for him in England. He experienced a deep sense of sinfulness, especially concerning self-will. Yet there was a certain peace which accompanied his surrender to the will of God.[40]

Newman later associated his three illnesses with three spiritual crises in his life. The first, when he was fifteen, "made him a Christian," by turning him away from skepticism; the second checked him, at twenty-six, when he

---

"Dear Mary seems embodied in every tree and hid behind every hill. What a veil and curtain this world of sense is. Beautiful, but still a veil." Over fifty years later, Newman wrote to Miss Giberne, now Sister Pia, 5 January 1882, in *LD* 30:48, about his love for his sister Mary. "This is the anniversary of my dear Mary's death in 1828, an age ago; but she is fresh in my memory and as dear to my heart, as if it were yesterday, and often I cannot mention her name without tears coming into my eyes." Four years later, he again referred to her death in a letter to Lord Blachford, 5 October 1886, in *LD* 31:167. See also his poem, "Consolations in Bereavement," written shortly after Mary's death in *Verses*, 26–28.

39. The Provost of Oriel, Edward Hawkins, disliked the reforms Newman was introducing into the tutorial system. Previously, tutors had simply delivered lectures, and if any undergraduate wanted individual attention, he had to pay for it. Newman thought such private supervision was what the tutors were already paid to do; he also thought they had a duty to take a personal interest in the young men—a pastoral care. Hawkins resolved the disagreement by assigning no more pupils to Newman and to the other tutors who agreed with him. Trevor, *Newman's Journey*, 41–42. Recalling how he understood his role as tutor in a pastoral sense, decades later, he mentioned to George Edwards, 25 February 1886, in *LD* 31:119: "And I know that before I became Tutor I resolved with God's help to resign the office if I could not make it a pastoral one, and that for this reason I did in the event actually resign it."

40. During his return voyage, he expressed his new spiritual growth in an intensely personal prayer which was to become his most famous poem, "The Pillar of the Cloud," better known by its opening words, "Lead, kindly light," in *Verses*, 152–53, written at sea, June 16, 1833.

was beginning to prefer intellectual excellence to moral; and the third acted as a purge for his self-will, forcing him to realize his own creatureliness as he lay helpless, struck down at the height of his powers, alone in the hands of strangers in a foreign country.

When Newman left England in December 1832, he was in a state of perplexity about his future; when he returned to Oxford in July 1833, he was a man with a mission—a mission to save the Church of England from the perils that encompassed her. Newman reached his mother's house near Littlemore on July 9, 1833. On July 14, Keble came to Oxford and preached from the pulpit at St. Mary's the Assize Sermon on "National Apostasy," which Newman considered the beginning of the Oxford Movement.[41]

The Oxford Movement basically began as an effort to defend the independence of the Church from the control of the State. Newman suggested to Keble and Froude an informal association to publish *Tracts for the Times* in defense of the Church's independence. Through the *Tracts* and other writings of its leaders, the Oxford Movement gradually attracted national attention. During the next half-dozen years, Newman's influence increased. As Gladstone later recalled (March 13, 1879): "I do not believe that there has been anything like his influence in Oxford, when it was at its height, since Abelard lectured in Paris. I myself, in my undergraduate days, saw just the commencement of it. It was beginning to be the custom to go and hear him on Sunday afternoon at St. Mary's."[42] Newman echoed the same words in the *Apologia*: "In the spring of 1839 my position in the Anglican Church was at its height. I had supreme confidence in my controversial *status*, and I had a great and still growing success in recommending it to others."[43]

During the long vacation of 1839, Newman was studying the history of the Church in the fifth century. One result of these studies was that his view of the Anglican Church as the *Via Media* between Protestantism and Roman Catholicism began to disintegrate. Newman's study of the Council of Chalcedon (451) indicated three parties: the Roman party led by Pope Leo the Great which had condemned Eutyches; the extreme Monophysites; in the middle however, a moderate Monophysite party emerged, claiming to reject Eutyches without fully accepting the decisions of the Council of Chalcedon.

---

41. Newman, *Autographical Writings*, 119. See also Dessain, *John Henry Newman*, 34. The immediate occasion of Keble's protest was the abolition of a number of unneeded Protestant bishoprics and parishes in Catholic Ireland by Parliament; in effect, the State, was interfering with the successors of the apostles.

42. Sir Mounstuart Duff, *Notes from a Diary, 1873–1881*, 2:121, as cited by Dessain, *John Henry Newman*, 43.

43. Newman, *Apologia*, 81.

John Henry Newman

"Rome was where she now is; and the Protestants were the Eutychians."[44] To Newman, it seemed that Anglicans were in the same position as the moderate Monophysites; it was difficult then to consider them heretics without saying the same thing about Anglicans; similarly, it was difficult to condemn the sixteenth-century popes and the Council of Trent without also condemning those of the fifth century and the Council of Chalcedon.

This upsetting analogy was followed almost immediately by another. In September 1839, Newman read an article on the Anglican claim to apostolical succession in the *Dublin Review* by Nicholas Wiseman, then Rector of the English College at Rome. Newman was not particularly bothered by the parallel Wiseman drew between schismatic Donatists in North Africa at the time of Augustine and Anglicans; but he was struck by Augustine's way of deciding the controversy, his appeal to the general consent of Christians. Newman later described graphically the effect upon him of this double shock. "He who has seen a ghost cannot be as if he has never seen it. The heavens had opened and closed again. The thought for the moment had been, 'The Church of Rome will be found right after all'; and then it had vanished. My old conviction remained as before."[45]

Until the summer of 1841, all had been well; then as Newman began translating the treatises of St. Athanasius against Arius, suddenly the history of the Arians and the semi-Arians appeared in a new light. The example of the Monophysites was repeated. The Arians were like the Protestants, the semi-Arians followed a *Via Media* like Anglicans; and again "Rome now was what it was then." The ghost had come a second time.[46]

On February 27, 1841, Newman published Tract 90, his last and most famous *Tract for the Times*. Writing it with the intention of keeping within the Anglican Church many who were beginning to move towards Rome, Tract 90 aimed at showing that the 39 Articles (the official doctrinal confession of the Anglican Church) did not necessarily contradict Catholic doctrine, and so could be accepted by those who believed the Catholic truths as expounded by the Tractarians. Tract 90 was a severe shock, because many Anglicans regarded the 39 Articles as a bulwark of Protestantism. Reaction was swift. At first an agreement was reached that the Anglican bishops would not condemn Tract 90 as long as no more tracts were published. However, this agreement was broken by individual bishops who spoke out against it.

It soon became clear to Newman that his position in the Church of England was untenable. A further blow in the autumn of 1841 was the

---

44. Ibid., 96.
45. Ibid., 99.
46. Ibid., 114–15.

establishment of a bishopric in Jerusalem that was jointly sponsored by the Church of England and the Evangelical Church of Prussia. At the same time that Newman was being denounced for moving closer to Rome, the Anglican Church was officially moving towards Protestantism; moreover, the establishment of an Anglo-Prussian bishopric in Eastern territory directly contradicted the "branch" theory of the Church. At the end of 1841, Newman decided to retire to Littlemore, where in an atmosphere of study, prayer and penance he could think out the problems that faced him.

His reflections, by the summer of 1843, were leading him towards Rome. On May 4, he wrote to Keble of "something which has at last been forced upon my full consciousness," so that "as far as I can realize my own convictions, I consider the Roman Catholic Communion the Church of the Apostles, and that what grace is among us (which, through God's mercy, is not little) is extraordinary, and from the overflowings of His Dispensation." Newman added: "I am very far more sure that England is in schism, than that the Roman additions to the Primitive Creed may not be developments, arousing out of a keen and vivid realising of the Divine Depositum of faith."[47] Five months later, on September 25, 1843, Newman preached his last sermon as an Anglican, "The Parting of Friends."

Newman continued to live at Littlemore, translating St. Athanasius, and agonizing over his growing conviction that it was his duty to join the Church of Rome. He feared that he was under an illusion, especially when men such as Keble and Pusey did not share his view. This fear could only be dispelled by waiting, by a life of penance, and by prayer and study. Second, since it was his teaching that had brought so many to the practice of a real Christian life, he feared that many would be thrown into confusion and would perhaps even fall into skepticism. He felt intense pain at the distress he was causing others.

The year 1844 was a "dark night" for Newman. To leave the Church of England meant leaving so much that he loved and breaking with so many friends to whom his move was incomprehensible. Even his own family lacked sympathy and understanding for his predicament. When he told his family and friends that he intended to resign his Fellowship at Oriel, his sister Jemima protested: "What can be worse than this? It is like hearing that some dear friend must die. I cannot shut my eyes to this overpowering event that threatens any longer."[48]

47. Newman, *Correspondence*, 218–19.

48. Trevor, *Newman: The Pillar*, 349. About a year and a half later, on Palm Sunday 1845, Newman wrote to his sister Jemima describing his anguish: "At my time of life men love ease. I love ease myself. I am giving up a maintenance involving no duties and adequate to all my wants. What in the world am I doing this for (I ask *myself* this) except

John Henry Newman

Personal considerations aside, Newman had to meet the objection that the Roman Church, in spite of its links with antiquity, had tampered with Revealed Religion and added to the revealed truths as they were to be found in primitive times. Newman gradually became convinced that modern Roman doctrines were legitimate developments of the teachings of the Early Church on the assumption that Divine Providence was guiding the Church through the centuries. By the end of 1844, Newman decided to work out fully this theory of doctrinal development in a treatise entitled *An Essay on the Development of Christian Doctrine*. "Before I got to the end," he said, "I resolved to be received."[49] On October 9, 1845, John Henry Newman was received into the Roman Catholic Church.

Newman's personal struggle in his own conversion process was very important not only for his own spiritual development, but also in his spiritual direction. Newman understood others who were experiencing turmoil in the process of conversion, because he had suffered through a similar experience. Prospective converts sought out Newman as one who would understand their difficulties.

Roman Catholic Experiences

In 1845, when John Henry Newman joined the Church of Rome, his Anglican bishop, Samuel Wilberforce, commented: "May God give him the grace of repentance before he falls through Rome into infidelity."[50] It was not an atypical reaction in Protestant England where many (including Newman a few years previously) saw Papal Rome as the antichrist of the Apocalypse. Quite different was the reaction of Edward Pusey, who was keenly pained by Newman's departure yet remained in the Church of England to continue the work of the Oxford Movement:

> He has gone as a simple act of duty with no view for himself, placing himself entirely in God's hands. And such are they whom God employs. He seems then to me not so much gone from me, as transported into another part of the Vineyard, where the full

---

that I think I am called to do so? I am making a large income by my sermons. I am, to say the very least, risking this; the chance is that my sermons will have no further sale at all. I have a good name with many; I am deliberately sacrificing it. I have a bad name with more. I am fulfilling all their worst wishes, and giving them their most coveted triumph. I am distressing all I love, unsettling all I have instructed or aided. I am going to those I do not know, and of whom I expect very little. Oh, what can it be but a stern necessity which causes this?" Bouyer, *Newman*, 241–42.

49. Newman, *Apologia*, 181.
50. Trevor, *Newman: The Pillar*, 370.

energies of his powerful mind can be employed, which here they were not. And who knows what in the mysterious purposes of God's good Providence may be the effect of such a person among them? . . . It is perhaps the greatest event which has happened since the communion of the Churches has been interrupted, that each one, so formed in Our Church, and the work of God's spirit as dwelling within her, should be transplanted to theirs.[51]

Pusey believed it to be providential that Newman, whose spirituality had been so completely formed in the Church of England, should now be given the opportunity of living out that spirituality in the Church of Rome. Moreover, Pusey anticipated the continuity between Newman's spirituality as an Anglican and that of his Catholic years. However, such tolerance was the exception, and even Newman's relationship with Pusey became strained. Furthermore, the loss of old friends was keenly felt by the new convert. Vincent Blehl has observed that the full testing of Newman's spiritual life took place in the Catholic period. "It is then that he meets the cross in the form of numerous trials and misunderstandings."[52]

Newman's life as a Catholic was plagued by a constant series of trials which became a succession of "purifications" in his spiritual growth and clearly helped shape his spiritual life. In chronological order, the most pertinent "tests" of Newman's spirituality included the following: the division of the two Oratories (1848–1856); the Achilli trial (1851–1853); the rectorship of the Catholic University in Dublin (1851–1857); the proposed translation of Scripture (1857–1860); the *Rambler* controversy (1859); Kingsley's attack (1863–1864); the Oxford Oratory project (1864–1867); the infallibility debate (1867–1875); and his Cardinalate and waning years (1875–1890).

The Oratory Dispute

On February 2, 1848, Newman officially established the Oratory in England with the admission of five priests, one novice, and three lay brothers. Several weeks earlier, Christmas 1847, he had been informed by Monsignor Wiseman that Frederick Faber and his seventeen "Wilfridians" wanted to join the new English Oratory. Newman referred to Faber's intention as "a most choice Christmas gift,"[53] but he expressed a note of realism by asking Faber to consider carefully such a decision.

---

51. Liddon, *Life*, 2:461.
52. Blehl, "Holiness," 327.
53. JHN to F. W. Faber, 2 January 1848, in *LD* 12:145.

> I will but say that, from the very wish I have that we may come to an understanding, I am anxious you should try if you have fully mastered *what* Oratorianism is. In many important respects it differs from what you are at present. It is not near so ascetic—indeed it is not ascetic. It is not poetical—it is not very devotional. . . . I am so desirous of our coming together, that I wince while I put down these objections, but no good will come of it, if we don't consider the matter in all its bearings.[54]

Faber effulgently responded that he and his community wanted to surrender themselves and their property, in "blind obedience." The Brothers of the Will of God were received by Newman at St. Wilfrid's on February 12, 1848. However, within a period of six months, difficulties arose between Newman and the young men in Faber's group. Newman mentioned his feeling of estrangement to his friend, Ambrose St. John:

> My great trouble is some of the *giovanni*—not that any thing new has occurred, but they have repelled any thing between us but what is external, shown so little kindness when I have done things for them, treated me with so little confidence, as to throw me back upon my self. . . . It is as if my time of work were gone by. Except that one has been led step by step to where one is, beginning in 1841 with going to Littlemore, one is tempted to say, "How much happier for me to have no liabilities (so to speak) but to be a single unfettered convert."[55]

Newman subsequently decided to bring the entire community to St. Wilfrid's while a site in Birmingham was being purchased for the first working Oratory house. Since he considered twelve to be the ideal number to foster a family atmosphere in an Oratory, he planned another Oratory for London and called for prayers that the division of personnel would be according to God's will. After the lists of names for the two Oratories were decided, Newman wrote to Coffin: "Give my best love to all and every one—and tell them, that, as they have all brought the matter before God for so long a time, with such a desire to know, and resolution to follow, His will, whatever it might be, so now they ought to rejoice and give thanks for what we may all trust is His decision."[56]

In the autumn of 1855, a quarrel began between the two houses of the Oratory which was to end in their official separation. Although the immediate issue was a dispute over the Rule, the cause lay deeper—in the increasing

---

54. JHN to F. W. Faber, 31 December 1847, in *LD* 12:140.
55. JHN to Ambrose St. John, 12 July 1848, in *LD* 12:243.
56. JHN to R. A. Coffin, 15 April 1849, in *LD* 13:114.

A Spiritual Biography of Newman

differences between the two groups, polarized by their different attitudes to the problems then facing the Church. The trouble began when the London Oratory, without telling Newman, wrote to the Office of Propaganda in Rome for an interpretation of the Rule on the question of hearing nuns' confessions. The spiritual direction of communities of women was an apostolate that Oratorians were not supposed to undertake, since it took them away from the community. The London Oratorians had assumed this work to oblige Wiseman. The idea of writing to Rome about it, however, was their own. By implication, it indicated their independence to correspond directly with Rome. Newman first learned of this appeal when Bishop Ullathorne said he was glad to hear a rescript from Rome was coming to dispense them from this provision of the Rule.

What disturbed Newman was the realization that because of the action of the London Oratory, the Birmingham Oratory could also be affected by a binding decree from Rome. Ullathorne was embarrassed to find that Newman had not been consulted and did not even know that Propaganda had written for his opinion, as bishop of a diocese in which an Oratory was situated. Subsequent correspondence between the Oratories only increased misunderstanding and mistrust. Eventually, in July 1856, a brief was obtained by the London Oratory to be completely independent of Newman's Birmingham Oratory.

Throughout this controversy, the nature of the Oratorian Rule was the central issue for Newman. To Richard Stanton, he wrote: "Our Rule is our vocation, as far as any thing external can be so called. Were our rule other than it is, without less devotion to St. Philip, perhaps we should never have been his children. To touch a Rule is to unsettle vocations; to create suspicions about its stability is to weaken the hope which those who have embraced it humbly entertain of their own perseverance."[57]

Newman did not see how he could defend himself against the attacks of the London Oratory without personally attacking Faber. He refused to do this and forbade the Birmingham Oratorians to talk to outsiders about the quarrel. Meanwhile, Faber was showing letters to his friends and justifying himself by creating an impression of Newman's sensitiveness. Newman still insisted on silence and shared his thoughts with John Flanagan: "I have never defended myself through life—I have been called all manner of names—but these things don't last. Such dirt does not stick. Nor am I allowing scandal to remain, by not speaking; scandal must be somewhere. If you talk of scandal, it is a less [sic] evil that I should be thought tyrannical than

---

57. JHN to Richard Stanton, 27 May 1856, in *LD* 17:248.

F. Faber proved to be double-dealing. Again, any one who defends himself, puts himself in the wrong."[58]

The Achilli Trial

In 1851, another storm overshadowed Newman's life. Giacinto Achilli, a former Dominican priest who had been imprisoned by the Roman Inquisition, had come to England under the auspices of the Protestant Alliance which sponsored his anti-Catholic lectures around the country. Cardinal Wiseman denounced him in an article in the *Dublin Review*, charging him with moral misconduct. Newman devoted one of his lectures on *The Present Position of Catholics in England* to an exposé of Achilli's rather sordid background in an attempt to show him to be a liar whose statements against Catholicism were false. Achilli, supported by the Protestant Alliance, filed charges, and Newman was brought to public trial on a libel suit.

Newman sensed that the Achilli trial was an opportunity for the Church to emerge stronger. "The Church is never more dangerous than when she seems helpless."[59] He recognized that he was probably being taken at his word for the times he had said, "Willingly would I suffer, if the Church is to gain."[60]

After a lengthy trial, Newman passed the last two days before the verdict in prayer in the presence of the Blessed Sacrament. He had stated during the trial: "I have all my life been speaking about suffering for the Truth,—now it has come upon me."[61] He was comparatively well prepared for the verdict of "guilty" which was delivered by the jury on June 25, 1852. The suspense of the trial had been a great penance for Newman. Writing to J. M. Capes shortly after the verdict, he said: "Suspense is the trial, not certainty—to have one's thoughts, prayer, masses occupied for months, without definite prospect of being released, to be an ocean of expense and responsibility with a receding horizon, this is a trial."[62]

His lawyers called for a new trial, and Newman became even more hopeful: "I recollect too the proverb, 'Man's necessity is God's opportunity,' and think it is probable that our adversity is over, and that the prayers of so many holy souls are now at length in the way to be answered."[63] On January 31, 1853, the request for a new trial was refused on technical grounds, and

58. JHN to John Flanagan, 10 July 1856, in *LD* 17:317.
59. JHN to J. M. Capes, 27 November 1851, in *LD* 14:443.
60. JHN to Richard Stanton, 4 December 1851, in *LD* 14:451.
61. JHN to Sister Mary Imelda Poole, 25 November 1851, in *LD* 14:438.
62. JHN to J. M. Capes, 4 July 1852, in *LD* 15:116.
63. JHN to Sister Mary Imelda Poole, 28 November 1852, in *LD* 15:206.

Newman was fined £100. His total court costs, amounting to over £10,000, were paid from a subscription fund to which many Catholics from different countries contributed. He celebrated a Mass of thanksgiving at the Oratory on February 21 for the outcome of the Achilli matter, and continued to remember his benefactors every Friday at Mass.

The Catholic University

In the midst of the Achilli trial, Newman was approached by Dr. Cullen, soon to become the Archbishop of Dublin, and asked to become the first rector of a Catholic University which was to be established in Ireland. The majority of Irish bishops were opposed to "mixed education," that is, the attendance of Catholics at secular colleges. Dr. Cullen headed a committee to establish an independent Catholic university in Ireland, and Newman was proposed as rector because of his educational background and prestige. After weighing the offer, Newman wrote on November 5, 1851, to Cullen: "I trust, through God's mercy, I shall be equal to any [work and responsibility] which the Committee puts before me—but at my age, when strength and spirits and vigour and health fail, one may well feel alarmed about it. I do earnestly trust my spirits may not go, or rather that grace may take their place—but, my dear Lord, I need your prayers, and those of all whom I can get to think of me."[64]

Newman's initial enthusiasm was slowly dampened by a series of embarrassing incidents. From the beginning, he was frustrated at not having the freedom to develop and implement his educational ideas. In fact, he was not actually installed as rector until three years after his acceptance; he was not permitted to choose his own vice-rector and could not freely negotiate contracts for professors. Furthermore, decisions were made without consulting or informing him.

Simultaneously, rumors began that he would be appointed Bishop of Liverpool or Nottingham. Being bishop of a diocese did not appeal to Newman, because it would take him away from both the University project and the Oratory. Meanwhile, Cardinal Wiseman decided it would be helpful for Newman to be made a titular bishop so as to be on an equal footing in his relationship with the Irish bishops. In January 1854, Wiseman had this appointment approved in principle at Rome, and proceeded to act as if it were an accomplished fact. The news spread quickly, and Newman's friends began to send gifts in anticipation of his consecration. When the Papal Brief of March 20, 1854, establishing the University, did not name him a bishop,

---

64. JHN to Archbishop Cullen, 5 November 1851, in *LD* 16:416.

Newman was surprised but remained silent. Time passed, and Newman never heard again from Wiseman or Cullen about the intended nomination.

In April 1857, Newman wrote to all the Irish bishops that he intended to resign as rector the following November.[65] He had experienced a mixture of success and frustration during his administration, and although he had accomplished a great deal, he was never able to have his hopes for the university realized. Nonetheless, his trust in God's wisdom and goodness remained steady; as he wrote to Bishop O'Brien of Waterford: "I have a sure confidence that the same Providence which has carried on the University to this date, will not be wanting to His own work and carry it on His own wise and good way. He has no need of men, and can find them, when He wills to use them."[66]

In 1858, several months after he had resigned the rectorship of the Catholic University in Dublin, Newman wrote Miss Holmes: "Don't forget to pray for me. We all must have trials in this life—they are for our good, or rather they are simply necessary for us. I have had accumulating trials for several years, and I expect that they will increase rather than diminish. But on the other hand, so great and many mercies, that the troubles are as nothing by the side of them."[67] A year later, Newman, expressing his conviction that time is the best judge of the validity of a work, wrote to Robert Ornsby:

> It does not prove that what I have written and planned will not take effect sometime and somewhere, because it does not at once. For 20 years my book on the Arians was not heard of, and then I began to hear it talked of. My Oxford University Sermons, preached out as long as 17 years, are now (in some passages) attracting attention at Oxford. When I am gone, something may come of what I have done in Dublin. And, since I hope I did what I did, not for the sake of man, not for the sake of the Irish Hierarchy, not even for the Pope's praise, but for the sake of God's Church and God's glory, I have nothing to regret, and nothing to desire, different from what is.[68]

Scripture Translation

Following his decision to resign the rectorship of the Catholic University in Dublin, Newman wrote to Ambrose St. John: "Do pray for me that I

---

65. JHN to Archbishop Cullen, 2 April 1857, in *LD* 18:5.
66. JHN to Bishop O'Brien, 14 April 1857, in *LD* 18:15.
67. JHN to Miss Holmes, 10 August 1858, in *LD* 18:438.
68. JHN to Robert Ornsby, 15 December 1859, in *LD* 19:254. These "University Sermons" are found in Newman, *Fifteen Sermons Preached before the University of Oxford*.

may find out what use God wishes to put me to, and may pursue it with great obedience."⁶⁹ A few months later, Cardinal Wiseman asked Newman to be in charge of "an accurate, idiomatic, well-annotated translation of the Bible."⁷⁰ Newman accepted this invitation with renewed enthusiasm: "A greater honour, I feel, could not possibly have been done me than that which your Eminence in that communication has conferred, in selecting me for the office of preparing an annotated English version of the Bible; and I beg your Eminence and through you the Episcopal Body, to receive the heartfelt and most humble acknowledgments, which so high and singular a mark of approbation and confidence demands at my hands."⁷¹

Newman set to work consulting heads of Catholic colleges and theology professors for their suggestions, and by November he presented his translation proposals and budget to Wiseman. The project became complicated by the news from America that Archbishop Kenrick of Baltimore had already published a translation from the Vulgate of the New Testament, the Psalms, and Sapiential Books, and the remainder of the Old Testament translation was ready for publication. The Ninth Provincial Council of Baltimore proposed that Newman should be asked to cooperate with Kenrick in producing a joint version that could be used in all English speaking countries. Newman referred that decision to the English hierarchy, but neither he nor the American bishops were ever formally answered. Newman had spent about £100 for books and materials in connection with the project, but finally decided to abandon it because of lack of communication and support from the English hierarchy. In spite of his disillusionment, Newman still publicly made excuses for Wiseman. In Meriol Trevor's appraisal, "The frustration of this unresolved mystery was only one, and not the worst, of Newman's tribulations at this time."⁷²

The Rambler

In 1848, J. M. Capes launched a Catholic periodical, the *Rambler*. The young Sir John Acton joined Richard Simpson as coeditor in 1857. The *Rambler's* influence was great in comparison with its small circulation of eight hundred copies per month. Its purpose was "to create a body of thought against the false intellectualism of the age, to surround Catholicism with the

---

69. JHN to Ambrose St. John, 7 May 1857, in *LD* 18:30.
70. Cardinal Wiseman to JHN, 26 August 1857, in *LD* 18:122.
71. JHN to Cardinal Wiseman, 14 September 1857, in *LD* 18:129.
72. Trevor, *Newman: Light*, 173.

defenses demanded by that age, to consider from the Catholic viewpoint the discoveries of that age and to give them a Catholic interpretation."[73]

Newman was quite happy to support such scholarship, but he recoiled from the hypercritical attitude of the editors towards ecclesiastical authority. The bishops were naturally displeased with this latter aspect, and they considered censuring the *Rambler* in a pastoral letter. Bishop Ullathorne asked Newman to intervene by helping to secure Simpson's resignation. Simpson agreed to resign, but threatened to publicize the whole transaction if the *Rambler* ceased to exist. Simpson also put pressure on Newman to become the editor, and Newman finally accepted the offer on March 21, after much prayer and consultation with the Oratorians and others. In the advertisement for the new series of the *Rambler*, Newman did not criticize previous indiscrete editorial policies but looked with hope to the future: "The Conductors of *The Rambler* indulge the hope that the zeal and labour expended on it in former years have not been without fruit; and, under the encouragement thereby given them, they recommend its future to the good prayers of those persons, not few, they trust, nor inconsiderable, who are interested in its well-being."[74]

When Simpson became bitter at Wiseman and the bishops for having forced him to resign as editor, Newman empathized:

> It seems hardly kind when you have so much to try you, to preach, yet I know you will excuse what comes from one who has had on various occasions already had to practise what he preaches. I assure you that the principal person who has unfairly used you, and whose wishes I have been executing in my negotiation with you, has been personally unkind to me, by word and by deed [viz. Cardinal Wiseman]. I consider myself much aggrieved, and, had not the experience of long years made me tire of indignation and complaint, I could indulge myself in both the one and the other.[75]

Newman continued with some practical advice on an appropriate response to unkind words or deeds: "But, depend upon it, no advice is better than that of the Holy Apostle, 'If our enemy hungers, to feed him—' [Romans 12:20] and to leave our cause simply in the Hands of the good God. He will plead our cause for us in His own way, and, even though it be not His high will to redress us openly, He can make compensation to us by inward blessings.... To fret,

---

73. Guitton, *Church*, 21.

74. JHN, March 1859, in *LD* 19:89. This advertisement was prefixed to the May 2 edition.

75. JHN to Richard Simpson, 25 February 1859, in *LD* 19:51–52.

and to be troubled, does not pay—it is like scratching a wound, instead of letting it heal."[76] This advice is characteristic of Newman, who after making his views known in the clearest manner possible, left the result to God's will, trusting that God would bring everything to its proper end.

After Newman had assumed the editorship of the *Rambler*, he expressed his reservations to Henry Wilberforce; yet his course of action was determined not by feelings, but by his desire to do God's will. "I have the extreme mortification of being Editor of *The Rambler*, I have never had in my life (in its time) so great a one. It is like a bad dream, and oppresses me at times inconceivably....

I take it in an extremely ill humour, except so far as I have done my best to find out God's will, and have the consolation of thinking I have found it. But you may be sure I don't feel indebted to any one for the complication."[77]

After the May issue, Bishop Ullathorne, still not satisfied with the tone of the *Rambler*, advised Newman to resign the editorship after the July issue. Newman promised to do so. "It is impossible, with the principles and feelings on which I have acted all through life, that I could have acted otherwise. I never have resisted, nor can resist the voice of a lawful Superior, speaking in his own province."[78] Newman again wrote Henry Wilberforce to share his reflections about the unexpected way that his editorship was prematurely curtailed. Once again, this letter manifests Newman's willingness to be patient for the opportune moment when his principles might be expressed.

> I did all I could to ascertain God's will, and that being the case, I am sure good will come of my taking it—I am of the opinion that the Bishops see only one side of things, and I have a mission, as far as my own internal feelings go, against evils which I see. On the other hand, I have always preached that things which are *really* useful, still are done, according to God's will, at one time, not at another—and that, if you attempt at a wrong time, what in itself is right, you perhaps become a heretic or schismatic. What I may aim at may be real and good, but it may be God's will it should be done a hundred years later.... When I am gone, it will be seen perhaps that persons stopped me from doing a work which I might have done. God overrules all things.[79]

In addition to the problem of the editorship, a controversy developed over his *Rambler* essay, "On Consulting the Faithful in Matters of Doctrine,"

---

76. Ibid., 52.
77. JHN to Henry Wilberforce, 31 March 1859, in *LD* 19:96.
78. JHN to Edward Thompson, 29 May 1859, in *LD* 19:150.
79. JHN to Henry Wilberforce, 17 July 1859, in *LD* 19:179–80.

which Newman published in the July issue. Bishop Brown of Newport deleted his article to Rome. The seriousness of this accusation was not conveyed to Newman at this time, and so he did not defend himself. At Rome, his orthodoxy was regarded with great suspicion; his reputation was "under a cloud." In December 1859, he wrote to W. G. Ward: "What I write may be mixed with a great deal of error—but if it is done honestly, in the sight of God, under the correction of the Church, good must come of it in some way or other, even though, certainly not in my day, it does not bring me any credit personally."[80] Newman's journal entry for December 15, 1859, stated: "I am writing on my knees, and in God's sight. May He be gracious unto me! as years go on, I have less sensible devotion and inward life.... I live more and more in the past, and in hopes that the past may revive in the future. My God, when shall I learn that I have so parted with the world, that, though I may wish to make friends with it, it will not make friends with me?"[81] Reflecting on how these recent events had affected his spiritual life, he prayed:

> O my God, not as a matter of sentiment, not as a matter of literary exhibition, do I put this down. O rid me of this frightful *cowardice*, for this is at the bottom of all my ills. When I was young, I was bold, because I was ignorant—now I have lost my boldness, because I have had advanced [sic] in experience. I am able to count the cost, better than I did, of being brave for Thy sake, and therefore I shrink from sacrifices. Here is a second reason, over and above the deadness of my soul, why I have so little faith or love in me.[82]

Newman certainly came near to a nervous breakdown in these years, although he carried on his normal work; Emily Bowles, a longtime friend of Newman, recorded her impressions after visiting him in Birmingham in 1861:

> She was welcomed by Newman "as only he can welcome." She would never forget "the brightness that lit up that worn face as he received me at the door, carrying in several packages himself." But when they were talking in the Guest Room, she noticed a change in him. He had not only aged disproportionately to the time but his grand massive face was scored with lines which no lapse of years had written there. They were too evidently lines of intense grief, disappointment, and the patient bearing up against the failure of hope. Whenever he spoke, the expression softened,

---

80. JHN to W. G. Ward, 3 December 1859, in *LD* 19:251.
81. Newman, *Autobiographical Writings*, 249.
82. Ibid., 251.

but when at rest, and his conversation was frequently broken by short fits of absence of mind, there was even a look of terrible weariness akin to lasting depression of mind—It gave me at first the idea of some personal displeasure, but I soon found that this idea could not be entertained.[83]

After the *Rambler* incident, Newman did not publish again until 1864. He occupied himself with the Oratory School which he had established in 1859, and with his pastoral duties as preacher and confessor. His disappointment was confided to his journal:

> "Not understood"—this is the point. I have seen great wants which had to be supplied among Catholics, especially as regards education, and of course those who laboured under those wants, did not know their state—and did not see or understand the want at all or what was the supply of the want, and felt no thankfulness at all, and no consideration towards a person who was doing something towards that supply, but rather thought him restless, or crotchetty, or in some way or other what he should not be. This has naturally made me shrink into myself, or rather it has made me think of turning more to God, if it has not actually turned me. It has made me feel that in the Blessed Sacrament is my great consolation, and that while I have Him who lives in the Church, my Superiors, though they may claim my obedience, have no claim on my admiration, and offer nothing for my inward trust. I have expressed this feeling, or rather implied it, in one of my Dublin Sermons (preached in 1856).[84]

He countered the temptation to look back, having put his hand to the plough, by praying for a greater spirit of detachment: "It has been my *lifelong* prayer, and Thou hast granted it, that I should be set aside in this world. Now then let me make it once again. O Lord, bless what I write and prosper it—let it have much success; but let no praise come to me on that account in my lifetime. Let me go on living, let me die, as I have hitherto lived."[85] In a memorandum which Newman wrote as a personal reflection on his delation to Rome, he

---

83. Trevor, *Newman's Journey*, 202.
84. Ibid., 251–52. Journal entry, January 8, 1860.
85. Newman, *Autobiographical Writings*, 252. He closed the entry for January 8 by praying for two concerns: "(1) Let not the contempt which comes on me, injure the future of my Oratory—about this I am anxious, though I ought to put it, and do put it simply, into Thy hands, O Lord. (2) And again, O teach me (for it is a subject which tries me very much just now, which I have prayed about, and have said Masses about), teach me how to employ myself most profitably, most to Thy glory, in such years as remain to me; for my apparent ill success discourages me very much." Ibid., 253.

considered himself as the "scapegoat" of a series of events. Providence had drawn him through a certain rhythm of purifying experiences, yet, although he was sensitive to misunderstanding, he was not bitter or cynical:

> I hope we shall be on our guard against the indignation or anger which in various ways may at this moment or that be in danger of besetting us. Pride and passion are bad counsellors. In saying this I do not at all forget that reason would lead one to be quiet and composed, but it is very difficult at all times to go by reason. For myself, I think it is a portion of the fate of my life—and, if I anticipated it beforehand, I really cannot with any reason be annoyed with the instruments of it, when it takes place, for nothing can happen without instruments.[86]

The Apologia

At the end of 1863, Newman received a book review that provided another such "instrument." At the time, Newman appeared to be a forgotten, powerless figure. His Birmingham Oratory included only six others, and he lived under a cloud of misunderstanding by Catholic authorities. On December 30, he received a copy of *Macmillan's Magazine* from William Pope, calling his attention to the following quotation from a book review of volumes 7 and 8 of James Froude's *History of England*: "Truth, for its own sake, had never been a virtue with the Roman clergy. Father Newman informs us that it need not, and on the whole ought not to be; that cunning is the weapon which Heaven has given to the saints wherewith to withstand the brute male force of the wicked world which marries and is given in marriage. Whether his notion be doctrinally correct or not, it is at least historically so."[87]

When he learned that the author of this article was Charles Kingsley, he realized he was not dealing with "a young scribe, who is making himself a cheap reputation by smart hits at the safe objects."[88] Kingsley was Professor of Modern History at Cambridge, a popular novelist, and tutor to the Prince of Wales. Newman entered into correspondence with Kingsley, but not receiving a satisfactory retraction, decided to publish their exchange of letters in a pamphlet: "Mr. Kingsley and Dr. Newman: A Correspondence on the Question whether Dr. Newman Teaches that Truth Is No Virtue?" Newman

---

86. Memorandum of Newman, 14 January, 1860, in *LD* 19:292.

87. JHN, 30 December, 1863, in *LD* 20:571, cited in a letter sent by Newman to Messrs. Macmillan and Co.

88. JHN to Alexander Macmillan, 8 January 1864, in *LD* 21:12.

had conflicting feelings about this type of publication but made his decision after deliberation, consultation, and prayer. Kingsley retorted by means of another pamphlet: "What then Does Dr. Newman Mean?" Feeling that Kingsley's accusations were not only a personal insult but an attack on the Roman Catholic priesthood, Newman decided there was only one way to answer the charge of untruthfulness against him.[89] "I must give the true key to my whole life; I must show what I am, that it may be seen what I am not, and that the phantom may be extinguished which gibbens instead of me."[90]

Two pamphlets appeared on April 21 and 22 in which Newman described Kingsley's behavior throughout the affair; each week thereafter until mid-June, a new installment was published and quickly read by an avid English public. As this strikingly personal history of his "religious opinions" unfolded, Newman presented his readers with a new perspective on the Oxford Movement. It was an exhausting ordeal for him to meet the publisher's weekly deadlines, and he pleaded with his friends for the support of their prayers,[91] so that he might be guided "to say that which is according to the Will of God."[92] On June 12, he sent his last proof to the printer; subsequently, to express his gratitude to his friends, he wrote letters such as this one to Mother Margaret Mary Hallahan: "I was like a man who had fallen overboard and had to swim to land, and found the distance he had to go greater and greater. At last I am ashore, and have crawled upon the beach, and there I lie; but I should not have got safe I know, but for the many good prayers which have been offered for me."[93]

Kingsley's chance remark unintentionally provided Newman with the opportunity of regaining his stature with the English public; Kingsley's insulting insinuation resulted in a spiritual classic. A century later, Basil Willey noted:

> The *Apologia*, though some of its themes belong to a dead past, will live as long as great literature itself has any survival-value. It will live because it is the record, in restrained yet impassioned prose, of the spiritual pilgrimage of a great and saintly man; it

---

89. Ibid., 4: "I was making my protest on behalf of a large body of men of high character, of honest and religious minds, and of sensitive honour,—who had their place and their rights in this world, though they were ministers of the world unseen, and who were insulted by my Accusor, as the above extracts from him sufficiently show, not only in my person, but directly and pointedly in their own."

90. Newman, *Apologia*, 11–12.

91. JHN to Miss. Holmes, 9 April 1864, in *LD* 21:92. "Only pray for me that I may not be overtired, for the toil is a fatigue, and that I may be guided what to say."

92. JHN to Edward Ryley, 26 April 1864, in *LD* 21:103.

93. JHN to Mother Margaret Mary Hallahan, 25 June 1864, in *LD* 21:131.

will live as a noble attempt to assert external Providence against the "all-corroding, all-dissolving skepticism of the intellect in religious inquiries."

The immediate effects of the *Apologia* can be expressed in less sweeping terms. First, it did more than any other single book to change the Englishman's image of the Roman Catholic Church; secondly, it dispelled the clouds of suspicion and misunderstanding which for a quarter of a century had hidden the real Newman from most of his contemporaries.[94]

The Proposed Oxford Oratory

Newman felt encouraged by the reception of his *Apologia*. Thus the proposal of Bishop Ullathorne that Newman should establish a Catholic mission in Oxford coincided with his hope to use his renewed influence at his alma mater. Although it was now possible for Catholics to attend English universities, the English bishops only reluctantly permitted it. Newman approached this new challenge enthusiastically, as can be seen in this letter to Sister Mary Imelda Poole: "We shall have plenty of trials in time, but at present the sky is very clear and bright, and the landscape is rose-colour. Alas! That bright mornings are the soonest over cast! So great a work cannot be done without great crosses—Yet I don't like to say so, for it is like prophesying against myself and I do not like trial at all. What is to happen if we are not preserved in health and strength? . . . But we must leave all this to Him who we trust in employing us."[95] To his old friend Pusey, he described the circumstances which led him to the Oxford scheme:

> Two or three things have combined—first, our youths are beginning to go to Oxford, and the Colleges are admitting them—secondly the late Mr. R. Smith suddenly offers me land—thirdly my diocesan puts, to my surprise, the Oxford Mission into my hands. These are independent of me—but, combined as they are, they have the force enough to make me think that it is God's will that I should accept the conclusion in which they issue. . . . I am too old

---

94. Willey, Introduction to *Apologia*, v–vi.

95. JHN to Sister Mary Imelda Poole, 16 November 1864, in *LD* 21:295. Newman wrote to Henry Wilberforce that same day: "As to Oxford, we are astonished at our own doings—and our only hope is that we are doing God's Will in thus portentously involving ourselves both in money matters and in work." JHN to Henry Wilberforce, 16 November 1864, in *LD* 21:297.

A Spiritual Biography of Newman

to be able to speculate on the future—and, if I found an Oratory at Oxford, it may be as much as Providence means me to do.[96]

The purchase price for the plot of land was £8,400, which Newman set about raising through subscriptions. Financial worries yielded to his trust in Providence, which he believed would bring him through the difficulty.[97]

Meanwhile there was influential opposition to Newman's involvement with Oxford: William G. Ward, Henry Manning, George Talbot, and Herbert Vaughan.[98] They used their influence at Rome to reinforce a strong stand against mixed education; on December 13, the English Bishops passed resolutions absolutely prohibiting Catholics from attending Oxford. Newman shared his disappointment with Sister Mary Imelda Poole: "As to the Oxford scheme, it is still the blessed will of God to send me baulks. On the whole, I suppose, looking through my life as a course, He is using me—but really viewed in its separate parts, it is but a life of failures."[99] Newman sold the property which had been acquired. Bishop Ullathorne, however, was still interested in having an Oxford Mission, and renewed his offer to Newman in April 1866. Newman's initial response was cautious and he listed five difficulties in his lengthy reply to Ullathorne.[100] He told Pusey that coming to Oxford "would be as painful a step" as he could be called to make, and that he "would not contemplate it except under the imperative call of duty."[101] The formal permission for an Oxford Mission was secured from Propaganda by Ullathorne, but with secret instructions—not communicated to Newman at the time—that he personally was to be dissuaded "blande suaviterque" (smoothly and sweetly) from residing at Oxford. Unsuspecting, Newman wrote to Catherine Bathurst at the end of 1866: "Incomprehensible as it is, great ecclesiastics in England, friends of mine, have set themselves with a feeling quite personal against me in the Oxford matter, and for two years have thwarted the plan. Our Bishop has triumphed over them, and we are to go there. The leave has come from Propaganda. Still, the same influence which has been so violent against me will bother me when I am there, I cannot doubt. So you must give me some good prayers."[102] A

---

96. JHN to Edward Pusey, 22 November 1864, in *LD* 21:303–4.
97. JHN to George Smith, 24 October 1864, in *LD* 21:269.
98. Bishop Ullathorne to JHN, 28 March 1867, in *LD* 23:3.
99. JHN to Sister Mary Imelda Poole, 28 December 1864, in *LD* 23:359.
100. JHN to Bishop Ullathorne, 23 April 1866, in *LD* 22:221–24.
101. JHN to Edward Pusey, 29 April 1866, in *LD* 22:227.
102. JHN to Catherine Bathurst, 31 December 1866, in *LD* 22:337. However, see JHN to Bishop Ullathorne, 1 January 1867, in *LD* 23: 4–5n4; this footnote indicates that Ullathorne sent Newman the letter from Propaganda on December 25, and that

few days later he shared his reflections with Emily Bowles in a letter which reveals his sensitivity of conscience:

> I have already asked the Bishop about our collecting money [for the Oxford scheme]. You speak as if I were dawdling and losing time. So I should be if the work were one which I had chosen as God's work. But on the contrary, it has been forced on me against my will, and certainly, if not against my judgment, yet not with it, or my will would not be against it. It *would* be a great inconsistency in me to let six months pass and do nothing were I convinced it was the will of Providence,—but I do not feel this. I only go because I fear to be deaf to a Divine call,—but, if anything happened in the six months to prevent it, that would be to me a sign that there never had been a Divine call.[103]

On April 6, 1867, William Neville and Newman went for a walk during which they talked happily about the prospects awaiting them in Oxford. When they returned to the Oratory, Newman was handed a long blue envelope delivered in his absence. It was a letter from Ullathorne revealing the secret instruction from Propaganda. Newman, after reading the letter, turned to Neville and said only: "All is over. I am not allowed to go."[104]

Newman's sense of interior peace and detachment can be sensed in a letter that he wrote to Henry Coleridge:

> It is my cross to have false stories circulated about me, and to be suspected in consequence. I could not have a lighter one. I would not change it for any other . . .
>
> For twenty years I have honestly and sensitively done my best to fulfill the letter and spirit of the directions of the Holy See and Propaganda—and I never have obtained the confidence of any one at Rome . . .
>
> I have lost any desire to gain the goodwill of those who thus look on me. I have abundant consolation in the unanimous sympathy of those around me. I trust I shall always give a hearty

---

Ullathorne knew at this time about the "secret instruction" which did not allow Newman to reside at Oxford; however, Ullathorne did not tell Newman about this constriction.

103. JHN to Emily Bowles, 8 January 1867, in *LD* 23:16.

104. Ward, *Life*, 2:138–39. The Roman correspondent for the *Weekly Register*, E. R. Martin, submitted a letter in the April 6 issue in which he attacked Newman, saying that the Pope himself had prohibited him from going to Oxford because of his doubtful orthodoxy. This provoked great indignation among Newman's friends, and they presented an address to him signed by about two hundred distinguished English Catholic laymen. They declared that "every blow that touches you [Newman] inflicts a wound upon the Catholic Church in this country." Ibid., 143.

obedience to Rome, but I never expect in my life time any recognition of it.[105]

Newman later wrote to Bishop Ullathorne to withdraw his offer to establish a Mission at Oxford: "Accordingly, I now ask your permission to withdraw from my engagement to undertake the Mission of Oxford, on the ground that I am not allowed by Propaganda the freedom to discharge its duties with effect."[106]

Vatican I

The proposal of convening a general council, which would be the first since Trent three hundred years earlier, was privately announced by Pius IX at the end of the year 1864. The public announcement came in June 1867, but the preparations took so long that it did not begin until December 8, 1869. Officially, the Council was convened to restate Catholic doctrine on issues under attack and to discuss proposed changes in Church discipline. However, there were persistent rumors that there would be a definition on the doctrine of "papal infallibility." English pro-infallibilists, also known as Ultramontanes, included Manning, Ward, and Talbot. Even prior to the opening of the Council, they had begun a campaign in favor of a declaration about infallibility and their exaggerated interpretations of infallibility aroused emotions to a high level. They insisted that their opinions were the only orthodox teaching. Newman maintained that Popes had always acted as if they had the right to the last word on disputed matters, thus sharing in Christ's guarantee to his Church that the Holy Spirit would guide it into all truth. What Newman rejected was a sweeping application of infallibility to all papal pronouncements as well as the way in which the pro-infallibilists characterized everyone else as unorthodox.

Although Newman had been invited to take part in the preparatory work of the Council, he declined the invitation because of his age and health. Instead he went to Rednall to finish writing *An Essay in Aid of a Grammar of Assent*, which appeared on March 15, 1870. On that very day, the *Standard* published Newman's private letter to Bishop Ullathorne protesting the methods of those who were campaigning to get the Council to promulgate a definition of papal infallibility. In his letter, Newman said the Ultramontanes were causing confusion and were spreading fear and dismay among

---

105. JHN to Henry Coleridge, 26 April 1867, in *LD* 23:191.
106. JHN to Bishop Ullathorne, 18 August 1867, in *LD* 23:312.

Catholics.[107] After lengthy debate, the Council approved the constitution *Pastor aeternus* on July 18, 1870. However, the triumph of Manning and other exaggerated proponents was limited by the modifications inserted into the text.[108]

When Newman saw the wording of the definition itself on July 23, he was pleased to find nothing in it that was startling. Nevertheless, he felt that it would not be easy for the ordinary person, whether Catholic or not, to understand the meaning of the decree, especially when Manning returned from Rome and began to pressure people to accept the new dogma. Many people were disturbed and wrote to Newman for advice.

During the months after the Council, Newman was frequently urged to write on the topic of infallibility, but a suitable opportunity did not present itself. In fact, he was again forced to defend his good faith—there were persistent rumors that he did not accept the decree, or that he had left or would leave the Church, that he was unhappy and longed to return to the Anglican Church. Finally, in 1874, an opportunity presented itself. William Gladstone published a book on *The Vatican Decrees in their Bearing on Civil Allegiance* that maintained that the Pope could command Catholics to act contrary to their civil allegiance under pain of eternal damnation. Newman needed no further urging. In defending the Church, Newman did not want to attack Gladstone personally; rather he wanted to attack both Gladstone's misunderstanding and the extreme views of Manning and Ward. Newman wanted to explain the definition in a legitimately minimizing sense, to clarify the relative position of conscience and papal authority and to disown Ultramontance exaggerations of the doctrine.

Newman decided to dedicate his pamphlet to his friend, the Duke of Norfolk, who had been educated at Newman's school, and who was England's leading Catholic layman. Since Newman's emphasis was on civil allegiance, he gave Gladstone no grounds for offense and Manning no grounds for attack. *The Letter to the Duke of Norfolk* was published early in January 1875. Like the *Apologia*, this work was immediately successful. The *Letter's* understanding of the Catholic position completely reversed public opinion, including that of Gladstone himself.

---

107. JHN to Bishop Ullathorne, 28 January 1870, in *LD* 25:18–19.

108. The following day, war was declared between France and Prussia, and many bishops returned to their dioceses. Although the Council met on three more occasions, attendance was small and nothing important was accomplished. Pius IX suspended the Council indefinitely on October 20; sessions never resumed.

Honors

Newman was almost seventy-four when his *Letter to the Duke of Norfolk* was published. Like many others his age, he was often saddened at the death of close friends who had stood by him in his trials and whose deaths left great voids in his life. Perhaps the greatest loss came not long after the success of the *Letter* when Ambrose St. John died on May 24, 1875, at the age of sixty. Newman's senior years were also the time of unexpected honors.

Just before Christmas 1877 came the surprising news that Trinity College wanted to make Newman its first Honorary Fellow; after anxiously consulting his fellow Oratorians and his bishop, he gladly accepted. And so it was in 1878 that Newman returned to Oxford for the first time since 1845. He called on Pusey and saw the new Keble College; he visited Thomas Short, his old tutor, age ninety and blind. The Trinity fellowship lifted the cloud which had overcast Newman in Anglican circles since he left Oxford a generation earlier.

However, Newman also lived under a cloud of suspicion in the communion which he joined. After the longest pontificate on record, (1846–1878), Pius IX died on February 7, 1878. His successor, Leo XIII, wanted to create Newman a cardinal. Rumors to this effect appeared in print in England in the summer of 1878, but Newman dismissed them as most improbable. The Duke of Norfolk, however, on behalf of the Catholic laity of England, took up the matter with enthusiasm. At that time, cardinals who were not diocesan bishops were expected to reside in Rome and Newman feared that he would have to leave the Birmingham Oratory; however, that fear was allayed when the official letter arrived at the Oratory on March 18, 1879. As cardinal, he was permitted to remain at his Oratory; Newman gladly accepted the cardinalate, regarding it as a sign of approval for his work. He felt as though the cloud had been lifted forever.

In 1886, Newman's health began to deteriorate. He celebrated his last Mass on Christmas Day 1889, but continued to see visitors on a limited basis. In August, 1890, Newman contracted pneumonia and after receiving the last rites on August 10, he died quietly the following day. At his request, he was buried next to his close friend and fellow Oratorian, Ambrose St. John, in the Oratorian cemetery at Rednal. As Newman's funeral procession passed through the streets from the Birmingham Oratory to Rednal, thousands lined the way to pay their final respects. In the cloister leading to the Oratory Church, there are tablets on the wall in memory of the deceased Oratorians. Newman, who had composed graceful Latin tributes to those who died before him, wrote a simple epitaph that summarizes his whole life: *Ex umbris et imaginibus in veritatem*—"From Shadows and Images into Truth."

At the time of Newman's death, the London *Times* remarked that "whether Rome canonizes him or not, he will be canonized in the thoughts of pious people of many creeds in England." On January 22, 1991, Pope John Paul II declared Newman "Venerable" since he had exercised the Christian virtues in an heroic degree.[109] After the Vatican recognized the cure of the severe spinal disorder of Deacon Jack Sullivan of Marshfield, Massachusetts, as an authentic miracle worked through Newman's intercession, on September 19, 2010, Pope Benedict XVI beatified John Henry Newman at Cofton Park, not far from the Oratorian house at Rednal. In his homily at the Mass of Newman's beatification, Pope Benedict XVI emphasized: "In Blessed John Henry, that tradition of gentle scholarship, deep human wisdom and profound love for the Lord has borne rich fruit, as a sign of the abiding presence of the Holy Spirit deep within the heart of God's people, bringing forth abundant gifts of holiness."[110]

---

109. The decree of beatification is available online at: http://www.newmanreader.org/canonization/promulgation.html.

110. The papal homily at the mass of beatification is available online at: http://www.vatican.va/holy_father/benedict_xvi/homilies/2010/documents/hf_ben-xvi_hom_20100919_beatif-newman_en.html.

2

Origins and Characteristics of Newman's Spirituality

"I ask not for comfort in comparison of sanctification"[1]

Origins of Newman's Spirituality

WHEN NEWMAN ENTERED THE Roman Catholic Church he was forty-four years old and had been an Anglican priest for twenty years. Both his spiritual life and theological outlook had already been largely formed. In leaving the Church of England and joining the Church of Rome, he looked for a more perfect realization of that faith which he had tried to live as an Anglican. Since the spiritual direction of others flows out of the director's personal beliefs, an analysis of the major elements of the director's own understanding of the spiritual life is helpful in understanding the foundation for his spiritual direction. Throughout Newman's life, there is a continuity in the influences which affected the development of his spiritual life. The first part of this chapter briefly examines the origins and characteristics of his spirituality and discusses the influences of biblical reading and patristic studies as well as certain influential Anglican authors on Newman's understanding of the spiritual life. The second part surveys the dominant characteristics of his spirituality: the unseen world, the holiness of God, providential guidance, and dependence on God. The third part considers the principal theological aspects of his doctrine on the spiritual life: personal experiences as theological *loci*, the indwelling of the Holy Spirit and the centrality of Christ.

---

1. Newman, *Autobiographical Writings*, 200.

John Henry Newman

Biblical

Newman was born into the rich heritage of Anglican piety, which is steeped in Scripture both in its themes and its language. His evangelical background strengthened his appreciation for the Bible. As a Roman Catholic, Newman recognized the value of "Bible religion," which consisted not in rites and creeds, but primarily in having the Bible read in Church, in the family, and in private. However, he also came to see that "Bible religion" had to be supplemented by creeds lest it remain only at the notional level of assent.[2]

The Bible revealed a living and personal God to Newman, a God whose providential care extends to every person in a unique way. This God is constantly taking the initiative in loving his people and the believer is invited to respond by generously detaching himself from anything incompatible with God's will. By watching and praying for opportunities to glorify God, the believer is led to share more deeply in the richness and joy of the community of his fellow believers. The Bible offers various examples of the attitudes and ascetical practices of holy people for admiration and instruction, and Newman incorporated these into his own understanding of the spiritual life. Moses and Paul were two particularly significant biblical figures for him. In 1853, Newman wrote to Mrs. William Froude concerning the importance of Moses: "The remarkable circumstance in the case of Moses, is, that the Almighty informs him of the sin of his people in order that he might intercede for them—which is just the object for which Catholics say the prayers of the faithful are revealed by Him to the saints."[3] Likewise, St. Paul was a special exemplar for Newman; Paul's life and writings greatly influenced Newman's theology and spirituality.[4] He considered the first chapters of the second letter to the Corinthians "one of the most soothing, comforting parts of Holy Scripture."[5] In these chapters St. Paul spoke openly of himself and of his sufferings, as well as of the transforming power of God contained in earthen vessels. In 1861, at a time when he was suffering from misunderstanding and lack of usefulness, Newman wrote to Sister Mary Gabriel du

---

2. Newman, *Essay in Aid*, 57. Newman, *Apologia*, 20–21, acknowledged learning the principle of tradition from Dr. Hawkins at Oxford: "He lays down a proposition, self-evident as soon as stated, to those who have at all examined the structure of Scripture, viz. that the sacred text was never intended to teach doctrine, but only to prove it, and that, if we would learn doctrine, we must have recourse to the formularies of the Church; for instance to the Catechism, and to the Creeds. He considers that, after learning from them the doctrines of Christianity, the inquirer must verify them by Scripture."

3. JHN to Mrs. William Froude, 8 March 1853, in *LD* 15:328.

4. Ivory, "Doctrine," 386.

5. JHN to Mrs. William Clarke, 10 October 1879, in *LD* 29:185.

Boulay: "For myself, I know I am deeply deficient in that higher life which lasts and grows in spite of the ills of mortality—but had I ever so much of supernatural love and devotion, I could not be in any different state from the Apostle, who in the most beautiful of his inspired epistles speaks with such touching and consoling vividness of those troubles, in the midst of which these earthen vessels of ours hold the treasure of grace and truth."[6]

Newman based his own spiritual life and his teaching on scriptural texts. Moreover, as a preacher, he consistently taught with the Bible in his hands, explaining its content and encouraging his congregation to read it themselves. C. S. Dessain has observed: "Newman never wrote like the great mystics, St. John of the Cross, St. Theresa, and the rest. He limited himself to expounding the scriptural ideal of holiness. He was preaching to ordinary people, not to enclosed contemplatives, and with his horror of unreality and unreal words in religion, he would not venture beyond the clear teaching of revelation."[7]

Patristics

As a young man, Newman was impressed by Joseph Milner's *History of the Church of Christ*, which awakened in him a love for the Fathers.[8] He was able to deepen his study of the church fathers in 1828 by setting out "to read them chronologically beginning with St. Ignatius and St. Justin."[9] Five years later he published *The Arians of the Fourth Century*, which reflected the thought of the Fathers of the Eastern Church. Newman viewed antiquity as the true exponent of the doctrines of Christianity, and the theology of Clement and Origen found resonance in his own thinking and activity. In his *Apologia*, he wrote:

> Some portions of their teaching, magnificent in themselves, came like music to my inward ear, as if the response to ideas, which, with little external to encourage them, I had cherished so long. These were based on the mystical and sacramental principle, and spoke of the various Economies or Dispensations of the Eternal. I understood these passages to mean that the exterior world, physical and historical, was but the manifestation to our sense of realities greater than itself. Nature was a parable: Scripture was an

---

6. JHN to Sister Mary Gabriel du Boulay, 18 August 1861, in *LD* 20:31.

7. Dessain, *Why Pray?*, 114.

8. Newman, *Apologia*, 18. "I read Joseph Milner's Church History, and was nothing short of enamoured of the long extracts from St. Augustine, St. Ambrose, and the other Fathers which I found there."

9. Ibid., 33.

allegory: pagan literature, philosophy, and mythology, properly understood, were but a preparation for the Gospel.[10]

The attitude with which he read Clement's *Stomata* and Origen's *De Principiis* was influenced by other books such as Joseph Butler's *Analogy* and John Keble's *Christian Year*. He was already favorably disposed toward a sacramental view of nature and the Church by reason of his literary background and personal experiences, and the patristic writings strengthened and developed it.

The respect and love for the Fathers which he acquired as an Anglican carried over into his Roman Catholic period. He was attracted to St. Philip Neri whose institute had the spirit of the primitive monks. He agreed with Cardinal Baronius that a beautiful apostolical method of spiritual life was renewed by means of St. Philip's rule. In his *Litany of St. Philip*, Newman included the phrase, "man of primitive times," which was a characteristic particularly appealing to his own spirituality grounded in Scripture and the Church Fathers. However, this patristic background was not appreciated by all his contemporaries: Archbishop Manning regarded Newman as the chief promoter of a dangerous attitude: "It is the old Anglican, patristic, literary, Oxford tone transplanted into the Church. It takes the line of deprecating exaggerations, foreign devotions, Ultramontanism, antinational sympathies."[11] In fact, Newman's strong foundation in patristic studies provided him with a mature view of the Church and spirituality which has come to be better appreciated in this century after the Second Vatican Council.

Anglican Authors

In addition to the biblical and patristic influences on the spiritual formation of Newman, various books which he read after his conversion experience in 1816 also played a significant role in his understanding of and growth in the spiritual life and influenced the way he directed others.

Thomas Scott (1747–1821) was the writer who made a deeper impression on Newman's mind than any other, and to whom he felt (in human terms) he almost owed his soul.[12] Scott's *Commentary on the Bible*, a widely acclaimed religious work at the time, first planted deep in Newman's mind the fundamental truth of Christianity, namely, faith in the Holy Trinity. Newman greatly admired Scott's unworldliness and the practical character

---

10. Ibid., 34.
11. Purcell, *Life*, 323.
12. Newman, *Apologia*, 17.

of his writings.[13] Newman was attracted by the manliness and independence of Scott's character, as one who was willing to stand on God's side against the world. Scott also influenced Newman's understanding of the value of prayer. Distinguishing between public, social, and secret prayer, Scott taught that secret prayer was the best means of maintaining communion with God, and keeping alive the power of religion in the soul.

Newman was also impressed by *A Serious Call to a Devout Life*, which was written by William Law (1686–1761), who greatly influenced Thomas Scott.[14] Stressing the practical implications of one who lives a spiritual life, Law emphasized the necessary link between moments of prayer and everyday activities to a church-going but easy-living age: "And as actions are of much more significance than words, it must be a much more acceptable worship of God to glorify Him in all the actions of our common life than with any little form of words at any particular time."[15]

A second aspect of Law's thought which impressed Newman was the close connection between prayer and asceticism. In Law's understanding, prayer had to be connected with mortification: "The spirit of indulgence and the spirit of prayer cannot subsist together."[16] In his chapter entitled "Daily Early Prayer," he wrote about the importance of self-denial in renouncing sleep in order to rise early for prayer: "It will best fit and prepare you for the reception of the Holy Spirit."[17]

The work of Joseph Milner (1744–1785) put Newman into contact with the Fathers of the Church who provided him with another strong basis for his spiritual life. Newman later acknowledged that he "was nothing short of enamored of the long extracts from St. Augustine, St. Ambrose, and the other Fathers" which he found in Milner's Church history:[18]

---

13. Ibid. Newman continued: "They show him to be a true Englishman, and I deeply felt his influence; and for years I used almost as proverbs what I considered to be the scope and issue of his doctrine, 'Holiness before peace,' and 'Growth is the only evidence of Life.'" In converting to Roman Catholicism, Newman scrupulously followed Scott's advice: "I sat down very coolly to search the truth, I proceeded very gradually, and with extreme caution." Scott, *Force*, 71.

14. Law, *Serious Call*. Concerning this work, Newman wrote, "The main Catholic doctrine of the warfare between the city of God and powers of darkness was also deeply impressed upon my mind by a work of a character very opposite to Calvinism, Law's *Serious Call*." *Apologia*, 18.

15. Ibid., 93.

16. Ibid., 146.

17. Ibid., 150.

18. Newman, *Apologia*, 18. See Milner, *History*.

John Henry Newman

> Even when I was a boy, my thoughts were turned to the early Church, and especially to the early Fathers, by the perusal of the Calvinist [Joseph] Milner's Church History, and I have never lost, I never have suffered a suspension of the impression, deep and most pleasurable, which his sketches of St. Ambrose and St. Augustine left on my mind. From that time the vision of the Fathers was always, to my imagination, I may say, a paradise of delight to the contemplation of which I directed my thoughts from time to time.[19]

Thomas Newton (1704–1782), Bishop of Bristol, is mentioned by Newman in negative tones with regard to his spiritual formation. Upon reading *Dissertations on the Prophecies*, Newman's imagination became stained by the effects of the teaching that the Pope was the antichrist predicted by Scripture.[20] The roots of Newman's initial prejudice against the invocation of the saints in prayer can also be traced to Newton.

Another influence on Newman was Bishop Joseph Butler (1692–1752) who introduced *The Analogy of Religion* by describing the general decay of religion in England: "It is come, I know not how, to be taken for granted, by many persons, that Christianity is not so much as a subject of inquiry; but that it is, now at length, discovered to be fictitious."[21] Newman listed some of Butler's teachings which were influential: a visible Church as an oracle of truth and a pattern of sanctity; the duties of external religion; the historical character of Revelation; and probability as the guide of life. The very idea of an analogy among the separate works of God led Newman to the conclusion that the system which is of less importance is economically or sacramentally connected with the more momentous system. Eventually this insight developed into Newman's sacramental principle, contributing to his understanding of the economy of salvation.

The *Private Thoughts* of William Beveridge (1637–1708) was not mentioned by Newman in his *Apologia* because "I am speaking there of the formation of my doctrinal opinions, and I do not think they were influenced by it."[22] Yet this work undoubtedly conditioned his devotional life. Walter Mayers had presented Newman with a copy on December 31, 1816, and in the spring of 1817 Newman wrote "reflections or sermonets" which were in the style of Beveridge of whom he was "very fond."[23] On the inside cover of

---

19. Newman, *Certain Difficulties*, 1:370–71.
20. Newman, *Apologia*, 18. See Newton, *Dissertations*.
21. Butler, *Analogy*, xvii.
22. Newman, *Correspondence*, 116.
23. Newman, *Autographical Writings*, 154; Newman added this additional note in 1873: "I have now burned them."

this same copy, Newman wrote on October 14, 1874: "No book was more dear to me, or exercised a more powerful influence over my devotion and my habitual thoughts. In my private memoranda I even wrote in its style."[24] Bishop Beveridge's labors earned for him, in his day, the title of "The Great Reviver and Restorer of Primitive Piety."[25] He maintained that our knowledge of God must be practical and experiential:

> For we must not think that it is enough to know in general that there is a God, and that he is wise and powerful, great and glorious, true and faithful, good and gracious; these things a Man may know in general, so as to be able to discourse of them, and dispute for them too, and yet come short of that knowledge which is requisite to our true serving of God: Which should be such a Knowledge as will not only swim in the Brain, but sink down into the Heart; whereby a Man is possessed with a due Sense of those Things he knows, so that he doth not only know, but in a manner feel them to be so . . . that is, feel and experience it in ourselves; which tho' it may seem a Paradox to many of us, yet there is none of us but may find it to be a real Truth, and attain unto it, if we but be careful and constant in our Meditations upon God, and sincere in performing our Devotions to him; for by these Means our Notions of God will be refined, our conceptions cleared, and our Affections, by consequences so moved towards him, that we shall *taste* and experience in ourselves, as well as know from others, that he is good, and that all Perfections are centered in him.[26]

C. S. Dessain has commented on Beveridge's combination of deep piety and compelling logic which is reminiscent of the *Spiritual Exercises* of St. Ignatius. For example, Beveridge reflected "on striving to enter in at the strait Gate" (John 6:44):

> But we can never expect that he should draw us, unless we desire it of him. And therefore it must be our daily Prayer and Petition at the Throne of Grace, that God would vouchsafe us his especial Grace and Assistance, without which I cannot see how any one that knows his own Heart, can expect to be saved. But our Comfort is, if we do what we can, God will hear our Prayers, and enable us to do what otherwise we cannot; for he never yet

---

24. Newman, *Correspondence*, 116.
25. Beveridge, *Theological Works*, 1:vii.
26. Beveridge, *Private Thoughts*, 22.

did, nor ever will fail any Man that sincerely endeavours to serve and honor him.[27]

Philip Doddridge (1702–1751) was the author of *The Rise and Progress of Religion in the Soul*, a manual which Newman used to prepare himself for the reception of the Eucharist. Doddridge provided an outline of his chapter, "The Christian Assisted in Examining into His Growth in Grace," which is important because of Newman's reflections in his journal:

> The examination [is] important. I. False marks of growth to be avoided. II. True marks proposed: such as (1) Increasing love to God. (2) Benevolence to men. (3) Candour of disposition. (4) Meekness under injuries. (5) Serenity amidst the uncertainties of life. (6) Humility, especially as expressed in Evangelic exercises of the mind towards Christ and the Spirit. (7) Zeal for the divine honour. (8) Habitual and chearful [sic] willingness to exchange worlds whenever God shall appoint. (9) Conclusion. (10) The Christian breathing after growth in grace.[28]

Besides proposing particular models for morning and evening prayer, Doddridge also exhorted the Christian to undertake the exercises of habitual love and joy in God, and to exert himself for purposes of usefulness.

In August 1821, Newman began using *The Communicant's Spiritual Companion; or, An Evangelical Preparation of the Lord's Supper* of Thomas Haweis (1734–1820).[29] Besides helping one to prepare for communion, this work also spoke about the element of fear in the spiritual life, which enables us better to understand this aspect of Newman's spirituality. In the form of a prayer, Haweis wrote:

> Lord, put thy fear into my soul; be thou ever sanctified in me; let me ever tremble before, and dread to offend thee. May the sense of thy omniscience and nearness ever over-awe my soul; when sin would tempt may I remember that thou art present; may my fear be as my love, filial; may thy displeasure be more grievous to me than thy punishment, and may I hate to offend

---

27. Ibid., 119.

28. Doddridge, *Rise*, 260–68. In *Autobiographical Writings*, 174, Newman's entry on August 4, 1821, responded to Doddridge's questions: "Praised be God, I think I am much more resigned to Him than I was, more contented, less careful of the morrow, less desirous of the things of the world.... I am very deficient in spirituality in prayer, brotherly love, humility, forgiveness of injuries, charity, benevolence, purity, truth and patience. I am very bad-tempered, vain, proud, arrogant, prone to anger, and vehement. ... I am also in great want of fervent love towards Christ."

29. Newman, *Autobiographical Writings*, 175, August 18, 1821: "I bought Haweis's Spiritual Communicant yesterday, and shall examine myself by that."

thee, because thou art my good and gracious Father, more than thou art withal the just and righteous Judge.[30]

Characteristics of Newman's Spirituality

To analyze and categorize the thought of another person is never a simple matter, and it becomes even more challenging when such analysis and systematization concerns something so personal as another's spiritual life. Yet, as a prelude to considering Newman's spiritual direction, it should be helpful to sketch the dominant characteristics of his spiritual life.

The Unseen World

In 1828 Newman wrote in an essay published in the *London Review* about how revealed religion should be especially poetical and bring us into a new world: "With Christians, a poetical view of things is a duty,—we are bid to colour all things with hues of faith, to see a Divine meaning in every event, and a super-human tendency."[31] Newman seems to have grown up with a poet's ability to penetrate beyond the surface of things, to discern God's immanence while respecting his transcendence. In his *Apologia*, he recalled the effect which the doctrine of final perseverance had on his youthful imaginations in isolating him from the objects surrounding him, in confirming him in his mistrust of the reality of material phenomena, and making him rest in the thought of two and only two absolute and luminously self-evident beings, himself and his Creator.[32] This view was presented in one of his sermons at St. Mary's: "To every one of us there are but two beings in the whole world, himself and God; for, as to this outward scene, its pleasure and pursuits, its honours and cares, its contrivances, its personages, its kingdoms, its multitude of busy slaves, what are they to us? Nothing—no more than a show."[33] This sense of separation from the visible world dated back to Newman's youth. Moreover, his reliance on the thought of himself and his Creator is to be understood, not as the worldview of an introspective self-centered youth, but as the re-echoing of the whole Christian ascetical

---

30. Haweis, *Communicant's*, 108.

31. Newman, "Poetry, with Reference to Aristotle's Poetics," in *Essays Critical and Historical*, 1:23.

32. Newman, *Apologia*, 16.

33. Newman, Sermon 2, in *Parochial and Plain Sermons*, 1:20; July 21, 1833.

tradition, from the Desert Fathers onwards, who aimed at seeking and living with God alone.

Newman's reading of Clement and Origen strengthened his attitude of looking beyond this visible world to that greater reality, which we experience sacramentally in this life. Beyond the veil of this world, Newman was conscious of an Invisible Presence which is more real than what is seen.

> We are born into a world of sense; that is, of real things which lie around us.
> . . . They act upon us and we know it; and we act upon them in turn and know we do.
> But all this does not interfere with the existence of that other world which I speak of, acting upon us, yet not impressing us with the consciousness that it does so. It may as really be present and exert an influence as that which reveals itself to us. And that such a world there is, Scripture tells us. Do you ask what it is, and what it contains? I will not say that all that belongs to it is vastly more important than what we see, for among things visible are our fellow-men, and nothing created is more precious and noble than a human soul. But still, taking the things which we see altogether, and the things we do not see altogether, the world we do not see is on the whole a much higher world than that which we do see. It appears, then, that the things which are seen are but a part, and but a secondary part of the beings about us. Once, and once only, for thirty three years has He condescended to become one of the beings that are seen, when, in the Person of His Only begotten Son, He was, by an unspeakable mercy, born of the Virgin Mary into this sensible world.[34]

The unseen world is a recurring theme in Newman's sermons, poetry and correspondence. This other world "exists now, though we see it not. It is among us and around us." The Christian must choose whether he will be dominated by the world he sees or the unseen world. He must be willing to walk by faith rather than by sight. The invisible presence of evil spirits and angels, for example, was very real for Newman, and he acknowledged it from childhood to old age.[35] Newman's lifestyle and personality conveyed his conviction about the invisible world, as Principal J. C. Shairp witnessed from his Oxford days: "From the seclusion of study and abstinence and

---

34. Ibid., Sermon 13, 4:201–3; July 16, 1837. Newman frequently referred to the unseen world in his correspondence during his Roman Catholic years.

35. Newman, *Apologia*, 14, 34–36. In Newman's Roman Catholic correspondence, there are numerous references to a person's Guardian Angel, as well as to St. Gabriel and St. Raphael.

prayer, from habitual dwelling in the Unseen, he seemed to come forth that one day of the week (Sunday) to speak to others of the things he had seen and known."[36] This outlook remained lifelong, as can be seen in a remark from the testimony of Elizabeth Mozley in 1874:

> One sees that Dr. Newman's great power . . . is a certain vivid realisation of the unseen, or rather that there is an unseen that you cannot see. "How can people say what is, or is not, natural to evil spirits? What is a grotesque manifestation to us may not be so to them. What do we know about an evil spirit?" The words were nothing, but there was an intensity of realisation in his face as he said them, of a reality of his ignorance about it, that was a key to me as to the source of his influence over others. The *sight* of belief in others is next to seeing yourself; and men cling to it.[37]

Newman's sense of the unseen world has led some authors to classify his spirituality as platonist, but this term must be understood with some nuances. His teaching must be distinguished from Platonism, insofar as he did not de-emphasize the reality of material phenomena to the extent that Plato did. For Newman, the invisible world was not simply a world of ideas but the world of christian revelation, the kingdom of a personal God, of Christ, the saints and the angels. As much as he involved himself in interpersonal relationships and pastoral responsibilities, the truth of his relationship with God and the reality of the unseen world remained primary.

Newman realized that some Christians are tempted to neglect their responsibilities in this world in order to contemplate the unseen world; however, when this occurs, "we may be sure that there is something wrong and unchristian, not in their thinking of the next world, but in their manner of thinking it."[38] Among the remedies suggested by Newman, thankfulness to Almighty God and the inward life of the Spirit will cause the Christian to labor diligently in his calling and to see God in all things:

> Accordingly, in whatever comes upon him, he will endeavour to discern and gaze (as it were) on the countenance of his Saviour. He will feel that the true contemplation of that Saviour lies in his worldly business; that as Christ is seen in the poor, and in the persecuted, and in children, so is He seen in the employments which He puts upon His chosen, whatever they may be; that in attending to his own calling he will be meeting Christ; that if he neglects it, he will not on that account enjoy His presence

---

36. May, *Cardinal Newman*, 30.
37. Mozley, *Letters*, 1:335.
38. Newman, Sermon 2, in *Parochial and Plain Sermons*, 8:155; November 1, 1836.

at all the more, but that while performing it, he will see Christ revealed to his soul amid the ordinary actions of the day, as by a sort of sacrament. Thus he will take his worldly business as a gift from Him, and will love it as much.[39]

In his own pastoral responsibilities, Newman was sensitive to following the signs which he thought were given to him by God in his providence. When he sensed a convergence of signs, he would pray and then move ahead and become actively involved in the project indicated. His ministry was always seen against the background of the unseen world insofar as Divine Providence granted such insights and revelations.

Holiness of God

Basic to Newman's teaching on the spiritual life is certitude about the existence of God. In his *Apologia*, he wondered, "Who can really pray to a Being about whose existence he is seriously in doubt?"[40] Similarly, he emphasised in his *Essay in Aid of a Grammar of Assent*: "Without certitude in religious faith there may be much decency of profession and of observance, but there can be no habit of prayer, no directness of devotion, no intercourse with the unseen, no generosity of self-sacrifice."[41] Newman preached "not a theory or philosophy of his own, but the Christian revelation—not Christian doctrine in the abstract, but the truths of faith in their concrete implications."[42] He always stood in awe at the mysteriousness and holiness of God, and this was reflected in his teaching and practice. When people encounter God, their reactions can range from extreme fear to powerful attraction. Usually there are elements of both fear and love in our reaction to the holiness of God. Newman certainly sensed the dialectic between the fear and the love of God, but scholars differ in their interpretation of which attitude predominated in his life and teaching. Geoffrey Faber thought that fear was the driving force of Newman's arguments: "Again and again in his sermons it seems as if he had to force himself to speak of God's love and mercy. The assurance of these is less real to him than the fear of condemnation and wrath."[43] Derek Stanford added that this is not to deprecate Newman's faith so much as to

39. Ibid., 165.
40. Newman, *Apologia*, 28.
41. Newman, *Essay in Aid*, 220.
42. Dessain, "Newman's Spirituality," 138.
43. Faber, *Oxford*, 170–71: "This was the inheritance from Evangelicalism which he was never able to discard, by which he was always to be distinguished from those happier spirits to whom the tidings of the Gospel were kindly tidings."

determine its kind.[44] Charles Sarolea wrote that Newman "has always dwelt far more on the idea of religion of wrath and retribution than on the idea of mercy and forgiveness."[45] In addition, Jan Walgrave called the fear of God the deepest motive of Newman's life which explains the course of his search after truth; however, he used the word "fear" in the more nuanced sense of a moral earnestness seeking after truth.[46] Newman sought to follow the inner light of his conscience step by step, but was fearful of being deceived by self-will. Newman's position seems to be clarified by Maurice Nedoncelle: "The fear of being unfaithful to the truth, of being a missing piece in the plan of God, this is what explains the evolution of Newman, and not the obsession of hell."[47] Certainly there is an element of fear in Newman's teaching, but in the sense which is so well expressed by the English word "awe."[48] Perhaps it would be best to let Newman speak for himself. In his Anglican sermon, "Shrinking from Christ's Coming," Newman preached:

> If indeed we have habitually lived to the world, then truly it is natural we should attempt to fly from Him whom we have pierced. . . . But if we have lived, however imperfectly, yet habitually, in His fear, if we trust that His Spirit is in us, then we need not be ashamed before Him. We shall then come before Him, as now we come to pray—with profound abasement, with awe, with self-renunciation, still as relying upon the Spirit which He has given us, with our faculties about us, with a collected and determined mind, and with hope. He who cannot pray for Christ's coming, ought not in consistency to pray at all.[49]

---

44. Newman, *Letters of John Henry Newman*, edited by Derek Stanford and Muriel Spark, 20: "The basis of religion in some men is joy; in some, love or praise; in others, fear. 'The fear of the Lord is the beginning of wisdom.' There is certainly a good case for believing this to be so of Newman."

45. Sarolea, *Cardinal Newman*, 41.

46. Walgrave, *Newman*, 22.

47. Nedoncelle, Introduction to *Apologia*, xliiin1.

48. Harrold, *John Henry Newman*, 328–29, offered a balanced view. "Yet we must do Newman the justice of observing that for him 'fear' was ordinarily more a 'holy awe' at the mysteriousness and dreadful seriousness of man's destiny, than the mere terror of the possibility of eternal damnation."

49. Newman, Sermon 4, in *Parochial and Plain Sermons*, 5:55–56; December 4, 1836. In one of his earliest sermons, Newman preached on repentance, on October 10, 1824: "But I would rather persuade you from love than urge you through fear." Ivory, "Doctrine," 408.

John Henry Newman

Providential Guidance

Newman could not imagine believing in God unless one also believed that God cares about his creatures and wills them good.[50] A person's happiness then is found in accepting the providential guidance which God's love speaks to his conscience.[51] Newman was especially conscious of God's providential concern throughout his life, and this awareness was reflected in his teaching and practice of the spiritual life. In his farewell sermon at St. Clement's, the twenty-five-year-old Newman set forth the ideals which were to characterize his entire life:

> For I have felt and feel now that it is only as He makes use of me that I can be useful—only as I put myself entirely into His hands that I can promote His glory, and that to attempt any slightest work in my own strength is an absurdity too great for words to express. He has been pleased to bring me into His ministry and to lay the weight of an high office upon me—And wherever His good providence may lead me I trust I shall never forget that I am dedicated and made over entirely to Him as the minister of Christ and that the grand and blessed object of my life must be to promote the interests of His cause, and to serve His Church, and contribute to the strength of His kingdom, and to make use of all my powers of mind and body, external and acquired, to bring sinners to Him, and to help in purifying a corrupt world—In this good work I willingly would be spent and I pray God to give me grace to keep me from failing.[52]

Various events in Newman's life provided indications of God's will. Even in the midst of his illness in Sicily, he could reflect confidently, "I thought God had some work for me."[53] He experienced the fact that God unfolds his will to us over a lifetime rather than revealing everything in one moment of great illumination.[54] His own experience was reflected in his direction to others to resign themselves to the divine will, to entrust

---

50. JHN to Mrs. F. R. Ward, 8 May 1849, in *LD* 19:127. "It would be easier for me to believe that there is no God at all, than to think he does not care."

51. Walgrave, *Newman*, 25 stated succinctly: "In Newman's thought, the primary factor is always conscience. It is his starting point in throwing a bridge across the external world, in 'situating' it in the perspective of Divine Providence, which is itself the first and supreme truth of religious experience."

52. Newman, *St. Clement's Sermon*, 150: unpublished manuscript, A. 17, 1, preached April 23, 1826, as cited by Ivory, "Doctrine," 410.

53. Newman, *Autobiographical Writings*, 122.

54. JHN to Mrs. William Froude, 23 February 1853, in *LD* 15:307. "He does not tell us everything at once—but first one thing, and then, when we act upon that, another."

their cares and anxieties to the hands of God's loving providence. In 1866, he wrote to Marianne Bowden: "Put yourself, then, my dear child, into the hands of your loving Father and Redeemer, who knows and loves you better than you know or love yourself. He has appointed every action of your life. He created you, sustains you, and has marked down the very way and hour when he will take you to Himself."[55] This doctrine of divine providence provided a source of inner strength and courage to Newman, as he experienced the difficulties involved in the realization of his mission. He entrusted himself as an instrument into the hands of God. He could witness by his own life to the truth of his preaching: "God's hand is ever over His own, and He leads them forward by a way they know not of."[56]

Dependence on God

A fourth characteristic of Newman's spirituality, which logically complements the other characteristics already mentioned, was the absolute dependence of a person upon God. This principle was not abstract but grounded in the events and relationships of Newman's life. He was a man who experienced and appreciated deep and lasting friendships, yet he was not totally dependent on the support of his friends. Human friendship pointed beyond itself to one's relationship with God. For example, there are autobiographical overtures in his sermon on "The Thought of God, the Stay of the Soul":

> We know that even our nearest friends enter into us but partially, and hold intercourse with us only at times; whereas the consciousness of a perfect and enduring Presence and it alone, keeps the heart open. Withdraw the Object on which it rests, and it will relapse again into its state of confinement and constraint; and in proportion as it is limited, either to certain seasons or to certain affections, the heart is straitened and distressed. If it be not over bold to say it, He who is infinite can alone be its measure; He alone can answer to the mysterious assemblage of feelings and thoughts which it has within it.[57]

---

55. JHN to Marianne Bowden, 5 June 1866, in *LD* 22:247.
56. Newman, Sermon 17, in *Parochial and Plain Sermons*, 4:261; May 7, 1837.

57. Ibid., Sermon 22, 5:318–19; June 9, 1839. The conclusion of this sermon reiterates the same idea: "Life passes, riches fly away, popularity is fickle, the senses decay, the world changes, friends die. One alone is constant; One alone can be all things to us; One alone can supply our needs; One alone can train us up to our full perfection; One alone can give a meaning to our complex and intricate nature; One alone can give us tune and harmony; One alone can form and possess us; Are we allowed to put ourselves under His guidance? This surely is the only question. Has He really made us his children, and

John Henry Newman

One Newman scholar, after a careful study of every stage of Newman's spiritual life, has judged that the principal motive of all his thoughts, words, and deeds was the will of God. "God's will is the 'Kindly Light' which led him step by step through the encircling gloom of his earthly existence."[58] From a study of Newman's life, it can be seen how he experienced the consequences of surrendering to the divine will. As the Christian grows in his realization of dependency, he advances in self-surrender and his realization of God's presence. As an Anglican, Newman challenged his congregation to "an honest purpose, an unreserved, entire submission of ourselves to our Maker, Redeemer, and Judge."[59] He taught that the true Christian enthrones the Son of God in his conscience and refers to Him as sovereign authority. He uses no reasoning with Him, but says, "Thou, God, seest me." God is felt to be too near to allow for argument, self-defense, excuse of objection.[60]

In his life as a Roman Catholic, Newman passed through various purifying events, remaining wholeheartedly convinced that he was in the hands of God. He was willing to be an instrument for the fulfillment of God's Will, and this demanded unconditional surrender. He urged people to unlock and open their hearts to God, and such advice was validated by his own experience.

Closely connected with Newman's sense of the unseen world and surrender to God was his spirit of detachment and unworldliness. The great and obvious characteristic of a Bible Christian, for Newman, was to be without worldly ties or objects, living in this world, but not for this world. The epitaph which he composed for himself and is displayed in the cloister of the Birmingham Oratory, expresses the dynamic of his whole life: *Ex umbris et imaginibus ad veritatem* ("From shadows and images into the truth").

Although the sense of unworldliness was a contributing factor to Newman's great spiritual strength and influence on others, it is also the reason why some critics attribute a lack of social concern to his attitude. Perhaps, in this respect, Newman did not transcend the "conventional wisdom" which led many preachers of his day to neglect the social evils of their age. Since he always served the poor, it seems that Newman's unworldliness led him to stress the individual conscience rather than social reforms. Moreover, by his own life and teaching, Newman has given a good example of the Christian productively living the tension between his spiritual life and his pastoral responsibilities. Newman's spirituality prompted him to use the present situation as the means *par excellence* of his sanctification.

---

taken possession of us by His Holy Spirit?" Ibid., 326.

58. Zeno, *John Henry Newman*, 274.
59. Newman, Sermon 17, in *Parochial and Plain Sermons*, 5:253; December 9, 1838.
60. Ibid., Sermon 16, in *Parochial and Plain Sermons*, 5:227; December 16, 1838.

Relation of Theology and Spirituality

Newman never elaborated an explicit theological treatise on the spiritual life. In fact, he even denied that he was a theologian.[61] His own refusal to describe himself as a theologian can be traced to three reasons: first, his acceptance of a conception of theological method which was prevalent during much of his life as a Roman Catholic: this neo-Aristotelean "scientific" method of theology, which dominated Roman schools, held that truth was gained in the sciences through induction and in theology by deduction. Since Newman customarily treated theological topics inductively, he did not consider himself a theologian.

The second reason for Newman's denial that he was a theologian was grounded in his belief that a "theologian" had to be a specialist with complete command of one particular field, and he was conscious of the fact that he was an amateur in many fields, rather than a specialist in one. For example, in 1874, in his *Letter to Norfolk*, Newman argued that "theology is a science, and a science of a special kind," and that "every science must be in the hands of a comparatively few people—that is, of those who have made it a study."[62]

Third, Newman knew his strength was less that of a theologian and more that of a controversialist, responding to particular needs, grappling with particular questions as they arose. He believed that he could best exercise his abilities if and when he was permitted to function as a private individual. Writing to Maria Giberne in 1869, he stated:

> Really and truly I am not a theologian. A theologian is one who has mastered theology . . . who can discriminate exactly between proposition and proposition, argument and argument, who can pronounce which are safe, which allowable, which dangerous—who can trace the history of doctrines in successive centuries, or apply the principles of former times to the conditions of the present. This is it to be a theologian—this and a hundred things besides. And this I am not, and never shall be. Like St. Gregory

---

61. This denial occurs chiefly in Newman's correspondence as a Roman Catholic and with increasing frequency during the years leading up to the First Vatican Council and the publication of the *Essay in Aid of a Grammar of Assent*. See the following letters:
JHN to Sir John Acton, 2 August 1859, in *LD* 28:433;
JHN to E. B. Pusey, 14 November 1867, in *LD* 23:369;
JHN to Maria Giberne, 10 February 1869, in *LD* 24:212–13;
JHN to E. B. Pusey, 4 November 1869, in *LD* 24:363;
JHN to R. H. Hutton, 16 February 1870, in *LD* 25:32;
JHN to Unknown Correspondent, July 1877, in *LD* 28:216;
JHN to Robert Whitty, 20 December 1878, in *LD* 28:431.
62. Newman, *Difficulties*, 294.

Nazianzen, I like going on my own way, and having my time my own, living without pomp or state, or pressing engagements. Put me into official garb, and I am worth nothing; leave me to myself, and every now and then I shall do something.[63]

Just as Newman did not consider himself a theologian and did not write a theological treatise on the spiritual life, it is not surprising that he did not develop a theology of prayer: "Newman seems never to have had a theory as to how prayer works. He did not get involved in the discussion of God's passivity, he did not ask how the immutable God could be acted upon by our prayers. He simply knew that Jesus has taught us to pray. He simply knew that prayer did work."[64]

Personal Experiences as Theological *Loci*

In 1868, J. M. Capes, reviewing Newman's *Verses on Various Occasions*, noted:

Dr. Newman's plea, in justification of the publication of this volume of his verses, revised and enlarged, is to be found in the fact that he cannot live in absolute isolation from his fellow-man. The ordinary companionship of the friends and acquaintances of one who, as he told us in his *Apologia*, early thought himself bound to celibacy, is not enough, even for a man whose inner resources are so varied, whose interest in human affairs is so sympathetic, and who is so penetrated with the sense, as he expresses it, that he is "*solus cum solo*" (alone with Alone) in the world.[65]

Responding to Capes' observations, Newman offered an interesting self-analysis: "I have often been puzzled at myself, that I should be both particularly fond of being alone, and particularly fond of being with my friends. Yet I know both the one and the other are true, though I can no more reconcile them than you can. You are the first, as far as I know, who have noticed an apparent inconsistency to which I can but plead guilty."[66] This "apparent inconsistency" perhaps explains the powerful influence of Newman on his contemporaries. The strength of his personality is still felt today in his writings. His fondness for being *solus cum solo* exemplifies the intimacy of his

---

63. JHN to Maria Giberne, 10 February 1869, in *LD* 24:212–13.

64. Swanston, "Newman Praying," 34.

65. Capes' review appeared in the *Fortnightly Review*, March 1, 1868, 342–45; cited in *LD* 24:53n1. The phrase *solus cum solo* (alone with oneself) is related to a longer phrase: *numquam minus solus quam cum solus* (never less alone than when alone).

66. JHN to J. M. Capes, 16 March 1868, in *LD* 24:53.

unique relationship with God, which was the source of his many human friendships and pastoral accomplishments.

Newman consistently emphasized the importance of honestly following God's voice as expressed in one's conscience. By being true to his conscience, Newman argued that a person could come to acknowledge the existence of God.[67] As people become more attentive to the voice of God in their consciences, they are drawn into a deeper personal relationship with God which is reflected in their spiritual life. As Jan Walgrave has observed: "The development of the religious man is a dialectic of fidelity to conscience."[68] Newman's spiritual life was not isolated from earthly realities, but rather his various experiences were theological *loci* in which he sensed the presence of God. In the solitude of his conscience he sought to integrate such events, penetrating to the more profound reality which is revealed only to the person of faith.

Various personal experiences either reminded Newman of his fundamental relationship with God or led him to deepen that relationship. His conversion experience as an adolescent, his pastoral ministry, his sister Mary's death and his illness in Sicily prepared him to exercise strong leadership in the Oxford Movement. His study of early Church history and patrology led him to seek admittance to the Roman Catholic Church, enduring all the pain which conversion involved at that time. As a Roman Catholic, a series of events purified his commitment to follow wherever God would lead him: the division of the two Oratories, the Achilli trial, the Catholic university in Ireland, the Scripture translation project, the *Rambler* editorship, the attack by Charles Kingsley, and the plans for an Oxford Oratory. In all of these situations, Newman suffered, but in his suffering he learned to confide himself to the hands of God. His personal experience of God's love revealed in Jesus Christ together with his faith in the Church's teaching authority enabled him to integrate his other experiences and to grow holier thereby.

This is not to suggest that the integration process was always smooth and rational. Newman was a man of strong feelings and sensitivity, and his interior emotional struggles in opening his soul to God are evident in his private journals. These private thoughts were not intended for the public's eye, but the demand for more information on Newman has publicized his personal thoughts to such a degree as to cause, in some cases, a negative

67. Newman, *Apologia*, 156: "I am a Catholic by virtue of my believing in a God; and if I am asked why I believe in a God, I answer that it is because I believe in myself, for I feel it impossible to believe in my own existence (and of that fact I am quite sure) without believing also in the existence of Him, who lives as a Personal, All-seeing, All-judging Being in my conscience."

68. Walgrave, *Newman*, 148.

reaction. Many saints probably experienced similar feelings but never wrote them down. What matters essentially is how Newman made the best use of his personality in his life. His consistency in generously responding to the Gospel was joined to his personal ascetical practices first initiated as a young man after reading Law's *A Serious Call to a Devout Life*.

The spiritual life must be based on the objectivity of God's existence and self-revelation, and the Christian should strive to conduct himself faithfully and peacefully. There must be no "unreal words," no sentiment without practice. The Christian has a personal knowledge of God and truly senses his presence. Newman sought to unify action with feeling and thought; he achieved this unity and simplicity by his faith in God and by his honesty with himself in the face of the events of his life. God speaks to us through the events and relationships of our lives. Our task is to have the right attitude toward these opportunities and this gives life its meaning.

Indwelling of the Holy Spirit

Another theological principle in Newman's doctrine on the spiritual life is his teaching on the Divine Indwelling in the soul of the Christian. This "unspeakable Gospel privilege," which has traditionally been ascribed to the agency of the Holy Spirit, became one of the doctrinal foundations for Newman's spirituality. The teachings of Thomas Scott, along with the study of Scripture and the Greek Fathers, influenced the young Newman's thought and spiritual life. His understanding of the time and the manner in which the presence of the Spirit inhabited the Christian underwent an evolution from the early years when he was influenced by evangelical thought. Because Newman preached what he believed, his sermons provide a rich source for understanding his personal faith experience. He understood that the foundation laid in the New Testament for the new life of union with God, which the Christian religion offered to mankind, was the doctrine of the indwelling in the soul of the Holy Spirit, and through the Spirit of the Father and the Son. True Christianity is therefore the presence of the Trinity: "God, the Son, has graciously vouchsafed to reveal the Father to His creatures from without; God, the Holy Ghost, by inward communications."[69] The Spirit is "the seal and earnest of an Unseen Saviour; being the present pledge of Him who is absent."[70]

Newman tried to describe this presence in order to help people realize this gift.

---

69. Newman, Sermon 19, in *Parochial and Plain Sermons*, 2:217; end of the year, 1834.

70. Ibid., 220.

> The Holy Ghost dwells in body and soul, as in a Temple. Evil spirits indeed have power to possess sinners, but His indwelling is far more perfect; for He is all-knowing and omnipresent, He is able to search into all our thoughts, and penetrate into every motive of the heart. Therefore, he pervades us (if it may be so said) as light pervades a building, or as a sweet perfume the folds of some honourable robe; so that in Scripture language, we are said to be in Him and He in us. It is plain that such an inhabitation brings the Christian into a state altogether new and marvelous, far above the possession of mere gifts.[71]

At the new birth of Baptism, the Christian enters the kingdom of Christ. "By this new birth the Divine Sheckinah is set up within him, pervading soul and body separating him really, not only in name, from those who are not Christians, raising him in the scale of being, drawing and fostering into life whatever remains in him of a higher nature."[72] Newman reminded his audience that they were temples of God. "We are assured of some real though mystical fellowship with the Father, Son, and Holy Spirit, in order to do this; so that both by a real presence in the soul, and by the fruits of grace, God is one with every believer, as in a consecrated Temple."[73] Moreover, he related the presence of the Spirit in the Christian to the Catholic Church by preaching that "the heart of every Christian ought to represent in miniature the Catholic Church, since one Spirit makes both the whole Church and every member of it to be His Temple."[74] Newman then encouraged his listeners to not only realize this presence, but to act on it.

> For ourselves, in proportion as we realize that higher view of the subject, which we may humbly trust is the true one, let us be careful to act up to it. Let us adore the Sacred Presence within us with all fear, and "rejoice with trembling." Let us offer our best gifts in sacrifice to Him who instead of abhorring, has taken up His abode in these sinful hearts of ours. . . . In this then consists our whole duty, to contemplate Almighty God as in heaven, so in our hearts and souls; and again to act the while towards Him and for Him in the works of every day.[75]

---

71. Ibid., 222.

72. Ibid., Sermon 18, 3:266; November 8, 1835. *Shekinah* ("dwelling" in Hebrew) refers to the dwelling place of God, i.e., the divine presence.

73. Ibid., Sermon 3, 2:35; December 25, 1834.

74. Ibid., Sermon 10, 2:132; June 4, 1843.

75. Ibid., Sermon 18, 3:269; November 8, 1835.

In 1838, Newman elaborated his teaching on the Divine Indwelling in his *Lectures on the Doctrine of Justification*. He carried this strong theological basis with him into the Roman Catholic Church, but he wrote little on the subject of uncreated grace after his conversion in 1845. By way of exception, in 1868, Newman wrote to W. J. Daunt: "In these later times it is usual to say that the Third Person of the Blessed Trinity resides in the soul by means of His grace—but it is still a theological opinion maintained by great divines (and I suspect the old opinion), that His Presence in the soul is not merely His grace but Himself."[76]

It is evident from his *Meditations and Devotions* that Newman personally had a special devotion to the Holy Spirit. From his lifelong appreciation of the indwelling of the Spirit flowed certain consequences in Newman's life: it made him watchful and detached, joyful and at peace, and substantiated his view of the unseen world. In particular, the Divine Indwelling was the dogmatic foundation for Newman's teaching on the spiritual life. His theology and piety are wedded beautifully in this 1838 sermon:

> A true Christian, then, may almost be defined as one who has a ruling sense of God's presence within him. As none but justified persons have that privilege, so none but the justified have that practical perception of it . . . In all circumstances, of joy or sorrow, hope or fear, let us aim at having Him in our inmost heart; let us have no secret apart from Him. Let us acknowledge Him as enthroned within us at the very spring of thought and affection. Let us submit ourselves to His guidance and sovereign direction; let us come to Him that He may forgive us, cleanse us, change us, guide us, and save us. This is the true life of the saints. This is to have the Spirit witnessing with our spirits that we are sons of God.[77]

Centrality of Christ

The centrality of Christ in Anglican spirituality provided a rich heritage upon which Newman based his spirituality. His patristic study led to a greater clarification and realization of the mediation of Christ in his spiritual life. His personal prayer books reflect his lifelong devotion to Jesus Christ. It is in union with the person of Christ that our prayers should be offered to God the Father, and the presence of Christ within us is a principle of sanctification. A study of

---

76. JHN to W. J. Daunt, 17 September 1868, in *LD* 24:144.

77. Newman, Sermon 16, in *Parochial and Plain Sermons*, 5:225–26, 236; December 16, 1838.

Newman's sermons reveals that the whole of his doctrinal message is centered in and consequent upon the mystery of the Incarnation.

Newman taught there were two reasons for the Incarnation: atonement for sin and renewal in holiness.[78] He made much of the Athanasian principle of the deification of a person by the incarnation, so that all Christians receive the power of mediation by the virtue of Him who is within them. In his *Essay on the Development of Christian Doctrine*, Newman called the incarnation the central aspect of Christianity, out of which the three main aspects of its teaching take their rise, the sacramental, the hierarchical, and the ascetic.[79] In effect, there are many other Christian principles which can be drawn from the truth of the incarnation, and it is important to examine three of these in relationship to his understanding of the spiritual life. By the dogmatic principle is meant that "supernatural truths have been irrevocably committed to human language, imperfect because it is human, but definitive and necessary because given from above."[80] Just how important this principle of dogma is in Newman's thought can be seen in his *Apologia*: "From the age of fifteen, dogma has been the fundamental principle of my religion; I know of no other religion; I cannot enter into the idea of any other sort of religion; religion, as a mere sentiment, is to me a dream and a mockery. As well can there be filial love without the fact of a father, as devotion without the fact of a Supreme Being. What I held in 1816, I held in 1833, and I hold in 1864. Please God, I shall hold it to the end."[81] Newman insisted on the dogmatic principle to counter the subjectivism of the liberals and the preoccupation of the Evangelicals with feelings and emotion. Newman believed that dogma was one of the means of expressing the faith of Christians. In the early Church, with which he was so familiar through the writings of the Fathers, the creeds were prayers which tried to describe objective realities. Each of the early Church councils would always incorporate the professions of faith, enunciated by previous councils. These credal formulations were part of the living tradition of the Church, and were not considered to be mere abstractions. They were an approach to the reality of God, which calls for real assent, and which provides the basis for our spiritual lives. Accordingly, Newman considered the Athanasian Creed as "the most simple and sublime, the most devotional formulary to which Christianity has given birth."[82] He faced his God in continuity with

---

78. Newman, *Select Treatises*, 189.
79. Newman, *Essay on the Development*, 36.
80. Ibid., 325.
81. Newman, *Apologia*, 51.
82. Newman, *Essay in Aid*, 133.

the whole of Christian tradition, ever striving to make his assent more real by his prayer and life.

For Newman, the doctrine of the Incarnation is "the announcement of a divine gift conveyed in a material and visible medium," and thus in the very idea of Christianity the sacramental principle is established as its characteristic.[83] The sacramental principle maintains that material phenomena are both the types and the instruments of real things unseen. The young Newman derived this understanding from Bishop Butler's *Analogy of Religion*, John Keble's *Christian Year*, and his study of the Alexandrine Fathers. The sacramental principle is easily connected with Newman's consciousness of living in the invisible world; everything that is seen is a revelation of the unseen world. Newman's use of various devotions and spiritual practices can be better understood in the light of the sacramental principle.

This idea of sacramentality found expression in Newman's understanding of prayer because he considered prayer a sacramental activity which draws people closer to the reality of God. By means of symbols such as words and gestures, prayer is a communication with God, acknowledging our complete dependence on Him. Prayer provides the means to come to a knowledge of God's will and enables us to participate more actively in his providential plan for the world. Just as the texts of Scripture can be understood in a mystical sense, so also our words in prayer are invested with a sacramental office. Because of Newman's sense of the holiness of God, he strongly advocated the use of set forms and times for prayer and reacted against the casual use of extemporary prayer.

The advantage of formulas is that they habituate us to an attitude of quiet reverence. As an Anglican, Newman prayed morning and evening from the Book of Common Prayer and employed the *Devotions* of Bishop Andrewes. From 1838 on, Newman prayed the Roman Breviary. In the prayers which he himself composed for private use, one can sense that he desired to have somewhat fixed forms for prayer as well as to recognize the influence of other traditional liturgical forms. He realized, however, that devotion is a highly personal matter and he never forced his preferences on anyone else. A letter written in 1863 affords insight into Newman's understanding of the dogmatic and sacramental principles.

> While private judgement is forbidden to Catholics in matters of divine revelation, it is fully accorded to them in matters of devotion. Worship is a free-will service. It is our response to God's voice. He speaks, and what He speaks is dogma—it cannot be altered—it never was ours—it comes to us, not from us—it is

---

83. Newman, *Essay on the Development*, 325.

objective—but worship is essentially subjective—it is what we give to God—and (under rational limits) we have power over our own acts. Therefore the Church is very loth to interfere with it. Catholics may choose *their* own saints to be devout to. They may honor this one, they may pass over that. They have their own "special devotion."[84]

The ecclesial principle is also important in Newman's understanding of the spiritual life. Although he insisted on the intimate relationship between the individual person and God, Newman experienced a developing appreciation of the Church and the value of public prayer. His sermons, especially at St. Mary's, reflected his theological conviction that the Church is the chief means of grace. As a Roman Catholic, his gratitude for the Communion of Saints increased; in 1848 he wrote to Mrs. William Froude: "To know too that you are in the Communion of Saints—to know that you have cast your lot among all those Blessed Servants of God who are the choice fruit of His Passion—that you have their intercessions on high—that you may address them—and above all the Glorious Mother of God, what thoughts can be greater than these"?[85] Newman also taught his parishioners that the Holy Spirit is given to individuals through the Church's sacrament of baptism. The Church celebrates the eucharist which strengthens and binds Christians together. The united prayers of Christians gathered for worship are particularly blessed and have a special place in the life of the Church.

Throughout the Oxford Movement, Newman was concerned with the significance of the Church. Just as the individual Christian enjoys the Divine Indwelling, so also does the Church possess an objective supernatural reality. Just as the individual Christian can serve as an instrument of God, so also does the Church serve as the means of communicating God's life to the faithful. The Church was considered by Newman as the sacramental reality of God's revelation, and he was willing to endure anything in order to be in true communion with it. The Church was presented as the Body of Christ, the Communion of Saints, adoring God and interceding for sinners. Ecclesiastical authority was an important ascetical value in Newman's spirituality. Reflecting on his Anglican days, Newman wrote in his *Apologia*: "I loved to act as feeling myself in my Bishop's sight, as if it were the sight of God."[86] He consistently lived and taught this principle throughout his life, expressing it by his personal faithful obedience to his ecclesiastical superiors.

---

84. JHN to Lady Chatterton, 16 June 1863, in *LD* 20:471.
85. JHN to Mrs. William Froudes, 16 June 1848, in *LD* 12:224.
86. Newman, *Apologia*, 52.

John Henry Newman

Summary

This chapter has highlighted some of the major influences on the origins and characteristics of Newman's approach to the spiritual life: its scriptural and patristic foundations as well as his worldview, integrating his consciousness of living in the unseen world with his personal experiences in this visible world. As he expressed in his famous poem, "The Pillar of the Cloud," he sought to surrender to the guidance and providence of God, leading him one step at a time toward his true home. His teaching on the holiness of God along with a person's absolute dependence upon God are characteristics which any authentic theology of the spiritual life must consider. Newman's spirituality was an expression of his theology. His belief in and explanation of the centrality of Christ and the indwelling of the Holy Spirit, as well as his dogmatic, sacramental and ecclesial principles give his understanding of the spiritual life a strong theological framework. The authenticity of his own spiritual life gives credibility to his teaching and contributes to the relevancy of his doctrine to people in other ages and cultures.

3

Spiritual Direction and the Providence of God

*"And He who all through my life has wounded
only to heal—will be with me still."*[1]

On June 5, 1869, with a frustrating experience fresh in his mind, Newman wrote in his journal: "The Providence of God has been wonderful with me all through my life. One thing struck me this morning as antithesis, which I have often thought of in its details, without observing the contrast they afford. It is this, that my troubles have come from those whom I have aided, and my success from my opponents."[2]

This observation was prompted by the opposition of Manning, Ward, and others, to the proposed foundation of an Oratory at Oxford. Embittered, yet enlightened by this most recent in a series of disappointments, he saw his whole life under a sign of contradiction in a dialectical succession of contrasts: "I suppose everyone has a great deal to say about the Providence of God over him. Everyone, doubtless, is so watched over and tended by Him that at the last day, whether he was saved or not he will confess that nothing could have been done for him more than had actually been done—and everyone will feel his own history as special and singular."[3] Since Newman felt "his own history to be special and singular" under Divine Providence, and since his spiritual direction flowed out of his own life experience, it is not surprising that "Divine Providence" is one of the dominant themes in his advice to others.

   1. JHN to John Pollen, 21 January 1862, in *LD* 20:131.
   2. Newman, *Autobiographical Writings*, 267.
   3. Ibid., 268.

A constant awareness of God's presence and an unshakable trust in divine guidance were basic factors in his life. Even as a youngster, he had "trust and hope in God, and abandoned himself without anxiety to his Providence."[4] When he entered Trinity College, Oxford, he chose as his favorite prayer the verse from the Psalms: "Thou shall guide me with Thy counsel."[5] Several years later at Oriel College, he felt himself "slowly advancing to what is good and holy, and led on by God's hand blindly, not knowing whither He is taking me."[6] Finally, he was led by unforeseen paths to the Catholic Church.

Newman's mother seems to have influenced his understanding of Providence, especially as regards resignation in sufferings or trials.[7] For example, when the family suffered from a financial crisis, she wrote to him:

> I thank God I just see and view our present afflictions in the light you do . . . My sorrows are not personal but they are divided and complicated. We are human beings, sent here to act a part full of trials, either from joys or sorrows . . . I anticipate in my anxiety for you all many evils that it may please God to avert, but yet I hope pardonable in the nature of a Mother's feelings . . . Many such feelings as these for my dear children will suggest themselves to my imagination; but with humble but sure confidence I resign me and mine to the Giver of all good, knowing that in due time we shall be relieved from our troubles, or enabled by His assistance to support them.[8]

In his life Newman perceived an almost regular succession of periods of darkness and periods of light, so that years later he could say: "I have ever tried to leave my cause in the Hands of God and to be patient—and He has not forgotten me."[9]

Newman's "first conversion" both rooted the concept of the "Providence of God" in his life, and also laid the fundamental groundwork for

---

4. Velocci, "Perception and Theology of Providence," 1.

5. Ibid., 2.

6. Ibid.

7. Newman, *Apologia*, 14. During his Anglican years, reflecting on his religious training, he wrote: "When I was a child, I was instructed in religious knowledge by kind and pious friends, who told me who my maker was, what great things He had done for me, how much I owed to Him, and how I was to serve Him. They not only taught me, but trained me; they were careful that I should not only know my duty, but do it. They obliged me to obey; they obliged me to begin a religious course of life." Newman, Sermon 8, in *Parochial and Plain Sermons*, 8:110–11; December 18, 1825.

8. "Family Letters," October 27, 1821, as cited by Zeno, *John Henry Newman*, 1:1–2.

9. JHN to R. W. Church, 11 March 1879, in *LD* 29:72.

his own spiritual life which later found expression in his spiritual direction. In particular, Newman considered that he had been providentially saved from religious liberalism by two events, first, a severe illness in the autumn of 1827, and second, by the sudden death of his beloved youngest sister, Mary. Her death reinforced an awareness that subsequently would play a dominant role in his direction of others—a vivid sense of the unseen world, invisible but more real than the material universe which acted as its veil. Thinking of Mary, he wrote to his sister Jemima: "What a veil and curtain this world of sense is! Beautiful, but still a veil."[10]

Similarly, Newman regarded his illness in Sicily as a period of probation, a kind of enforced retreat, which God had designed for him in preparation for the part he was to play in the Oxford Movement. A half century later, Dean Church, in response to a question from Anne Mozley as to the propriety of publishing some material during this period of illness in Newman's life, wrote: "He so plainly always looked on the fever in all its features as a *crisis in his life*, partly judgment on past self-will, partly a sign of special electing and directing favor, that the prominence given to it is quite accounted for by those who knew him, and explains why all these strange pictures of fever are given."[11]

After the condemnation of Tract 90 by the Anglican bishops, Newman reflected: "I felt that by this event the uproar caused by the Tract a kind of Providence had saved me from an impossible position in the future."[12] The thought of Providence kept returning during this stormy period: "May we not leave them (these matters concerning the Church and the Tracts) meanwhile to the will of Providence? I *cannot* believe this work has been of man; God has a right to his own work, to do what He will with it. May we not try to leave it in His hands, and be content?"[13]

Newman, who had retired to Littlemore in 1842 in order to study and pray, wrote to his sister Jemima, on March 15, 1845: "I cannot at all make out why I should determine on moving, except as thinking I should offend God by not doing so ... Oh, what can it be but a stern necessity that causes this? ... Think that perhaps you have a right to believe that He who has led me hitherto will not suffer me to go wrong ... His ways are not our ways, nor His thoughts as our thoughts. He may have purposes as merciful as they are beyond us. Let us do our best, and leave the event to Him."[14]

10. Mozley, *Letters*, 1:184.
11. Ibid.
12. Newman, *Apologia*, 79.
13. Ibid., 129.
14. Mozley, *Letters*, 2:459–61.

John Henry Newman

The Providence of God

The "Providence of God" was a major unifying element in the development of Newman's spiritual life, and constantly finds expression in his spiritual direction. Although this fundamental belief was deeply rooted, its implications both for him and for others could only be worked out in daily life. The major events in his own life—both trials and successes—plus his experience in directing others, gave rise to a continual emphasis on the importance of the Providence of God in each person's life. For example, at the age of seventy-nine, after years of both success and sorrow, Newman reflected:

> Looking beyond this life, my first prayer, aim, and hope is that I may see God. The thought of being blest with the sight of earthly friends pales before that thought. I believe that I shall never die; this awful prospect could crush me, were it not that I trusted and prayed that it would be an eternity in God's presence. How is eternity a boon, unless He goes with it?
>
> And for others dear to me, my one prayer is that they may see God. It is the thought of God, His presence, His strength, which makes up, which repairs all bereavements. "Give what thou wilt, without Thee we are poor, And with thee rich, take what Thou wilt away."[15]

After becoming a Roman Catholic, while studying theology in Rome at the College of the Propaganda, Newman was concerned about how God would use him when he returned to England; expressing his trust in the will of God, he wrote to Mrs. J. W. Bowden:

> But I cannot tell, and I think I am very indifferent about it—for if Providence means to use me He will—and if He wills to put me aside, it is with Him—as I have no wish one way or the other, as far as I know myself . . . but as I think I am indifferent . . . I am content to let all things take their course. . . . You see I have a good deal upon me, and need the prayers of all my friends. I cannot believe, as I have said above, that I have been brought to where I am for nothing—but God's ways are mysterious. He uses one man for one purpose, another for another. He breaks His instruments when He will—He may intend to have done with me—but, if He means to use me, He will find a way.[16]

Similarly, several months later, he wrote: "We do not deserve such protection, but I hope St. Mary and St. Philip will stand by us still—'Lead Thou me

---

15. JHN to John Mozley, 26 February 1880, in *LD* 29:241.
16. JHN to Mrs. J. W. Bowden, 13 January 1847, in *LD* 12:13–14.

Spiritual Direction and the Providence of God

on' is quite as appropriate to my state as ever, for what I shall be called to do when I get back, or how I shall be used, is quite a mystery to me."[17]

In Rome, Newman had to settle his vocation and that of the small group who wished to join him. After considering various religious orders, he concluded that he could best work as an Oratorian. Nevertheless, as he confided to Mrs. J. W. Bowden, he felt a very real anxiety about beginning a new life:

> My letters are always dull ones, for somehow I have lost all spring in writing—sometimes I wonder whether I shall be so wooden in preaching and other work when I get to Birmingham—but this is all in His hands who can make and break His instruments as He pleases. I am sure I ought to be most thankful for the abundant blessing which has attended me hitherto. Everything as yet has turned out well, and will continue to do so, I firmly believe, whatever be the will of Providence about my personal powers and exertions. We are on the brink now of Birmingham—and, as you may fancy, it is an awful thing, an awful thing, to begin a new life at my age.[18]

Returning to England in 1848, Newman was convinced that he "had a work to do." In February, the first Oratorian house was established at Old Oscott, rechristened Maryvale, with Newman as superior. Shortly afterwards, at Wiseman's wish and against his own judgment, Newman admitted as novices to the Oratory another convert group headed by the exuberant Frederick Faber. Early in 1849, Newman moved to Birmingham, where an Oratory and a church were established. When a second house of the Oratory was proposed for London, the question arose whether he should remain in Birmingham or go to London. In his exchange of letters with various people, one can observe his process of discernment, which included not only his own assessment of the situation, but also his search for the will of God. He wrote to R. A. Coffin, an early companion, "I will oppose nothing which seems God's will, but I will not promise to go to London."[19] In a letter to Faber several days later, he listed the reasons, pro and contra:

> Now as to the state of the case. You have all of you, through kindness to me, made it turn on *what is my place*, much more than I like or judge right. We must decide for the *long run*, and for all. However, I will speak of myself—I say then:
> 1. That one of two incompatible courses is open to me, for the rest of my life, between which I have to choose, viz.

---

17. JHN to Henry Wilberforce, 11 August 1847, in *LD* 12:107.
18. JHN to Mrs. J. W. Bowden, 14 January 1849, in *LD* 13:9.
19. JHN to R. A. Coffin, 27 March 1849, in *LD* 13:93.

either a life which admits of leisure for reading and writing, or a life of unmixed missionary or quasi-missionary work. What I do, is indifferent, if I could know God's will; but, as far as I can see His will, it is to take the former.

2. To take the former is to be in Birmingham; to take the latter is to be in London.

3. In saying that London is more suited to me than Birmingham, I mean more suited to me as a missioner; *therefore* it would absorb my time in mission, etc. work, while Birmingham does not.

4. Did I go to London, I should have various work for which I am well-fitted; to preach, lecture, converse, etc. Also much semi-religious work, far less suited to me, measures for the good of Catholicism, projects for bills in Parliament, etc. And much merely routine business,—Golden Square soirees, Committees, preaching for public objects, speeches at meetings. These engagements, with my correspondence, would absorb my time. In Birmingham, on the other hand, my day is mainly free; I am busy two or three hours in the evening, and confessions etc. drop in through the day. It is just the life I have ever coveted, time for study, yet missionary work of the most intimate kind, confessing, preaching, catechising. It is most suitable to my years, especially as they increase, and to my turn of mind, etc. I might be laying the foundation of a school, for which a London life is too busy. If I have certain talents which I must use in the best way, I ought to *find* that way, and this seems it.

5. It follows that my Library would be wasted on me, (for I am speaking of myself), in London; whereas, next to my own claim on it, is Birmingham's. Accordingly my Library stops here, whether I go to London or not. Here I am with it. This is irrevocable.

Thus then I bring my own case to an issue, and I wish to decide on it *first of all,* and thereby to simplify the arrangements which follow. Therefore I ask you all your opinion on the above alternative of disposing of myself; which course shall I take of the two, or have you nothing to say? *Shall I go to London without my Library, or remain here with it?* Do not do me the injustice to suppose that I am putting out a reduction ad absurdum, or driving you into a corner. I could make up my mind readily to leave my books here, and go to London. It would be a relief to me, though in some respects a pain. The only real misery to me, would be to go to London with them; I will not do so, for I should then have conflicting duties. I have had too much of this misery in past times to incur it again. A man cannot do everything, even that he is fitted for. He must make a choice out of his capabilities, and cultivate one or the other to the neglect of the rest. Now, my dear F. Wilfrid, we have arrived at the first step forward; the caravan is in motion; give me the general opinion (if there be any) on the above question, and after settling that I will proceed to step to the second.[20]

That same day, Newman wrote another letter to Faber asking him to solicit the opinion of the other Oratorians in order to help him determine God's will for him.

In my letter of today I will observe that from all you have said I have drawn the conclusion that to leave myself unfixed is impracticable. I must settle it first. I will settle it by myself, or I will take into consideration anything which may be said by any of you; but after my best thought, after the thought of months, I cannot see why I am to leave Birmingham; and (if left to myself) I shall settle for remaining in B. If, however, anything is put before me to the effect that I ought to devote myself to a missionary life in London (leaving my library here), I will give it the most serious and anxious attention. I have been saying Mass on the subject continually, and giving the intentions of St. Wilfrid's Masses to it.

I don't know whether I seem to you to have varied in my judgement during these discussions—and therefore it is hardly worth speaking about it. But if so, and F. Ambrose sometimes accuses me of it, it has risen from these two feelings—1) a great desire (for which you have blamed me) to please you all and 2) a great fear lest Divine Providence should by the means of others be offering me light which I was rejecting. Else from first to last, my own immovable view has been that I ought to stay where I am.[21]

After further consultation, Newman decided to stay in Birmingham and Faber was designated the superior of the house in London. Newman was convinced that Divine Providence had been continually leading them. "Give my best love to all and every one—and tell them that as they all have brought the matter before God for so long a time, with such a desire to

---

20. JHN to F. W. Faber, 29 March 1849, in *LD* 12:94-95.
21. JHN to F. W. Faber, 29 March 1849, in *LD* 12:96.

know, and resolution to follow, His Will, whatever it might be, so now they ought to rejoice and give thanks for what we may all trust is His decision."[22]

As the months continued, Newman's belief that this entire development was the will of God solidified:

> Almighty God is, I trust, leading us all separately not in our own way, but in His way, to His glory—and it matters not whether we see one another here or not, so that He is with us, and brings us one and all about His Throne in His Kingdom. For us, we are in Birmingham, a place which in one way has a sufficient omen of good, in that its name so little recommends it. When men wonder that the Pope's Brief should have placed us here I think of the inquiry of old, "can any good come out of Nazareth?" . . . But nothing can fail which is done in God's name and with the desire to please Him, and in dependence on His grace.[23]

Achilli Trial

In 1851, Newman began a series of lectures in Birmingham which were eventually published as *Lectures on the Present Position of Catholicism in England*; their purpose was to respond to Protestant misconceptions of Catholicism. One of the unforeseen results of this work was that Newman became involved in a trial for libel. His fifth lecture denounced an ex-Dominican, Giacinto Achilli, who had been lecturing on the corruptions of Rome and detailing his own sufferings at the hands of the Inquisition. In fact, Achilli had been in trouble for immoral conduct. Cardinal Wiseman had previously documented Achilli's guilt in the *Dublin Review*.

Relying on Wiseman's article, Newman denounced Achilli, who in turn sued for libel. Unfortunately Wiseman failed to produce the pertinent documents which might have staved off a trial, and Newman spent a frustrating eighteen months involved in legal proceedings with the threat of imprisonment. His correspondence connected with this trying experience provides glimpses of three aspects of his spiritual life: his mental anguish as he faced the prospect of a trial and the possibility of a prison sentence; the

---

22. JHN to R. A. Coffin, 15 April 1849, in *LD* 12:114.

23. JHN to Sister Mary Columba Poole, 9 July 1849, in *LD* 13:208–9. Similarly, he wrote to Mrs. John Mozley on January 27, 1850: "Our year here is finished on the Purification. I need not boast, but we have been wonderfully prospered within and without. . . . He who has carried me on through my whole life, will not desert me and mine." *LD* 13:399–400.

importance that he attached to prayer; and the manner in which he viewed this entire affair as being the will of God.

Prior to publishing his lecture against Achilli, Newman wrote two lawyers asking their opinion on whether he could be held for libel. Both replied in the negative. With that assurance, Newman proceeded to publication. Nonetheless, in November a libel suit was brought by Achilli against Newman. After an attempted compromise between the lawyers failed, it became clear that the case would go to trial. To complicate matters, Newman could not obtain the necessary documents from Wiseman who had misplaced them. An attempt to obtain Inquisition documents from Rome was unproductive; these documents arrived—six days too late.

By late November, it was clear to everyone that the process was going to be lengthy. Newman expressed his feelings in a letter to Richard Stanton:

> I have been very anxious since the middle of August. Things have gotten about as bad as they can be. The previous state of the affidavits is past—the Judges to the *utter surprise* of our lawyers would give *no time* to get them. Talbot delayed at Rome. I wrote him the most pressing letters. I urged him to send off at once what he had. He kept what he had 12 days—they came six days too late. Now, we go on trial; it comes in February. Humanly speaking, I am certain of being found guilty, for any one point unproved is enough. . . . I have not had any interruption to the simple feeling that I shall be borne thro' everything—I cannot at all divine the event, but that it will be good in some way or other, I am *sure*. . . . But you must all pray— . . . All through the year, I have said we should have some cross on account of our new building, and when the report of this matter came in August, I said "Behold, the cross."—I did what I did most deliberately. I went before the Blessed Sacrament and begged to be kept from doing it, if wrong. I have no misgiving. I cannot wish it otherwise. It is God's hand; it is His purpose. We shall see in time why. Many people think it will hurt my influence. It will not. I have said in print more than once, "Willingly would I suffer, if the Church is to gain." I seem to be taken at my word.[24]

Two major concerns dominated his correspondence concerning the Achilli trial. First was a significant increase in his requests for prayer, especially for strength to do God's will; second, many of his letters describe the suffering involved in matters related to the trial. Many of his friends, when they realized the seriousness of his predicament, wrote to him expressing their concern and offering him their support. In response, Newman

---

24. JHN to Richard Stanton, 4 December 1851, in *LD* 14:450–51.

frequently asked for their prayers: "The need . . . is that we all may have strength to bear God's blessed will. Tomorrow we begin a Novena to the Holy Ghost for that object. Your good Mother may if she will, and I will thank her, add the intention of my deliverance from the snare of the hunter, but let the main intention be, that we,—that I, may have the fortitude, patience, peace, to bear His sweet will withal."[25]

The trial date had been set for February 1852, but when Achilli learned that Newman had brought personal witnesses from Italy prepared to testify, he managed to delay the trial until the beginning of May on the hope that the witnesses would become restless and return to their homes. The delay caused Newman more pain and mental suffering; to his good friend, Ambrose St. John, he wrote on February 22:

> The opposite party is simply wearing us out, and knows it. I begin almost to think it will be given against me. I *should* think so, but for the great mercy (of God) that has already been shown me. Never have I had such a Christmas, never such a birthday. I think I could make up my mind to anything—but the suspense and the spending money, and the keeping witnesses in good humour, are such great trials. I only hope my pain [will] go to some good purpose—it is so like physical, that I seem to understand how the soul can physically suffer in purgatory.[26]

On June 24, Newman was found guilty of libel for failing to prove every point in his accusation. Newman's correspondence after this experience illustrated how deeply rooted was his understanding of the working of Divine Providence in his life. The day after the verdict he reminded Faber:

> It strikes me to say, *you must none of you be doleful*. We are floored, if we think ourselves floored, whether we think ourselves so or not, in a worldly standard—but we must steadily recollect that we are above the feelings of society, and therefore must cultivate a lightness of heart and elasticity of feeling, which, while deeply based on faith, looks at the first sight to others as mere good spirits. Mere good spirits are not enough—but bad spirits will be a positive hallucination. We are done if we feel beaten. We must have no indignation against Judge and Jury, or anything else—they act according to their nature—and accomplish according to God's will. Poor shadows, what are they to us!

---

25. JHN to Sister Mary Imelda Poole, 25 November 1851, in *LD* 14:437–38. "Mother" in this quote refers to Mother Margaret Hallahan, from whom Newman often requested prayers.

26. JHN to Ambrose St. John, 22 February 1852, in *LD* 15:40–41.

You must make your Brothers meditate on the nothingness of the world unless the subject be too intellectual.

P.S. You must bear this in mind, viz, that we always thought the verdict would be unfavorable—and relied on the *moral effect of* the evidence—now the article in today's *Times* is sufficient to prove that we have attained the moral effect.[27]

The anguish which Newman experienced during these months was reflected in his correspondence once the verdict had been pronounced. The day after the verdict, he wrote to Mrs. J. W. Bowden: "I hope you are not cast down by the verdict yesterday—for I am not. There is no doubt I have justified myself *morally*, in the eyes of everyone—and, though the party who upheld Achilli will call it a triumph, no one else but will call it, not a triumph for him, but simply a triumph over me."[28] Time and again in response to people writing to him to express their concern, he made it clear that he was thankful that the trial was ended. "Thank you for your most kind letter and all your good thoughts on my behalf. Anxiety, suspense, care, all this is pain, certainty is no pain. The last two days of the trial I was not in any pain compared with what I had had, but I felt I should have to reproach myself if I did not pass the time in prayer, and so I saw no one, for had I seen one, I must have seen many, and should have had no time to myself."[29]

---

27. JHN to F. W. Faber, 25 June 1852, in *LD* 15:107-8. The *Times* was known to be unfavorable to Catholics. This postscript must have been added on June 26, after the leading article of that day in the *Times*, 5, which strongly criticized the conduct of the trial and the verdict.

28. JHN to Mrs. J. W. Bowden, 25 January 1852, in *LD* 15:195.

29. JHN to T. W. Allies, 27 June 1852, in *LD* 15:110. On June 27, Newman wrote four other letters with the same theme. He tried to reassure and console his friends. There are two letters to Francis Kenrick, Archbishop of Baltimore, thanking him for the prayerful and monetary support of American Catholics. On November 9, Archbishop Kenrick sent Newman the resolutions passed by the American Bishops on October 4, when they met at Louisville, Kentucky, for the consecration of its cathedral. The resolutions expressed sympathy with Newman and recommended diocesan collections for his expenses. The Archbishop closed his letter: "In common with my colleagues, and the Clergy and Laity at large, I entertain sincere admiration for your zeal, and unqualified confidence in the integrity of your faith." This extract was twice printed in the *Tablet*, December 11 and 18, 1852, 791, 804. See Francis Kenrick to JHN, 3 December 1852, in *LD* 15:212n2.

Newman responded to Kendrick on December 3, 1852: "I have received with feelings of the deepest veneration and gratitude the Resolutions, which your grace has condescended to transmit to me by his Lordship the Bishop of Louisville, passed by a large meeting of Catholic Prelates in that city; and I hope they will indulgently receive the few and imperfect words, in which I attempt to express my sense of the great honour and kindness, which those Resolutions have conferred upon me.

"Did I need a fresh proof, in addition to the many which have already been showered

Throughout the summer and early autumn of 1852, while Newman was waiting to be sentenced, he wrote many letters of gratitude to those who had supported him. In November, he was called into court only to find his own lawyers wanting to request a new trial. Acceding to the wishes of his lawyers and friends, Newman agreed. On January 20, 1853, arguments were heard for a new trial in London, but the judges refused. On January 31 the sentence was given: a fine of £100. The comparatively light sentence surprised everyone. Newman's counsel and friends were elated; Achilli was plainly disappointed.

The one dominant characteristic throughout the Achilli affair was Newman's belief even in the darkest moments that Providence was guiding him, and that he was accomplishing the will of God. In a letter to Robert Whitty, written about a month after the sentencing, Newman summarized his thought:

> What is good, endures; what is evil, comes to nought. As time goes on, the memory will simply pass away from me of whatever has been done in the course of these proceedings, in hostility to me or in insult, whether on the part of those who invoked, or those who administered the law; but the intimate sense will never fade away, will possess me more and more, of that true and tender Providence which has always watched over me for good, and of the power of that religion which is not degenerate from its ancient glory, of zeal for God, and of compassion towards the oppressed.[30]

---

upon me, how the Loving Providence of God defeats evil and turns trial into joy and triumph, I should find it in the course and issue of the proceedings to which those Resolutions relate. And I did look for an evidence of the unity of object and the world-encircling charity which are the characteristics of Catholicism, I should find an instance, even more impressive than occurs in Apostolic times, . . . in the vigilant paternal solicitude, which has fixed the eyes of an exalted Hierarchy, with a whole continent to engage them, upon one person, over the great ocean, who happens in a particular instance to have been made the sport of the common Enemy of Christians in every land." *LD* 15:212–13. See Newman's other letter to Kendrick on December 2, 1852, in *LD* 15:211–12.

Newman also wrote to John Hughes, Archbishop of New York, on July 12, 1854: "I am quite overpowered at receiving from Dublin the letter with its munificent enclosure, which has come to me from your Grace. . . . As to my past anxieties, to which your Grace alludes, I adore the mercy of a good Providence, who has never forsaken me in trial, and who, on this occasion has, by the instrumentality of Catholic liberality, carried me so triumphantly through them." *LD* 16:195.

30. JHN to Robert Whitty, 2 March 1853, in *LD* 15:320.

Submission to the Will of God

The importance of his decision to be an Oratorian and the experience of the Achilli trial cannot be overemphasized in understanding Newman's own understanding of the Providence of God. Immediately following the conclusion of the Achilli trial, the theme of the Providence of God frequently appeared in his correspondence. From his own experience of the mysterious ways in which God was directing him, Newman believed that one of the basic elements of the spiritual life lay in the process of submitting oneself to the will of God in everything. He constantly encouraged others to see so many facets of life in this way—in sickness, in death, in trials of various kinds.

Newman believed that God unfolds his will to us; as he wrote to Mrs. William Froude: "He does not tell us everything at once—but first one thing, and then, when we act upon that, another."[31] He was convinced that God would reveal his will to those who persevered in seeking to do it. He advised Mrs. Houldsworth to ask God for "tokens to distinguish between the side which He owns and the side which He rejects."[32] God's will can be manifested through failures, through the instrumentality of people, and by means of sickness and death.

Newman often reminded his correspondents that they were entirely in God's hands, and that "He orders us about, each in his own way; happy for us, only, if we can realise this, and submit as children to a dear Father, whatever He may please to do with us."[33] He asks, then, that people put themselves trustingly into the hands of their loving Father, as he advised Marianne Bowden: "Put yourself then, my dear Child, into the hands of your loving Father and Redeemer, who knows and loves you better than you know or love yourself. He has appointed every action of your life. He created you, sustains you, and has marked down the very day and hour when He will take you to himself."[34] Similarly he told Miss Tennant: "You must put

---

31. JHN to Mrs. William Froude, 23 February 1853, in *LD* 15:307. To S. S. Shiel, he wrote in January 1870: "I would gladly help you in your difficulties of faith, if I could—but, as you know well, you must wait upon God, and he will hear you and not forsake you. If you ask him to teach you the truth, He will do so, slowly perhaps, but surely." JHN to S. S. Shiel, 25 January 1870, in *LD* 25:13.

32. JHN to Mrs. Houldsworth, 16 May 1971, in *LD* 25:331. There seems to be a link here with the Evangelical influences on Newman's early life. "Ask of God to give you *tokens*, which side is true, as He condescended to give tokens to Gideon. I don't mean miraculous tokens, but tokens appropriate to your position and case."

33. JHN to John Bowden, 21 September 1849, in *LD* 13:261.

34. JHN to Marianne Bowden, 5 June 1866, in *LD* 22:247.

yourself into His hands, and ask Him Himself, Him, not mortal man, not me, to bring you out of your perplexities."[35]

Occasionally Newman spoke of "the rule of God's Providence"[36] or "a sort of law in Providence"[37] which purified people through suffering. His basic attitude, however, was always one of trust and confidence in God's support in trials. For example, he advised Mrs. Keon:

> Of course no one but yourself can know what your trial is—that is, none but God and yourself—and He, who knows you so much better than you know yourself, will support you, and the more you lean upon Him, the more He will do for you. It is no comfort to tell a soul in trouble that others have suffered before it, and as keenly—but it ought to be a great comfort to be told that in trouble God never disappointed those who trusted Him, and that is the experience, not of one person only, but of many. He is a sure friend and makes openings for us, when we least expect it.[38]

Newman's response to a letter written by Mrs. William Froude indicates how difficult it is to be resigned to the will of God. She had stated in a letter of August 21, 1877, that due to a death in her family, she found that resignation to the will of God "requires a tremendous effort." Newman responded:

> What a wonderful Providence! Strange to say that I who had no right to feel it, in one way felt it as I have rarely felt anything which God has sent—and I say so to show I can sympathize with you. I mean, when I first heard of the blow from Fr. Ignatius, I could not at once respond "thy will be done."
>
> But God knows what is good. This I have observed, that such dreadful blows do issue in great blessings, and when we look back upon them years afterwards, we see what mercy there is in them, and learn with all our hearts to kiss the scourge to use the common phrase) which has made our hearts bleed. This is after the wound is healed, but oh! how long it will be in healing.[39]

---

35. JHN to Miss Tennant, 14 April 1878, in *LD* 28:344. On May 2, 1878, he wrote to her again: "He will heal all the wounds which you receive in His service." *LD* 28:354.

36. JHN to Duchess of Norfolk, 26 July 1862, in *LD* 20:245. "I suppose it is the rule of God's Providence towards us, that, the better we bear trial, the more He gives us to bear."

37. JHN to Catherine Bathurst, 28 April 1863, in *LD* 20:436. "I assure you, those persons like yourself, whom I know best, whom I have known longest, who have been most faithful to me and open with me, are so driven to and fro, that there seems a sort of law in Providence bringing it about."

38. JHN to Mrs. Keon, 27 November 1878, in *LD* 28:426.

39. JHN to Mrs. William Froude, 2 September 1877, in *LD* 28:235–36.

Similarly, in 1858 Newman told Henry Bittleston that up until the previous year it had never been difficult for him to be resigned. "How heavily the Hand of God weighs upon us—never in my life till this last year have I felt it any thing of a difficulty even for a moment to feel resignation."[40]

Sometimes it was not so much an event that prompted his spiritual direction about resignation, but rather the "suspense" of not knowing the outcome of life. Such had been his own experience during the Achilli trial, and it was reflected in his spiritual direction. For example, Miss Hope-Scott, who had been ill, wrote to Newman as she was recuperating; he replied:

> Thanks for your encouraging letter. God grant that this rally may be a respite and more. I suppose there might be a great amelioration without a miracle. A respite is a call upon us to pray more earnestly.
>
> I trust the long suspense and the alternation of hope and disappointment do not try you. I sometimes think that God tries us with suspense in order to teach us perfect resignation, and when we have no will of our own, no will but His, when we can look in the face steadily and accept what our natural heart shrinks from then He sees the time is come to end the time of waiting, and either to take away the desire of our eyes because we can bear the loss, or to grant it because we have merited the restoration.[41]

Similarly, after receiving the cardinalate in Rome in 1879, Newman hoped to visit his longtime friend, Miss Giberne, now Sister Maria Pia, at her convent in Autun, France on his return trip to England. Because of his ill health and the heavy rainfall, his doctor refused him permission to cut across the sixty miles from Mâcon to visit her at Autun, and so the two old friends never met again. Newman wrote to tell her the sad news: "We must submit ourselves to the Will of God. What is our religion, if we can't?"[42] Such a reflection is characteristic of Newman's spirituality. Submission to the loving will of God was fundamental to his guidance of others. This was closely connected with his teaching on prayer, since the Christian must "gravely and continually pray to God that His Will may be taught to him."[43] As he wrote to an unknown correspondent in 1867, "God Himself, the Holy

---

40. JHN to Henry Bittleston, 8 August 1858, in *LD* 18:436. See Newman's letter to John Flanagan on May 19, 1858: "I never have, nor have had (thank God) any temptation to murmur against His dispositions—for, *whatever* I receive of good . . . is ten thousand times more than I deserve." *LD* 18:351.

41. JHN to Miss Hope-Scott, 4 November 1872, in *LD* 26:196–97.

42. JHN to Miss. Giberne, 3 July 1879, in *LD* 19:148.

43. JHN to Robert Froude, 3 August 1864, in *LD* 21:181.

Ghost, is the only Teacher and He is every where and sees your heart—and for His grace you must importune Him without ceasing."[44]

Yet Newman's counsel to others was not always a passive acceptance of whatever came one's way in life. Very often he would advise people to do all in their power to seek a Christian solution, trusting that God was with them. In his later years, however, there is an interesting series of letters to Lady Herbert of Lea who was anxiously concerned that her son had lost his faith and had become a skeptic. Newman advised her to accept the situation and to do nothing: "I suppose my letter did not do—it would not at all surprise me, for it is only after a long time, and after many experiments, that a soul is brought right.

"I write now to say so. Don't be discouraged—you must not be impatient. Recollect what St. Ambrose said to St. Monica. The less you attempt the better. I am sure this is good advice. We must learn perfect submission to the will of God before we have a right to expect anything from Him."[45]

Newman often tried to help people view their failures in life as part of God's Providence. For example, in reply to Catherine Bathurst, a long time friend who had difficulty finding permanent residence and success in her work, he wrote:

---

44. JHN to Unknown Correspondent, 3 July 1867, in *LD* 23:260.

45. JHN to Lady Herbert of Lea, 31 August 1879, in *LD* 29:174. In two subsequent letters Newman repeated the same counsel. On September 8, 1879, he wrote Lady Herbert: "From my experience of such cases, a soul must be left to itself and its God. I know a case such as this lately. The young man's friends were in great distress, and he was as miserable. He cried for help and seemed not [to] be heard. I corresponded with him, and nothing seemed to come of it. Several great trials befell him. I heard lately that he was much easier in mind, and I have reason to believe that he is coming round. Such cases are so like that of St. Augustine as to be very hopeful; but they try our faith and patience." *LD* 29:175. A month later, on October 6, 1879, he wrote Lady Herbert again: "I have been thinking much about my best way, were I you, to affect your dear son, and to secure his restoration, and I feel strongly, though it may seem cruel, that it is decidedly the best treatment to leave him quite to himself. I take a great responsibility on me in saying this—for supposing this way did not succeed, I should be laying myself open to the charge of having by my do-nothing policy brought about that sad result.

"But, you know, it frequently happens that medical men say of a patient—'Leave him alone—give him no physic—let nature act.'

"Now I think that controversy is Lord P's *food*. He is supported, as on crutches on asking and urging difficulties on the one hand and demolishing answers on the other. The best hope of his changing lies in his having no one to combat with him. Especially no one whom he loves or knows about. There is no *substance* in his scepticism, and this is most likely to come home upon him, if a silence is offered to his restless activity of mind, and he has nothing brought before him to make him think that he is an object of anxiety to others. I doubt whether he would like to have his own way. Excuse this, but I feel it strongly—it gives him the best chance." *LD* 29:181.

I rejoice to hear about you. God be with you, and He will be, wherever you are. How glad I shall be to hear you are in settled, and further, permanent work. . . .

If we attain to the Life to come, it will be a joyful contemplation to understand how all our failures, borne well, tended to God's glory and our own salvation. I assure you, those persons like yourself, whom I know best, whom I have known longest, who have been most faithful to me and open with me, are so driven to and fro, that there seems a sort of law in Providence bringing it about. I do not mean simply locally driven, but in their aims, in their work, in their prospects. I feel it intensely of myself—my life seems wasted in attempting many things and doing nothing.[46]

Basically, Newman saw life as a series of opportunities, from seemingly insignificant events to more personal ones, that God gives us as a way of resigning ourselves to his will. Yet he was never naive or simplistic in believing that resignation was an easy process. Newman allowed for God's extraordinary intervention in our lives. Providence, in his view, did not neutralize the laws of nature, but completed them: "The whole divine system is a system of compensations and recapitulations. Revelation itself is an extraordinary system compared to nature."[47]

Sickness and Death

Newman wrote to his friends when they were sick, assuring them of his prayers and encouraging them to be resigned to the will of God. His anxiety over John Keble's health in 1866 gave way to an expression of trust in God's

---

46. JHN to Catherine Bathurst, 28 April 1863, in *LD* 20:436. Another letter written on the very same day to Miss Holmes expresses similar sentiments. "What has made you write so sadly? Your letter has quite distressed me. I have been saying various Masses for you lately. I am so sorry, and always am, that you have not a clearer prospect before you. You must not suppose I do not often think, whether there is no suggestion, advice, or opening which I could make you, but, in very truth, I myself, though I have a fixed place to live in, and so far have a great blessing, am in the most strange way cut off from other People. Out of sight, out of mind, I suppose—but so it is, that I know nothing of how things are going on, what there is to do, and who is doing it. Only I see, that it is very hard indeed, that, after the many trials you have had, you have not yet a resting place. When we get to heaven, if we are worthy, we shall enjoy the sight of how, all our failures and disappointments, if borne well, have been for God's glory and our own salvation." JHN to Miss Holmes, 28 April 1863, in *LD* 20:436–37.

47. JHN to R. B. Seeley, 15 August 1851, in *LD* 14:327.

care for him: "I can do no more than think of you and love you, I wish I could do more—but there is only One who is powerful, One who can will and do."[48]

This same theme of confidence is found in his letter to Mrs. F. J. Watt, whom he had known since her birth: "What shall I say to you, but that you are in the hands of Him who loves you more than anyone on earth can love you? and who can and will protect all who are dear to you on earth, better than anyone else."[49]

Similarly, when he learned of Dr. Dunne's illness in 1861, he wrote him a supportive letter, saying:

> I have long intended to send you a line to express the great concern I have felt on hearing of your unsatisfactory state of health. This is not written with any purpose of giving you the trouble of answering it—but merely that you may know that I feel great interest in all that befalls you, and that you have my earnest prayers, that, if it be according to His will, God may remove your trial. It must be a great trial over and above the illness itself, for a mind so active and zealous as yours to be thrown out of work.[50]

In 1864, Newman learned that the Froudes' youngest daughter, Mary, who was their only child to remain a Protestant, was sick and dying. Immediately he wrote saying: "I have thought of you especially in the way in which you speak of yourself. To see a child die slowly before one's eyes seems an incredible trial.... But what you think about most is whether you are doing all that you ought to do for her. I think you certainly are—and may leave things simply in God's hands."[51] After the agonizing last hours of her death on May 31, Newman wrote to her father: "Dear Child, she is gone to heaven and is safe; so how can I but rejoice that your long pain is at an end—? At least, I trust it is so with you. I think that the trial you have had, though it is not more than many others have, to see a young life cut off, and that by such a slow and certain process, is one of the greatest pains possible in this world."[52]

---

48. JHN to John Keble, 7 February 1866, in *LD* 22:148.
49. JHN to Mrs. F. J. Watt, 12 November 1873, in *LD* 26:385.
50. JHN to D. B. Dunne, 14 June 1861, in *LD* 19:514.
51. JHN to Mrs. William Froude, 16 March 1864, in *LD* 21:80. On March 21, William Froude responded: "It may be, as you say that none but parents can quite sympathise with parents, when such an event as we fear, is approaching. Yet I am inclined to think that in this particular case there can be few parents who can enter into and sympathise with what we feel, so truly as yourself." See Ibid., n4.
52. JHN to William Froude, 1 June 1864, in *LD* 21:111–12.

Spiritual Direction and the Providence of God

Similarly, having learned about the illness of his good friend Emily Bowles, he said:

> It is very sad indeed to hear you have been so ill. I thought of course you were abroad. Well, it seems a token of God's will towards you. What trials you have had I do hope you are getting well. Please, keep me au courant about yourself. Oh what a thing life is and how objectless to most of us, unless there were a future! We seem to live and die as the leaves; but there is One who notes the fragrance of every one of them, and when their hour comes, places them between the pages of His great Book.[53]

During his friend James Hope-Scott's last illness, Newman corresponded extensively with his family, indicating his conviction in the power of prayer, and joining in their various novenas. Newman assured Lady Henry Kerr, Hope-Scott's sister: "He who loves us has the times and season in His own hand, and if we saw all things we should see how good His will is, though in our ignorance and our banishment it is so hard to accept."[54] He conveyed his confidence in Divine Providence to Miss Hope-Scott: "There is nothing like the blessedness of feeling oneself in God's hands, to do what He will with us—to be lodged there, without a will of our own, knowing that with Him we are safe."[55] His profound reflections on resignation to the Divine Will were expressed in another letter to Miss Hope-Scott:

> I trust the long suspense and the alternation of hope and disappointment do not try you. I sometimes think that God tries us with suspense in order to teach us perfect resignation and when we have no will of our own, no will but His, when we look in the face steadily and accept what our natural heart shrinks from, then He sees the time is come to end the time of waiting, and either to take away the desire of our eyes because we can bear the loss, or to grant it because we have merited the restoration.[56]

---

53. JHN to Emily Bowles, 13 February 1864, in *LD* 21:50–51.

54. JHN to Lady Henry Kerr, 21 October 1872, in *LD* 29:183. To the Duke of Norfolk Newman wrote on October 27, 1872: "He is in better hands than ours. He who made him what he is, loves him more than we can love him. And as He cares for him, so He cares for all his also." *LD* 26:190.

55. JHN to Miss Hope-Scott, 29 October 1872, in *LD* 26:191–92.

56. JHN to Miss Hope-Scott, 4 November 1872, in *LD* 26:197. On November 12, he wrote to her again: "Distress in some shape or other is in this world the necessary condition of having foretastes of the world to come." JHN to Miss Hope-Scott, 12 November 1872, in *LD* 26:200.

John Henry Newman

When the doctors spoke of improvement in Hope-Scott's condition, Newman was cautious about their opinion: "St. Philip cautions us against leaving off prayers too soon and taking things too easy. We must still pray and still make acts of resignation."[57] Finally, when Hope-Scott died on April 29, 1873, his daughter received this letter of consolation from Newman: "You alone can know what it is to be bereaved of such a Father. You never can have a heavier blow, because you are so young and so untried in suffering. But God is more than enough to make up all to you, and He will. You will look back with tender affection, not only on happy past days, but on this long sad time, when hope rose and fell again, and you felt weary of the changes."[58]

Never was Newman's conviction about the unseen world more clearly articulated than when he sought to console those mourning a deceased relative. When Robert Monteith's daughter died in 1877, Newman wrote: "Few losses are greater than that of a daughter . . .—but there is nothing, under God's blessing, which tends so greatly to detach one from the world as such bereavements, and when time has passed and we look back, we see how much we owe to the Hand which afflicted us in mercy."[59] Twenty years earlier, when he learned that Ambrose Phillipps' son had been killed in Delhi, India, Newman empathized by saying:

> Nothing, I know well, that others can say, can enable you and Mrs. Phillipps to support such a blow. It is the consolation which comes from above, and that alone, which can aid you—and that you have abundantly. And as time goes on, the pain will be less and less, and the light of divine consolation will become brighter and brighter—for you will understand, more than anyone else, how great a thing it is to have a son, secured from the ten thousand temptations of the world, and safely lodged in unchangeable blessedness.[60]

Similarly, he consoled Mrs. F. R. Ward on the loss of her twenty-year-old son:

> May we all be as ready for death, when our time comes, as that dear boy was. He could never be more fit to die than now, and so God took him. And for what, my dear Mrs. Ward, was he given you, what was your mission in cherishing and rearing him up so carefully, except to bring him to heaven? . . . That was your work,

---

57. JHN to Miss Hope-Scott, 12 December 1872, in *LD* 26:213.

58. JHN to Miss Hope-Scott, 30 April 1873, in *LD* 26:300. Newman concluded: "For me, his departure is a memento that my day must come. May I be as well prepared as he."

59. JHN to Robert Monteith, 9 July 1877, in *LD* 28, 220.

60. JHN to Ambrose Phillipps, 24 November 1857, in *LD* 18:183.

and through God's grace you have done it.... Your loving Lord has fulfilled all your largest prayers—and now your dear boy will pay them back to you a hundred fold by praying for you and for all who are so dear to him.[61]

Consoling Lady Simeon on the loss of her husband, Newman paid tribute to his integrity and assured her: "Shadows have departed for him, and he is with his God. Those who have gone before us, have, so far, a blessing which the best and holiest of men cannot have here."[62] Moreover, when Mrs. Bowden wrote and told Newman that her father, Sir John Swinburne, who had been baptized a Roman Catholic, but was reared and died an Anglican, without receiving the "consolations of the Church," Newman reassured her: "No one but the Creator Himself reads our hearts and is able to decide on our responsibilities. None loves the soul so well as He—none wishes for its salvation as He wishes for it. To Him we must leave our nearest and dearest, with a full confidence that not one of those pleas, which we are able to urge for them, but are understood much better by Him."[63] Likewise, he advised Isy Froude, whose grandfather had died under similar circumstances, to trust in the mercy of God: "It must be an extreme trial to your mother and aunt—but God orders all things, and we must recollect that He is infinitely more tender and kind and merciful to every one of us, than we can be, and that, in going to Him, we are going to One who knows of what we are made, and, as knowing us, is able to be indulgent in a way in which we cannot be to those even whom we know best."[64]

Newman's affection and compassion, as well as his trust in the Providence of God, was often manifest in his counsel to the surviving relatives of his personal friends. To the children of Mrs. Henry Bowden he wrote: "It is indeed most piercing to see the pain of those we love, and not be able to help them—a wall of separation between oneself and them! But it is all over—and don't doubt that all the suffering which she has had, borne so bravely and lovingly, has brought her near to God, and to a state of peace and rest."[65]

---

61. JHN to Mrs. F. R. Ward, 22 September 1866, in *LD* 22:299.

62. JHN to Lady Simeon, 30 May 1870, in *LD* 25:136–37. Newman continued: "He is beyond sin, trial, fear and uncertainty. If we had the power of bringing him back by wishing, we could not bring ourselves to wish it."

63. JHN to Mrs. J. W. Bowden, 30 September 1860, in *LD* 19:408.

64. JHN to Isy Froude, 16 May 1860, in *LD* 19:337.

65. JHN to Henry Bowden's children, 28 June 1864, in *LD* 21:136. On the same day Newman also wrote to Henry Bowden: "God has struck you most heavily but your dear children will rise up and console you. And God Himself, who has afflicted you, will be your best Comforter and Friend.

"She is now in peace and rest—... I feel that I have a great loss myself, the loss of one

At the death of Edward Bellasis, he wrote to his widow: "I know my pain is nothing to yours and those about you—but I feel deeply I have lost one of my best, my most constant, dearest friends—still it is a great consolation beyond words to think that I have such a friend with God, who I am sure still loves me, (though he is now cleansed from all sin and infirmity and I am still encompassed by both,) that I have such an intimate friend so near to my Saviour and my Judge."[66]

In comforting the widower of Lady Chatterton, Newman told him: "There are wounds of the spirit which never close—and are intended in God's mercy to bring us nearer to Him, and to prevent us leaving Him, by their very perpetuity."[67] He then shared his thoughts on the loss of his closest friend, Ambrose St. John, who had died unexpectedly the previous year: "I never had so great a loss. He had been my life, under God, for thirty-two years. I don't expect the wound will ever heal, but from my heart I bless God, and would not have it otherwise, for I am sure that the bereavement is one of those Divine Providences necessary for my attaining that heavenly Rest which he, through God's mercy, has already secured."[68]

"Wounded to Heal": Trials, Trust, and Providence

"To fret, and to be troubled, does not pay—it is like scratching a wound, instead of letting it heal."[69] Much of Newman's spiritual direction in relation to the Providence of God dealt with trust. He encouraged persons in every kind of trial to trust God, to believe that in their present situation God was with them. Emerging in this context is a very unique quality that we find permeating Newman's direction of others, that of sensitivity. Many people felt comfortable with Newman and wrote to him about their personal trials. His advice was both encouraging and conscious of personal circumstances, and his direction was adapted to each individual. He believed that "all events in life form one system of Providence, and depend on one another. One cannot be

---

so kind, so gentle, so open and true a friend, whom I sincerely admired and loved, who talked with me so frankly and familiarly, and made me know her by that most winning ease of her conversation." Ibid., 135–36.

66. JHN to Mrs. Edward Bellasis, 27 January 1873, in *LD* 26:240. On the same day he wrote to her daughter Monica Bellasis: "He was one of the best men I ever knew." Ibid., 241.

67. JHN to Edward Dering, 10 February 1876, in *LD* 28:22. Newman went on to elaborate: "Such wounds then may almost be taken as a pledge, or at least as a ground for humble trust, that God will give us the great gift of perseverance to the end."

68. Ibid., 22–23.

69. JHN to Richard Simpson, 25 February 1859, in *LD* 19:52.

Spiritual Direction and the Providence of God

sure that the loss of these blessings is not the condition of the grant of these."[70] Both the happy occasions in life and the difficult ones he saw in relation to God's Providence and consequently directed others in this way.

One of the most evident themes in Newman's correspondence is that trials of all kinds are a mark of God's love. For example, the death of Lady Georgiana Fullerton's only child at the age of twenty-one was the great tragedy of her life. When Newman learned of her son's death, he wrote:

> It would be presumptuous in me to speak to you and Mr. Fullerton of submission. However, let me bear witness not only as a matter of faith, which we all receive, but as a point, which the experience of life had ever been impressing on me, more and more deeply, from my early youth down to this day, that unusual afflictions, coming on religious persons, are proofs that they are objects, more than others, of the love of God. Those whom He singularly and specially loves, He pursues with His blows, sometimes on one and the same wound, till perhaps they are tempted to cry out for mercy.
>
> He loves you in proportion to the trials he sends you. I am telling you no news: but a testimony, external to oneself, strengthens one's own: and perhaps my testimony may be given with greater energy and fervency of conviction than another's. We are in His hands—and cannot be in better.[71]

The following month, in a similar manner, Newman advised the Countess of Arundel to view her present sorrow as a mark of God's love for her.

> I would not write to you, did I think you would suppose I expected an answer. Nay, I almost fear to intrude upon you at all, yet the many kindnesses I have received from you and Lord Arundel make me earnestly desire to express to you how much I feel the succession of trials which a good Providence has brought upon you.
>
> However, such a visitation (as you know so well,) is the greatest mark of His love:—or rather, who would have any encouragement to hope that his name was written in heaven, if he passed through this life without affliction! Be sure, you are dearer to God and His Angels than ever you were, now that you are suffering so much, and, unwelcome as suffering is, so willingly.[72]

---

70. JHN to Henry Ryder, 25 April 1879, in *LD* 29:108.
71. JHN to Lady Georgina Fullerton, 4 June 1855, in *LD* 16:475–76.
72. JHN to Countess of Arundel, 29 July 1855, in *LD* 16:517–18.

It was Newman's conviction that in the midst of anxieties and trials the Christian is invited to place his trust in God who reads his heart "as no one on earth can read it and will supply all its needs." To Mrs. Bellasis, who was concerned about the future, Newman counseled her to trust God:

> You have indeed a heavy cross to bear just now—one which none but yourself can understand—for it is so mixed up with feelings to and fro, with the past and the future, with fond memories of those who are no longer here, and affectionate solicitude for those who are nearest and dearest to you, with reverence and disappointment. However, there is One above who reads your heart as no one on earth can read it, who will supply all its needs, and can and will do more for those, whose future is so anxious to you, than could have been done for them, had every thing happened as you wish. So do not be cast down, but put your trust in God, and be sure that every thing happens in the best way for those who love Him.[73]

Empathizing with Mrs. Keon in her time of difficulty, Newman encouraged her:

> Of course no one but yourself can know what your trial is—that is, none but God and yourself—and He, who knows you so much better than you know yourself will support you, and the more you lean upon Him, the more He will do for you. It is no comfort to tell a soul in trouble that others have suffered before it, and as keenly—but it ought to be a great comfort to be told that in trouble God never disappointed those who trusted Him, and that is the experience, not of one person only, but of many. He is a sure friend and makes openings for us, when we least expect it. And your letter just received shows me how fully in your secret heart you respond to such sure truths.[74]

In Newman's view, trials were meant to induce a person to turn to God for consolation and strength as the center and object of their hope and confidence. "After a time of excitement, perhaps of spiritual exultation," Newman warned, "there is often in turn a season of re-action. . . . Then a despondency comes on, and then is our enemy's time to suggest difficulties or murmurings."[75] He counseled Miss Emily Buchanan: "If such happens to you, you must be brave, and call on God to help you, and go straight forward in spite of all difficulties, and cherish a sure trust that your Lord

---

73. JHN to Mrs. Edward Bellasis, 21 May 1863, in *LD* 20:449–50.
74. JHN to Mrs. Keon, 27 November 1878, in *LD* 28:426.
75. JHN to Miss Emily Buchanan, 16 April 1875, in *LD* 27:278.

and Saviour will in His own time bring your trial to an end."[76] He advised Margaret Dunn: "Humble yourself when He gives you comfort—be grateful when He gives you pain. All things turn out well to those who love Him."[77] How a Christian conducts himself under affliction is more indicative of his spiritual maturity than when in a state of consolation.[78] For Newman, what was important was not a matter of feeling but of constancy and confidence in God's mercy and love:

> You must not suppose your present state of peace and joy will always continue. It is God's mercy to bring us over difficulties. As time goes on, you may be cast down to find that your warmth of feeling does not last as it once was, and instead of it you may have trials of various kinds. Never mind; be brave; make acts of faith, hope, and charity; put yourself into God's hands, and thank Him for all that He sends you, pleasant or painful. The Psalms and St. Paul's Epistles will be your great and abiding consolation.
>
> "Rejoice with trembling." I say all this, not as dissuading you from enjoying your present joy and peace, but that you may enjoy them religiously.[79]

An administrative problem at the Oratory school provided Newman with another occasion to reflect on the importance of trusting in God. In a letter to John Pollen, who had supported him in a conflict about the dismissal of the headmaster, he wrote: "All important undertakings are subject to such trial, at least in their commencements. . . . And He, who all through my life has wounded only to heal—will be with me still."[80]

Marriage problems were another human situation in which Newman directed people to have confidence in God. Responding to Margaret Dunn in 1878, he encouraged her:

> I have not forgotten you. You have a severe trial—but it will turn out well—as you will understand when this life is over. . . . My intention for you shall be that God may comfort and guide you. Trust Him fully—you cannot trust Him too much. Beware of all

---

76. Ibid.
77. JHN to Margaret Dunn, 12 April 1869, in *LD* 24:237.
78. JHN to Miss M. R. Giberne, 5 December 1880, in *LD* 29:324. Speaking of a trial she was experiencing, he wrote: "It is no proof that you are less pleasing to God; perhaps you are more so. One may fairly argue that it is indeed a special honour to you that you are thus tried. It is easy to serve God, when consolations abound. Think of the lives of the Saints; consider what desolations weighed upon them for years."
79. JHN to Miss Emily Fortey, 3 October 1884, in *LD* 30:404.
80. JHN to John Pollen, 21 January 1862, in *LD* 20:131.

> rash steps—I was relieved when you told me that matter was at an end. The Blessed Virgin will not be unmindful of you, and your Guardian Angel is the most faithful of all friends. Don't forget that He is always with you, and invoke him continually.[81]

Newman was frequently in the center of controversy, and quite naturally others disagreed with his position and even tended to be unkind. On one such occasion, he explicitly spoke of the Providence of God.

> If I did not in my answer allude to any controversial matter contained in it, it was because I did not see the good of it. All one can do is to act according to one's best light, and leave all things to God. I consider He has brought me to what I am—but, while I hold there is a right and a wrong, and only one right, still if I were impatient of any one differing from me, I should be impatient with God's Providence, who has all souls in His hand, and does with them whatever He will.[82]

In 1859, Richard Simpson wrote to Newman saying that he was being treated unkindly by Cardinal Wiseman. Newman, who had had similar experiences, shared his feelings with Simpson:

> I assure you that the principal person who has unfairly used you, and whose wishes I have been executing in my negotiation with you, has been personally unkind to me, by word and by deed. I consider myself much aggrieved, and, had not the experience of long years made me tire of indignation and complaint, I could indulge myself in both the one and the other.
>
> But, depend upon it, no advice is better than that of the Holy Apostle, "If our enemy hungers, to feed him—" and to leave our cause simply in the Hands of the good God. He will plead our cause for us in His own way, and, even though it be not His high will to redress us openly, He can make compensation to us by inward blessings.[83]

Finally, advancing years and impending death provided another occasion for Newman to advise about the importance of trust in life. One can grasp through his personal correspondence his growing sensitivity to the anxiety of the unknown.

> It is natural that you should look with anxiety towards the future. The better you are, the more will the prospect before you

---

81. JHN to Margaret Dunn, 30 September 1878, in *LD* 28:401.
82. JHN to Charles Crawley, 22 February 1863, in *LD* 20:410.
83. JHN to Richard Simpson, 25 February 1859, in *LD* 19:52.

Spiritual Direction and the Providence of God

be solemn. Again, the older you are, the more you realise what is to come. To younger people the unseen state is a matter of words—but, as to people of our age they say to themselves, "For what I know I shall be in that unknown state tomorrow," and that is very awful.

So you must not allow yourself to be disturbed—but the more you feel that you have to give an account, you must look in faith, hope, and love, towards our Lord Jesus, the Supreme Lover of souls, and your abiding Strength, towards the Blessed Virgin, and to St. Francis. They won't forsake you in your extremity—and your Guardian Angel will be faithful to the end.[84]

In a similar vein, Newman wrote to the Duchess of Argyll, whose sister had just died:

How awful the Future is, when one is approaching the threshold, behind which it lies!—so impenetrable what is reserved for one. We can but pray for each other, and cling to the Cross. If it were not for the memory of so many, many mercies shown us personally, and the deep conviction that we are separately and personally objects of His love, who is Almighty, how could we bear the prospect which lies before us! He who has brought us on to what we are, who has led us on step by step into His Church, will lead us on safely into His eternal heaven.[85]

Even the place in which a person was residing was viewed by Newman in terms of Providence. When Eleanor Bretherton wrote, saying how well things were going for her at Stone, he responded:

I am glad to hear from Mama so good an account of you. I do not at all doubt, that, if God's good providence gives you many years, you will look back on the time spent at Stone as one of the happiest seasons of your life. It is a great blessing to be in peace and quiet, to be storing up good lessons, and to be in the midst of holy persons and to be in the immediate presence of your dear Lord.

Enjoy what is really your *Holy day*, and determine that, through God's grace, it shall tell upon your whole life.[86]

On the other hand, when Mrs. Henry Bowden wrote to say she had to leave Chiselhurst, he observed: "You are under a very heavy trial in leaving

---

84. JHN to Miss M. R. Giberne, 22 January 1878, in *LD* 28:306.
85. JHN to Richard Simpson, 25 January 1859, in *LD* 19:52.
86. JHN to Eleanor Bretherton, 17 November 1862, in *LD* 20:355–56.

Chiselhurst—and one, alas! which is more difficult than most to get over—for nothing can supply the loss of a dear place full of happy associations.

"May God support you in that and all trials—and He will—I am sorry to hear from you so poor an account of your health."[87]

Waiting on Providence was characteristic of Newman's own spiritual development and one which deepened over the years. His own inner struggle to abandon himself to God's Providence was characterized by another Oratorian as "his passivity—making no attempt to fashion the course of his life, but waiting on Providence."[88] In his life he perceived an almost regular succession of periods of darkness and then light, so that years later he was able to say: "I have ever tried to leave my cause in the Hands of God and to be patient—and he has not forgotten me."[89] It is not surprising, then, that Newman frequently encouraged people to incorporate a sense of "patiently waiting" into their own lives. For example, he advised Emily Bowles: "I consider that Time is the great remedy and Avenger of all wrongs, as far as this world goes. If only we are patient, God works for those who do not work for themselves. Of course an inward brooding over injuries is not patience, but a recollecting with a view to the future is prudence."[90]

Particularly when persons were thinking about entering the Church, Newman advised patient waiting and trust as part of his direction. For example, Mrs. William Froude was concerned about her daughter who was dying and had not yet entered the Church. In response to her letter, Newman said:

> As to dear Mary, I cannot be surprised at your being down about her. As to your anxiety about her religion, I think you may simply dismiss it from your mind. Of course it is indescribably better in every way, in this life, and on the death bed, and between death and judgement, and after that in eternity, to have been in Catholic communion, but it cannot be said that she is old enough or has seen or thought enough to have *rejected* grace offered her—and, while you do all you can to make her a Catholic, up to the point of teasing or unsettling her, which would only be so much harm, you must leave her to that God who loves her more than you can love her, and as to whom you can only say that, while He loves her, He has shown greater mercies to her sister and brothers. It still may be His purpose to convert her,

---

87. JHN to Mrs. Henry Bowden, 17 March 1862, in *LD* 20:173.
88. Ward, *Life*, 1:15.
89. JHN to R. W. Church, 11 March 1879, in *LD* 29:72.
90. JHN to Emily Bowles, 8 January 1867, in *LD* 23:16.

Spiritual Direction and the Providence of God

but you may have a cheerful hope about her even though she died a Protestant.[91]

The same was true when a person experienced questions or doubts about faith; for example, in writing another member of the Froude family, Newman advised:

> Then, as to your doubts, it is wonderful if they never had come upon you. I have expected you would have them all along. It is impossible that a young and opening mind, such as yours, should not have them sooner or later. There are large questions which cannot be taken in all at once—and they must come as questions before they admit of answers. They are like plus and minus quantities, equal to each other severally, in an equation. The plus come first, I mean objections—then come the minus, the answers; and the equation is left at the end, as it began. God is not a hard master—nor is the Church severe—you have an honest heart, and desire to do what is right. Sacraments are not snares—privileges are not burdens. Put off your trouble as much as you can, put yourself into God's hands and be patient.[92]

Very often with a unique insight into the person writing to him, Newman gently encouraged others to trust with patience in times of doubt.

> I would gladly help you, if I could—but every soul is individual, and solitary, and what affects one, does not affect another.
>
> But God is One too—and if you are one, as you must be, He too is as much your God as if there were no other soul in the world for Him to care for. He made you, He sees you through and through, He can do all things for you, as knowing all your needs. If your present unsettlement is your own fault, you must take the pain and misery of it as your punishment—any how you must be patient under it. Impatience won't bring you out of it.
>
> You must put yourself into His hands, and ask Him Himself, Him, not mortal man, not me, to bring you out of your perplexities. You say, "What duties do creatures owe to their Creator?" "Do they owe Him any duty?" Ask Him, He will not answer you at once—but in time He will hear you. He will try you, but He will reward you for your earnestness.

---

91. JHN to Mrs. William Froude, 7 February 1864, in *LD* 21:43–44.
92. JHN to Robert Froude, 20 April 1866, in *LD* 22:220.

> This is all I can say to you—but it is a good deal. I don't think you have so little faith as you suppose. You would not be so disturbed if you had none.[93]

His own ministry provided Newman with yet another area of life in which to advise others to trust patiently even in the face of failure. Commenting to a friend about the difficulty of establishing an Oratory school due to lack of funds, Newman said:

> Thus I have just committed myself in *order* to fail. This is a fresh great mortification to me, and I hope I shall bear it well. But it is plain I am being put aside in all hands as in some way or other unpractical and unsuccessful. . . .
>
> Only the other day I was saying that I wanted to know God's will *clearly*. The misery is the beginning in twilight—Well, I had rather a thousand times not begun it, than be in doubt whether He wished it or not. I shall dismiss it from my thoughts. It is never difficult to *reconcile* one's mind to any thing—the trial is the being in *suspense*.[94]

In 1867, when some wanted Newman to establish an Oratory at Oxford for the sake of Catholic students there, Emily Bowles wrote a letter to him chiding him for "dragging his feet."[95] She too was very much in favor of this project and yet Newman himself hesitated.

> I have already asked the Bishop about our collecting money. You speak as if I were dawdling and losing time. So I should be, if the work was one which I had chosen as God's work. But on the contrary, it has been *forced* on me against my will, and certainly, if not against my judgement, yet not with it, or my will would

---

93. JHN to Mrs. Tennant, 14 April 1878, in *LD* 28:344. See his letter to her on August 13, 1878, which suggests that his advice had been helpful. "I am indeed made very happy by your tidings about yourself, and thank God with all my heart.

"I was very anxious to hear from you and knew not what to think.

"Now all is well and clear—but don't indulge your feelings of happiness overmuch. They are given you in mercy, to overcome the difficulties and trials from within and without, which may beset you—but you must embrace whatever comes, and stand prepared to welcome whatever is God's will, pleasant or painful. He is your sure defence and stay—and the longer you live, the more you will be able to witness to His goodness—but you must begin with trusting Him fully, and resolving by His grace to be His good servant and child." *LD* 28:396.

94. JHN to Henry Bittleston, 21 May 1859, in *LD* 18:352.

95. Initially the Bishops favored this plan, but in the end did not want an Oratory established at Oxford. Newman felt that the concept was a sound one, i.e., of strengthening the faith of the Catholic students attending Oxford. His hesitancy involved the issue of property, finances, etc.

not be against it. It *would* be a great inconsistency in me to let six months pass and do nothing, were I convinced it was the will of Providence—but I do not feel this. I only go because I fear to be deaf to a divine call—but, if any thing happened in these six months to prevent it, that would be to me a sign that there never had been a divine call. It is cowardice not to fight when you feel it to be your duty to fight—but, when you do not feel it is your duty, to fight is, not bravery, but self will.

As to defending myself, you may make yourself quite sure I never will, unless it is a simple duty. Such is a charge against my religious faith—such against my veracity—such any charge in which the cause of religion is involved. But, did I go out and battle commonly I should lose my time, my peace, my strength, and only show a detestable sensitiveness. I consider that Time is the great remedy and Avenger of all wrongs, as far as this world goes. If only we are patient, God works for us—He works for those who do not work for themselves.[96]

Finally, Newman believed that it was God's Providence that had brought him to the Catholic Church: "This day was quite a turning point in my life—and, humanly speaking, I should never have been a Catholic but for God's Providence to me upon it."[97] And when he became a cardinal thirty-four years later, he continued to believe that God's Providence had vindicated him from those Roman Catholics who were suspicious of him.

I knew what gladness it would cause to you and your's, to hear of the high honour to be conferred on me by the Holy Father. It has a special value in my case, who have suffered so much from the suspicions which have been so widely prevalent about me. My writing and publishing days are over, and I am looking for a far more solemn Tribunal than any on earth; but one naturally likes the good opinion of one's Catholic brethren, and it was hard to receive letters to the effect that I was under a cloud. . . . Now, the Pope in his generosity has taken this reproach simply away, and it is a wonderful Providence, that even before my death that acquittal of me comes, which I knew would come some day or other, though not in my life time.[98]

---

96. JHN to Emily Bowles, 8 January 1867, in *LD* 23:15–16.
97. JHN to Mrs. J. W. Bowden, 12 April 1849, in *LD* 13:108.
98. JHN to Mother Mary Imelda Poole, 6 March 1879, in *LD* 29:63.

John Henry Newman

Detachment and Providence: "Singleness of Mind and Purpose"

In the *Catholic University Gazette* in 1854, Newman wrote about a characteristic virtue of the Popes—detachment. His description of this virtue revealed not only another vital facet of his personal spirituality, but also of his spiritual direction:

> Detachment, as we know from spiritual books, is a rare and high Christian virtue; a great Saint, St. Philip Neri, said that, if he had a dozen really detached men, he should be able to convert the world. To be detached is to be loosened from every tie which binds the soul to the earth, to be dependent on nothing sublunary, to lean on nothing temporal; it is to care simply nothing what other men choose to think or say of us, or to do to us; to go about our own work, because it is our duty, as soldiers go to battle, without a care for the consequences: to account credit, honour, name, easy circumstances, comfort, human affections, just nothing at all, when any religious obligation involves the sacrifice of them.[99]

Newman understood detachment to be closely connected with the Providence of God. The more people believed and trusted that God was guiding them, the less need they would have to care what others might think or say about them. To possess this quality, Newman believed, was to have "singleness of mind and purpose."[100] It was a virtue that was important for St. Philip Neri, the founder of the Oratorians, and yet it was one that Newman felt he did not adequately possess—at least in 1858, when writing to Ambrose St. John:

> Yet for myself I know too well, how infinitely more I have from the Giver of all good than my deserts, to have any [even] *temptation* to complain. But, when I think of St. Philip, I argue thus— "There is just one virtue he asks for, detachment, [which at the same time he prevents me having.]" Now the only external thing which keeps me from being perfectly detached, is that I have made myself his servant. What wish have I for life, or for success of any kind, except that I have got his Congregation upon my hands? He has implicated me in the world, in a way in which I never was before.[101]

---

99. Newman, *Historical Sketches*, 3:130.
100. JHN to Sir James Stephen, 17 July 1853, in *LD* 15:398.
101. JHN to Ambrose St. John, 13 June 1858, in *LD* 18:377.

Newman's description indicated three dimensions that find expression in his spiritual direction: detachment from the world; detachment from the opinion of others; and detachment from the desire for praise.

Newman did not despise the world as such; rather, given the passing and temporal value of things, he came to emphasize the unseen world and to be indifferent as to what the world thought of him. He advised Henry Wilberforce in 1846: "My dear Henry, this world is such a vanity—let us look at things as we should wish to have looked at them at the last."[102] Thirty-four years later, in 1880, when Lord Coleridge was appointed Lord Chief Justice, Newman again expressed these same sentiments: "I was just about to write to you to congratulate you on your new position, when your letter came. My sincere congratulations were coupled, of course, with the sorrowful thought to which you refer, and which is one of those mementoes given us all, in one way or another, as life goes on, what a *Vanitas Vanitatis* is all here below."[103]

In 1884, Newman was disturbed by a publication of his brother-in-law; Thomas Mozley's *Reminiscences Chiefly of Oriel and the Oxford Movement* not only quoted from one of Newman's letters without his permission, but also, in his judgment, was loaded with inaccuracies. Newman shared his concerns with George Edwards: "It is one of those incidents which are intended I believe by a good Providence to deepen one's indifference as to what the world thinks of one."[104] Four days later he wrote again, saying: "This is what makes me feel keenly, that one must look out for what God thinks of one, and care nothing for the judgment or the testimony about one of man."[105]

During his Roman Catholic years, Newman's counsel on detachment became more and more explicit. Several days after his conversion, his sister Jemima wrote to him lamenting the fact that now his influence would be lost; Newman replied: "Nothing you say about my loss of influence has any tendency to hurt me, as you kindly fear it should. I never have thought about any influence I had had—I never have mastered what it was—it is simply no effort whatever to give it up. The pain indeed, which I knew I was giving individuals, has affected me much—but as to influence, the whole world is one great vanity, and I trust I am not set on any thing in it—I trust not."[106] Similarly, after the Achilli trial, but before he knew whether he was going to be imprisoned or not, Newman reminisced: "I am but inheriting the lot of Catholics, to suffer and to triumph. Did not I refer you to my words, said 15

---

102. JHN to Henry Wilberforce, 10 March 1846, in *LD* 11:135.
103. JHN to Lord Coleridge, 2 December 1880, in *LD* 29:322–23.
104. JHN to George T. Edwards, 22 February 1884, in *LD* 30:312.
105. JHN to George T. Edwards, 26 February 1884, in *LD* 30:316.
106. JHN to Mrs. John Mozley, 14 October 1845, in *LD* 11:16.

years ago, repeated a year (to the day) before the beginning of this affair, that I had parted with the world—that I was prepared for its worst, and should triumph thro' it! I am the last person who has a right to complain of such a matter, nor do I dream of complaining."[107] Several months later he spoke to the Oratorians:

> I do not suppose that either you or I feel able simply to rejoice and exalt today in our secret hearts, yet reason tells us that we ought to do so. It is *natural* we should be depressed; it is *reasonable* we should triumph. It is from human feeling that we are sad; it will be from grace, if we are satisfied and thankful. Human feeling is not wrong; but grace is better.
>
> Nor need one exclude the other. Our Lord's soul was in heaviness in Gethsemani, though it was in personal union with His All-blissful Divinity; and in our best estate we cannot surpass the Apostles, who were in sadness, yet in continual joy. I do not wonder that we feel pain just now; but I wish a supernatural consolation to consecrate that pain, and to raise it from earth to heaven.[108]

Although this theme of detachment found its way into his preaching, it was usually specific events which occasioned Newman's advice on detachment. For example, when J. M. Capes retired from the editorship of the *Rambler*, Newman told him not to look for any reward in this world.

> I think the Catholic body in this country owes you much gratitude, from the animus and object of your undertaking, the devotion you have shown to it for so long a time, and the various important benefits it has done us. But it is well for us, my dear Capes, that we do not look out for any reward for what we do in this world, for, whether we do or not, we are sure not to get it here—for what we do imperfectly or wrongly affects the public ten times more than what we do well, even though the good may be ten times as much as the amiss. But this is God's merciful dispensation to oblige us to look up to Him, and lay up treasures above, whether we will or no.[109]

The joyful occasion of Eleanor Bretherton's birthday in 1863 provided Newman with another context in which to speak about detachment from the world: "May every year make you more devout, more loving, and more

---

107. JHN to Mrs. William Froude, 4 July 1852, in *LD* 15:120.

108. Newman, "In Sadness Yet in Continual Joy," February 2, 1853, in *Newman the Oratorian*, 14.

109. JHN to J. M. Capes, 17 May 1858, in *LD* 18:349.

detached from the world. May you be clad cap-a-pie [protected] in Divine armour, so that no deceit may mislead you, and no sorrow may sadden you. And may your light burn brighter and brighter in the sight of Angel guardians and earthly friends, till such time as shall seem fit to the Highest, to absorb it into His own Eternal Beatific Splendour."[110] On the other hand, the sad occasion of Manuel Johnson's death caused him to reflect: "Those who knew him will have, each his own grief, in this unexpected blow, and feel it in his own way. To me it comes as a warning of the approach of another world, considering he was some years younger than myself."[111] Finally, in a letter to Miss Holmes in 1855, after elaborating on the fact of instability in the lives of people they both knew, Newman advised her: "Times goes on silently but powerfully, and is making all sorts of changes. . . . May all this instability teach us to love more what is unseen."[112]

Part of Newman's description of detachment was "to care simply nothing what other men choose to think or say of us, or to do to us."[113] Because he was misunderstood and at times mistrusted, he struggled, especially during his Catholic years, to free himself so that he could accomplish what he thought was right in the sight of God. Soon after his conversion, Henry Wilberforce wrote that some Protestants were accusing him of being a Romanist all along. Newman responded: "Thank you for the kind sollicitude [sic] of your letter just received; but I do not partake of your fears. Whatever I do, false reports will get about, and wrong motives and acts be credited. I have outlived many slanders, and, please God, shall outlive many more. I have done nothing, I have not shaken them off; they have fallen off. So will it be with any such absurd belief as you mention."[114]

"Unless a call of duty interfered," Newman never responded to accusations against him because he believed that time would clear up all errors; that eventually truth would conquer falsehood. For example, Newman explained his usual way of handling attacks in a letter in 1850 to Philip Howard, a member of Parliament and a prominent Catholic.

> To tell the truth I have been now for seventeen years the subject of so much daily misrepresentation, in the public prints and at public meetings, that I never think at all about what ever is said against me in the one or at the other. Did I attempt to answer them all, my life would be spent in the occupation; if I answered

---

110. JHN to Eleanor Bretherton, 15 July 1863, in *LD* 20:494. Brackets added.
111. JHN to Mrs. J. W. Bowden, 2 March 1859, in *LD* 19:58.
112. JHN to Miss Holmes, 8 June 1855, in *LD* 16:481.
113. Newman, *Historical Sketches*, 3:130.
114. JHN to Henry Wilberforce, 20 October 1845, in *LD* 11:19–20.

only some, the rest would be taken for granted as true. Moreover, time clears up all errors; the untruth of today is driven out by the contrary untruth of tomorrow, and many-coloured impressions of particular minds are all eventually absorbed by the consistent light of truth. In consequence, I have never done anything but smile at the extravagant things which have been said against me, unless a call of duty interfered.[115]

Similarly, in 1853, when Sir James Stephen wrote criticizing Newman's novel *Loss and Gain*, Newman replied that he was indifferent to what others thought or said about him and what was important was to possess a singleness of mind and purpose with a clear conscience. After stating that the criticisms had not bothered him, Newman continued:

An honorable-minded man, like the Author of them, will easily understand how little an external opinion affects one's feelings, when there is no secret consciousness concurring with it within. Now I have never been dissatisfied with my Tale on the grounds which have caused you to introduce it into your Essay: and I shall not feel the adverse judgement even of good and sagacious men, till I have reason to accuse myself. Moreover this clearness of conscience gives me a sort of prophetic confidence, which the experience of the past justifies, that not a few of those excellent persons, who criticize me now, will see cause at length to soften their unfavorable sentiments.

It used to be a proverb often in the mouth of Dr. Whately, "Fling dirt enough and some will stick." I have not found it true in my own case. Misconceptions from many quarters have been attached to my words, acts, and motives, for 20 years and more. But they have been inconsistent with each other, and unreal in themselves; and having no life, have faded away. It has been so in time past, it will be so in time to come. Do not think me arrogant when I say, that, with ten thousand failings, I have a witness within me to singleness of mind and purpose, and to a heart bared before my Maker and Judge. Time is test of facts. What I am conscious of myself now, I think will one day be granted by others.[116]

Another aspect of Newman's spirituality was his conviction that instead of doing things in order to receive praise, one should act with the realization that God, whose Providence is guiding everyone, will in his own time reward everyone. "I wish you would not be set on human praise,"[117]

115. JHN to Philip Howard, 24 November 1850, in *LD* 14:141.
116. JHN to Sir James Stephen, 17 July 1853, in *LD* 15:398.
117. JHN to Ambrose St. John, 17 November 1857, in *LD* 18:175.

he said to his friend Ambrose St. John, in 1857. Then, revealing his own interior disposition towards the praise of superiors in a letter in 1861 in which he tried to bolster the spirits of Sir John Acton who was thinking of giving up public life, he observed:

> Of course you know very well, without my telling you, that any one who wishes to do good of any kind, must start with the full understanding that he will get no thanks for doing it from any one—and must be content to look for his reward in that quarter only, towards which he looked, in faith and prayer, when he began it. The poet calls fame "the last infirmity—" but I think for my part that the last infirmity is the wish to be praised by our superiors, and intimate friends, and good men—and that we must set out by believing that God's highest tribunals on earth, whether ecclesiastical or moral, will be, for the time, or till we are gone, unfavorable in their view of those deeds of ours which God Himself most approves. And therefore we must, with the holy Apostle, put ourselves above human judgment of every kind.[118]

The following month Robert Ornsby sent Newman a newspaper report of Bartholomew Woodlock's installation as rector of the Catholic University in the University church on June 23, 1861. In commenting on the ceremony, Ornsby noted that hardly any allusion had been made about Newman and his work there. Newman's response manifested his desire to be detached from praise:

> Thank you for the Newspaper and your letter. It is very kind in you to be so anxious about my feelings—but you need not fear. I have had so long a schooling, now nearly for 30 years, of being put on one side, that it is simple truth to say that I expect nothing else, and wish nothing else. I have said in print that it is my wish to have all my reward hereafter, and no reward here—and this is the sort of wish, as to which I have observed that Providence takes one at one's word. As I had occasion to say the other day to a friend, it seems to me a mistake in Milton to make the desire of fame the "last infirmity." I think rather it is the desire to approve oneself to one's superiors and to those whom one respects and pays homage to. I have tried it all my life, and failed to gain it—and in one of the Sermons I preached at Dublin, I say virtually that I have given up the effort. Indeed, I have cause to give it up, if I desire to be at peace, for it has been my lot never to succeed in it. One thing, however, I have been blessed in—that

---

118. JHN to Sir John Acton, 7 June 1861, in *LD* 19:505.

those, whom I have been thrown with intimately, have seldom been unkind to me.[119]

Newman's reason for emphasizing the value of detachment from the desire for praise was expressed in a letter to Miss Giberne in 1858: "If we waited, if I waited till people valued what I did, I should do nothing at all—because, I suppose, the very precept of the gospel, which we all have to practise, is, 'do good, hoping for nothing thereby,' for thus we become the sons of the Highest. If we do a good work, it does not become 'odious,' because God has to reward us, and not man."[120]

Moreover, he was confident that if he undertook a task for God and not for the acclaim of others, eventually God, in his Providence, would prosper it. When some of his plans for the Catholic University in Ireland were being thwarted, Newman calmly reassured Robert Ornsby:

> Don't fancy I feel annoyance at my plans being put aside. 1. I always felt, as I have said in print, that it was quite a chance *what line* things would take. The great thing was to *set up*, and then leave the direction of things to the currents which would determine it. 2. If I *was* to begin, I must begin with some plan. I began with that plan which I thought best. I could not have begun with any other. 3. It does not prove that what I have written and planned will not take effect sometime and somewhere, because it does not at once. For 20 years my book on the Arians was not heard of, and then I began to hear it talked of. My Oxford University Sermons, preached out as long as 17 years, are now (in some passages) attracting attention at Oxford. When I am gone, something may come of what I have done at Dublin. And, since I hope I did what I did, not for the sake of man, not for the sake of the Irish Hierarchy, not even for the Pope's praise, but for the sake of God's Church and God's glory, I have nothing to regret and nothing to desire, different from what it is.[121]

Summary

Cuthbert Butler, in *The Life and Times of Bishop Ullathorne*, summarized Newman's life as a Catholic: "But for the Cardinalate at the end . . . Newman's Catholic life was, from the human point of view, a sad one. The trials

---

119. JHN to Robert Ornsby, 11 July 1861, in *LD* 20:10.
120. JHN to Miss M. R. Giberne, 24 June 1858, in *LD* 18:391.
121. JHN to Robert Ornsby, 15 December 1859, in *LD* 19:253–54.

Spiritual Direction and the Providence of God

were very real, and beyond the lot of most of us. . . . His life was, from the standpoint of this world, a long drawn tragedy. . . . It was indeed the way of the Obscure Night. The explanation of it all is to be found in the spiritual diaries and the intimate letters reproduced by Ward: not insensibility but acceptance, resignation, faith, trust, are the dominant notes."[122] As Butler pointed out, and as the completed publication of Newman's Roman Catholic letters confirms, reflections on the "Providence of God" permeated Newman's life. This theme was a major unifying element in the development of his own spiritual life and constantly found expression in his spiritual direction. "Divine Providence" served as the horizon in which he came to see the ways that God was working in his life.

Experientially, Newman's understanding of Providence was rooted in his intense awareness of God and the unseen world. From his childhood to his "first conversion," through his years at Oxford, Newman believed that Providence was guiding him. For example, the sudden death of his youngest sister, Mary, reinforced in him a vivid sense of the unseen world, invisible but more real than the material universe which acted as its veil; thinking of Mary, he wrote to his sister Jemima: "What a veil and curtain this world of sense is! Beautiful, but still a veil."[123]

Similarly, he saw his conversion to the Church of Rome as part of God's plan for him. Because of his conviction about the reality of the unseen world, it is not surprising to find in his correspondence many letters encouraging people to trust in the Providence of God.

Newman's correspondence does not present a complete treatise on the "Providence of God," for Newman was primarily concerned with answering particular questions or responding to particular concerns in the lives of individuals. However, certain occasions, such as sickness and death, different kinds of human trials, difficulties in belief, failures in ministry, and the need for detachment offered Newman the opportunity of sharing with others his understanding of Providence which was derived from his own spiritual pilgrimage and his theological reflections.

Yet it was not always easy for Newman to discern the Providence of God operative in his life. As Butler has observed, Newman's life was filled with trials, and as his letters indicate, Newman sometimes had to struggle to become resigned to the will of God. For example, in 1859, Newman began to record his thoughts in an exercise book as part of an effort to understand the spiritual implications of the many failures of the previous years.[124] As a

---

122. Butler, *Life and Times*, 2:312–13.
123. Mozley, *Letters*, 1:184.
124. Trevor, *Newman's Journey*, 199. These entries began on December 15 with the

result of these reflections, he saw the rhythm of his life as one of darkness and light in which God was the key figure, providentially guiding him.

It is hardly surprising, then, that this theme of "Providence" permeated his personal correspondence. In guiding others in the Christian life, he encouraged them both to see the events of their lives as directed by Providence and to be responsive to the will of God. Newman, believing that a person was "wounded to heal," also encouraged his inquirers to wait patiently, to trust that their particular trial was for a purpose, and to believe that Providence was guiding them. What assumed importance in his direction was the need to possess a "singleness of mind and purpose," to be detached from the world and people, so that God could become the motivating force of one's life and actions.

The implications of this fundamental trust in Providence were worked out in his daily life and were reflected in his correspondence. The major events of his own life—both trials and successes—plus his experience in directing others, occasioned a continual emphasis on the importance of Providence first in his own life and then in the lives of others. In particular, Newman's spiritual direction reflected not only his personal experiences but also his platonic view of the world. Newman's belief that "the visible is but a copy of the invisible" had discernible implications for both his own spiritual life and his direction of others. First, this belief catalyzed his relationship to God by confirming him in his "mistrust of the reality of material phenomena" and by making him "rest in the thought of two and two only absolutely and luminously self-evident beings, myself and my Creator."[125] Second, for Newman the world was a veil which hides the mysteries of the divine; thus, the task of the believer is to discover the spiritual behind the material. Finally, his view of Providence helped him personally to face obstacles and defeats with astonishing courage, invincible independence and indifference to the world's judgment.

Theologically, Newman's view of Providence reflects a traditional Catholic understanding of an infinite God whose providence "causes, cares for, and directs all creatures to their particular ends, in attaining which each one contributes to his final purpose of the universe—the manifestation of His eternal glory."[126] Underlying Newman's understanding of Providence, however, was his Platonic view of the material world as a veil hiding the spiritual world. This Platonic presupposition shaped his theological understanding of Providence and influenced his advice to others.

---

words: "I am writing on my knees and in God's sight."

125. Newman, *Apologia*, 16.

126. Carney, "Theology of Providence of God," 184.

4

Spiritual Direction and Faith

"These earthen vessels of ours hold the treasure of grace and truth."[1]

FAITH IS AT THE heart of spiritual direction. The way a spiritual director understands faith implicitly underlies the way that director directs another. This was certainly true for Newman. Many people wrote to him about various aspects of faith or about some particular belief of the Catholic Church. There was an intimate connection between his understanding of the nature of faith as such, and his belief in the Catholic Church; consequently, it is often difficult to separate one from the other. Accordingly, this chapter on faith and the subsequent chapter on the Church should be viewed as a unit. In presenting this aspect of his spiritual direction, this chapter on faith deals with what Newman believed about faith and the ways in which he directed others either to prepare themselves to receive this gift of faith or to deepen their belief. The following chapter investigates his spiritual direction on particular aspects of faith in the Catholic Church.

Coming to Faith

From a theoretical perspective, Newman can be seen as investigating faith on two levels. On one level he addressed his own countrymen who, he felt, generally lacked real faith. They might hold the opinion that Christianity is probably true, but for Newman religious faith must be an absolute assent to what God has revealed. "Is it possible . . . that faith in Revelation is

---

1. JHN to Sister Mary Gabriel du Boulay, 18 August 1861, in *LD* 20:19.

nothing beyond the thought, 'Perhaps after all God may have spoken?' . . . Who would call this an act of faith? Was such Abraham's faith?"[2] On this level Newman was concerned with explaining and defending the certitude of faith.[3] On a second level Newman faced a growing skepticism and relativism which denied the possibility of objectively certain knowledge. Consequently he explained and defended the certitude of human knowledge. The certitude of our human way of knowing is found in that reasoning which leads people to make a judgment that they ought to believe; this judgment, when made with a right will and an honest hope and prompted by divine grace, grounds an act of faith, that is certain and salvific.[4]

Newman was deeply aware of the difficulties that trouble those in doubt. He was equally aware of mysterious facts which he could not ignore; he had an unshakable faith in God's word. Yet Newman was not the kind of individual who could be satisfied with quick solutions that left questions unresolved. Nor could he be satisfied with a quick retreat to "religious feeling" that in effect abandoned the issue to the skeptic. Either to deny the facts or to affirm them too abruptly was unsatisfactory because it was superficial. Instead he sought to balance fidelity to the facts with humility before the mysteries. He sought to present the truths of faith, yet to respect friends who were honestly in doubt.

From Newman's correspondence, two dimensions emerge in his spiritual direction concerning faith. First, many letters are concerned with helping individuals understand the gift of faith that God was offering them and attempting to resolve their difficulties and doubts so that they might be able to respond to this gift. Second, other letters attempt to help a person understand and appreciate faith in their own lives, and suggest how these people might deepen their faith.

Faith as a Gift

Since Newman understood faith as a gift from God, he sought to understand the human process by which persons disposed themselves to receive this gift. In fact, much of his correspondence centered on helping individuals understand

---

2. Newman, *Lectures on the Present*, x–xi.

3. In some of his correspondence, Newman spoke of the "certainty" of faith; in his *Essay in Aid* (1870), chapter 7, he used "certainty" in reference to "formal inference" (e.g., mathematical or logical conclusions) and "certitude" in relation to matters of "informed reference" (e.g., matters of trust, faith, etc.).

4. Fey, *Faith*, xii.

Spiritual Direction and Faith

some facet of this process. In three letters written to his good friend Mrs. William Froude, Newman spoke of the importance of faith as a gift:

> I wish you would consider whether you have a right notion of how to gain faith. It is, we know, the Gift of God, but I am speaking of it as a human process and attained by human means. Faith then is not a conclusion from premises, but the result of an act of the *will*, following upon a conviction that to believe is a *duty*. The simple question you have to ask yourself is "Have I a *conviction* that I *ought* to accept the Catholic Faith as God's Word?" if not, at least, "do I *tend* to such a conviction?" or "am I *near* upon it?" For directly you have a conviction that you *ought* to believe, reason has done its part, and what is wanted for faith is, not proof but will. *We can believe what we choose.*⁵

In this same letter, he emphasized the determination of the will rather than the object of belief.

> Is it not plain that many of Dr. Pusey's followers are at this very time exerting an act of *will, commanding* their minds, to believe, on this ground, be it sufficient or be it not, *because* Dr. Pusey believes? And is not he believing, because he is *determined* he will believe so and so? So you think they could not in like manner, if they pleased, believe what the Catholic Church teaches? The simple question with them is, which of the two creeds their *reason* tells them they ought to believe; and their reason tells them they ought to believe, not what the ancient widely spreading (Roman) Catholic Church believes, but what Dr. Pusey believes—but the belief itself is the result of an act of *their will.*
>
> Now can you, my dear Mrs. Froude, say this, that, directly you feel sure you ought to believe the Catholic Faith, you will begin making efforts to control your mind into belief? You see, I will not admit your language, that "you *cannot believe*," you can. The simple question is, whether you *ought*. If you do not feel you ought, (I hope such a state of mind will not last—but) that is a reason, because it is not true, to say, "I don't believe because I can't."⁶

Eight months later, however, Newman again wrote Mrs. Froude about the importance of cooperating with God and of accepting the gift He was offering her.

---

5. JHN to Mrs. William Froude, 27 June 1848, in *LD* 12:228.

6. Ibid. In another letter a week later, July 3, 1848, to Mrs. Froude, Newman repeated: "Though you can believe what you choose, you must believe that you ought." *LD* 12:233.

> My fears may certainly be groundless—but O what an awful thing it is, should you be in the way of losing your faith. If God has for many years past been forming a habit of faith in you, and at length has put before you the true object of that faith, and you have refused to accept it, and so have lost a state of mind which cannot live except in its Object! Alas, how many instances do we see around us of a wrecked and ruined faith! Of those who either deliberately, or at least virtually, have preferred scepticism to Rome! Surely faith is the gift of God, as it was in St. Paul's day, and the divine election is as wonderful now as then.
>
> . . . No, the election is with God; we can but co-operate with him—and we must submit to His decision.[7]

Writing Mrs. Froude several years later, he underscored the importance of faith as a gift in relation to prayer:

> I am quite sure you wish to please God, and would do any thing He told you. On the other hand, I know well He does not tell us everything at once—but first one thing, and then, when we act upon that, another. No one ought to enter the Church without faith—no one can have faith for it by wishing or willing it, at the moment. Faith is a Gift of God; we can gain it by prayer, we cannot gain it at once; but we can gain it at last. I will quarrel with no one simply for not entering into the holiest and happiest of states on the spur of the instant—faith must be preceded by reason—but I will quarrel with him much, if he does not earnestly and continually ask of God the illumination which leads reason to faith.[8]

In 1870, he wrote to Mrs. Wilson, a convert who had been prematurely received into the Church, reiterating the link between faith as a gift and prayer.

> I can easily believe you were received too soon—for many persons are. They do not know their religion, and difficulties come upon them afterwards, which they ought to have considered before they become Catholics. Faith is a gift of God, and a mere wish or a decision to join the Church is not necessarily faith.
>
> However, I would not say that you have not faith—but your faith is weak—and I speak of its being a gift of God to

---

7. JHN to Mrs. William Froude, 14 July 1849, in *LD* 13:218–19.

8. JHN to Mrs. William Froude, 23 February 1853, in *LD* 15:307–8. Newman continued to stress this idea as late as December 11, 1886 in a letter to Alfred Spurrier: "Faith is a divine gift. It is gained by prayer. Prayer must be patient and persevering." *LD* 31:177.

Spiritual Direction and Faith

believe, to remind you, what it must be right to say, even tho' you do not need reminding, that you must *pray* for it.[9]

Four years later, Newman wrote a much sterner letter, since he apparently felt that she was not doing enough herself to dispose herself to receive this gift.

> As far as I see, I do not think you have with a resolute heart, and with earnestness fought the battle of your soul. I know others who, with greater disadvantages than I suppose yours are, have been brave, and determined, and, though they have been knocked down, have got up again, and fought on. They will have their reward, and it will be great. St. Philip says "Paradise is not meant for cowards," and, when I see such instances of courage, I feel how little I have myself done in that line—and I think you have done very little too.
>
> It seems to me that, instead of going straight-forward to your work, you indulge yourself in finding faults with priests, whom you should not come near, and are not unwilling to provoke them—that you do not make the best of things, but take pleasure in complaints. I may be wrong in points of detail in my view of you, and beg you to pardon me, if I am—but I don't think I am wrong on the whole. We cannot do without *faith*, and faith is the *gift of God*. You do not seem to me to keep before your mind and to realize, these two awful truths.[10]

Similarly, in Newman's *Loss and Gain*, a novel about an Oxford student's conversion, the central figure, Charles Reding asked, "If a man finds himself unable, though wishing, to believe, for he has not evidence enough to subdue his reason, what is to make him believe?" The priest answered, "What is to make him believe! the *will*, his *will*."[11] Catherine Ward read this and asked Newman, "How am I to know when I ought to believe?" He replied that reason proves what ought to be believed. It does not prove what is true "as it proves that mathematical conclusions are true." There are many questions left unanswered. Yet the "grounds are sufficient for conviction. This is not the same thing as conviction . . . while there is enough evidence for conviction, whether we will be convinced or not rests with ourselves."[12] A few weeks later, he wrote to the same correspondent about doubt before faith: "You cannot be rid of those doubts without grace; as you distinctly say,

---

9. JHN to Mrs. Wilson, 8 January 1870, in *LD* 25:6.
10. JHN to Mrs. Wilson, 3 August 1874, in *LD* 27:102–3.
11. Newman, *Loss and Gain*, 383–84.
12. JHN to Catherine Ward, 12 October 1848, in *LD* 12:289n1.

they are *not* intellectual doubts; your intellect is convinced, but in spite of that conviction, you are haunted with doubts."[13]

In October 1853, Newman had tried to avoid speaking "of divine grace, where it comes in, or what it does."[14] But in December he wrote a paper, "On the Certainty of Faith," where he recognized that a treatment of the certainty of faith demanded a discussion of "the process of supernatural faith, and the portion of it which is supernatural."[15] In this paper, Newman hesitated to speak of a "fides humana . . . aided by grace" preceding the act of "fides divina." However, the next month, on January 17, 1854, he wrote a further paper on the object of divine faith. "I may believe things from reason etc. and then the form of belief is demonstration. But faith is belief in God telling me—i.e. in God, as God revealing."[16] Newman then summarized his meaning: "The Formal Object of Faith is God . . . God, as God Revealing . . . or, as it is commonly said, Divine Revelation . . . that is, the Divine Authority in revealing . . . or (if we would consider the matter more accurately), the truth of God in speaking . . . or even the truth of God, all-knowing and all-wise, in speaking . . . or the wisdom and veracity of God."[17]

It was this notion of "a speaker" which distinguished the grace-created act of divine faith from every grace supported act of human faith. As he developed this essential feature of divine faith, he clarified these two distinct operations of grace. Newman believed that in divine faith grace enables one to believe, not arguments and evidence, but "the Divine Speaker." Moreover, it was because divine faith follows the logic of testimony that the operation of grace, reason and will before faith must be distinguished from their operation in faith.

In 1855, in a letter to Mrs. William Froude, Newman explained the role of grace before faith: "Perhaps what divines call grace, the supernatural assistance of the Father of Lights, may be the necessary preparation for our understanding the force of the arguments in the subject matter of religion; and perhaps prayer may be the human means . . . of gaining that supernatural assistance."[18] In other words, grace may be necessary to aid the will in putting down "a wild unhealthy state of mind" comparable to the state of mind

---

13. JHN to Catherine Ward, 30 November 1848, in *LD* 12:356.

14. JHN to Edward Thompson, 11 October 1853, in *LD* 15:467.

15. Newman, "Papers of 1853 on the Certainty of Faith," in *Theological Papers of John Henry Newman*, 36.

16. Fey, *Faith*, 175.

17. Ibid.

18. JHN to Mrs. William Froude, 1855, in *LD* 16:108.

which unreasonably suggests, "perhaps there is poison in my breakfast."[19] In this way grace indirectly brings about "that moral condition of which the recognition of certain intellectual truths" is the "natural result."[20]

Wanting to encourage his Anglican friend Henry Wilberforce, Newman emphasized the need of cooperating with grace in coming to faith:

> I think I quite understand your state of mind, and earnestly trust and believe that God is leading you forward to the sure test of His True Fold. It would not annoy me that you delay, could I be sure that you are keeping pace with the guidance given you—but of course to any one who does not see the heart, it is a source of continual anxiety lest you should be letting a precious time slip past you. You know what an awful overcoming view Catholics take of the grace of God—as that which we cannot merit, which may be withheld without any injustice to us, which is not given to all in the same measure. The immediate consequence of such a belief is to make one fear intensely, as for myself, so for one's friends—certainly if they are outside the Church, and may be receiving an infinite condescension on God's part, which may never be repeated. Charissime, be sure you do not trifle with God's grace.[21]

After speaking of one of the effects of grace in bringing one to faith, he continued:

> Keep before your mind that, when you are once convinced, you must act. Conviction is a state of mind—it is not the mere perception of a conclusion, for then it would vary about with the strength of the premises—but it is a state, which follows on a conclusion, sometimes more, sometimes less strictly logical. It is no proof then that you are not *convinced in your heart*, because there are objections in *reason* which you cannot answer. It often happens in this life that, when we are convinced, we *refuse* further proofs, though cogent—we say "Take them away, my mind is made up, is clear." Charissime, you will have a great deal to go through. I do not undervalue it—but in proportion to your suffering, will be your reward.[22]

For Newman, the entire process of coming to faith is touched by grace. For example, in response to J. Walker of Scarborough he wrote:

---

19. Newman, *Philosophical Notebook*, 195.
20. Ibid., 195–97.
21. JHN to Henry Wilberforce, 1 October 1849, in *LD* 13:266–67.
22. Ibid.

> I maintain that probabilities lead to a speculative certainty legitimately; so that it is quite rational to come to that conviction, that human faith, which is rewarded by divine faith. In thus speaking, of course I do not mean to say, that, in matter of fact, that human conclusion is reached, or the reward of divine certainty given, without the influence of actual grace, both being present and being obeyed. And so, in like manner, human charitableness, honesty, fortitude, patience, in the case of a heathen, may be assisted by actual grace, and bring the soul forward towards conversion, and have a congruous merit—but still they do not cease to be acts of human nature.[23]

Whenever Newman wrote to an unbeliever, he discussed the operation of reason, will, and grace before faith. Yet in speaking of an ability to know (be certain) that revelation is credible, he was not speaking of the certainty of faith itself which is the direct result of grace. Accordingly, at the end of his last letter to Froude, he compared the situation of a believer with that of someone who is certain of his friend's loyalty despite irrational doubts: "And if it be said that his friend is visibly present, and the object of faith invisible, there the action of supernatural grace comes in, which I cannot enter upon here."[24]

But when writing to believers, Newman did not hesitate to discuss the unique role of grace in faith itself. In 1862 he wrote to William Ward: "Human faith lies in the intellect as well as Divine faith; but the former is created there by previous acts of mere human reason, the latter is the creation of supernatural grace."[25] Newman believed that reason's role is "critical" not "creative."[26] Reason might provide arguments which "will be a stay, a refuge, and encouragement, a rallying point for faith."[27] It might lead us to faith. Nevertheless, "the two things are quite distinct from each other, seeing you ought to believe, and believing; reason, if left to itself, will bring you to the conclusion that you have sufficient grounds for believing, but belief is the gift of grace."[28] Emphasizing the importance of grace in the human process, Newman wrote to J. Walker of Scarborough in 1864, saying that the human conclusion cannot

---

23. JHN to J. Walker of Scarborough, 24 October 1864, in *LD* 21:270–71. See also JHN to Mrs. William Froude, 23 February 1853, in *LD* 15:307–8.
24. JHN to Mrs. William Froude, 29 April 1879, in *LD* 29:120.
25. JHN to W. G. Ward, 15 March 1862, in *LD* 20:171.
26. Newman, "Faith and Reason Contrasted," in *Fifteen Sermons*, 183.
27. Ibid., 199.
28. Newman, "Faith and Private Judgement," in *Discourses*, 211.

be reached, "or the reward of divine certainty given, *without* the influence of *actual* grace, both being present and being obeyed."[29]

Newman was interested, not in theoretical questions about nature and grace, but in the process that an individual followed in coming to faith. In stressing the concrete situation he did not mean to imply that faith is merely the result of an informal argument aided by grace. Nor did he mean to imply that grace merely lends supernatural value to a natural act. Divine faith is completely reasonable, but it is also completely the free gift of grace which enables a person not only to appreciate the force of arguments but to grasp in faith God testifying to Himself. Thus, he called divine faith "spiritual sight,"[30] or "an original means of knowledge."[31] Accordingly, he compared the unbeliever to a blind man who has access only to notions and inferences but lacks a real familiarity with the object of his discourse.[32]

Persons coming to faith will recognize the truth "dimly, though certainly, as the sun through mists and clouds" but "it is the office of grace to clear up gloom and haziness, to steady that fitful vision, to perfect reason by faith, and to convert a logical conclusion into an object of intellectual sight."[33] Divine faith is not the acceptance of the conclusion of an argument, nor the acceptance of a particular way of looking at the world; it is an acceptance of God revealing a definite message.

Faith and Certitude

Newman believed that certitude in religious matters was essential for living a spiritual life; he stated in his *Essay in Aid of a Grammar of Assent*: "Without certitude in religious faith there may be much decency of profession and of observance, but there can be no habit of prayer, no directness of devotion, no intercourse with the unseen, no generosity of self-sacrifice. Certitude then is essential to the Christian; and if he is to persevere to the end, his certitude must include in it a principle of persistence."[34]

Much of Newman's spiritual direction for persons in the process of coming to faith dealt with various difficulties in the area of certitude. A convert himself, he understood what they were experiencing. Through his

---

29. JHN to J. Walker of Scarborough, 24 October 1864, in *LD* 21:270.
30. Newman, Sermon 14, in *Parochial and Plain Sermons*, 2:151–52; January or February 1836.
31. Newman, *Lectures on the Doctrine of Justification*, 267.
32. Newman, *Fifteen Sermons*, 61–62.
33. Newman, *Discourses*, 187.
34. Newman, *Essay in Aid*, 220.

correspondence, he patiently helped individuals to clarify their own thinking on certain issues while at the same time attempting to answer their questions, doubts or difficulties. Sometimes his correspondent evoked a single letter; with others, their correspondence spanned many years.[35]

Since Newman believed that faith is a gift personally granted by God as a result of a quest, he often advised people to continue their search, to pray for the grace of believing. To Louisa Simeon, who was searching for religious certitude, he wrote in 1869:

> You must begin all thought about religion by mastering what is the fact, that any how the question has an inherent, irradicable difficulty in it. As in tuning a piano, you may throw the fault here or there, but no theory can any one take up without that difficulty remaining. It will come up in one shape or other. If we say, "Well, I will not believe anything," there is a difficulty in believing nothing, an intellectual difficulty. There is a difficulty in doubting; a difficulty in determining there is no truth; in saying that there is a truth, but that no one can find it out; in saying that all religious opinions are true; or one is good as another; a difficulty in saying there is no God; that there is a God but that He has not revealed Himself except in the way of nature; and there is doubtless a difficulty in Christianity. The question is, whether on the whole our reason does not tell us that it is a duty to accept the arguments commonly urged for its truth as sufficient, and a duty in consequence to believe heartily in Scripture and the Church.[36]

In 1871, Newman described an act of certitude to William Brownlow: "I may wish both to act and to believe—though I can do neither—and, as I ask God for grace to enable me to act, so I ask Him for grace to enable me to believe.

"'It is the gift of God—why does He not give it to me?' Because you do not perseveringly come to Him for the gift, and do your part by putting aside all those untrue and unreal and superfluous arguings."[37]

---

35. See, e.g., his extensive correspondence with William Froude from 1860 to 1879:
William Froude to JHN, 15 January 1860, in *LD* 19:283–84;
JHN to William Froude, 18 January 1860, in *LD* 19:284–85;
William Froude to JHN, 25 January 1860, in *LD* 19:296–98;
JHN to William Froude, 26 January 1860, in *LD* 19:298–99;
JHN, Memorandum of Conversation with William Froude, 14 December 1860, in *LD* 19:440–42;
JHN to William Froude, 9 April 1863, in *LD* 20:430;
JHN to William Froude, 30 September 1864, in *LD* 21:245;
William Froude to JHN, 29 April 1879, in *LD* 29:119–20.

36. JHN to Louisa Simeon, 25 June 1869, in *LD* 24:275.

37. JHN to William Brownlow, 29 April 1871, in *LD* 25:324.

Spiritual Direction and Faith

Newman realized that finding certitude in religious matters was not an easy task. Mrs. William Froude, who had been influenced by her skeptical husband, had been writing to Newman about faith and certitude. After acknowledging her objections, he emphasized the importance of prayer in her quest:

> Men who have lived in the dark, see things with a clearness unintelligible to those who enter it from the broad day. That religious truth is an obscure subject is granted; but that does not prove that we cannot find out its roads and their termination.
> ... Perhaps prayer may be the human means, in the way of cause and effect, of gaining that supernatural assistance ...
> I should like an inquirer to say continually, "O my God, I confess that *Thou canst* enlighten my darkness—I confess that Thou *only* canst. I *wish* my darkness to be enlightened. I do not know whether Thou wilt; but that Thou canst, and that I wish, are sufficient reasons for me to ask, what Thou at least has [sic] not forbidden my asking. I hereby promise thee that, by Thy grace which I am seeking, I *will embrace* whatever I at length feel certain is the truth, if ever I come to be certain. And by Thy grace I will guard against all self deceit which may lead me to take what nature would have, rather than what reason approves."
> If a man tells me he has thus heroically cast himself upon God, and persisted in such a prayer, and yet is in the dark, of course my argument with him is at an end. I retire from the discussion, and leave the matter to God.[38]

In 1881, Newman repeated this same theme. Mrs. Christie had become a Catholic in 1879, and she had been corresponding with a relative as to whether he should follow her example. After explaining the difficulties involved, she asked Newman's advice. Newman responded:

> As to Mr. C. and his not having a "call," in Catholic language he means he has not *faith*. It is not infrequent for men to be intellectually convinced, and to add that "they wish they *could* believe, but they can't." Your friend throws into language which pleases him better the same confession, and says "I have not a call." ...
> Mr. C. seems to feel that membership with the Catholic Church, is the *normal* state of a Christian, and therefore it is his duty to pray earnestly, to pray continually, for that living faith, for that true call, which comes to him indeed from God but which withal comes thro' himself. God gives to all liberally, and

---

38. JHN to Mrs. William Froude, 1854 or 1855, in *LD* 16:108–9.

it will be a grevious thing to find some day that it is through his own fault that the call has not come to him.[39]

Besides advising prayer, Newman also wrote many letters to people concerning some particular aspect of the search for certitude. When William Goodwin, who had been brought up a Methodist, wrote that he felt the need for certitude in religious matters, Newman told him that a person's first principles were crucial in order to find certitude.

> It seems to me that the great differences in religion between man and man arise from their difference from each other in first principles, so that according to their first principles such is the religion which they severally adopt.
>
> For instance—one man thinks sin to be so great an evil, as not to be named in the same breath with any other evil, but to stand simply by itself. Another thinks it nothing but a coming short of ethical perfection, more or less, not involving any sense of guilt.
>
> And first principles *hold together* so that these imply those. I fear I may seem running very far back for a beginning, but I now come to my answer to what you seem to ask of me. What you, as all men, need, is *true* first principles, and who can give them to you, but He who made you?
>
> I say then to every one who feels the pain and unnaturalness of scepticism, it may be a hard matter for a man to *detect* and recognize his own first principles, and you may *never* know them, nor is it necessary that you *should* know them, but it is necessary that they should be true—and, I repeat, who can give you them but God?
>
> It is usual to say that the choice of a religion is an intellectual work and matter of reasoning—it may be an object of the *intellect* but as a work of reasoning, it is subordinate to first principles, which is that very intellectual gift, which God alone can give us, and from which reasonings follow.[40]

Newman spoke of certitude as a state of mind in several letters and the method he employed in order to help people understand was an appeal to common sense. William Brownlow had been advising a woman and wrote to Newman for clarification concerning evidence, assent and certitude. Newman replied:

---

39. JHN to Mrs. Christie, 20 December 1881, in *LD* 30:33.
40. JHN to William Goodwin, 13 August 1884, in *LD* 30:389–90.

Spiritual Direction and Faith

As you will see, she confuses the *conclusion* from *evidence*, with the act of *assent* which depends on the *will*. No one on earth can have evidence strictly *sufficient* for an *absolute* conclusion, but I may have evidence so strong that I may see it is my duty to give my absolute assent to it. I have not absolute demonstration that my father was not a murderer, or my intimate friend a sharper, but it would not only be heartless, but irrational not to disbelieve these hypotheses or possibilities utterly—and, anyhow, in matter of fact men generally do disbelieve them absolutely—and therefore the Church, as the Minister of God, asks us for nothing more in things supernatural than common sense, as nature asks of us in matters of this world. I believe absolutely that there is a North America—and that the United States is a Republic with a President—why then do I not absolutely believe, though I see it not, that there is a Heaven and that God is there? If you say that there is *more* evidence for the United States than for Heaven; that is intelligible—but it is not a question of more or less; since the *utmost* evidence only leads to probability and *yet* you believe absolutely in the United States, it is no reason against believing in heaven absolutely, though you have no "experience" of it . . .

She says there are persons who are *certain* of the Christian religion *because* they have strictly proved it—no one is certain for this reason. Every one believes by an act of will, more or less ruling his intellect (as a matter of duty) to believe absolutely *beyond* the evidence.

She says "acts of certitude are always made about things of which our senses or our reason do, or can take cognizance"—our senses do not tell us that there is a "United States" and our reason does not demonstrate it, only makes it possible. We not only do not, but we *could* not make a demonstration; yet we assent absolutely.

"How can any human testimony make me *quite certain* that I am hearing a message from God?" None can, but human testimony may be such as to make me see it is my *duty* to be certain. *Action* is distinct from a conclusion—yet a conclusion may be such as to make me see that action is a *duty*—and so *belief* is not a conclusion—yet it may be such as to make me see that belief is a *duty*—And, as I cannot act merely because I ought to act, so I cannot believe merely because I ought to believe.

I may wish both to act and to believe—though I can do neither—and, as I ask God for grace to enable me to act, so I ask Him for grace to enable me to believe.[41]

---

41. JHN to William Brownlow, 29 April 1871, in *LD* 25:323–24.

Similarly, he told Henry Wilberforce that conviction being a state of mind, was different than having a feeling in one's heart:

> Keep before your mind that, when you are once convinced, you must act. Conviction is a state of mind—it is not the mere perception of a conclusion, for then it would vary about with the strength of the premises—but it is a state, which follows on a conclusion, sometimes more, sometimes less strictly logical. It is no proof then that you are not *convinced in your heart*, because there are objections in *reason* which you cannot answer. It often happens in this life that, when we are convinced, we *refuse* further proofs, thought cogent—we say "Take them away, my mind is made up, is clear."[42]

In a letter to Frank Haydon, Newman expressed his understanding of faith in relation to certitude:

> In my *judgement* then the evidence [of mathematical proofs] is not simply demonstrative—but *certainty* is a state of mind, and in spite of this *judgement*, I suppose we are *certain* without any sort of fear of mistake, that the proposition in question is true. At the same time I think that state of mental certainty depends ultimately on the will—and that the will could so act upon the mind as to lead it morbidly to make that microscopic objection an occasion of doubt in the truth of that proposition. In like manner when I say that the proof of a certain person or body being the oracle of the God who can neither deceive nor be deceived is sufficient to lead to certainty, I mean no more than that it is such that certainty is the state of mind to which it legitimately leads, and will lead unless an act of the will interferes to hinder it.[43]

Ten years later, Newman again wrote to Henry Wilberforce indicating that the certitude of faith is not based on the same kind of demonstration that is possible in the sciences:

> Yet on the other hand it is a paradox to say there is not such a state of mind as certitude. It is as well ascertained a state of mind, as doubt—to say that such a phenomenon in the human mind is a mere extravagance or weakness is a monstrous assertion which I cannot swallow. Of course there may be abuses and mistakes in particular cases of certitude, but that is another matter. It is a law

---

42. JHN to Henry Wilberforce, 1 October 1849, in *LD* 13:267.
43. JHN to Frank Haydon, 24 April 1858, in *LD* 18:333–36.

of our *nature* then, that we are certain on premisses which do not touch <reach> demonstration. This seems to me undeniable.[44]

Faith and Reason

Newman's question on the certitude of faith shaped his remarks on the role of reason in faith and it was a topic on which he frequently corresponded during his life as a Roman Catholic. He encouraged people to search, to inquire about their faith in order to make it personal. At the same time, he was deeply concerned about an individual's approach to the problem and felt that God needed to help a person use their reason in a correct way in their search for faith. Encouraging George Boag to continue his investigation, Newman wrote in 1881:

> I am with you entirely in holding that every inquiring mind must inquire for itself and cannot content itself with the conclusions of others and nothing more. Where I should perhaps not go with you would be in the special view you took of your relations towards the Supreme Being. It may be that I construe what you say wrongly, but, as I read your letter it seemed to me that you did not dwell sufficiently on the need of God's teaching you, his promise to do so, and the duty of every one of us, if we would find what is the Truth, to ask that great blessing from Him.
>
> I am conscious that I may have made a great mistake—but, when you say that a man must shelter himself from doubt with such aid as shall be given him from on high, you may be saying all that any sober Catholic could ask of you, (for one does not necessarily deny what one does not affirm), but the question arose in my mind, whether you threw yourself on God's grace and said to Him "Teach me" with such exercise of reason as was your duty to; whether God came first or reason.[45]

Catherine Ward wrote to him in 1848 concerning her inner confusion about converting to Catholicism. At times she had strong convictions about joining the Church and yet she was also fearful. Her questions gave Newman the opportunity to explain his understanding of the role of reason in faith:

> The Catholic doctrine concerning faith and reason is this, that reason proves that Catholicism *ought to be* believed, and that in that form it comes *before the will*, which accepts it or rejects it,

---

44. JHN to Henry Wilberforce, 27 July 1868, in *LD* 24:104.
45. JHN to George Boag, 25 February 1881, in *LD* 29:343.

> as moved by grace or not. Reason does not prove that Catholicism is *true*, as it proves that mathematical conclusions are true, e.g., that the 3 angles of a triangle are equal to two right angles; but it proves that there is a *case* for it so strong that we see we ought to accept it. There may be many difficulties which we cannot answer, but still we see on the whole that grounds are sufficient for conviction. This is not the same thing as conviction. If conviction were unavoidable, we might be said to be forced to believe, as we are forced to mathematical conclusions—but while there is enough evidence for conviction, whether we *will* be convinced or not, rests with ourselves—this is what the priest means, when he is first asked "If a man has not evidence enough to *subdue* his reason, what is to make him believe?" and then answers "His will." and this is just our trial—and one man rejects what another accepts—On the contrary, were we forced to believe, as we are forced to admit that two sides of a triangle are greater than the third, there would be no trial of our affections, nothing morally right in believing, or wrong in not believing.
>
> The simple question then with you is, Have you sufficient grounds for being convinced that the Catholic Church is from God?—if you have, it is nothing to the purpose that you find it difficult to believe—of course it is, for belief is a supernatural act—you must pray to God for the will to believe—for the will has the power to command the mind. *You can believe what you will*; the only question is whether your reason tells you that you *ought* to believe; and I think it does.[46]

In addition to these letters expressing Newman's basic belief on the role of reason in faith, two other letters indicate a broader horizon. The first concerned the area of "faith and mystery." An unknown correspondent had written to him: "That which is a conclusion in reason cannot also be an object of faith; since then the being of a God is an object of faith, it is not a conclusion of the reason."[47] Newman responded:

> Now here a great deal might be said, did my paper admit of it, on the difference between a conclusion and an object; but I will only say this, that the same truth may at once be proved by reason and held by faith. For instance, the truth of the Newtonian system is a conclusion in reason; yet by the mass of the community it is held, not as a conclusion which they have proved, but as a truth received on faith in scientific men. Or, (what is

---

46. JHN to Catherine Ward, 12 October 1848, in *LD* 12:289–90.
47. JHN to Unknown Correspondent, 23 September 1864, in *LD* 21:236.

more simple,) the fact that, contrary to the evidence of sight, the earth turns on its axis, some conclude on grounds of reason, most men only believe "because every one says so, because men of science say so." Nay, the very same person may hold the same fact at once upon faith and upon reason. 1) I may have satisfactorily proved to myself by pure reason that the nebular theory is true; and then, on turning to Scripture, may find that light was created before the sun. Here faith confirms reason, or I hold a fact first by reason, and then in addition by faith. 2) I may receive on faith that the whole human race descends from Adam, and at some future time may be able to prove it from philology, ethnology, geology, and archeology. Here reason confirms faith, or I hold a fact, first by faith, and then in addition by reason. 1) I do not cease to conclude because I believe. 2) I do not cease to believe because I conclude.[48]

A letter to Newman from Louisa Simeon gave Newman the opportunity of helping her come to faith by emphasizing the importance of the role of reason in finding the correct starting points for religious truth. He felt this search was intimately bound up with living a moral life and one's conscience:

> You must not suppose that I am denying the intellect its real place in the discovery of truth; but it must ever be borne in mind that its exercise mainly consists in reasoning,—that is, in comparing things, classifying them, and inferring. It ever needs points to start from, first principles, and these it does not provide—but it can no more move one step without these starting points, than a stick, which supports a man, can move without the man's action. In physical matters, it is the senses which gives us the first start—and what the senses give is physical fact—and physical facts do not lie on the surface of things, but are gained with pains and by genius, through experiment. . . . In like manner we have to ascertain the starting points for arriving at religious truth. The intellect will be useful in gaining them and after gaining them—but to attempt to see them by means of the intellect is like attempting by the intellect to see the physical facts which are the basis of physical exercises of the intellect. . . . To gain religious starting points, we must in a parallel way, interrogate our hearts, and (since it is a personal, individual matter,) our own hearts,—interrogate our own consciences, interrogate, I will say, the God who dwells there.
>
> I think you must ask the God of Conscience to enable you to do your duty in this matter. I think you should, with prayer to

48. Ibid.

> Him for help, meditate upon the Gospels, and on St. Paul's second Epistle to the Corinthians . . .; and this with an earnest desire to know the truth and a sincere intention of following it.[49]

Probability and Faith

Much of Newman's direction in helping people to arrive at faith centered on the concept of probability.[50] He felt that an assemblage of probabilities represented a moral demonstration of religious truth which gave a person certitude, and which was quite different from acting as if one were certain. Using the example of a cable, he explained his position to J. Walker of Scarborough:

> The best illustration of what I hold is that of a *cable* which is made up of a number of separate threads, each feeble, yet together as sufficient as an iron rod.
>
> An iron rod represents mathematical or strict demonstration; a cable represents moral demonstration, which is an assemblage of probabilities, separately insufficient for certainty, but, when put together, irrefragable. A man who said "I cannot trust a cable, I must have an iron bar," would, in *certain given cases*, be irrational and unreasonable:—so too is a man who says I must have a rigid demonstration, not moral demonstration, of religious truth.[51]

Newman commented on the opinion of Catholic theologians:

> Thus I thought as a Protestant; and I observe there are Catholic theologians of authority who go *further* in their estimate of the legitimate pace of probability in creating certitude than I went,—maintaining that the *greater* probability is a sufficient, or rather the intended and ordinary, ground of certainty with men in general; or that that Religion, which is evidently more credible than the rest, is that very religion which is revealed by God, and therefore most certainly true, or demonstrated, for there is a way, by which the highest certainty of religion may be arrived at by fundamental articles which are only *more* probable.
>
> For myself, I never, that I recollect, took this ground of "the more probable," but of a certitude which lay in an assemblage

---

49. JHN to Louisa Simeon, 25 June 1869, in *LD* 24:275–76.
50. Newman, *Apologia*, 21 and *Essay in Aid*, 58–59, 159–64, 237–40.
51. JHN to J. Walker of Scarborough, 6 July 1864, in *LD* 21:146.

and accumulation of probabilities, which *rationally demanded* to be considered sufficient for certitude.[52]

Writing again to the same inquirer several months later, Newman elaborated:

> As to the question of "certainty," I conceive that the certainty, (human) arising from the cumulus of probabilities, is rewarded by the certainty of faith, which is firmer and more satisfying. The aggregate of probabilities does not create the faith, or its certainty, which is a gift direct from God—but they create the same sort of certainty, which an infidel may have that our Lord suffered under Pontius Pilate. If then Manning meant (as I do not suppose) that the probabilities did not create legitimately a human certainty, he differed from me—but if he meant that the human certainty was swallowed up by the faith from God's grace, which is its reward, (and I think he meant this) I agree with him. However, in my book I have nothing to do with supernatural faith—but with the human process. Children may have divine faith without any logical process whatever—but Butler is speaking of the logical value of probabilities, and so was I. Butler *tends* to reduce the certainty to a *practical certainty*, viz that it is *safer to act*, as if the conclusion were true; I maintain that probabilities lead to a speculative certainty legitimately; so that it is quite *rational* to come to that conviction, that human faith, which is rewarded by divine faith. In thus speaking, of course I do not mean to say, that, in matter of fact, that human conclusion is reached, or the reward of divine certainty given, *without* the influence of *actual* grace, both being present and being obeyed. And so, in the manner, human charitableness, honesty, fortitude, patience, in the case of heathen, may be assisted by actual grace, and bring the soul forward towards conversion, and have a congruous merit—but still they do not cease to be acts of human nature.[53]

Twenty years later as a Cardinal, he wrote to Mr. Lilly:

> As to the question of probability I think you have said somewhere that you follow Butler in considering probability to be the guide of life. This has a good sense and a bad. I think Anglicans, even Keble(?) mean by probability a mere *practical* probability i.e. what is safe to act upon, whether true or not; whereas Catholics hold

---

52. Ibid.
53. JHN to J. Walker of Scarborough, 24 October 1864, in *LD* 21:270–71.

that it is a real speculative assent (or certitude) to a truth, to which I add "speculative, true, but arising, not from demonstration, but from the result of a combination and joint force, equivalent to demonstration, of many separate probabilities."[54]

Both of these letters, the one to J. Walker in 1864 and the one to Mr. Lilly in 1884, represent Newman's mature position on probability and faith. Yet it was his correspondence, spanning many years, with three individuals—J. M. Capes, Edward Thompson, and William Froude—that prodded Newman to refine and clarify his own thought. From his letters it can be seen that it was their questions and challenges that brought his ideas to maturity.

On January 27, 1850, Newman wrote to J. M. Capes who had published three articles in the *Rambler* under the title "Four Years' Experience of the Catholic Religion" defending his conversion as an act of "embracing the more probable of two momentous alternatives."[55] Newman advised Capes that his position would be sound only if it were certain "that the *more probable* alternative is the *true* one." But this would have to be proved since it is not always or necessarily the case. In fact, Capes seemed to take the "unsound position" that "it is *not certain* that Catholicism is true, but only *more* probable than that it is not."[56] Credibility is not probability but neither is it the evident certainty of syllogistic reasoning. "The simple question," as he wrote later, "is whether enough has been done to *reduce* the difficulties so far as to hinder them absolutely blocking up the way, or excluding these direct and large arguments on which the reasonableness of faith is built."[57]

Discussing the same issue the following year with Francis Wegg-Prosser, Newman maintained that insofar as there are objections to the contrary, one's judgment of credibility must be only a judgment about the degree or probability. Newman replied that "Unanswerable objections need not interfere with a moral proof." By a moral proof he did not mean "a mere balance of probabilities" where the side with "greater weight" is considered true. "On the contrary," he wrote, "a proof is something such that it can only be on one side." There may be many unanswered questions, but they "do not form a proof of some . . . incompatible conclusion."[58] In other words, a person may grasp by an informal use of reason what is true, but may be unable to answer difficulties, yet will be sure they cannot prove the contrary.

54. JHN to Mr. Lilly, 15 October 1884, in *LD* 30:415.
55. Capes, "Four Years," 4; July 1849, 164.
56. JHN to J. M. Capes, 27 January 1850, in *LD* 13:398.
57. JHN to J. M. Capes, 20 November 1850, in *LD* 14:134.
58. JHN to Francis Wegg-Prosser, 7 September 1851, in *LD* 14:348.

In October, Newman admitted to Edward Thompson, that "left to myself, I should be very much tempted" to adopt Butler's view and understand credibility as probability upon which it is safe to act."[59] But Newman again was not left to himself. He read works on faith and reason written by traditional authors; he read letters written by friends struggling toward an act of faith. Together they led him to admit that a safe probability is not enough. He wrote to Thompson, stating that it is not enough to say "to believe is the safe side, or *rather*, to act as if you believed is the safer side."[60] It was not enough to understand "moral certainty" as "the highest step of mounting probabilities, not differing from probability in kind, but only in degree."[61] Newman then stated that it was part of our everyday experience "that we are positively and absolutely and speculatively (not practically only) certain of a thing by a combination of arguments, each of which is only probable."[62]

What occurs in ordinary matters also occurs in religious matters. Someone might have begun with a "practical certainty, or certainty that it is a duty to do this or that" but "if this were all, there was not faith." If one is to have divine faith then "true *motiva* credibilitatis, (motives of credibility) leading *prudentia* (prudence) under the guidance of *pia affectio* (good will) to induce the will to command the intellect to assent, would gradually be evolved."[63] Thompson, not satisfied with this explanation, objected that the will often commands us "to *act* on probabilities, to act, in fact, *as if* we believed, but I do not see that it ever commands *belief* itself, where the grounds are such as produce *opinion*, a probable opinion, but still opinion."[64] He allowed that "faith corresponds to certainty," but he would not allow us to take "probabilities as certainties" by an act of will. The will could be called upon to put down fear and doubt, but only after the intellect has determined that the doubt is, in fact, unreasonable.[65]

Although it might appear that someone embraced faith without "certain intellectual evidence" Thompson suspected there existed "moral evidence ... impossible to put into words" yet "amply sufficient." Thompson was not denying that persons may be "*bound to act* on probabilities previous to certainty." "But," he added, "I believe if they did so, God would provide them with proof

---

59. JHN to Edward Thompson, 7 October 1853, in *LD* 15:456.
60. Ibid.
61. Ibid.
62. Ibid., 457.
63. JHN to Edward Thompson, 7 October 1853, in *LD* 15:460.
64. Edward Thompson to JHN, 8 October 1853, in *LD* 15:464.
65. Ibid.

sufficient to produce certainty."[66] Newman responded: "I shall be surprised if I have called, or implied, the conclusion to which human faith comes, as *probable*." Reason judges that a revelation is credible and this implies that the will, under the guidance of prudence, ought to direct the intellect to accept it as true without reservation. Moreover, "'Probable' means that which has certain grounds, *greater* or less, to be *opined;* whereas 'credible' means that which has *sufficient* grounds to be thoroughly *believed*."[67]

Newman then explained the process of faith in four points:

1. The object to be contemplated is this, the Christian doctrines, as revealed, or the revelatio (Revelation) and res revelata (matters that have been revealed);—these two are indivisible in this matter, being respectively the formal and the material objects of faith....

2. Next this object of faith, is it to be made to appear to us *true,* or to be proved in the strict sense of the word; or, on the other hand, is it to remain *obscure* and inevident?

3. If then the *Revelatio* and *Res Revelata*, that is, the Revealed Creed, is not to be made *evident* as true ... what *is* to be made evident? ... The use of arguments, the *motiva* (motives of credibility) is to prove evidently, not that the revelation and revealed doctrines, are true, but credible—*digna fide* (worthy of belief).... Which arguments are in consequence called "*motiva credibilitatis*," not "*veritatis*" (motives of credibility not of truth).

4. Lastly when the mind is convinced that the *Revelatio* and the *res revelata* are *digna fide, credibilia* (worthy of belief), the *prudentia* (prudent people) sees that the intellect must fittingly, naturally, conscientiously believe them, and the *pia motio voluntatis* (good disposition of the will) draws the same way. Accordingly the intellect *does* assent to that as *true*, which has been evidently proved to it to be credible. And... it sees that if it believes at all, it cannot believe by halves—for to believe in *God's word*, which by the hypothesis it is doing, is to believe in that which claims the *firmest* and most *absolute* assent, or certainty in its highest form.[68]

66. Ibid., 465.

67. JHN to Edward Thompson, 11 October 1853, in *LD* 15:465. Above "*sufficient* grounds" Newman wrote "*motiva.*"

68. Ibid., 466–67. Newman spent the next two months expanding this summary into a long paper entitled "On the Certainty of Faith" which is now published in *Theological Papers*, 3–38.

Spiritual Direction and Faith

On September 29, 1858, J. M. Capes again brought forward the objection which Thompson had raised five years earlier. "To act upon an uncertainty . . . involves nothing absurd or morally false" but to force certainty is "logically absurd and morally wrong." If it can be demonstrated that Christian revelation is more probably true than false, then "it is wise to act on the hypothesis of its certain truth; but to profess that *one is certain that it is true*, is to utter a direct falsehood and nothing less."[69] Newman's reply reaffirmed his 1853 position, but instead of outlining his solution as he had done for Thompson, he shifted his approach and appealed to parallel cases in everyday life where "no complete proof is possible":[70]

> It is a property of the human mind, to be certain, speculativè, not *merely* practicè, in certain cases in which no complete proof is possible, but only proof that the point in question "demands our belief," or is *credible*.
>
> I have no demonstration that I shall die—but I am as speculativècertus of it, as if I *had* demonstration. For the evidence is such and so much, as to make it clear to me that I should be a fool not absolutely and implicitly to believe it.
>
> It has a claim on my speculative belief that England is an island, even though I have no demonstration of it. Reason goes just so far, not as to prove it, but to tell me it is but common sense in one to order my mind to believe, or to direct my mind to believe it. I do not merely say to myself, "It is safe to act as if I believed it."
>
> I am speculativè certain that intemperate habits lead to loss of health; and that, in consequence, not of my having direct proof of it, but in consequence of my having just enough evidence to show me that I *ought* to believe it. Say, a temptation to drink comes and obscures this clear conviction, and in consequence I do not believe it. Here, it is not, as you seem to say, that, when I believe it, my will "forces" my mind to believe, reason disapproving, but that, when I do not believe, my will, reason disapproving, keeps my mind *from* belief.
>
> I cannot see that induction is ever a demonstration—but it makes the conclusion "credible"—viz "claiming belief."
>
> I cannot understand the state of mind which can love our Lord really with the feeling upon it, "After all, perhaps there is no such person." It is loving a mere vision or picture, and is so

---

69. JHN to J. M. Capes, 1 October 1858, in *LD* 18:471n1.

70. Ibid. Newman's intention in the second part of his *Essay in Aid of a Grammar of Assent* was to show that one can believe what one cannot absolutely prove.

> unreal as to be degrading. I cannot fancy (you will say perhaps from an idiosyncrasy) this existence of devotion without certainty. I could not throw myself upon any one here below, of whom I had the suspicion, "perhaps he is not trustworthy." On the other hand, I daily control and direct my mind into a firm belief, or speculative certainty, of truths which I cannot prove, on the ground that I should be a fool not to believe them, or, that reason bids my will to bid my mind to believe.[71]

The third correspondent whose questions helped Newman refine his thought was William Froude, the younger brother of Richard Hurrell Froude, Newman's closest friend in the Tractarian Movement, who died prematurely in 1836. William, who entered Oriel College in 1828 and began a lifelong friendship with Newman, eventually gained professional recognition in hydrodynamic research with the Royal Navy. His wife and four of their children became Catholics, largely through Newman's influence, but William remained agnostic. From 1844 until Froude's death in 1879, they corresponded regularly. Froude gave Newman firsthand information about trends in nineteenth-century science, while at the same time confronting him with the relativist outlook accepted by many scientists of the day.

Froude maintained that anyone who sought intellectual integrity must withhold certain assent in religious matters since they must be qualified as tentative and revisable in the same way that scientific statements must be qualified as open to change. Froude came to visit Newman on December 11, 1860, and after their conversation, Newman wrote a memorandum outlining points on which they differed.

> He [Froude] maintained that every additional piece of evidence made a man *more certain*, i.e. (absolute certainty being impossible) more disposed towards certainty: e.g., a man was more certain, if there were 12 witnesses to the point than if there were 11—more certain if there were no objections on the other side than if there were such.
>
> On the contrary, I maintained, that, the laws of the human mind being assumed as facts and authorities, according to which we must conduct our thinking, if we would think at all, that in *fact* a man was *not* more certain, if he had 12 witnesses than if he had 11—he might, under circumstances, rejoice in the 12th as a confirmation, as it is called—as if he proved a mathematical problem by a second process, or gained the world's praise for an action, which already was to himself a duty from the approbation of his conscience, but he was not more certain;

71. Ibid., 471–72.

that it was the nature of the human mind to fall into, or to take up, that state and habit called certainty, after certain preliminary evidence—so that probabilities in an object conspired to certainty in the subject or mind contemplating them.[72]

Several months earlier, in response to a question concerning the possibility of sophistry in the proofs of truth in general versus religious truth, Newman had replied:

1. That I not only do not mean that there is any thing sophisticated in the principles on which non-religious truth is pursued at present, but that theologians all affirm that Christianity is proved by the same rigorous scientific processes by which it is proved that we have an Indian Empire or that the earth goes round the sun. I mean, the proof is in the same line or order, for of course it is difficult to say whether we have more right or less or neither more or less, to be certain that the earth goes round the sun, than that India belongs to England.

2. But the scientific proof of Christianity, is not the popular, practical, personal evidence on which a given individual believes in it. And here I think it is where your question really comes in. I should differ from you, if I understood you, in thinking that there is a popular and personal way of arriving at certainty in Christianity as logical as that which is arrived at by scientific methods in subjects non-religious.

    Nay I go further—I think there is a sophism in considering the certainty of secular science so far superior to the certainty or persuasion, as you would call it, of the personal evidence for Christianity. I suspect, that, when all scientific proof, even for the existence of India, is examined microscopically, there will be found hiatuses in the logical sequence, so considerable, as to lead to the question, "Are there no broad first principles of knowledge which will protect us from scepticism as to all reasoning on things external to us, both scientific and popular?"[73]

---

72. JHN, Memorandum of Conversation with William Froude, 14 December 1860, in *LD* 19:440.

73. JHN to William Froude, 18 January 1860, in *LD* 19:284–85. See the extensive correspondence in chronological order between Newman and Froude:
JHN to William Froude, 28 December 1850, in *LD* 14:178;
JHN to William Froude, 10 April 1854, in *LD* 16:104;
JHN to William Froude, 1854, in *LD* 16:108;

Newman felt that his discussion of antecedent dispositions was his most promising contribution to a realistic theory of faith. For example, he felt that the most "original" feature of his University Sermons was their insistence "that antecedent probability is the great instrument of conviction in religious (nay in all) matters."[74] Accordingly, Newman believed "a good and bad man will think very different things probable."[75] Realizing that temperament and inclination affect our judgments in many matters, he felt that people are often ready to believe what they wish were true. They are slow to admit the failure of their own projects, or accept disappointing news, while they "readily believe reports unfavourable to persons they dislike, or confirmations of theories of their own."[76] Some antecedent dispositions are inevitable, but they are not always reasonable. They are "inducements to belief which prevail with all of us, by a law of our nature . . . whether they are in the particular case reasonable or not."[77] They cannot be eliminated but sometimes they must be corrected.

JHN to William Froude, 29 December 1859, in *LD* 19:270;
JHN to William Froude, 2 January 1860, in *LD* 19:172;
William Froude to JHN, 15 January 1860, in *LD* 19:283–84;
JHN to William Froude, 18 January 1860, in *LD* 19:284–85;
William Froude to JHN, 25 January 1860, in *LD* 19:296–98;
JHN to William Froude, 26 January 1860, in *LD* 19:298–99;
JHN, Memorandum of Conversation with William Froude, 14 December 1860, in *LD* 19:440–42;
JHN to William Froude, 9 April 1863, in *LD* 20:430;
JHN to William Froude, 30 September 1864, in *LD* 21:245;
William Froude to JHN, 29 April 1879, in *LD* 29:109–12;
JHN to William Froude, 29 April 1879, in *LD* 29:112–20;
Also for a thorough and detailed explanation of Froude's position and Newman's response, see Fey, *Faith*, 127–35. For other correspondence with persons having questions concerning science in relation to faith, see:
JHN to John Mozley, 19 April 1874, in *LD* 27:54–56;
JHN to John Mozley, 3 December 1875, in *LD* 27:385–89;
JHN to John Mozley, 10 November 1877, in *LD* 28:265–68;
JHN to Henry Bellairs, 21 March 1882, in *LD* 30:69–70;
JHN to W. S. Lilly, 7 December 1882, in *LD* 30:159–60;

74. JHN to W. G. Penny, 13 December 1846, in *LD* 11:293. See also JHN to J. D. Dalgairns, 8 February 1847, in *LD* 12:32, describing the University Sermons as "the best things I have written"; and JHN to Edward Thompson, 12 June 1853, in *LD* 15:381. Newman put the University Sermons on a par with his *Essay on the Development of Christian Doctrine*, his *Idea of a University*, and his *Essay in Aid of a Grammar of Assent* as his best achievements.

75. Newman, *Fifteen Sermons*, 190–91 (January 6, 1839).

76. Ibid., 189.

77. Ibid.

Faith and Doubt

From Newman's letters, it can be seen that when anyone approached him with doubts, he was extremely sensitive and empathetic. It was in such a pastoral milieu that his spiritual direction developed. He did not favor sheltering faith from the world or avoiding confrontation with people or positions that challenged one's faith. As he wrote to Mrs. Ward in 1859: "Faith ought to be tried and tested, if it be faith. I don't like that faith, which, (as I have seen written to a new convert) is a 'precious tender plant,' to be sedulously guarded under a glass cover, or in a hot-house—an exotic—if so, our religion is a mere 'alien religion,' and 'Oriental faith and worship'—but it is a tough principle within us, bearing heavy weights and hard work, or it is worth very little."[78]

Newman directed people from every walk of life who had doubts of faith. In 1883, at the end of October, Arthur Hutton, an Oratorian, announced to his fellow community members that he had lost belief in the existence of a personal God. After speaking to Newman personally, Hutton wrote a letter to Ignatius Ryder who shared it with Newman: "Even if you were willing to receive me back, I could not honestly return to my work as a priest. I can only say that I believe I am acting rightly in coming to this decision; and I will add that if at any future time I can see my way to make a sincere act of faith in Catholicism, wherever I am I will seek to be reconciled to the Church, and will accept any penance that may be laid upon me."[79]

After reading this letter, Newman responded to Hutton with great sensitivity.

> Francis has shown me the last page of your letter to him. I will not allow that you are, as you say, "irrevocably cut off" from your friends (all that is dear to you),—and since your letter to me came, I have wished to say so. I treasure the words in that letter in which you almost anticipate (may I not use the term?) that the time will come, when you will "make a sincere act of faith in Catholicism." That will be a joyful day, and I assure you of our united prayers that God will hasten its coming. You believe more than you think you do, and God loves you better than, in your dishonouring thought of Him, you allow yourself to fancy. He will overcome you in spite of yourself.[80]

---

78. JHN to Mrs. F. R. Ward, 8 May 1859, in *LD* 19:128.

79. Arthur Hutton to Ignatius Ryder, 15 November 1883, in *LD* 30:274n2. See also JHN to Henry Ryder, 4 November 1883, in *LD* 30:271–72.

80. Ibid., 274–75.

Lady Chatterton also had doubts and difficulties with faith which she did not overcome for almost a decade. In advising her, Newman manifested his understanding of her struggle:

> It grieves me deeply that you should be suffering so much, knowing as I do how much you desire to do God's will, and knowing too how much it must distress you to differ from Mr. Dering and your niece, and how it must distress them to differ from you.
>
> These are trials, which God puts upon us; and we cannot at our will put them aside. You have been so kind as to state fully your difficulties, and to say that you do not wish for an answer. Nor could I, without writing a volume, go through them all. Nor do I think, any more than you do, that it would fulfill any good purpose to attempt an elaborate answer to them. To make you happy, as a Catholic, is the work of God alone; if you put yourself into His hands, and ask for His grace perseveringly, He will gradually remove all your doubts and perplexities; of this I am most confident.[81]

Later, when she thought that she was causing her doubts or that they were sinful, Newman reassured her:

> I am glad to think that, as you so kindly say, that I have been of service to you, when your spirits have been oppressed. It is a received religious truth that nothing can really harm us, if we make it our duty to try to please God. The doubts you are troubled with are not your fault, nor are you answerable for them, if you do not consent to them, but repel them. You should do what you can, and nothing will harm you. If you are careful to go to Mass, when your health or the weather allow you, if you go duly to Confession and Communion . . . then doubt is only temptation. I say this, because persons who are in low spirits sometimes from a sort of despondency or despair, neglect their religious duties.[82]

When Fräulein M. experienced doubts of faith, Newman directed her first to seek out a spiritual director; and second, to cherish a deep conviction that God loves her by trying to put herself into His hands and grow in trust.[83] Likewise, when William Froude began to write about his difficulties with faith, Newman not only corresponded with him at length but wrote

---

81. JHN to Lady Chatterton, Holy Thursday 1866, in *LD* 22:193–94.

82. JHN to Lady Chatterton, 29 January 1873, in *LD* 26:241–42. See also JHN to Lady Chatterton, 13 June 1873, in *LD* 26:325.

83. JHN to Fräulein M., 27 November 1883, in *LD* 30:276.

his wife about her husband's difficulties, so that she would understand the problem and hopefully help in her own way.[84]

The fact that Newman was a convert made other converts feel more comfortable in writing to him about their doubts; for example, after Isy Froude was received into the Church, she began to experience reservations. Newman responded in a calm and reassuring way: "Don't you wonder, though your feelings go up and down, and though the long suspense which has excited your mind, should be followed by a re-action. Your heart and soul are fixed on the Rock of Truth—which remains fixed, though the waters around it rise and fall."[85] Continuing his encouragement, he wrote again four days later:

> I am not at all surprised that you should be tried in the way you describe. If you were older, your trials would be of a different kind. The wise man says, "If thou wouldest serve the Lord, prepare thy soul for temptation." What you must do, is to beg our Lord to give you what you need. Recollect the man who cried out to Him "I do believe, Lord—help my unbelief." He will help you. I know—and He is teaching you and giving you experience about yourself.
>
> It is very difficult for anyone like myself at a distance from you to say anything which will quite meet your wishes. I will do my best for you in prayer; it is by prayer, my dear Child, and in no other way that you have been brought forward hitherto, and you and all of us must still pray for you.[86]

Newman also wrote another letter to Mrs. F. R. Ward, Isy Froude's sister, who was concerned about her. By helping her understand the difficulty, he hoped that she would be able to help her sister. He said: "Young people look forward for some great sensible effect to follow upon their reception, and are disappointed that they seem to themselves what they were before. And any excitement is sure to be followed with a re-action. Here the reaction is contemporaneous with the disappointment. Older people can by an act of reason, set themselves right—it is more difficult to a child and a girl. However, your and her mother's influence must do for her what she cannot do for herself."[87]

To another recent convert who was experiencing difficulties with the "newness" of Catholic ways, he advised:

---

84. See Newman's very lengthy letter to Mrs. William Froude, 1854 or 1855, in *LD* 16:105–9.
85. JHN to Isy Froude, 4 May 1859, in *LD* 19:120.
86. JHN to Isy Froude, 8 May 1859, in *LD* 19:122.
87. JHN to Mrs. F. R. Ward, 8 May 1859, in *LD* 19:126.

> I can quite understand your state of mind—and really I do feel much sympathy in your trial. It is what many have had before you, but I cannot conceal from myself that you are at a point in your religious history when you may gain great peace and comfort or implicate yourself in much mental embarrassment . . .
>
> The greatest trial a Convert has to sustain, and to women it is often greater than to men, is the strangeness at first sight of everything in the Catholic Church. Mass, devotions, conversation, all may be a perplexity to you, so I am not at all surprised at what you say about the Mass. You must be brave and determined, and resolutely beg of God's grace to carry you through your difficulties. Every nation, every body of people, has its own ways—Catholics have their own ways—we may not at first like them—and the question is where is religious *Truth*, where is *salvation?*—*not* is this habit, this fashion pleasant to me or not?[88]

Similarly, when Miss Emily Buchanan wrote to Newman telling him of her recent conversion, he counseled her to be realistic about future difficulties. In this case, his advice was given in advance in order to help a convert anticipate doubts and avoid difficulties. However, if they should come, he suggests ways to handle them constructively.

> I am very glad to receive from you the tidings of your conversion, and am thankful to God both for it and for the circumstances under which it occurred.
>
> God has been very gracious to you—and you may feel confident that He who has done so much for you will do still more. You must guard against your spiritual enemy, who will try to use you against yourself. After a time of excitement, perhaps of spiritual exultation, such as often is the attendant on conversion, there is often in turn a season of re-action, from the mere weariness of the mind, as we are apt to feel in the parallel case of bodily exertion. Then a despondency comes on, and then is our enemy's time to suggest difficulties or murmurings. And the shorter has been the process of conversion, the more severe is likely to be the reverse. If such happens to you, you must be brave, and call on God to help you, and go straight forward in spite of all difficulties, and cherish a sure trust that your Lord and Saviour will in His own time bring your trial to an end.[89]

---

88. JHN to Miss Ellen Fox, 25 February 1868, in *LD* 24:41.
89. JHN to Miss Emily Buchanan, 16 April 1875, in *LD* 27:278.

Spiritual Direction and Faith

Newman manifested great sympathy to people who seemed to have been received into the Church prematurely. To Helen Forbes, who wrote for advice about the second thoughts she was experiencing, he replied;

> I have read your very painful letter with great interest. No apology was necessary for your writing to me—at the same time I cannot argue on the subject, nor do you wish it, as I understand you . . .
>
> From what you tell me, I dare say it is as you consider—you were received prematurely. You ought to have been more fully prepared for the step before you took it. I have known some men, and more women, who have been in your case. We cannot escape much mental uneasiness and trial in the course of so great a change—and, if we do not patiently go through with it before reception, it comes upon us afterwards. This is my experience; if you had waited till your convictions were fully formed, I believe you would have been spared this great suffering since your change of religion.[90]

However, to Edward Walford, a convert who seemed to have simply grown weary of his faith and who wanted to abandon it without sufficiently serious reflection or adequate reasons, Newman was much sterner:

> I plainly gather from the tone of your letter that you have virtually made up your mind on the subject of it already.
>
> Besides this, you say that "Every year the peculiar doctrines of the Catholic Creed have sat lighter and lighter upon you." That is, I should not have to answer your questions, but to change habitual courses of thought and frames of mind.
>
> And further still, I must ask your permission to say that your letter is not written with that seriousness which so momentous a question demands. When a man in your position has advanced so far as not to feel that a change of religion is a solemn act, in the highest degree pleasing or displeasing to his Maker and Judge, he has practically decided one way.[91]

Faith and Doctrine

For Newman faith and doctrine were intimately connected. To believe meant to have faith in something—a creed, and in someone—an authority,

90. JHN to Helen Forbes, 4 October 1864, in *LD* 21:248–49.

91. JHN to Edward Walford, 10 May 1860, in *LD* 19:336. See also another letter to Walford three days later, May 13, 1860, in *LD* 19:336–37.

who will not mislead you. But what is unique about this aspect of his faith life, was the way in which he employed it. Newman emphasized the importance of having a creed and an authority as a method to help others to come to faith. To Mrs. Froude in 1848 he wrote: "Though you can believe what you choose, you must believe what you ought. Now, assuming *duty* proved, still you cannot believe without 1. a *creed.* 2. an *authority* which will not mislead you. At least put these first *before you*, even if (as you imply) you do not think in your position you need *prove* them. E.g., the Catholic makes his act of faith 1. in the *Creed*, and the so called Creed of Pope Pius, and the other dogmatic teaching of the Roman Church—2. in the *authority* of the Roman Church. This at least is intelligible."[92]

Especially when writing to Anglicans, Newman would appeal to the importance of authority and doctrine for the person who believed, pointing out the great difference in the way Catholics and Anglicans understood these things. In a lengthy letter to E. J. Phipps, Newman pointed out major differences in belief between Catholics and Anglicans:

> Consider the vast difference between believing in a living authority, unerring because divine, in matters of doctrine, and believing none;—between believing what an external authority defines, and believing what we ourselves happen to define as contained in Scripture and the Fathers, where no two individuals define quite the same set of doctrines; between believing a creed, which, as far as such definitions go, is ever increasing, and believing the letter of Creeds which we may expand and explain for ourselves. In the one case, the living authority, deciding the controversies of faith, is the Church, in the other (whatever men pretend,) it is we ourselves who are the ultimate authority.[93]

As a former member of the Church of England, Newman was in a special position to advise Anglican correspondents who were considering becoming Roman Catholics; he understood their beliefs. By emphasizing the weakness of not having a definite creed or an established authority, by pointing out the dangers of private judgment in matters of faith, he hoped to show that these lacunae led to confusion and uncertainty; then, he tried to emphasize the benefits of believing in a definite creed and authority. For example, he pointed out the benefits of Catholicism to Catherine Ward: "All the *details* of a Church, how to get pardon, how to get grace, what to worship, what to believe,—confession, absolution, the Real Presence, the Creed, the list of duties,

---

92. JHN to Mrs. William Froude, 3 July 1848, in *LD* 12:233.

93. JHN to E. J. Phipps, 3 July 1848, in *LD* 12:234–35. See also JHN to T. W. Allies, 6 September 1848, in *LD* 12:260; JHN to Robert Jenkins, 5 January 1881, in *LD* 29:330.

Spiritual Direction and Faith

the distinction of sins, all are set down with an exactness such as is implied by a gift from heaven, not a vague generality, not an idea, but by a working religion. Its visible unity answers to the scriptural prophecy of a *kingdom*."[94]

Newman wrote again one month later. Intellectually convinced that she ought to convert, but still fearful, she had asked: "How am I to know that my present convictions are truth?"[95] In response, Newman appealed to his similar experience, and that of many other converts. "Having experienced for many months, nay I would say for a year or two before I became a Catholic, while my convictions were growing, that very distressing feeling which you describe, 'How do I know, confident as I may be, that it may not be a false confidence, that I am not in a dream, and the act of conversion will break it? I am sure, but how can I be sure that I ought to be sure?'—I can both sympathise with you, and perhaps have some right to advise you."[96]

Because she had been brought to her conviction through the "notes" of the Church, Newman continued:

> Take then this test, as you surely may, that the notes of the Church are not like other professed tokens of Revelation, deceptive, but the very properties and indications of Divine truth, viz that that Creed, to which they lead, *keeps fast hold* of those who trust them. It is not that you only were carried to and then from Calvinism or Dissent; but how few there are who find in the long run any Communion, but the Catholic, what they fancied it would be, when they joined it! Converts to Evangelicalism or to Millenarianism, tire of it as easily as they take up with it. They go further or they fall back—and how they change. I am not denying exceptions, but such is the rule. Your own experience is but the experience of a multitude.
>
> Look on the other hand to Catholics. It is notorious generally, however you account for it, that the Catholic Church takes hold of the mind with a grasp which no sect can rival or imitate. And as to converts, may we not fairly offer you our testimony, that you will find with us that rest which you can find no where else? There are now, as at all times, a thousand disorders within and without the Church—her head is in exile[97]—her subject countries in political strife—her members full of imperfection—but there is *that* in her which is what she peculiarly

---

94. JHN to Catherine Ward, 18 November 1848, in *LD* 12:336.
95. Catherine Ward to JHN, 19 December 1848, in *LD* 12:377n1.
96. JHN to Catherine Ward, 19 December 1848, in *LD* 12:377.

97. During the revolution of 1848 and the establishment of the Roman Republic, Pope Pius IX (1789–1878; Pope: 1846–1878) went into exile from November 24, 1848 to April 12, 1850, in Gaeta in the Kingdom of the Two Sicilies.

> promises, which no other body promises, and in which she does not deceive; she *can* present a creed, she alone can do what a Messenger from heaven ought to do; and her children feel this and are satisfied. If you join the Catholic Church for fine services, for splendid temples, for outward show or appearance of any kind, if it were in you an indulgence of sentiment or imagination, you might in this event be disappointed;—you cannot be disappointed in seeking in it these great attributes, which our reason tells us belong to the oracle of heaven and the Vicar of Christ. *We* give you this our testimony; not the testimony of one or two persons, but of many; of persons of education, of active and inquiring minds, who would, if any, have temptations to become sceptical or discontented, but who have had in fact not any temptation to doubt ever since they were Catholics. Such is the power, intellectual and spiritual, such is the *grace* lodged in the Catholic Church. I suppose (I speak it humbly) we should be ready to die for our certainty that it is true and the oracle of faith. Who would die for the truth of any other body?[98]

So, when George Forbes wrote to Newman expressing his sympathy at being "locked in" to a doctrinal system, it gave Newman an opportunity to explain: "Also it is one of the special comforts for which I thank God that since I have been a Catholic I have a peace and satisfaction as regards the authoritative doctrinal system under which I now live; and you call it my cross!"[99]

Finally, in response to a question from Isy Froude, Newman maintained that the act of faith is of the nature of an act of obedience.

> Speaking under necessary corrections which must be ever made, when we lay down an abstract proposition in a concrete and practical matter, I would make the following statement:
>
> "No one will be punished hereafter merely for holding or not holding a given proposition." A man must do, or have done, something more than this to incur punishment.
>
> This being said, I have two important explanations or provisos to add to it.
>
> 1. I have said "holding" not "believing." There may be no merit in holding or not holding, and yet merit in believing or not believing, and demerit too.
>
> "Our Lord died on the Cross for sinners"—this we are to *believe*—we cannot prove it—there would be no merit in holding it on the ground that we *could* prove it. But we are to believe it,

---

98. JHN to Catherine Ward, 19 December 1848, in *LD* 12:377–78.
99. JHN to George Forbes, 11 August 1871, in *LD* 25:378.

because it is told us on *trustworthy authority*; and according as we believe it or not, we have merit or demerit. This responsibility arises out of the duty of believing the *Authority* which reveals it to us. Thus the act of faith is of the nature of an act of obedience, and faith, though considered as the acceptance of a proposition, it is an act of the intellect, yet indirectly it is a moral act, and is rewarded or punished as such.

If you go on to ask *why* we are commanded to believe on authority, instead of holding on proof, it is enough to answer that such a duty is a trial of our trust and obedience to Him, who has a right to demand our trust and obedience. But I add, ex abundanti, [out of an abundance (of caution)] that such a belief, bringing in a new set of motives, has an important effect upon our moral state, or tends, to use the common phrase, to change the heart etc. etc.

Both reasons are exemplified in the Gospels. Our Lord asked the faith of those whom he healed, first, as appears in the narrative, as an act of submission and devotion to Himself, and secondly because we may suppose that in some cases that faith may have been the medium of the cure.[100]

Growing in Faith

Although many of Newman's letters dealt specifically with helping others come to faith, there are nevertheless a significant number that suggest ways of growing in one's faith. By encouraging and guiding individuals to become more sensitive to God's grace, by instilling a deeper realization that faith is both personal and communal, Newman sought to help people mature in faith.

Newman was deeply aware of difficulties present in Christian belief, yet he spoke of divine faith as "a clear certainty greater than any other certainty" but added that "this is wrought in the mind by the grace of God and by it alone."[101] For Newman, it was important that a person not only do those things which might keep him from receiving the gift of faith, but

---

100. JHN to Isy Froude, 9 April 1873, in *LD* 26:287. In a letter on November 20, 1879, encouraging Mrs. Christie to submit to this trustworthy authority, Newman emphasized the fact she should not do it blindly, but rather to make an act of the will. "I don't ask you to 'shut your eyes', but to do it with your eyes open. Here the 'Will' comes in." *LD* 29:200.

101. Newman, *Discourses*, 224. Teresa of Avila, in her *Interior Castle*, 252, wrote: "How, you will ask, can we become so convinced of what we have not seen? That I do not know; it is the work of God." John of the Cross, in his *Dark Night of the Soul*, 159, spoke of a "secret wisdom ... communicated and infused into the soul through love ... hidden from the work of the understanding."

it was also necessary to be sensitive to the ways that God's grace moved a person. To Mrs. William Froude he asked: "Are you quite sure that you respond, as you should, to God's grace leading you on?"[102]

Because faith is a free gift of God, it necessarily solicits a free response. So, for Newman, the basic stance of the Christian ought to be one of receptivity and patient waiting for God. To grow in faith it is necessary to become more and more open to a deeper realization of who has spoken in the depths of a person's heart. At the same time the ability to wait patiently is also important. Yet, it is not a passive kind of waiting, but active—one in which a person is doing those things that will prepare one's mind and heart to receive this gift when God chooses to grant it. In 1853 he wrote to Mrs. William Froude: "I am quite sure you wish to please God, and would do any thing He told you. On the other hand, I know well He does not tell us everything at once—but first one thing, and then, when we act upon that another.... Faith is a gift of God; we can gain it by prayer, we cannot gain it at once, but we can gain it at last."[103]

Over twenty years later, a recent convert, Miss Emily Buchanan, asked Newman's advice about growing in one's faith. After directing her to be prepared to experience a reaction common to many converts, he encouraged her to pray, to patiently trust in the Lord, and "to go straight forward in spite of all difficulties."[104]

For Newman, faith is essentially personal; it is to believe someone. So in order to grow in faith, a person needs to know, love, and surrender more completely to God who is revealing Himself. For Newman, there were three means to accomplish this: prayer, reading Scripture, and associating with other believing people.

Newman felt that after reasoning there must come invocation—a calling out to a real Being who acts in history and in individual human lives. For this reason, prayer assumes a role of great significance both in coming to faith and in growing in faith. Henry Goodwin had felt the need of certainty in religious belief and asked Newman for "the secret ... of combining real religious spirituality with perfect freedom to accept all knowledge."[105] Newman responded: "You ask me for a 'secret'. The secret is prayer."[106] Mrs. Wilson, a convert, was

---

102. JHN to Mrs. William Froude, 27 June 1848, in *LD* 12:227.

103. JHN to Mrs. William Froude, 23 February 1853, in *LD* 15:307–8. See also JHN to James Budin, 10 May 1886, in *LD* 31:137–38.

104. JHN to Miss Emily Buchanan, 16 April 1875, in *LD* 27:278.

105. JHN to William Goodwin, 13 August 1884, in *LD* 30:389n5.

106. Ibid., 390.

experiencing difficulties in faith and asked Newman's direction. His supportive response emphasized the Apostles' increase in faith.

> However, I would not say that you have not faith—but your faith is weak—and I speak of its being a gift of God to believe, to remind you, what it must be right to say, even tho' you do not need reminding, that you must pray for it. The Apostles said to our Lord "Increase our faith." They were not discouraged—they did not go back and fall away because their faith in Him was tried—they did (not) allow themselves to say, "Perhaps after all He is not the Christ—why should we attempt to believe Him"—but they said "Increase our faith." So be sure, my dear Madam, that He will increase yours. He loves you. He has done great things for you, and He will do more still.[107]

When Fräulein M. wrote to him about the doubts of faith she was having, Newman suggested that she seek spiritual direction and pray. "But he [Newman] feels, as far as his eyes will allow him to read her letter, that what she needs is a good Priest to direct her.

"She ought to do what he tells her to do . . .

"She ought to cherish a deep conviction that God loves her and desires her salvation. She must not despond, but put herself into God's Hands and say: 'o Lord guide me'. The more we trust Him the more He will do for us."[108]

A second means that Newman advocated for growing in awareness of God was by reading the Scriptures. After writing to Louisa Simeon about the importance of starting points for arriving at religious truth, he concluded: "I think you must ask the God of Conscience to enable you to do your duty in this matter. I think you should, with prayer to Him for help, meditate upon the Gospels, and on St. Paul's second Epistle to the Corinthians."[109]

---

107. JHN to Mrs. Wilson, 8 January 1870, in *LD* 25:6.

108. JHN to Fräulein M., 27 November 1883, in *LD* 30:176. For other letters treating prayer and faith see:
JHN to Mrs. William Froude, 27 June 1848, in *LD* 12:227–28;
JHN to Catherine Ward, 12 October 1848, in *LD* 12:289–90;
JHN to William Monsell, 9 December 1850, in *LD* 14:164;
JHN to Mrs. William Froude, 1854 or 1855, in *LD* 16:105–9;
JHN to William Brownlow, 29 April 1871, in *LD* 25:323–25;
JHN to George Boag, 25 February 1881, in *LD* 29:342–43;
JHN to Mrs. Christie, 20 December 1881, in *LD* 30:33–34.

109. JHN to Louisa Simeon, 25 June 1869, in *LD* 24:276. In two other letters, Newman wrote about the power of the Gospel and the power contained in them in reference to a defense against skepticism:
JHN to J. R. Bloxam, 20 February 1883, in *LD* 30:186;
JHN to Emily Bowles, 10 March 1883, in *LD* 30:194.

Newman understood that Christian faith is lived in a social context. A believing community is surrounded by an unbelieving one and therefore one of the means of growing in faith is to associate with a community of believers in order to find strength and support.[110] Within and by this believing community a message is announced and declared to have a divine origin and authority; there are signs and evidence given to defend that this is accepted not as the word of man, but of God. Newman felt that an individual was called to believe the "word" socially present in this believing community in an intensely personal way. To mature in the community one must believe those who teach the word; yet, if one believed just the apostle or teacher or society, he would not have divine faith. Only one who believed in God, bearing witness to Himself in this community has come to full Christian faith. Only then can one enter into the spirit of a particular community which is created by the personal faith of its members.

This was one of Newman's major concerns in the controversy over whether Catholics ought to be able to attend the Protestant-oriented universities. In principle he was opposed to the idea; he thought that it could be very detrimental to their faith. Because of the agnostic climate that prevailed at these universities, Newman believed it would be very difficult to find a community of believers to support and strengthen a person's faith and consequently attendance at these universities would be a serious danger to faith. His proposed solution was not a prohibition against attending these universities, but the establishment of an Oratory at Oxford, which might serve as a source of strength, support and protection for Catholic students. However, because the bishops of England wanted to begin their own Catholic college, they did not accept Newman's proposal.

Summary

It was not the purpose of Newman's correspondence to present a complete treatise on the nature of faith. Rather, he attempted to respond to particular questions of people in concrete situations in order to guide them to a correct understanding of faith and to help them in authentically living their faith. By putting together these pieces of advice, one can grasp Newman's essential views on faith. What emerges from his letters is first, the content—how Newman understood faith, and second, the method—how he went about directing others to come to believe.

---

110. JHN to Emily Bowles, 5 January 1882, in *LD* 30:48. In this letter Newman advised against associating with groups of people who would be a detriment to faith.

Newman portrayed faith as an absolute assent to what God has revealed because God has spoken. Through faith, a person's assent to what is revealed rests directly on the authoritative testimony of God. When faith is absent, the judgment that one ought to believe rests on natural evidence. Yet because God enables the believer to accept revealed truths on His word, the act of faith is absolutely certain beyond all other judgments. While denying that divine faith is the conclusion of an argument, Newman believed that a human process of reasoning that honestly considers evidence is a necessary condition if the act of faith is to be made in a way which conforms to the rational nature of the human person.

Newman also believed that the entire process leading to faith is guided by the grace of God. Through grace, God draws a person to share personally in His own knowing. The "illumination" of grace does not merely give a new dignity, but a new inner structure to the faith-knowledge of the believer. God is the formal object of this Divine faith-knowledge because the believer now knows revealed truths through a unique share in God's knowledge. Prior to faith, grace enables a person to appreciate the force of arguments that God exists and that revelation is credible. In faith, grace enables one to grasp God's revelation.

Newman acknowledged that his own thought on faith had developed over the years. His correspondence shows his thought gradually taking shape through a dialogue with both old friends and new critics. Sometimes there was a clarification of questions which previously had been confused; sometimes an awareness of new questions which had been overlooked. The view of faith that Newman worked out in his correspondence ultimately was given systematic form in his *Essay in Aid of a Grammar of Assent*, published in 1870.

In his correspondence, Newman did not define faith according to some *a priori* theory. Rather, he took faith as he found it—both in personal experience and as described in Scripture, expressed in creeds, and practiced in the Church from Apostolic times. In 1849, he told a Birmingham audience that faith has always consisted in submitting to God's word, not in judging for one's self.[111] Newman considered faith a "venture" that includes a variety of paradoxical properties. There are antecedent dispositions before evidence, a readiness to obey, to love, and to venture everything on God's word.[112]

---

111. Newman, "Faith and Private Judgement," in *Discourses*, 200–201, 195–96.

112. On February 10, 1848, Newman wrote to A. J. Hammer about the "venture" of faith: "You speak against making *ventures* in matters of faith—but did not Abraham, my dear Sir, make a venture, when he went out, not knowing whither he went?—he had not even the opportunity, which you have, of asking persons who had gone before him—And now, though circumstances may be different, yet so far is the same—that without faith nothing good will be done." *LD* 12:168.

For Newman, faith is not a conclusion that comes from argument, rather, faith comes by hearing; faith simply "accepts testimony. As testimony is distinct from experience, so is Faith from Reason."[113] In human faith however, we take someone's word "for what it is worth"; we more or less accept and act on it, yet we retain the right of questioning its validity at any time. In divine faith, however, the situation is quite different: "He who believes that God is true, and that this is His word, which He has committed to man, has no doubt at all . . . he is certain, because God is true, because God has spoken, not because he sees its truth or can prove its truth.[114]

Newman attacked a variety of inadequate solutions to the problem of faith and reason under the general term "liberalism."[115] For example, in 1845 Newman described an "anti-dogmatic principle" which seemed to emerge whenever men lost confidence in reason's ability to prove the mysteries of revelation. "That truth and falsehood in religion are but matter of opinion; that one doctrine is as good as another; . . . that there is no truth; that we are not acceptable to God by believing this than by believing that; . . . that we may take up and lay down opinions at pleasure; that belief belongs to the mere intellect, not to the heart also; that we may safely trust to ourselves in matters of Faith, and need no other guide,—this is the principle of philosophies and heresies, which is very weakness."[116] This attitude had become so pervasive among Newman's countrymen that he complained: "It is not at all easy (humanly speaking) to wind up an Englishman to a dogmatic level."[117]

Newman's correspondence reveals the unique parallel that exists between his personal direction of others and his own understanding of faith. From his *Fifteen Sermons Preached before the University of Oxford* (1826–1843), through his "Papers of 1853 on the Certainty of Faith,"[118] to his systematic position enunciated in *An Essay in Aid of a Grammar of Assent* in 1870, the topic of faith continued to mature in his mind. Accordingly, his spiritual direction during these years reflected both his own questions

---

113. Newman, "Faith and Reason Contrasted," in *Fifteen Sermons*, 180 (January 6, 1839).

114. Newman, "Faith and Private Judgement," in *Discourses*, 195.

115. Newman, *Apologia*, 218. "Liberalism," he wrote, "is the mistake of subjecting to human judgement those revealed doctrines which are in their nature beyond and independent of it; and claiming to determine on intrinsic grounds the truth and value of propositions which rest for their reception on the external authority of the Divine Word." See also 50–51, 200–201. In 1887, Newman was still writing about liberalism as the development of rationalism. See JHN to Richard Armstrong, 23 March 1887, in *LD* 31:198.

116. Newman, *Essay on the Development*, 357–58. See also *Essay in Aid*, 316.

117. Newman, *Apologia*, 185.

118. In *Theological Papers of John Henry Newman*.

and the progression of his thought. His understanding of faith gradually assumed a deeper doctrinal orientation which can similarly be detected in his spiritual direction. Not only did his spiritual direction reflect his own thought on faith, but often his direction of others seems to have provided the occasion for deepening his own faith.

Emerging from his correspondence are certain important qualities of Newman as a spiritual director. First, Newman had the gift of accepting people as they were and of working with them patiently over a period of many years; he realized that helping a person come to faith was a slow process often involving many complex human factors. Second, his letters show that he did not impose his views on others, but tried to understand their positions and their backgrounds before responding to their questions. In this respect, he was particularly adept at writing Anglicans, whose background and beliefs he understood. Third, his willingness to dialogue with others on issues of faith seems endless. Often his letters were long, involved and detailed yet written in such a way that they not only invited a response but even allowed a correspondent to feel comfortable in disagreeing with him. His persistence and perseverance in writing had the effect of making people feel that both they and their questions were important. In sum, Newman believed that faith "is a particular mode of thinking and acting,"[119] yet it is not merely speculative. It is entirely free and entirely reasonable. It is absolute, yet a believer may seek to uncover the grounds of his belief. It is reasonable, but not the conclusion of an argued proof. What he gradually worked out in his writing was an account of how these ingredients combine in faith.

---

119. Newman, "Faith and Private Judgement," in *Discourses*, 193.

5

Spiritual Direction and the Roman Catholic Church

" . . . it was like coming into port after a rough sea."[1]

ALTHOUGH NEWMAN NEVER WROTE a systematic ecclesiology, ideas about the Church permeate his thought and were the bulwark of much of his spiritual direction. For example, his conversion to Rome was accompanied by much soul-searching and anxiety, including long reflection on the nature of the Church. However, the absence of an articulated ecclesiology is not so surprising, if one recalls that the Church Fathers never wrote ecclesiologies; for the Fathers, the Church was fundamental to their thinking; it operated as a first principle and never became a direct object of study. Similarly, for Newman the Church is a given.

While the fundamental principles of his ecclesiology developed during his Anglican years, the full maturation of his thought on the Church came after his conversion.[2] Both in his correspondence, and in his celebrated *Apologia*, he described and justified his conversion from the Church of England

---

1. Newman, *Aplogia*, 184.
2. Reflecting forty-two years later on how his thinking had matured in the Catholic Church, Newman wrote to George Edwards on February 24, 1887: "I will not close our correspondence without testifying my simple love and adhesion to the Catholic Roman Church, not that I think you doubt this; and did I wish to give a reason for this full and absolute devotion, what should, what can, I say, but that those great and burning truths, which I learned when a boy from evangelical teaching, I have found impressed upon my heart with fresh and ever increasing force by the Holy Roman Church? That Church has added to the simple evangelism of my first teachers, but it has obscured, diluted, enfeebled, nothing of it—on the contrary, I have found a power, a resource, a comfort, a consolation in our Lord's divinity and atonement, in His Real Presence, in communion in His Divine and Human Person, which all good Catholics indeed have, but which Evangelical Christians have but faintly." *LD* 31:189.

to the Church of Rome. His conversion meant leaving family and friends; it meant foregoing a secure and respected position in the Church of England; it meant losing a podium of influence in the Nation; it meant the possibility of scandalizing Anglicans who had followed his religious leadership; it meant entering among people whose culture was strange and new to him. His conversion cost so much in human terms that his option had to be clear and his decision compelling.

From a theological perspective, Newman's conversion was an ecclesiological decision: Where was the Church of Christ? What should it look like? How can one be sure that this institution, rather than that, is the true Church? After his conversion, Newman had to respond to so many questions about the Church that his correspondence forms an intimate account of why he left Canterbury for Rome. His conversion placed him in a unique position to direct others in understanding both the nature of the Church and many facets of Church life.

Newman's Conversion and the Importance of Apostolicity

Newman was often asked by his correspondents why he became a Roman Catholic or what they should look for in considering that possibility. His letters indicate what were the most important considerations which led him to accept the Roman Catholic Church as true. First, his study of the Fathers was pivotal to his thinking, as a letter written a quarter-century after his conversion clearly emphasizes. When Mrs. Houldsworth asked Newman why he had left the Anglican Church, he answered:

> As to your question, suggested by your friends, it is not at all the case that I left the Anglican Church from despair—but for two reasons concurrent, as I have stated in my *Apologia*—first, which I felt *before* any strong act had been taken against the Tracts or me, namely, in 1839, that the Anglican Church *now* was in the position of the Arian Churches of the fourth century, and Monophysite Churches of the fifth, and this was such a shock to me that I at once made arrangements for giving up the editorship of *The British Critic*, and in no long time I contemplated giving up St. Mary's. This shock was the *cause* of my writing Number 90 which excited so much commotion. Number 90 which roused the Protestant world against me, most likely never would have been written except for this shock. Thus you see my condemnation of the Anglican Church arose not out of despair, but, when everything was hopeful, *out of my study of the Fathers*. Then, as to the second cause, it began in the autumn of 1841,

six months after Number 90, when the Bishops began to change against me. This brought home to me that *I had no business in the Anglican Church*. It was not that I despaired of the Anglican Church, but that their opposition confirmed the interpretation which I had put upon the Fathers, *that they who love the Fathers, could have no place in the Church of England*.³

The more that Newman read in the Church Fathers, the more he became convinced that the Patristic Church continued on in the Roman Church, not in the Anglican Church. Soon after his conversion, he wrote H. W. Banner:

> Pray be quite assured that I would not have left the English Church, had I thought it possible for me to remain in God's favor and remain a member of it. To my own mind it is as clear as light that it is a Church which the Fathers would not have acknowledged. I had no alternative but to leave it, unless I gave up the Fathers, nay all revealed religion. It would have been a gross hypocrisy in me, to profess to rule myself by the early Church, and yet to remain in a communion which resembled the Donatists, or Nestorians, or Monophysites, and not the ancient Catholic Church.⁴

In 1862 a correspondent sent Newman objections against Rome's apostolicity. After noting that he himself, as an Anglican, had raised much the same objections, Newman declined to enter into controversy:

> I cannot undertake that answer, both because I am at a distance from books, and because really I am too tired with controversy, to give myself to the consideration of objections, which the thought and experience of thirty years makes me feel vividly to be nothing more than objections, however plausible, not positive arguments the other way. I say to myself, if a mind can come to a solid immoveable conclusion, mine has done so—I have a clear anticipation that there is no possible argument which has a chance of interfering with my conviction that what is called the "Roman communion" is a continuation of that ecclesiastical body to which St. Cyprian belonged, and which the Apostles founded.⁵

The question of apostolicity also loomed large in the *Essay on Development*; as he wrote to his friend Henry Wilberforce:

---

3. JHN to Mrs. Houldsworth, 3 July 1871, in *LD* 25:352–53.
4. JHN to H. W. Banner, 18 November 1845, in *LD* 11:26–27.
5. JHN to Daniel Radford, 15 October 1862, in *LD* 20:304.

> As to my Essay, you mistake in one minor matter, it is not the argument from unity or Catholicity which immediately weighs with me (in it) but from Apostolicity. If that book is asked, why does its author join the Catholic Church? The answer is, because it is the church of St. Athanasius and St. Ambrose . . . And it is an argument *natural* to weigh with me, who have so many years been engaged in the meditation of early Church History—and it is as natural that the difficulties I had felt, and the difficulties I there answer should be difficulties of doctrine, since I have studied in Church History the history of doctrine more than any thing else.[6]

Once Newman saw Rome as the apostolic Church continuing on into the present, it became a matter of duty to join it: "For myself, I came into the Church to save my soul, which I considered I could not save by remaining in the Establishment."[7] This imperative overrode all considerations, even the pain of hurting and confusing those whom he influenced in the Anglican Church.

> I felt, the question was one of personal duty in the most solemn of matters—and that, if I saw that there was one Church to which the promises were made, and that I as yet was not in it, I must join it, and leave to the Providence of God to overrule all consequences, and must act on faith that He who called me could order things better than I could, with a higher wisdom and in unknown ways—and, sad as it has been to me to see that my anticipations have been fulfilled, I have never for an instant repented of the step which gave occasion to them.[8]

Although the question of the Pope's office was much discussed during the decades prior to the Vatican Council (1870), it was the apostolicity of the Church alone, not the papal function, which attracted Newman to Rome. "I was not converted by 'the claims of the Pope,' but by the claims of the Church—And the question seems to me to be, has the Catholic Church a claim upon us?"[9] Eight years before the Council, Newman wrote:

> How then do I know which is the true Church? I know it by the tokens of its unity, its apostolicity, its pretentions etc. etc. I admit that there are able men who have been led into the Church through belief in the Pope's prerogatives. But a man need not

---

6. JHN to Henry Wilberforce, 7 March 1849, in *LD* 13:78–79.
7. JHN to Edward Walford, 10 May 1860, in *LD* 19:336.
8. JHN to Lady Chatterton, 19 July 1863, in *LD* 20:495.
9. JHN to J. R. Bloxam, 18 January 1876, in *LD* 28:17.

> believe in the jus divinum of the see of St. Peter in order to submit himself to the Church which is in communion with it. This was my own case. I did not distinctly believe in the jus divinum of the Holy See till I joined the Church. I then believed in it as I believed in any other doctrine of the Church because she *was* the Church, the oracle of Christ.[10]

Fourteen years later in 1876, he stated:

> There are men, as I suppose T. W. Allies, who have been converted to the Catholic Church by their belief in the divine Mission of St. Peter and his successors; I on the contrary, . . . mainly received it on the word of the Universal Church, that is, on faith. I believed that our Lord had instituted a Teaching, Sacramental, organized Body called the Church, and that the Roman communion was as an historical fact its present representative and continuation—and therefore, since that communion received the Successor of St. Peter as the Vicar of Christ and the Visible Head of the Church such he was . . .[11]

After he had accepted the Roman Church as the Church of Christ, Newman could accept what was taught about the Church and about its Pontiff. To a frequent correspondent he wrote: "I think there *are* abundant reasons for holding the R. C. Church to be the true Church, quite distinct from any argument (which to some is so convincing) *through* the infallibility of Rome. A point which to some people is the *proof*, is to me a *doctrine* of the Church."[12] Thus, Newman's emphasis on apostolicity corroborated his conviction of the Church's divine origin; as he wrote to William Gladstone: "From the time I took that step, close to 30 years ago, I never have had a moment's misgiving in my conviction that the Catholic Roman Church comes from God, and that the Anglican is external to it, or again in my sense of duty which lay upon me to act on that conviction."[13]

In directing others, Newman insisted that prospective converts act neither precipitously nor haphazardly, but only after they had a clear conviction that the Roman Church alone is true. To Miss Alice Smith, he wrote in 1870, "I advise you by all means to become a Catholic on one condition—viz. if you can say deliberately and from your heart 'I believe the

---

10. JHN to Daniel Radford, 15 October 1862, in *LD* 20:307–8.
11. JHN to Henry Wilberforce, 4 July 1846, in *LD* 11:190–91.
12. JHN to F. R. Wegg-Prosser, 22 February 1852, in *LD* 15:42. In numerous letters about the "infallibility controversy," Newman reiterated that the initial question centers on the trueness of the Church, and only subsequently on the Papacy.
13. JHN to W. E. Gladstone, 26 February 1875, in *LD* 27:236.

Holy Catholic Roman Church to be the one and only Fold of Christ and Ark of Salvation, and I believe whatever she teaches, has taught, or shall teach, to be the Word of God committed by our Lord to his Apostles in the beginning."[14] Similarly, to a priest counseling an inquirer, he advised, "not that her motive is not sufficient, 'that Catholicism is the best religion,' but it ought to have been accompanied by the conviction that the best religion is the true religion."[15]

Newman's advice was also motivated by his knowledge that many converts would be confused by the cultural strangeness of Catholicism.

> The greatest trial a Convert has to sustain, and to women it is often greater than to men, is the strangeness at first sight of everything in the Catholic Church. Mass, devotions, conversation, all may be a perplexity to you, so I am not at all surprised at what you say about the Mass. You must be brave and determined, and resolutely beg of God's grace to carry you through your difficulties. Every nation, every body of people, has its own ways—Catholics have their own ways—we may not at first like them—and the question is where is religious *Truth*, where is *salvation?*—not is this habit, this fashion pleasant to me or not?[16]

Above all, Newman wanted converts to "count the cost," lest they be disappointed. In contrast to some of his contemporaries who accepted converts hastily, Newman wanted a slow enduring commitment that could adjust to changes and accept abuses, which, in his view of the Church, were inevitable. To the President of Oscott, he wrote:

> I dare say I have said to many Protestants that they would be disappointed in the Catholic body, if they knew it experimentally; and I have said so, in order that *anticipation*, to hinder them from being disappointed in fact. Protestants not unfrequently view us in an imaginative way, and are in consequence likely to suffer a reaction of mind.
>
> I have said that they ought to be prepared for disappointment. 1. because they considered that we were a powerful *organization*, whereas we acted and we conquered by *faith* . . . first rate direction is rare . . . theological schools are sparse.
>
> I certainly think it very dangerous for persons to pass out of educated Protestantism, without "counting the cost." I always

---

14. JHN to Miss Alice Smith, 3 November 1870, in *LD* 25:225.
15. JHN to William Brownlow, 23 April 1871, in *LD* 25:231.
16. JHN to Miss Ellen Fox, 25 February 1868, in *LD* 24:41.

have thus felt and acted, and I cannot change . . . I have a dread of haste.[17]

A slow process of decision-making alleviated two difficulties: first, acting in a state of enthusiasm usually led to future problems; second, a measured approach lessened the likelihood of "a mere outward conformity to the Church or rebellion of the reason after joining it."[18] Yet, in Newman's opinion, a convert need not solve every single difficulty before converting. Human decisions are not that neat and tidy. Accordingly, he counseled F. R. Wegg-Prosser in 1851:

> I do not deny, far from it, that there are objections to a doctrine *so great* as to be sufficient to overturn the authority of the person who propounds them. Did the (Roman) Catholic Church say that impurity was a virtue, there would be no way of solving the opposition which our moral sense would make to it—there would be arguments so decisive against so monstrous a position, as to suffice simply to overturn the Church's authority—all proofs for that authority notwithstanding—and so doubtless there might be historical arguments against our Lord's Divinity or Papal Infallibility such as to destroy the credit of the oracle which asserted either. On the other hand there might be arguments against the doctrines of the church, unanswerable, yet insufficient to overturn the authority propounding them, which had a just claim to be believed in its propounding, in spite of those arguments; and this, whether against its moral precepts, or its theology, or the economy of grace.[19]

The mind leads a person to a broad and sound base on which to accept the Church as true. Apostolicity was the base for Newman. The will, however, embraces the Church, not under a single aspect, but as a *totum*, with all its doctrine, with its virtues, with its abuses. Accordingly, when asked whether it is not sort of "intellectual tyranny," for a Catholic to be cautioned not to raise doubts about the Church, Newman answered: "A Catholic is kept from scepticism, not by any external prohibition, but by admiration, trust, and love. While he admires, trusts, and loves our Lord and His Church, those feelings prohibit him from doubt; they guard and protect his faith; the real prohibition is from within."[20] The support to continue steadfast in one's faith is not from the vividness or strength of one's personal experience of Christ. Newman

17. JHN to Spencer Northcote, 18 June 1862, in *LD* 20:209–10.
18. JHN to A. J. Hammer, 10 February 1849, in *LD* 12:168.
19. JHN to F. R. Wegg-Prosser, 24 September 1851, in *LD* 14:367.
20. JHN to William Froude, 7 April 1863, in *LD* 20:430.

stressed that the support of faith is one's trust and love of the Church. While many would be tempted to say that they are supported by their love *of Christ*, the object of this support is internal. Newman perceived that the object of support needed to be *outside*, without denying that the experience of Christ is important, yet *within*. Newman simply asked why did those who placed such stress on a personal experience of Christ no longer believe?

> I should myself consider that this personal hold upon Him is the immediate evidence of divine truth to every consistent Christian; who has no need of having his answer in hand to every one of the multiform, many headed objections which from day to day he may hear urged against his faith.

But I consider too, that the Lover of souls and Searcher of hearts has not thought it enough for us, has not felt it safe for our poor nature, to have no other safeguard for our faith than this. Religious experiences and convictions, when right, come from God; but Satan can counterfeit them; and those may feel assurances who have no claim to them. And in matter of fact, men who have professed the most beautiful things, and with the utmost earnestness and sincerity believed in their union with our Lord, have often slipped away into some form of error on the ground of new experiences and assurances, nay into scepticism and infidelity. Looking over the letters of early friends, who are now unbelievers, I have before now come upon the expression of their faith and hope in Christ so simple and fervent, and of their experimental certitude so vivid, as to fill one with awe and tearful pity at the vision of such a change.

> Here it is that I see the wisdom and mercy of God in setting up a Catholic Church for the protection of His elect children.[21]

In Newman's view, in accepting Catholicism, one is first and primarily accepting the Church *as such*. On that basis, one accepts the doctrines of the Church. Furthermore, although one accepts the Church's practical system in *globo*, one must find one's own genuine expression. For example, English devotion should not be Italian; thus in Newman's judgment, Italian devotion should not be imported into England.

Directing Others to Recognize the Church

Much of Newman's spiritual direction was intended to help people recognize the Catholic Church as the one, true Church established by Christ. By

21. JHN to Unknown Correspondent, 19 August 1874, in *LD* 27:109–10.

patiently answering questions, by responding to difficulties and especially by sharing his own beliefs concerning the nature of the Church, he was able to direct prospective converts while leading others to a deeper understanding and a richer participation in the life of the Church. In directing others towards the Church, Newman made frequent use of the "notes of the Church" not as a systematic theological treatment, but as a practical pastoral approach.

Notes of the Church

The first characteristic of a Note is that it is easily perceptible. It recommends itself, directly and immediately; it is not subtle but based on common sense evidence. In his correspondence with Catherine Ward, Newman pointed out that discovering the Church is not reserved to the wise and learned, but open to the simple.

> As to the question of *inquiring* about religion, *surely* religion is not like the "philosophy of Plato and Aristotle," for the learned only. What a condemnation of any man's religious system, for him to *allow* that it is like a heathen science. To the poor is the Gospel preached. Accordingly the notes of the Church are simple and easy, and obvious to all capacities. Let a poor man look at the Church of Rome, and he will see that it has *that* which no other Church has. He has nothing to do with books or controversy. The *world calls* it "the Catholic Church"; the world allows that all the sects have separated from it, though it may justify them; the world calls the Anglican communion *Protestant*. And so on with the grand outlines. All the details of a Church, how to get pardon, how to get grace, what to worship, what to believe—confession, absolution, the Real Presence, the Creed, the list of duties, the distinction of sins, all are set down with an exactness such as is implied by a gift from heaven, not a vague generality, not an idea, but a working religion. Its visible unity answers to the scriptural prophecy of a kingdom. And so on with other notes. *Keep* them from books, *keep* him from his letters, and he will join it. But when you go to private teachers, and they bring down St. Basil, and St. Cyprian and St. Chrysostom from their shelves, *then* the confusion Dr. Pusey spoke of *begins*, and it *begins with those who begin it*.[22]

Perception of a note, however, must not be solely subjective. As external, the note is valid to the extent that it can impress itself on people

---

22. JHN to Catherine Ward, 18 November 1848, in *LD* 12:335–36.

generally. "It is nothing to the purpose then that this communion or that says that itself has the Notes of the Church; or that divines of this or that say so; for the *fact* is to be decided, not by any such private judgement, but by the consent of the world . . . The appeal and the decision lie with the bulk of mankind. Take then the Roman Church, and take the Anglican in a large town; let each *call* itself the Church, and just see what the people say to it."[23] On the negative side, if a "note" does not make a general appeal, Newman would not allow it.

> This persuasion, conviction, impression, call it what you will, felt by the large mass of Protestants as well as Catholics, may be analyzed variously and the heads of arguments, into which it is resolved, are called Notes. But I say frankly, that if this conviction, and the heads of arguments or Notes, into which it is resolvable, be not assented to by the mass of enemies as well as friends, be not independent of particular persons, independent of me, I give up the very theory of the Notes of the Church, and will look for other arguments in contending for the Roman Church against the Anglican.[24]

Thus Newman was emphasizing that a note must make a general appeal, *as note;* however, this does not mean that a note convinces the general multitude, nor is it equally convincing for each Catholic. Different persons are attracted by different notes. Indeed, some people are not attracted to any notes and never become Catholics, even though they will admit that the Roman Church is "catholic" or "visible" or possesses other notes.

> In the middle ages, when it [the Church] was without rival and supreme, it seemed to have a divine blessing with a luminousness and force of evidence, which is now wanting to it. But it must be considered, that at that time the minds of a race or a population were for the most part homogeneous, because education had not brought out their individual differences. A broad, shining assemblage of Notes, one and the same, confronted the popular mind. Now that every mind stands (so to say) by itself, it is not wonderful that the Notes of truth, necessary for conversion, are various and relative to individuals; that one has one reason for believing, another another; and that our duty is to look at ourselves, not at others, not to try to make out why *they* do not embrace the truth, but to ask whether there is not evidence enough for us personally . . .

23. JHN to Catherine Ward, 30 November 1848, in *LD* 12:354.
24. Ibid., 354–55.

> And thus I think that in every age every man may find a sufficient evidence in his own line of thought. One aspect of the Church will be the instrument of conversion with one man, another with another; but some or other for every one. For myself, what made me a Catholic was the fact, as it came home to me, that the present Catholics are in all essential respects the successors and representatives of the first Christians.[25]

Newman's "broad view of matters" also extended to his treatment of notes, and he employed this technique in his spiritual direction. He wrote to Lady Heywood who became a Catholic two months later: "No truth, no conclusion about what is true, is without its difficulties. You must give up faith, if you will not believe till all objections are solved. . . . Take then a broad view of Catholicism and Anglicanism. . . . Which has ever spoken to the whole truth? Which has ever felt it a duty to propagate religion and has carried out its profession? Which has succeeded in converting men of all races, countries, ranks, classes, callings, descriptions, rich and poor, learned and ignorant."[26] Newman went through a litany of such external notes and concluded: "Which in its genius and look, in its tone of teaching and in the character of its devotions, is more like the Church of the early centuries?—So I might go on, and fill another sheet. This is a *broad view*."[27]

This appeal to notes cannot be separated from God's grace; as he pointed out to Mrs. Houldsworth: "Ask of God to give you *tokens* . . . I don't mean *miraculous* things, but tokens appropriate to your position and case . . . Pray to God to give you *tokens* to distinguish between the side which He owns and the side which He rejects—and beg of him faith and patience."[28].

In his correspondence, Newman utilized three notes of the Church: *visibility, unity*—which he closely connected with catholicity—and *apostolicity*, which was so persuasive for him personally. The note of *sanctity* received occasional mention.

Visibility is a feature of the Church that was generally accepted by Anglicans in Newman's time when the Established Church in England was very visible. Newman's letters contain little on the Church's visibility, except for two letters where he developed the idea of Church as visible kingdom. To Lord Charles Thynne in 1852 he wrote:

> If your Lordship asks me *why* I maintain that my communion is *the* Church, the answer (to me) is so plain, that I do not know

---

25. JHN to Unknown Correspondent, 19 June 1870, in *LD* 25:147.
26. JHN to Lady Heywood, 8 March 1876, in *LD* 28:38.
27. Ibid., 39.
28. JHN to Mrs. Houldsworth, 16 May 1871, in *LD* 25:330–31.

what can be said against it. I felt its force when I was a Protestant, and have done my utmost to overcome it, but in vain. The reason is this:—the Church is a *kingdom*—so our Lord says. Now does this mean a kingdom only as when we talk of the "animal kingdom," or the "vegetable kingdom"? Impossible. Is it an *invisible* kingdom? No Anglican will say so. Well then if it be a visible kingdom, *where* is such a kingdom, visible and yet spiritual, all over the earth except the Catholic Church? I do not know what can be said for Buddhism or some other Eastern Superstitions; but, putting such aside, I want to know *what* religion is embodied in a kingdom except the Catholic?[29]

Eighteen years later, Newman, took a common sense approach to the note of visibility:

In Scripture, we are told that to become interested in the promises, we must *join* the Church. The first Christians are represented as continuing in the *fellowship* of the Apostles—and those who were to be saved are said to have been added by Almighty God to His *Church*. The Apostles were visible men—the Church was a visible body, St. Paul speaks of the Church as "the pillar and ground of the Truth," thereupon it was a visible teaching body. If a man commit a fault against another, that other is directed by our Lord to "tell it to the Church,"—therefore, the Church was a visible body. And the earliest Fathers, as the Martyrs St. Ignatius and St. Cyprian, both of them in the clearest way speak of the Church as a visible body. Therefore the Church is the Ark of Salvation, and it is necessary to join a visible body. I can understand a man doubting, *which is* the Church, at first sight, but not his doubting that it is a duty to join the Church, if he can find it. As to the question "Which is the Church of *Christ*?" Of course it would puzzle any one—but there is a question which would puzzle no one. In the Creed we profess belief in "the *Catholic* Church"—Now then go into any town, and ask for "the Catholic Church," and you know whether you would be directed.[30]

In corresponding with Anglicans, Newman often emphasized the note of *unity*, because the unity of the Roman Church seemed evident in contrast

---

29. JHN to Lord Charles Thynne, 18 January 1852, in *LD* 15:19–20.
30. JHN to S. S. Shiel, 25 January 1870, in *LD* 25:12–14. For other letters related to the Church's visibility, see:
JHN to Miss Rowe, 16 September 1873, in *LD* 26:364–67;
JHN to John Mozley, 1 April 1875, in *LD* 27:259–63;
JHN to James McCarten, 24 October 1878, in *LD* 28:412–13.

to the apparent divisions in the Anglican Church. To Miss Rowe in 1873, he wrote: "The Church is a *visible* body—and one body. It is not two bodies—to be a visible body, there must be a visible unity between its portions. Where is the visible unity between the Church of Rome and the Church of England? If indeed a man says there is an invisible unity between them, I deny it, but if he tells me there is a visible unity between the two,—he is uttering the greatest paradox that ingenuity can invent and he refutes himself."[31]

In a long letter to an Edinburgh lawyer, Newman first defined his terms and then presented his case; he described the Anglican view of the Church as follows:

> The Church is the aggregate of certain visible congregations which are descended from one stock (this by ordination from the Apostles), marked by a certain government, episcopacy, and professing one faith (Apostles' or Nicene Creed)—When then the Catholic Church is spoken of, the word Church is not analogous to a singular noun, as John or Thomas, marking an individual, but a general term as a man or Englishman or again as manhood or humanity. The Church of Jerusalem, or the Apostolic College in the beginning, was the only instance of a Church meaning a social individual or corporation. Ever since Christianity spread into the world, it denotes a collection of small and real corporations, which are severally individual Churches, and viewed all together make up a generalized or Catholic Church.[32]

In contrast, the Catholic Church "is a social individual, answering to a singular noun, or corporation, having inter-communion in a political form."[33] Newman then explained to Campbell the difference between the Anglican and Catholic understanding of unity:

> What [is] in our view the Catholic Church, is in the Anglican view the particular diocese. The Church of Smyrna, or of Exeter does precisely in the Anglican view answer to that idea to which the whole collection of dioceses answers in our view. By Catholic Church we mean a thing, and the Anglicans a name. When we call the Catholic Church one, we mean it to be one in the same sense in which we popularly speak of a body of men being one; e.g., there is one Royal Society, one Royal Academy, one British Association, viz. a social or political unit; when Anglicans call the Catholic Church one, they mean it in the sense

---

31. JHN to Miss Rowe, 16 September 1873, in *LD* 26:365.
32. JHN to Robert Campbell, 23 October 1851, in *LD* 14:401.
33. Ibid.

in which we might call Whigs and Tories one, because they both are loyal subjects to the monarchy, or England and the United States one because their race and language are one.

We call the Church one in a sense analogous to that in which the Nicene Catholics called the Father and Son one, viz, one individual; Anglicans call the Church one in the sense in which the Arians called the Father and the Son one, viz. in will and love and (according to the high-Semi-arians) nature.[34]

Eleven years later, in 1862, Newman again utilized this polity-approach in response to an inquiry from Daniel Radford: "Anglicanism does not surpass the limits of the English race—where the English power colonises, there it goes. It does not take roots, it does not win hearts, any where else. It is in no sense a polity in many countries—a spiritual imperium one and the same, stretching over the nations. Nay, it is barely in communion with its own branches in Scotland, United States, Canada, Australia etc. It has no certainty, over and above the provision of Acts of Parliament, that what a Bishop does or teaches in England, other Bishops will do and teach elsewhere."[35] Newman then described Roman Catholic unity as being based on a polity, having a unified structure, and having effective authority.

> There are 200 millions of Christians poured over the earth, who, while they maintain somewhat more unanimously than Anglicans that they are the primitive and medieval Church, are in *matter of fact* in unity. In what aspect of the Sacramentum Unitatis is the modern Roman Catholic communion inferior to the Church of St. Cyprian's Age, or of St. Athanasius's or of St. Leo's or St. Gregory the first's. Is it not more populous? is it not more widely diffused? is it not less troubled with heresy and dissensions? is it not more minutely the same everywhere, in profession of faith, in theological language, in ritual, in legislation, in moral teaching, in devotions, in spirit? Do Bishops quarrel with Bishops within its pale now, as they did within the Ancient Church? Do Archbishops initiate heresies? Is Easter of England different from the Easter of Brazil or of the Philippines? It may be objected that there are great outstanding bodies, as the Greeks with their many millions etc. etc. Well, and this was so in ancient times—at one time the Nestorians and Eutychians together equalled or out-numbered the subjects of the Church.[36]

---

34. JHN to Robert Campbell, 21 October 1851, in *LD* 14:402.
35. JHN to Daniel Radford, 15 October 1862, in *LD* 20:305.
36. Ibid., 306.

Although Newman maintained that the Anglican Church does not possesses the *unity* that Rome possesses, one could still ask: Are there "degrees" of unity? Even if the Anglican Church has less unity than Rome, could it not possess some type of unity? In response to Lord Charles Thynne who asked this question, Newman replied: "Unity does not admit of degrees but of kinds—sanctity admits of degrees. You cannot talk of 'more one,' you can talk of 'more holy.' The degree of holiness, to which the Church should attain, is not specified—we cannot say that anything has failed—on the contrary our Lord distinctly foretold 'Offences'—and said His Church was to be a net. But if he has said His Church should be one, it either is one or it is not."[37]

Since Newman's approach was pastoral, he appealed to a perceptible unity. However, this unity did not mean that he favored a deadening uniformity; in fact he advocated freedom in both devotions and theological thought. In matters not *de fide*, diversity is allowable and *desired*. "in those things which are not of faith, there has been considerable difference of opinion among Catholics, and often serious and bitter quarrels. I have treated of the subject in the 10th Lecture of my volume on 'Anglican Difficulties.' Religion is so deeply interesting and sovereign a matter, and so possesses the whole man, when it once gains its due entrance into the mind, that it is not wonderful, that, as worldly men quarrel fiercely about worldly things, so, through the weakness of human nature, particular theologians have had unchristian disputes about Christian truths."[38] The same letter also responded to a question about whether the Church was one in doctrine: "As to your first question, 'Are you indeed one in doctrine in the Roman Catholic Church?' the only true answer is, that we are and ever have been one, and that is one of the special notes of our being the true Church. It is one which has had a special effect on intellectual men not Catholics, when they have happened to become intimate with Catholics and to witness the action of the Church. Our faith is one."[39]

Newman understood "apostolicity" as the continuation in the *style* of the primitive Church, and, secondarily, the ability to teach accurately what the Apostles taught. He discussed this continuation in *style* in a letter to A. J. Hammer in 1849:

> The question is, "Is the communion of Rome the Catholic Church?" ... To my mind the overbearingly convincing proof is this: that were St. Athanasius and St. Ambrose in London now, they would go to worship, not to St. Paul"s Cathedral, but to

---

37. JHN to Lord Charles Thynne, 24 March 1852, in *LD* 15:58–59.
38. JHN to Albert Smith, 8 January 1868, in *LD* 24:5–6.
39. Ibid., 5.

Warwick Street or Moor Fields. This my own reading of history has made to me an axiom, and it converted me, though I cannot of course communicate the force of it to others ... I hardly see a trace of the Church of the Fathers, as a *living, acting* being, in the Anglican communion. Whereas e.g., the Eucharistic Service of the Ancients and our High Mass would strike a stranger as the same, a priestly action with the congregation assisting and uniting with voice and posture; and so of other peculiarities. Again, an active intercommunion is a special characteristic of the Ancient Church; again, a combination of many nations in one etc. etc. Again, a one government.[40]

The reason for Newman's insistence on apostolicity is that it ensures the identity of the contemporary Church with the apostolic. "All these things *make up* together a great note of the Church. The Church was to be one and the same from Christ's first coming to His second. The modern Roman communion is unmistakeably like the Church of the Fathers; and this great argument is confirmed by finding that the Church of England is unmistakeably unlike it."[41]

Other churches could not claim "apostolicity"; thus, Newman rejected the "branch theory" which maintained that there are three authentic branches to the Church: English and Greek as well as Latin. For example, regarding the Greek Church, which some Anglicans considered a living branch of the Church, he asked: "Did our Lord intend Councils to cease with the seventh? Why has not the Greek Church held a council these last 1000 years? In the Latin, there is a continuation of all the functions which went on in the early Church—there is no suspended animation."[42]

The teaching role of the Church played a significant role in Newman's ecclesiology and he understood that teaching as an apostolic function. "A Catholic believes that the Church is, so to call it, a standing Apostolic committee—to answer questions, which the Apostles are not here to answer, concerning what they received and preached. As the Church does not know more than the Apostles knew, there are many questions which the Church cannot answer—but it can put before us clearly, what the Apostles (being in heaven) cannot, what their doctrine is, what is to be believed, and what is not such."[43]

In his correspondence, Newman did not develop the creedal note of *sanctity* to any great extent; when he did discuss *sanctity*, he usually wrote about it in reference to some abuse in the Church. To Lord Charles Thynne,

---

40. JHN to A. J. Hammer, 18 November 1849, in *LD* 13:295–96.
41. Ibid., 296.
42. JHN to J. F. Seccombe, 14 December 1869, in *LD* 24:390.
43. JHN to R. F. Hutton, 20 October 1871, in *LD* 25:418.

who found visible sanctity in the Church very problematic, Newman suggested a more balanced position. "The degree of holiness, to which the Church should attain, is not specified—we cannot say that any thing has failed—On the contrary our Lord distinctly foretold 'Offences' and said His Church was to be a net...

"You say 'the sanctity is lost visibly'—but I say 'it is not lost visibly'—it is only not so great as it might be. It *never* could (from the nature of the case) be as great as it might be. It is as great now as ever it was, even in Apostolic times."[44]

However, there is a noticeable difference in tone between two letters, one written in 1846, shortly after his conversion, and another written nearly thirty years later, after Newman had had personal experience of sanctity in the Catholic Church. The earlier letter displays some of the enthusiasm of a new convert for his new communion and a hint of disdain for his former Church. To Henry Wilberforce who argued that the note of sanctity had been obscured at times and the same could be the case with unity, Newman wrote:

> Day by day, am I more and more struck with this note in the Roman Church as contrasted with the Anglican. The series of evidences depending on the inward work of the Spirit, from miracles to personal graces, has been most wonderfully unfolded to me since my conversion, in the natural intercourse and conversation I have had with Catholics. As to personal graces, as far as I have had experience, I have been extremely struck with their rigid purity. Evidence of this has come before me in a way not to be mistaken. How low the Anglican Church is here. Of course, I am speaking of religious [Newman later added pious] persons in both communions. Again, I have a passage in my first volume of Sermons, about the inconsistencies of good men.[45]

Writing to his nephew nearly thirty years later, the tone of the letter is quite different.

> As to your other question, the virtues peculiar to Catholics, I think there are various such—but here we enter upon another large question—I do not think they make a show—that is, are such as to constitute what is called a Note of the Church. Our Lord Himself foretold that His net would contain fish of every kind—He speaks of rulers who would be tyrannical and gluttonous—and it was one of the first great controversies of the Christian Church, issuing in the novatian schism, whether

---

44. JHN to Lord Charles Thynne, 24 March 1852, in *LD* 15:58–59.
45. JHN to Henry Wilberforce, 4 July 1845, in *LD* 11:191.

extraordinary means should or should not be taken to keep the Church pure—and it was decided in the negative, as (in fact) a thing impossible. Now when this is once allowed, considering how evil in its own nature flaunts itself and is bad, and how true virtue is both in itself a matter of the heart and in its nature retiring and unostentatious, it is very difficult to manage to make a "Note of the Church" out of the conduct of Catholics viewed as a visible body. Besides it must be recollected that the Church is a militant body, and its work lies quite as much in rescuing souls from the dominion of sin as in leading them on to any height of moral excellence.[46]

Oracle of God and Ark of Salvation

Newman frequently described the Church as the Ark of Salvation and Oracle of Truth. He repeatedly advised prospective converts that they must firmly confess this truth before they could enter the Roman Catholic Church. Since most of Newman's inquirers believed that Christ established a Church in and through which one was saved, their question was, how do I recognize where this Church is today? Accordingly, his purpose was not so much to analyze how the Church functioned as a saving Ark but rather *where* this Ark was to be found.

In his correspondence, Newman commented on the Church's special function of proclaiming and teaching revealed truth. This duty of the Church assumed particular importance in light of the controversies occasioned by the publication of the Syllabus of Errors (1864) and the decisions of the First Vatican Council (1869–70). Not surprisingly, the focus in Newman's spiritual direction on helping people to recognize the Roman Catholic Church as identical with the primitive Church, was paralleled by his effort to help people to identify the Roman Catholic Church as the faithful teacher of the Revelation in Jesus Christ. A letter written in 1870 to William Gainsford clearly situates the context of revelation.

> There are two or three large questions which carry us on—Is there a God? is there a particular providence? is there a Moral Governance? what are the relations between man and His Maker? Do we need supernatural assistance that is, a revelation? does not a revelation imply an organ of revelation? is that revelation really made, if there is no organ, or if that organ can mislead or go wrong—that is, if it be not infallible? can a book be such an

---

46. JHN to John Mozley, 19 April 1847, in *LD* 27:55.

organ—especially such a book as the Bible, written in a language not our own, and full of difficulties? In this way we are able to see where the shoe pinches—that is, where it is our difficulty lies.[47]

In contrast to those theologians who would search the New Testament to extract a definition of the Church, Newman approached the question differently. He argued from the notion of *prophet* and the common testimony of mankind; as he stated at the conclusion of a letter to William Pope: "You will observe, from my way of treating the subject, I have superseded your question about arguing from Scriptures—for I do not see that it is necessary to bring in Scripture into the proof of a Church."[48]

William Pope had asked if he was to follow private judgment in becoming a Catholic. Newman replied that, in becoming a member of the Church, one's private judgment which was used in discovering the Church in the first place, gives way to Revelation, as to a superseding truth. Tying together his understanding of the Church as prophet in relation to private judgment, he replied:

> Now when you once fix your mind on this principle steadily, that, if God has spoken, He must have His organ of Prophet, I think you will see at once that the Catholic (or Roman Catholic) Church is that Prophet. Consider what is meant by the word Prophet, what *is the idea* which it conveys. I am not asking you to go by taste, or imagination, or feeling, or previous notions, or whatever is often included under the name and the exercise of *private* judgement in deciding what "Prophet" means, but use the judgement not of a private person, not of yourself, but of all mankind, use what may be called *public* judgement in determining this question, *what must a prophet be like*.
>
> Now surely it is no private judgement, but it is a mere explanation of the word to which all will assent to say that a Prophet must come from God, must say that he comes from God, must know what he has to tell, must be able to answer all questions which are put to him on the subject of his message, must be *firm and resolute* against all opposers or corrupters of it. He must be up to his office, up to emergencies, and consistent in his view to his duty. Has any so called Church any claim to answer such a description, (which I say is involved in the very idea of a prophet) but the Church of Rome? Is not the question reduced to this—either the Church of Rome is God's organ or He has none? And is not this conclusion arrived at without

---

47. JHN to William Gainsford, 10 November 1870, in *LD* 25:227.
48. JHN to William Pope, 15 April 1853, in *LD* 15:350.

any private judgement at all? for my description of it with the Church of Rome, of England, the Presbyterian Church, the Lutheran etc. etc. has nothing private either.[49]

Newman maintained that if God has spoken, then there must be an organ, an agent, for this revelation. In other words, there must be a prophet who claims to speak for God; not only in biblical times but today as well.

> The question then is brought to this? *is there* a Prophet of God on earth now? or, in other words, is there a Church? Now I do not think that even here private judgement comes prominently in, though it does partially. It is true, Protestants and Infidels deny that God has an organ of revelation or Church. The Infidel says He never had—the Protestant says, He once had—viz. the 12 Apostles, that they wrote the New Testament, and handed over the Old to us; that the Bible is their legacy, the record of revelation made through Apostles and Prophets—but that Prophet on the earth there now is none.
>
> On the other hand, a large body of even your own communion have ever said that there is and ever will be a Prophet on earth—the followers of Laud, of Bull, of the Non-jurors, and of Dr. Pusey. Now it is not a violent private judgement to go by them—But further extend your view across the channel and let it range the earth—go back into past history for 1800 years; and it is a matter, not of private judgement, but of public fact, that the immense majority of Christians have ever said that there is a Church, that there is a Prophet of God. Count up all Christian countries from the Apostles age till now, and see what a very small minority on the whole will be found to deny the existence of a Church. At this very time the (Roman) Catholic Church is, I believe, nearly equal to all other forms of Christianity together—and of those other forms the largest (the Greek) and besides, the Monophysite, the Nestorian, the Copt, the Armenian, a good part of the Episcopalian, all maintain that *there is a Church*. Which is most like Private Judgement, to deny it or to affirm it?[50]

Numerous correspondents wrote Newman concerning their doubts about and objections to various doctrines of the Roman Catholic Church. One pattern found in his responses was not to focus on a specific issue, but to raise the more fundamental question: "Do you accept the Church as Teacher?" For example, shortly after Newman's conversion, his friend,

---

49. Ibid., 349.
50. Ibid., 349–50.

Henry Wilberforce, wrote about the disturbing doctrine of Papal Supremacy; Newman responded:

> It seems to me extravagant or unreasonable in you to demand proof of one certain particular tenet which it so naturally comes to the Church to decide. If the Roman [Catholic] Church be the Church, I take it [and submit to it] whatever it is [monarchical, aristocratic or democratic]—and if I find that Papal Supremacy is a point of faith in it, this point of faith [though not capable of proof on its own merits] is not to my imagination so strange, to my reason so incredible, to my historical knowledge so utterly without evidence, as to warrant me in saying "I cannot take it on faith."[51]

Many years later, Newman wrote in the same way to another prospective convert about the basic condition for becoming a Catholic: "If you can say deliberately and from your heart 'I believe the Holy Catholic Roman Church to be the one and only Fold of Christ and Ark of Salvation, and I believe whatever she teaches, has taught or shall teach, to be the Word of God committed by our Lord to his Apostles in the beginning.'"[52] The basic and *broad* truth was the Church-as-Teacher.

This emphasis can be seen in a letter reacting to Edward Pusey's *Irenicon;* Newman indicated that the attitude, "enumerate the doctrines I must believe and I will say if I can become one of you," was misplaced.

> I have made this long talk by way of protest against the principle of the "Minimum," which both you and De Forbes stand upon, and which we never can accept as a principle, or as a basis of an Irenicon. It seems to us false, and we must ever hold, on the contrary, that the object of faith is *not* simply certain articles, ABCD, contained in dumb documents, but the whole word of God, explicit and implicit, as dispensed by His living Church. On this point I am sure there can be no Irenicon; for it marks a fundamental, elementary difference between the Anglican view and ours.[53]

Newman's belief that Christ spoke through the Church and that individuals receive Church doctrines on faith, gives an incarnational perspective to his spiritual direction: "We rely, not on the word of man, but on the word of God. *However,* thro' *whatever* instrument, He speaks to us, if he speaks to us, we are bound to believe. The voice of the Church is but the

---

51. JHN to Henry Wilberforce, 4 July 1846, in *LD* 11:190–91.
52. JHN to Alice Smith, 3 November 1870, in *LD* 25:225.
53. JHN to E. B. Pusey, 23 March 1867, in *LD* 23:105.

particular mode under our Dispensation, and the usual and ordinary under it, in which the word of God is proposed to us. If Almighty God spoke to Abraham, Abraham was bound to believe, and (by divine grace) did believe, without the voice of the Church."[54]

The normal and ordinary vehicle of Revelation is the Church. For a Revelation apart from the Church, namely, a direct communication from God to an individual, only that recipient is bound to belief. Similarly, a person is not obliged to believe what is not formally taught by the Church. For example, a year before the publication of *Ineffabilis Deus*, Newman wrote: "The Immaculate Conception may be a point of faith in this way to the individual, though not to the faithful generally, because the Church has not proposed it."[55]

Implied in the belief that the Church is the instrument of God's word, is the idea that the Church alone can determine what that word is: "The rule of the Church is never to decree any doctrine to be of faith but what comes by tradition; but the Infallible Church, while she always appeals to tradition, is the true judge and interpreter of it, not you or I."[56] The Church, as instrument, is not mechanical; it must bring its judgment to bear on what has been revealed to it; it speaks from out of its own faith, and so it alone can judge what its faith is.

The process, of course, is difficult, ambiguous, slow, and sometimes discordant. There are times, when the voice of one age seems to contradict that of another age. Criticizing Newman's *Letter to Pusey*, Robert Jenkins cited the denial of the Immaculate Conception by the Dominican Cardinal, Blessed John Dominic. Newman answered that the meaning of the term "Immaculate Conception" was determined by the Church in the Definition of 1854 and other uses of the phrase must be judged on their own merits.

> As to Cardinal Dominic's judgement and that of many other Divines you speak of, I do not feel it is to the purpose, because they all meant something different from what we mean now in speaking of the "Immaculate Conception." There is a sense doubtless in which the words may be taken, which would be, if not heretical, very like heresy. The history of the word Homousion is a parallel. The Great Council of Antioch, 70 years before Nicea, rejected it in *the sense* in which Paul of Samosata and the Manichees understood it. And even long after the Council of Nicea, orthodox Catholics had a difficulty in taking the word in what to them was a new sense upon the word and introduced it

---

54. JHN to W. J. O'Neill, 13 December 1853, in *LD* 15:499.
55. Ibid.
56. JHN to Mrs. Helbert, 28 September 1869, in *LD* 24:339.

> into the Creed—and in like manner, after a far longer controversy and probation, the Infallible Church has rejected certain old notions attached to the words "Immaculate Conception" and has used the phrase to express that old truth conveyed in the doctrine of the "Second Eve."[57]

Newman then saw the Church as an instrument speaking God's word today and determining the sense of that word. Newman's satisfaction with this position is apparent in a letter to Catherine Ward, who, under Newman's direction, later became a convert: "There are now, as at all times, a thousand disorders within and without the Church—her members full of imperfection—but there is *that* in her which is what she peculiarly promises, which no other body promises, and in which she does not deceive; she *can* present a Creed, she alone can do what a Messenger from heaven ought to do; and her children feel this and are satisfied."[58]

Characteristics of Newman's Spiritual Direction

Since many of Newman's letters were responses to concrete problems, his ecclesiology in these letters was practical and pastoral. Simultaneously, his spiritual direction about the church is characterized by recurring themes.

The most consistent element of Newman's spiritual direction is his encouragement of persons in their search for the Church and his support in their difficulties. He realized that recognizing and believing in the Catholic Church was no easy matter. The painful process of his own conversion offered a unique vantage point from which to direct others.

Letters abound in Newman's correspondence in which he supports persons at various stages in their investigation into the Church. Newman advised others that individuals are not bound to join the Church until they have considered the arguments for Catholicism; once they are convinced, then it is their duty to join. As he wrote to Albert Smith: "You are not bound to become a Catholic till you feel it your duty to be one, and then you are bound . . . it is better to consider all the difficulties in the argument for Catholicism before becoming a Catholic, than to let them come upon you after you are a Catholic."[59] Similarly, after explaining the visibility of the Church to S. S. Shiel in 1870, he wrote: "I can understand a man doubting, *which*

---

57. JHN to R. C. Jenkins, 19 February 1866, in *LD* 22:160.
58. JHN to Catherine Ward, 19 December 1848, in *LD* 12:378.
59. JHN to Albert Smith, 6 January 1869, in *LD* 24:204.

is the Church, at first sight, but not his doubting that it is a duty to join the Church, if he can find it.[60]

Noteworthy in Newman's encouragement is the empathy he expressed for people struggling with the question of conversion. Because Newman had himself gone through a similar struggle, he appreciated the internal turmoil that others were experiencing. Two months after his own conversion, Newman wrote the Marquise de Salvo about her desire to enter the Church yet her fear at causing pain to relatives and friends:

> I earnestly exhort you to join the Catholic Church. It is necessary for your salvation, considering your present state of mind. Believe me to feel very much for you, which I do— . . . You say you have to pain relatives by your step—alas, that is the trial which *all* have to go through. You hardly can be called on to inflict such pain as has been my own duty to inflict. But God will support you under every trial He puts upon you—and you will have the strength of the whole Church of all saints who ever lived. You will be one of a body who have gone through far more than any of us are called to undergo—and their prayers and their sanctity will operate in you, and raise you above yourself. I am not speaking necessarily of *sensible* comfort, but of real power which will be yours in God's presence.[61]

Similarly, he wrote an understanding letter to his friend Henry Wilberforce about how the trial of conversion is one of the ways in which God prepares us for new birth:

> The distress of mind at this moment of other friends of mine, of a different kind—I mean, their struggling to know whether or not they should join the Church of Rome, and not seeing their way—[is] a most consuming, exhausting trial. Yet it will, doubtless, all turn to good. Perhaps, if we knew all, we should know it is impossible for the elect of God to emerge from darkness to light in any other way. Such travail is necessary for the new birth. Perhaps if we saw our way too soon, there might be a re-action and old habits and associations might come over one again. I know too well the state [of mind] of those in doubt, not to understand that the long trial of some is no sin of theirs, but God's way with them, imparting light slowly that He may impart it more effectually. My only dread is, and it is in some cases very great, when they are not, to all appearance, using the light given them, but shutting their eyes. And as doubt long continued may

---

60. JHN to S. S. Shiel, 25 January 1870, in *LD* 25:14.
61. JHN to Marquise de Salvo, 18 December 1845, in *LD* 11:71.

be the fiery process by which one person is brought into the Church, so the loss or alienation of friends by their conversion may be the divinely sent trial of others. It may be the gradual operation, by which God prepares their own souls for the truth.[62]

In 1875, in a letter to Lady Heywood, Newman compared the inner turmoil of converting in the nineteenth century to the struggle of the early Church.

> Your case is the case of many others, and a very painful one. But I suppose the inward conflict of mind which was the inevitable lot of those who in the first age of the Church had to face the prospect of loss of friends, home, familiar habits, the happy and secure routine of life, life-long beliefs and opinions and human authority and favour, with the chance of persecution and death, in order to win Christ, was still more painful, but even the trial to which the soul is subjected now and in this country, ere it can get free of the world and follow Christ, is great indeed. And bystanders can only pray for souls in this distress; for it is God, and none else, who must help them.[63]

An additional instance occurred in the case of Lord Fielding whose father, the Earl of Denbigh, threatened to disinherit him for joining the Catholic Church. Since Newman had experienced the painful reaction of family and friends at his conversion he could write:

> It was with deep sorrow I read what you told me about your family matters. Time, however, please God, will set all to rights, or at least indefinitely soften the acuteness of feeling which such steps as you tell me of express. Such feeling in course of time may give place to a very different sentiment. For such a change you must pray unceasingly.
>
> ... Be of good cheer, my dear Lord, the first months of a convert's life, though filled with joy of their own, have a pain and dreariness of their own too. We feel the latter when nature overcomes grace—the former, when grace triumphs over nature. But no one made a sacrifice without effect. God does not forget what we do for Him—and whatever trouble you may have now, it will be repaid to you a hundred fold.[64]

62. JHN to Henry Wilberforce, 29 May 1846, in *LD* 11:166–67.

63. JHN to Lady Heywood, 15 November 1875, in *LD* 27:376.

64. JHN to Viscount Fielding, 15 November 1850, in *LD* 14:129–30. For similar letters manifesting empathy, see the following:
JHN to A. J. Hammer, 17 November 1849, in *LD* 13:311;
JHN to Lord Charles Thynne, 30 January 1852, in *LD* 15:25;

Spiritual Direction and the Roman Catholic Church

Another element that emerged in Newman's guidance of others towards the Church was his personal testimony. Newman was willing to share his own struggles, questions, and trials. Frequently, his personal witness became a way of helping others to resolve their own difficulties. With the Marquise de Salvo, he employed this method in advising in her to join the Church.

> You will see from the letter which has already gone all I have to say—and how idle the report is that I repent of having joined the Catholic Church. This is said of every one in turn—and in every case which I am acquainted with most falsely—there is but one feeling of joy and happiness among those persons with whom I am acquainted who have become Catholics—and as to *finding* things we did not expect in the Church, I do not know what is meant by "*finding*." I inquired into the system of religion I was joining before I submitted to it. Many things indeed I have found—extreme kindness and unsuspicious cordiality far beyond my deserts—and great excellence of life and character among a circle of persons with whom I was hitherto unacquainted: I earnestly exhort you to join the Catholic Church.[65]

A week earlier, Newman had written to A. J. Hammer about his own new found certitude in relation to the Church: "Then I was in doubt about things of which I am now sure. When one is sure that a certain thing is in itself right, one feels far less scruple in recommending it to a given individual, than when one is in doubt about its truth or propriety. I am now so convinced of the truth and divinity of the Catholic Church, that I am pained about persons who are external to it in a way in which I was not before."[66]

Similarly, when Mrs. J. W. Bowden was trying to decide whether to convert or not, one of her concerns revolved around the issue of certainty. Newman responded:

> But among the anticipations you must entertain, I think must be this—that you *cannot* have "certainty," to use your words. The class of minds to which I just now referred have certainty—that is, they have no doubt at all. But calmer and more sober minds from the nature of the case see difficulties on all sides of them,

---

JHN to Unknown Correspondent, March 1871, in *LD* 25:294;
JHN to Frederick Capes, 24 May 1865, in *LD* 21:475;
JHN to Mrs. William Clark, 30 August 1873, in *LD* 26:357–58;
JHN to Mrs. William Clark, 22 November 1875, in *LD* 27:381;
JHN to Lady Heywood, 8 March 1876, in *LD* 28:37–39;
JHN to Mrs. Frederick Lee, 2 April 1881, in *LD* 29:356–57.

65. JHN to Marquise de Salvo, 18 December 1845, in *LD* 11:71.
66. JHN to A. J. Hammer, 11 December 1845, in *LD* 11:60.

> in every course of action—and must in a certain sense act in the dark, and have their reward, and perhaps greater merit, in thus looking up to God and doing what they really do trust on the whole is pleasing to Him, though they have much hesitation while they act. Perhaps one speaks from oneself—not for one moment have I felt otherwise than most grateful to God that I did what I did last October—and it comes to me sometimes with affright "what if I had missed the moment and lost my election!" and day by day I seem to gain a nearer approach to Him who condescends to dwell with man upon earth under sensible forms—but what would I have given for a clearer view at the time of acting, and for a year before![67]

Later in this letter Newman cautioned Mrs. Bowden about what to expect by way of final temptations.

> Another thought about you is this—that, did you make up your mind to the step of which I have been speaking, you might have great temptations at the last minute, to make you change it. This occurs to many persons, and in various ways. Of course, I should call them artifices of the enemy to hinder what seems inevitable. The moment before acting may be, as can easily be imagined, peculiarly dreary—the mind may be, confused—no reason for acting may be forthcoming in our mind—and the awful greatness of the step in itself, and without any distinct apprehension of its consequences, may weigh on us. Some persons like to be left to themselves in such a crisis—others find a comfort in the presence of others. I could do nothing but shut myself up in my room and lie down on my bed. In addition to this, a person may very easily be tried, in a way I was not, by strong misgivings that perhaps he is doing wrong.[68]

Newman's own conversion had been a lengthy process; understandably, he insisted that others take their time and not rush their decision. When Mrs. Bowden was considering joining the Church in 1846, Newman wrote to her:

> I cannot wish you to be otherwise than slow in your decisions, were I to choose for you, in those very solemn matters which at present press upon you. There are persons who must be taken at a moment or they will not act—and whose minds are so variable

---

67. JHN to Mrs. J. W. Bowden, 22 March 1846, in *LD* 11:140–41. Mrs. Bowden entered the Roman Catholic Church in October, the previous year.

68. Ibid., 141.

and who go so little by reason that they are incapable of going through a *process* of change. But you, I suppose, are very different—and I should not like you, as you would not like yourself, not to contemplate the consequences of a great step, and so to leave no place afterwards for re-action of mind or the rise of difficulties or distresses which you had anticipated.[69]

Some months later, however, on learning that she was very confused by the conflicting advice she was receiving, Newman advised her to join the Church immediately.

> It really seems now that time has come when I ought to speak. You know how very much I have kept in the background. You have not been allowed to make up your mind calmly for yourself. You have (naturally) had kind friends urging you to stay—those on the other side who might have spoken, have not urged you to go. Much as I have felt, earnestly as you may conceive I have prayed, I wished you to make up your mind slowly and for yourself, because I thought that you had a right to do so, and were equal to doing so. You may think how hard it has been to be patient—but I really reverence you too much to have the same temptation to impatience which I should have with other people.
>
> Now I only claim this—to be able to judge that really you see you ought not to remain where you are. You have no faith in the system you are in—you cannot have the Christian grace of faith where you are. You do not know what to believe and what not—you have no one to tell you. As to corresponding with Pusey, nothing will come of it but weariness and disappointment to him, and pain to yourself. I do seriously counsel you to join the Church at once.[70]

Yet Newman did not want people considering conversion to act impetuously or on the spur of the moment because he felt that trouble would arise later and the conversion would not last. Thus he advised Lady Heywood:

> Certainly you have a great trial and I wish that you could be relieved from or under it—but God knows what is best for you, and will reward you for all you suffer for conscience sake. You wish to do God's will; He will not forget you. Have a full trust in Him; go to Him with an open heart and you will find how good He is. Of course you should not act in a state of enthusiasm, and

---

69. Ibid.
70. JHN to Mrs. J. W. Bowden, 7 June 1846, in *LD* 11:173–74.

John Henry Newman

of course too, I cannot know whether such is your state. I doubt not you pray God to keep you from enthusiasm.[71]

Similarly, Newman cautioned Gilbert Simmons who was inquiring about the Church:

> But when the question is asked *who* are those who are called, and *when* are they bound to act upon it, of course caution is necessary in dealing with individuals. I have long determined, though I find it difficult to keep my rule, not to give definite advice to anyone I have not seen. How do I know you are not a person who have taken up a fancy today, and will give it up tomorrow? There is nothing in your letter like this, and I am not supposing it—but there are those who have come to the Church with but an imperfect idea of its teaching and its usages, and when they knew it better have, like the disciples at Capernaum (John VI) left it again.[72]

For Newman, knowing an individual personally was an important factor in spiritual direction; in fact, he hesitated to advise anyone if he did not know them personally.[73] Similarly, when a person asked advice on guiding a

---

71. JHN to Lady Heywood, 8 March 1876, in *LD* 28:37.

72. JHN to Gilbert Simmons, 28 June 1868, in *LD* 24:95–96. For similar letters where Newman advised acting slowly see:

JHN to William Maskell, 7 January 1850, in *LD* 13:371–73;
JHN to Mrs. William Froude, 20 May 1856, in *LD* 17:243–44;
JHN to Baroness von Köller, 1 July 1864, in *LD* 21:140–41;
JHN to Henry Coleridge, 22 February 1873, in *LD* 26:265;
JHN to James McCarten, 24 October 1878, in *LD* 28:412–13;

Newman seemed particularly concerned with young people who wanted to convert; for his counsel to them see:

JHN to Charles Williamson, 7 June 1874, in *LD* 27:74;
JHN to Mr. Hutton, 17 April 1878, in *LD* 28:345–46;
JHN to Emily Fortey, 6 July 1882, in *LD* 30:109–10;
JHN to Marion Tucker, 4 September 1882, in *LD* 30:124.

73. On a number of occasions Newman explicitly declined to advise someone whom he did not know personally. Most of these occurred in his later years. However, he answered their questions or responded in a general way:

JHN to Miss Bristowe, 15 April 1866, in *LD* 22:212–13;
JHN to Gilbert Simmons, 28 June 1868, in *LD* 24:95–96;
JHN to Fanny Pearson, 31 October 1870, in *LD* 25:222;
JHN to Unknown Correspondent, March 1871, in *LD* 25:294;
JHN to Archibald Maccall, 27 April 1874, in *LD* 27:57–58;
JHN to Lady Heywood, 15 November 1875, in *LD* 27:376–78;
JHN to Mr. Hutton, 17 April 1878, in *LD* 28:345–46;
JHN to Mrs. Christie, 29 December 1881, in *LD* 30:40;
JHN to Marion Tucker, 4 September 1882, in *LD* 30:124.

prospective convert, again his counsel was not to hurry, but to take the time needed. For example, Mrs. Bowden was anxious to have her son become a convert; Newman advised her:

> You must not be anxious about John as regards yourself. It is as clear to you, as it is to me, that you could not have done, that you cannot be doing, anything more than you have done and do. We cannot change wills at pleasure. You cannot force a boy of his age. To join the Church would not profit him, if he did it against his will. And you must not be troubled with ups and downs of hope and fears which his conduct gives you. . . . For myself I know not how to doubt, looking at the case externally that you will ultimately have him. Meanwhile the delay is doubtless intended to quicken your prayers for him.[74]

Since Newman felt that his own conversion was "coming out of shadows into truth," he wanted converts to join the Church for the right reasons. Accordingly, he was constantly advising persons to be sure of their motives before joining the Church. Newman believed a person ought to come to the Church "in the spirit of a child" in order to be "taught and with the intention of submitting to her teaching."[75] Ultimately, it was a question of salvation. As he wrote to the Marquise de Salvo: "You may suppose I can have no doubt on the point, considering how much I have given up for it. I never could think it right to change my religion on any ground short of the *absolute necessity* of the act, as a condition of *everlasting salvation*."[76]

In discussing the correct motives for conversion with Mrs. Froude, Newman wrote: "You must come to the Church, not to avoid it, i.e., trial but to save your soul. If this is the motive, all is right—you cannot be disappointed."[77] Twenty-two years later he wrote almost the exact same thing to Fanny Pearson: "Do you come to the Church to save your soul? That is the only true motive."[78]

Newman was sometimes faced with situations where people wanted to join the Church for incorrect or inadequate reasons. Whenever this occurred, he patiently attempted to guide the person to what he believed to be correct reasons. For example, in 1848 Newman wrote A. J. Hammer that it was not enough to possess a "mere outward conformity to the Church";[79]

---

74. JHN to Mrs. J. W. Bowden, 22 August 1846, in *LD* 11:230.
75. JHN to Richard Hutton, 16 February 1870, in *LD* 25:30.
76. JHN to Marquise de Salvo, 14 December 1845, in *LD* 11:63.
77. JHN to Mrs. William Froude, 16 June 1848, in *LD* 12:223–24.
78. JHN to Fanny Pearson, 31 October 1870, in *LD* 25:222.
79. JHN to A. J. Hammer, 10 February 1848, in *LD* 12:168.

rather a sincere internal faith is needed. Another external factor is human respect, which can be employed to pressure an individual to join the Church or to keep a person from converting. The latter was the case with his friend Henry Wilberforce. Newman agreed that a person ought not to join the Catholic Church out of human respect, yet he observed: "And they tell you to be aware of human feelings and human respect, as if there were none on the side of staying where you are."[80]

Perhaps the most unusual motive for wanting to become a Catholic appeared in his correspondence in 1864 with Baroness von Köller. She apparently believed that she would be supported from Catholic sources if she became a convert; she wrote to Newman to confirm this. Newman quickly assured her that this would not happen, and hoped that she would not become a Catholic for this motive.[81]

At least four different persons, at various times, told Newman that they were thinking of converting because they "liked" the Catholic Church. Newman replied to one: "You must not become a Catholic merely because you like our doctrines and devotions, but because you believe the Catholic Church to be the Ark of Salvation."[82]

Another person apparently wanted to convert "merely to get rid of painful doubts." Newman felt that such doubts would simply return later, and the second state of the person would be worse than the first. Writing to Richard Hutton in 1870, he explained: "I never shall wish you to become a Catholic, merely to get rid of your painful doubts. I don't see that it is a sufficient motive—and I do see at least the danger of their reviving when you were in the Church, if you had not let them die a natural death before you came into it."[83]

Another inadequate motive was suggested by James Le Quesne who wanted to join the Church because he thought he could be more "religious." Newman pointed out that this kind of fervor dies away quickly and that unless an individual believes what the Church teaches, this person will not persevere.

> In answer to your question, I would observe that there is a great temptation, (as it is to some people) without believing that the Catholic Church is the One authoritative Oracle of God and the one Ark of Salvation, to join it merely because they can pray better in it, or have more fervency than in the Anglican Church, and in consequence conceive a *"hope"* of becoming more religious

---

80. JHN to Henry Wilberforce, 10 October 1840, in *LD* 13:270.
81. JHN to Baroness von Köller, 1 July 1864, in *LD* 21:140.
82. JHN to Mrs. William Clark, 31 December 1875, in *LD* 27:397.
83. JHN to Richard Hutton, 16 February 1870, in *LD* 25:30.

Spiritual Direction and the Roman Catholic Church

in it than they are at present, whereas the demand which the Church of God makes on them is to *believe* her *teaching* as the teaching of God. We will say, perhaps they become Catholics; their fervour after a while dies away, their faith is demanded for some doctrine which as yet they have not heard of or considered—and they stumble at it and fall away.[84]

Even when Newman was eighty years old, this concern continued to appear in his correspondence; he wrote to an unknown correspondent that the desire to become a missionary was an insufficient motive for wanting to join the Church, "If you become a Catholic, it must be in order to save your soul, not in order to become, or on condition of becoming a missionary."[85]

A final characteristic of Newman's spiritual direction is honesty. Newman directed prospective converts to be honest with others even when that was very painful. By so doing, he hoped to prevent more serious difficulties in the future. He advised Mrs. Newdigate, whose husband was an Anglican clergyman, that she do nothing without her husband's knowledge.

> Whether he would have you join at once, or not at once, delaying either for instruction in our faith or for other reasons, I should advise you to do nothing without your husband's knowledge. I know it is a most cruel thing to have to tell him, but it is more cruel not to tell him. I know too how sadly it must embarrass him as an Anglican clergyman, but on the other hand an underhand conversion will be the beginning of a long train of miseries. Better meet the trial at once—it is the honest and the expedient course.[86]

Similarly, he directed young people who were contemplating conversion, to be honest with their parents.[87]

In guiding many different persons in their process of conversion, Newman wanted them to know that they were not alone. He knew the importance of waiting patiently on God, who was directing the process; the person's job was to pray and be receptive to God's action in them. For example, he wrote Mrs. Froude, who was having a difficult time accepting the Church:

> My dear Mrs. Froude, *do* you pray for "effectual grace"—? Suppose I come to a high wall—I cannot jump it—such are the

---

84. JHN to James Le Quesne, 11 October 1879, in *LD* 29:185.

85. JHN to Unknown Correspondent, 19 June 1881, in *LD* 29:287.

86. JHN to Mrs. Alfred Newdigate, 23 July 1873, in *LD* 26:341. Both husband and wife were received into the Catholic Church in 1875.

87. JHN to Mrs. Hutton, 17 April 1878, in *LD* 28:345-46.

moral obstacles which keep us from the Church. We see the Heavenly City before us, we go on and on along the road, till a wall simply crosses it. Human effort cannot clear it—there is no scaling, no vaulting over. Grace enables us to cross it—and that grace is called effectual grace. Our first grace is sufficient to enable us to pray for that second effectual grace—and God gives grace for grace.[88]

Directing Others in Particular Aspects of Church Life

After his own conversion, Newman experienced a period of adjustment; it took him time before he felt at home in his new communion. First of all, he encountered the suspicious attitude of English Roman Catholics toward converts. He was also embarrassed by publicity and display: "I was the gaze of so many eyes at Oscott, as if some wild incomprehensible beast, caught by the hunter, and a spectacle for Dr. Wiseman to exhibit to strangers as himself being the hunter who captured it !"[89] Nonetheless, his letters written soon after his conversion reveal a brighter aspect of his experience. On December 13, 1846, he wrote from Rome to Henry Wilberforce: "I was happy at Oriel, happier at Littlemore, as happy or happier still at Maryvale—and happiest here."[90]

For most of his life rumors kept arising that Newman was unhappy as a Roman Catholic or that he was returning to the Anglican Church. Nothing could have been more unfounded. From his letters it can be seen that not only had he discovered truth and happiness, but that he never had any intentions of returning to Anglicanism. In 1848 he wrote to Henry Bourne: "I can only say, if it is necessary to say it, that from the moment I became a Catholic, I never have had, through God's grace, a single doubt or misgiving on my mind that I did wrong in becoming one. I have not had any feeling whatever but one of joy and gratitude that God called me out of an insecure state into one which is sure and safe, out of the war of tongues into a realm of peace and assurance."[91]

In 1862, the *Globe* published a report that Newman was about to leave the Oratory and return to the Church of England. This occasioned Newman's strongest language in his response. Without desiring to offend anyone, but at the same time wanting to squelch the growing number of rumors, Newman replied:

88. JHN to Mrs. William Froude, 2 March 1854, in *LD* 16:65–66.
89. Newman, *Autobiographical Writings*, 255.
90. JHN to Henry Wilberforce, 13 December 1846, in *LD* 11:294.
91. JHN to Henry Bourne, 13 June 1848, in *LD* 12:218.

> I have not had one moment's wavering of trust in the Catholic Church ever since I was received into her fold. I hold, and ever have held, that her Sovereign Pontiff is the centre of unity and the Vicar of Christ. And I ever have had, and have still, an unclouded faith in her creed in all its articles; a supreme satisfaction in her worship, discipline, and teaching; and an eager longing and a hope against hope that the many dear friends whom I have left in Protestantism may be partakers of my happiness.
>
> This being my state of mind, to add, as I hereby go on to do, that I have no intention, and never had had any intention, of leaving the Catholic Church and becoming a Protestant again, would be superfluous, except that Protestants are always on the look-out for some loophole or evasion in a Catholic's statement of fact. Therefore, in order to give them full satisfaction, if I can, I do hereby profess *ex animo*, with an absolute internal assent and consent, that Protestantism is the dreariest of possible religions; that the thought of the Anglican service makes me shiver, and the thought of the thirty-nine Articles makes me shudder. Return to the Church of England: no; "the net is broken, and we are delivered." I should be a consummate fool (to use a mild term) if in my old age I left "the land flowing with milk and honey" for the city of confusion and the house of bondage.[92]

Newman was quick to point out that his conversion to the Roman Catholic Church and his desire to remain in it was a matter of faith and did not depend on personalities or how he was treated by others in the Church. He wrote a letter to Sir Frederic Rogers in 1868 reminiscing about his life in the church:

> I have found in the Catholic Church abundance of courtesy, but very little sympathy, among persons in high places, except a few—but there is a depth and a power in the Catholic religion, a fulness of satisfaction in its creed, its theology, its rites, its sacraments, its discipline, a freedom yet a support also, before which the neglect or the misapprehension about oneself on the part of individual living persons, however exalted, is as so much dust, when weighed in the balance. This is the true secret of the Church's strength, the principle of its indefectibility, and the bond of its indissoluble unity. It is the earnest and the beginning of the repose of Heaven.[93]

---

92. JHN to the Editor of *The Globe*, 28 June 1862, in *LD* 20:215.
93. JHN to Sir Frederic Rogers, 2 February 1868, in *LD* 24:25.

John Henry Newman

Infallibility

The specific ecclesiological topic which received the most attention in Newman's letters during his Catholic years was infallibility.[94] For over four decades it was a recurring theme. His letters do not offer a complete theological treatise on this topic since his inquirers were usually asking specific questions. Nevertheless it is possible to trace chronologically his own progression of thought concerning infallibility and to see how he directed others.[95]

Newman had been a Roman Catholic for only two months when the first letters concerning infallibility arrived. His earliest explanation of the role of infallibility in the Church focused not on infallibility as such, but rather on the consistency of the contemporary Roman Church with the primitive Church. When Mrs. Anstice wrote on December 18, 1845, concerning Mr. Northcote's difficulties with infallibility which were keeping him from joining the Church, Newman suggested taking "large and broad views of the subject, instead of entangling ourselves with particular questions."[96] He went on to say "that some things perhaps must ever be difficulties, but

---

94. Although a number of studies have been done on Newman's views on infallibility, his correspondence abounds with material about the pastoral problems occasioned by the debate on and the definition of infallibility. Altogether there are 138 letters concerning some aspect of infallibility:

LD 11 (1845–1846): 4 letters;
LD 13 (1849–1850): 2 letters;
LD 14 (1850–1851): 5 letters;
LD 15 (1852–1853): 2 letters;
LD 19 (1859–1861): 2 letters;
LD 20 (1861–1863): 1 letter;
LD 21 (1864–1865): 4 letters;
LD 22 (1865–1866): 3 letters;
LD 23 (1866–1867): 5 letters;
LD 24 (1868–1869): 9 letters;
LD 25 (1870–1871): 60 letters;
LD 26 (1872–1873): 15 letters;
LD 27 (1874–1875): 29 letters;
LD 31 (1885–1890): 3 letters;

LD Supplement, 31: 2 letters. Both of these letters were written in 1858. As the prospect of a definition became more likely and immediately after it occurred, the number of letters on this subject increased.

95. Chronologically, five periods can be distinguished: (1) 1845–April 24, 1870; (2) April 24, 1870–July 18, 1870, the period when it became clear that the doctrine of infallibility would be defined; (3) July 18, 1870, when *Pastor Aeternus* (the Dogmatic Constitution which included the Definition of the infallible magisterium of the Pope) was promulgated until the end of the year when it became clear that opposition would not continue and the Council would not be reconvened; (4) 1871–1875; (5) after the publication of his *Letter to the Duke of Norfolk* (1875).

96. JHN to Mrs. Anstice, 15 December 1845, in *LD* 11:69.

that on the whole and in proportion as persons come *nearer* to the system, there is a *growing evidence* of consistency."[97]

Several months later he asked his friend, Henry Wilberforce, who was also having problems with infallibility, to examine his own inconsistency, "You must go one way or the other. You may shut your eyes for a time to the fact of your on inconsistency, but it will break upon you."[98] The following month he wrote again with more precision:

> If we can get a tolerable notion *which* is the Church, and know (as we do) that it may be trusted because it is the Church, then comes the question why should not the Pope's Supremacy be one of the points on which it may be trusted? For myself I have had so great experience of the correctness of the Roman view where once I thought otherwise, that I should be a beast if I were unwilling to take the rest on faith, from a confidence that what is still obscure to me . . . is explainable. And it seems to me extravagant or unreasonable in you to demand proof of one certain particular tenet which it so naturally comes to the Church to decide. If the Roman Church be the Church, I take it whatever it is—and if I find that Papal Supremacy is a point of faith in it, this point of faith is not to my imagination so strange, to my reason so incredible, to my historical knowledge so utterly without evidence, as to warrant me in saying, "I *cannot* take it on faith."[99]

In 1849, in response to A. J. Hammer, who still had not settled his difficulties about infallibility, Newman discussed, not the issue itself, but his understanding of the Church. "Next, I cast my eyes over your ten difficulties, and I see that not one of them is (as I think) to your purpose. The question is, 'Is the communion of Rome the Catholic Church?' and you answer in these ten difficulties that the Pope is not infallible. How does the argument run, 'The Pope is not infallible, therefore the Church in communion with him is not the Catholic Church'?"[100] Then taking a more strategic approach to the question he continued: "Now, it is the old fallacy of division, and nothing else, to say, '*This* (infallibility) is not necessary to the Church, nor *that*, nor the *other*; therefore not *all together*.' All these things *make up* together a great note of the Church. The Church was to be one and the same from Christ's first coming to His Second. The modern Roman communion is unmistakeably like the

---

97. Ibid..
98. JHN to Henry Wilberforce, 8 June 1846, in *LD* 11:174.
99. JHN to Henry Wilberforce, 4 July 1846, in *LD* 11:190.
100. JHN to A. J. Hammer, 18 November 1849, in *LD* 13:295.

Church of the Fathers; and this great argument is confirmed by finding that the Church of England is unmistakeably unlike it."[101]

Between September 1851 and February 1852, Newman wrote a series of seven lengthy letters to Francis Wegg-Prosser, which presented his most comprehensive treatment of infallibility prior to its definition in 1870. Wegg-Prosser found difficulty in accepting papal infallibility. Newman's approach was to present the infallibility of the Church and then, within this context, to encourage an acceptance in faith of the infallibility of the Pope.

> Did I not in my letter make the infallibility of the *Pope* a doctrine to be taken in faith on the Church's word (so far as the Church says it): If I have not said so clearly (at the end of my letter) it is what I meant to say. The way I wished to put the question is this: 1. There must be ever in the world a continuation of the Primitive Church. 2. That continuation is infallible. 3. It is no other than the Roman. 4. What the Roman says is to be received. 5. The Roman teaches (if so) the infallibility of the Pope. I mean, submit yourself to the Roman Church, and *then* take the infallibility of the Pope, if the Roman Church teaches it.[102]

Two weeks later, when Wegg-Prosser tried to make Papal infallibility the basis of Catholic faith, Newman was quick to point out that the infallibility of the Pope is not the basis of the Catholic religion, but a doctrine of the Church which the Church teaches along with many other doctrines.

> I must protest with all my might against what I consider an assumption, that the infallibility of the Pope is the *basis* of the Catholic Religion looked at controversially, and I will not meet you on a point, the admission of which seems to me a mistake...
>
> For me, I maintain it is a *doctrine of the church*, (whether a dogma or not, I am not going into) but I mean, as far as it is to be received, it is to be received on the church's authority...
>
> I conceive that the fundamental proof of Catholicism, (i.e., the basis according to *my* conception of Catholicism,) is the promise that the Primitive Church shall continue to the end, the likeness of the (Roman) Catholic church to the Primitive, and the dissimilarity of every other body—The (Roman) Catholic Church then, being proved to be the organ of revelation, or infallible in matters of faith, will *teach* the Pope's infallibility, as far as it is a doctrine, just as it teaches the Divinity of our Lord, or

---

101. Ibid., 295–96.
102. JHN to Francis Wegg-Prosser, 10 September 1851, in *LD* 14:354.

original sin—and its teaching must, as regards the one doctrine and the other, be received on faith.[103]

Moreover, the infallibility of the Catholic Church is an inference from its teaching office. Four years after the definition, Newman said that infallibility is "a doctrine *derived from*, a *consequence* of, an Apostolical and Divine doctrine, viz., that the Church is the *authoritative teacher*—She cannot teach without infallibility."[104]

During the two decades prior to the First Vatican Council (1869–1870), most of Newman's correspondence concerning infallibility was an explanation of his fundamental belief that the Roman Catholic Church was the descendent of the Primitive Church which had received the true revelation of God and, consequently, the authority to teach infallibly. Accordingly, this ecclesial infallibility provided the context for belief in the infallibility of the Pope.

After extensive preparations, the First Vatican Council officially commenced on December 8, 1869. Although the topic of "infallibility" was not on the official agenda, there were persistent rumors that there would be a definition of the Pope's infallibility. An Ultramontane[105] campaign had already begun in favor of a definition and the debate was carried on in popular newspapers with passionate partisanship.

Wilfrid Ward teamed with Cardinal Manning and Monsignor Tabot to advocate the doctrine of infallibility. These "infallibilists" insisted that their opinion was the only orthodox teaching and wrote as if they alone represented the Roman Catholics of England. Two years earlier, Newman had accused Ward of making a church within a church, like the Novatians of old or the Evangelicals within the Establishment, "by exalting your opinions into dogmas, and shocking to say, by declaring to me, as you do, that those Catholics who do not accept them are of a different religion to yours. I protest then again, not against your tenets, but your schismatical spirit."[106]

---

103. JHN to Francis Wegg-Prosser, 24 September 1851, in *LD* 14:365–68. For the remaining correspondence with Wegg-Prosser, see the following:
JHN to Francis Wegg-Prosser, 7 September 1851, in *LD* 14:348–51;
JHN to Francis Wegg-Prosser, 18 September 1851, in *LD* 14:360–61;
JHN to Francis Wegg-Prosser, 20 February 1852, in *LD* 15:39–40;
JHN to Francis Wegg-Prosser, 22 February 1852, in *LD* 15:41–42.

104. JHN to J. H. Nevins, 25 June 1874, in *LD* 27:84.

105. Ultramontanism is a term used to describe a strong emphasis on centralization in the Church, or on papal authority in matters of ecclesiastical government and doctrine. It was especially applied to those favoring the definition of infallibility prior to Vatican I.

106. JHN to Wilfrid Ward, 9 May 1867, in *LD* 23:217.

Two months later, Newman expressed his feelings about Ward to his friend Henry Wilberforce:

> From all I have heard Ward has hindered various people from becoming Catholics by his extreme views, and I believe is unsettling the minds of I can't tell how many Catholics. He is free to have his own opinion, but, when he makes it part of the faith, when he stigmatizes those who do not follow him as bad Catholics, when he saves them only on the plea of invincible ignorance, when he declines to meet those Catholics who differ from him and prefers the company of infidels to theirs . . . when the spontaneous instinct of his mind is rather that Protestants should not be converted than converted by certain Catholics who differ from him, what is he (as I have told him) but a Novatian, making a Church within a Church, or an Evangelical preacher, deciding that the Gospel is preached here, and is not preached there.[107]

Newman's position was all the more delicate at this time because those who opposed the Ultramontane line most vigorously were former students or close associates. While the historical objections they raised were valid, their style was often as pugnacious as Ward's and they sometimes repudiated every form of infallibility, which Newman never did. He objected to a sweeping application of infallibility to all the pronouncements of a Pope and to the way in which the proponents of such views anathematized everyone else as unorthodox.

A few years before the opening of the Council, Newman spoke of the infallibility of the Pope as a doctrine of the Church. As he wrote to F. C. Burnand: "Many writers, like Mr. Allies, rest the argument for Catholicity on the Pope's authority. . . . But I was not converted by it, and I never use it myself.

"What I believe about the Pope, I believe, as I believe any other doctrine—because the Church teaches it—but, for me, the Church directs me to the Pope not the Pope directs me to the Church."[108]

In 1865, when he learned that his friend Thomas Arnold was leaving the Church because of infallibility, Newman decided not to engage in discussion, but rather to express his confidence:

> Do not suppose I write these lines to trouble you with controversy, or to exact an answer—but I cannot bear to let you go from the one foundation of grace and spiritual strength, without saying a word, not of farewell, for well it cannot be so to direct your course, but to express my deep sorrowfulness at hearing

---

107. JHN to Henry Wilberforce, 21 July 1867, in *LD* 23:274.
108. JHN to F. C. Burnand, 5 November 1865, in *LD* 22:94–95.

the news. I will not believe that you have not found strength and comfort in Masses and Sacraments, and I do not think you will find the like elsewhere. Nor shall I easily be led to believe that the time will not come when you will acknowledge this yourself, and will return to the Fold which you are leaving.[109]

As the controversy on infallibility became public in the years immediately prior to the Council, more people wrote to Newman for some advice. His responses at this time became more personal; he shared his own beliefs about papal infallibility without trying to force them on anyone else; he realized that others did not share this belief. For example, he told J. Walker of Scarborough, "I have myself ever professed to hold the Pope's Infallibility as a theological opinion—but, as so holding it, of course I imply there are other opinions on the subject, and, though it would be no hard matter to me to accept it as a dogma, yet it isn't a dogma."[110] Twice within a period of five months he wrote almost identical words to Peter Le Page Renouf: "I hold the Pope's Infallibility, not as a dogma, but as a theological opinion; that is, not as a certainty, but as a probability."[111]

When Mrs. Helbert acknowledged her confusion over the issue of infallibility since so many people were saying different things, Newman began by directing her to trust in God. When she mentioned that she had been reading many of the current books and pamphlets but didn't know what to believe, Newman replied:

> I do not know the book called "England and Christendom"— and I have not read Archbishop Manning's. There are very false opinions afloat about the Catholic Church—it is thought it does not allow of private judgement, but it allows a great deal—and this is the reason you are perplexed by hearing different Catholics say different things. If you want to know what we believe, go to our standard authoritative books—if you wish to hear what individuals think, go to pamphlets, reviews, and the like. . . . When a man is perplexed by a difference between different teachers, if he cannot solve the difficulty at once, it is his duty to

---

109. JHN to Thomas Arnold, 4 June 1865, in *LD* 21:484. In 1876, Arnold became a catholic once more.

110. JHN to J. Walker of Scarborough, 15 December 1868, in *LD* 24:188.

111. JHN to Peter Le Page Renouf, 21 June 1868, in *LD* 24:92. In a second letter to Renouf on November 30, 1868, Newman stated: "I have ever held the Pope's Infallibility, that is, held it as a theological opinion, the most probable amid conflicting historical arguments." *LD* 24:180.

say "I believe what the Church holds and teaches." He cannot go wrong in that.[112]

As the time for convening the Council approached, people began to expect a definition of papal infallibility. This prospect marked another phase in his correspondence; Newman began stating more directly that while he personally had no difficulty with infallibility, he opposed a formal definition of the doctrine because he thought such a definition was unnecessary. His letters indicated five basic reasons for his view: first, there was no heresy to quiet; second, a definition would harm the Church's missionary efforts by unsettling people's minds; third, a definition would occasion greater centralization in Rome; fourth, the Church would be burdened with a great many historical objections to answer; fifth, people needed to be better prepared to understand and receive it: "We are not ripe yet for the Pope's Infallibility."[113]

At first, Newman did not really think that the Council would define the doctrine. As late as April 7, 1870, he consoled Ambrose de Lisle: "Anxious as I am, I will not believe that the Pope's Infallibility can be defined at the Council till I see it actually done. Seeing is believing. We are in God's Hands—not in the hands of men, however high—exalted. Man proposes, God disposes. When it is actually done, I will accept it as His act; but, till then, I will believe it impossible."[114]

On March 15, 1870, the *Standard* printed a private letter, which Newman had written on January 28 to Bishop Ullathorne at Rome. It was "one of the most confidential letters that I ever wrote in my life,"[115] he told Charlotte Wood. His letter was a protest at the methods of those who were campaigning to get the definition of papal infallibility on the agenda of the Council. In his letter to Ullathorne, Newman accused the Ultramontane papers of spreading fear and dismay among Catholics who "practically, not to say doctrinally, hold the Holy Father to be infallible."

> Suddenly there is thunder in a clear sky, and we are told to prepare for something, we know not what, to try our faith, we know

---

112. JHN to Mrs. Helbert, 30 August 1869, in *LD* 24:324.
113. For letters presenting his reasons for his opposition to the Definition, see: JHN to Mrs. William Froude, 21 November 1869, in *LD* 24:377–78; JHN to David Moriarty, Bishop of Kerry, 28 January 1870, in *LD* 25:16–17. JHN to Alfred Plummer, 28 February 1872, in *LD* 26:34–35; JHN to Alfred Plummer, 19 July 1872, in *LD* 26:138–39. JHN to Ambrose St. John, 21 August 1870, in *LD* 25:192. JHN to Richard Hutton, 16 February 1870, in *LD* 25:30–32. JHN to Robert Whitty, 12 April 1870, in *LD* 25:92–96.
114. JHN to Ambrose de Lisle, 7 April 1870, in *LD* 25:82.
115. JHN to Charlotte Wood, 14 April 1870, in *LD* 25:99.

not how. No impending danger is to be averted, but a great difficulty created. Is this the proper work of an Ecumenical Council? . . . When has a definition *de fide* been a luxury of devotion and not a stern painful necessity? Why should an aggressive and insolent faction be allowed to "make the heart of the just sad, whom the Lord hath not made sorrowful?"

I am continually asking myself whether I ought not to make my feelings public. . . . If it is God's will that the Pope's Infallibility is defined, then it is God's will to throw back "the times and the moments" of that triumph which He has destined for His Kingdom; and I shall feel I have but to bow my head to His adorable inscrutable Providence.[116]

Once this private letter was leaked to the press, more and more people began to write to Newman for his opinion and advice. He felt that a dogmatic declaration was being rushed through like a political measure in an emergency. "You are going too fast at Rome," he wrote to Robert Whitty,[117] who had once desired to be an Oratorian but subsequently became a Jesuit: "We do not move at railroad pace in theological matters even in the 19th century. We must be patient and that for two reasons: first, in order to get at the truth ourselves, and next in order to carry others with us.

"The Church moves as a whole: it is not a mere philosophy, it is a communion; it not only discovers but it teaches; it is bound to consult for charity, as well as for faith."[118]

By the end of April 1870, it had become clear that infallibility would be defined. Newman continued to express his opposition and to ask others to trust in God. To Francis Wackerbarth, a Cambridge man, who had become a Catholic in 1841, he said: "I will not believe that this definition about Papal Infallibility is passed, till it actually is passed. It seems to me a duty, out of devotion to the Pope and charity to the souls of men, to resist it, while resistance is possible . . .

"We can but leave the matter to God, and rest confidently in His protection of His Infallible Church and the guidance of the Holy Ghost."[119]

During the two months prior to the official definition, a new emphasis appeared in two of his letters which made the distinction between "inexpedient" and "inopportune."[120] Newman believed the impending definition

---

116. JHN to Bishop Ullathorne, 29 January 1870, in *LD* 25:18–19.
117. JHN to Robert Whitty, 12 April 1870, in *LD* 25:93.
118. Ibid., 92–93.
119. JHN to Francis Wackerbarth, 28 June 1870, in *LD* 25:153–54.
120. JHN, 27 June 1870, in *LD* 25:151, Memorandum on the Definition of Infallibility. Explaining the difference between "inexpedient" and "inopportune" he wrote:

was inexpedient, as he wrote to W. J. Daunt: "I certainly think this agitation of the Pope's Infallibility most unfortunate and ill-advised . . . there are truths which are inexpedient."[121]

After the Definition was proclaimed (July 18, 1870), there was some uncertainty about its binding force because the Council had not officially ended and the bishops had not signed the decree.[122] The Council was supposed to reconvene, but was unable to do so because of the political situation. By December, it had become clear that opposition to the decree would not continue and that the Council would not be reconvened in the immediate future. William Clifford, Bishop of Clifton, an opponent of the Definition, told Newman: "There is now no reasonable prospect of the Bishops meeting again in Council for a long time to come, the doctrine, has everywhere been openly taught without any organized stand having been made against it by the Bishops of the minority, several of whom have openly expressed their adhesion to it. . . . Even if opposition were offered by a few Bishops, this could only result in a schism. The Definition therefore must be accepted as the voice of the Church and as such, undoubtedly true."[123]

When Newman saw the wording of the definition on July 23, he was pleased at what he considered its restrictive terminology. Accordingly, when Ambrose de Lisle wrote a worried letter, Newman replied: "I saw the new Definition yesterday, and am pleased at its moderation, that is, if the doctrine in question is to be defined at all. The terms used are vague and comprehensive; and personally, I have no difficulty in admitting to it."[124] Newman saw that the eventual effect of the terminology might even be to restrict the Pope's power. "As to this particular doctrine [Papal infallibility], I am not at all sure it will increase the Pope's power—it may restrict it. Hitherto he has done what he would, because its limits were not defined—now he must act by rule," he wrote to Anna Whitty.[125] But it was not easy for an ordinary person whether Catholic or not, to understand the meaning of the

---

"inopportune

To Him who sees the end from the beginning, whatever he does is *expedient* i.e. in the long run but it may be inexpedient for *the time*.

Inopportune means 1. uncharitable

2. unecclesiastical—a false step."

121. JHN to W. J. Daunt, 27 June 1870, in *LD* 25:150.

122. Political events overtook the Council: The Franco-Prussian war broke out on July 19; Italian troops entered Rome on September 20. The Council was suspended on October 20.

123. William Clifford, Bishop of Clifton to JHN, 9 December 1870, in *LD* 25:246.

124. JHN to Ambrose de Lisle, 24 July 1870, in *LD* 25:164.

125. JHN to Anna Whitty, 9 September 1870, in *LD* 25:204.

decree, especially when Manning returned from Rome and began to pressure people to accept the new dogma (as interpreted by the Ultramontanes party). Many whose consciences were strained wrote to Newman who thus became more and more aware of the immediate effects of the definition. He consoled Lady Chatterton:

> I grieve, as much as you can, at the news from Rome, because it will pain and perplex so many good people—and I think lightly of the charity of those, who seem as if they wished to increase that pain and perplexity by exaggerated statements and words of triumph...
>
> You must not fancy that any very stringent definition has passed—on the contrary it is very mild in its tenor, and has been acted on by the Pope at least for the last 300 years. And as, he has done nothing extravagant, now also, when it is declared authoritatively, we may reasonably expect that all things will go on quietly as before. So I hope you will not make yourself unhappy, when it may be all for nothing.[126]

Newman was opposed to putting pressure on people to submit quickly to the Definition; he felt that people needed time to digest and accept it. Referring to Manning and the Ultramontanes, Newman expressed his feelings to Bishop Moriarty of Kerry:

> The definition, if we are to suppose it legitimately passed, is producing most untoward effects, as far as I have experience of it—and, when poor people ask me categorically "Is is binding?" I don't know what to say. That *"securus judicat orbis terrarum,"* ["the whole world judges with confidence"] I am sure—but time has not been given yet to ascertain this, and the very cruelty of certain people, of which I complain is, *that they will not let people have time.* They would come round quietly if you gave them time—but, when you hold a pistol to their heads and say, "Believe this doctrine, however new to you, as you believe the Holy Trinity, under pain of damnation," THEY CAN'T. Their breath is taken away—they seem to say "Give me time, give me time—" And their confessors all about the country, say "No, not an hour—believe or be damned—we want to sift the Catholic body of all half Catholics."

---

126. JHN to Lady Chatterton, 4 August 1870, in *LD* 25:172–73.

> I assure you this so pierces my heart, I do not know what to do—and I rise in indignation against such cruelty.[127]

Similarly, several weeks later when Manning's exaggerated interpretation of the doctrine disturbed Lady Simeon, Newman responded:

> God has certainly brought upon you a dreadful weight of suffering, but He will enable you to bear it, and will bless you in it and after it. The day will come when you will look back upon it, and praise Him for it, though it is so difficult to feel this before that day comes.
> ... The Archbishop only does what he has done all along—he ever has exaggerated things, and ever has acted towards individuals in a way which they felt to be unfeeling. ... Therefore, I say confidently, you may dismiss all such exaggerations from your mind.[128]

Because the issue of infallibility was so complex and emotionally charged, Newman's method of direction at this time was many-faceted, depending on the difficulty of the individual. Some he guided by sharing his own personal belief in the doctrine. To others, he simply explained a moderate interpretation of the definition, apparently with the hope that people would understand it and be more peaceful with it.

When some individuals objected that "infallibility" was a novel doctrine, unknown to the Apostolic Church, Newman responded that perhaps there were no claims to infallibility, in such words, in the early Church; nevertheless, the Church and the Pope have always acted as if they were claiming infallibility, that is, they presented their formal teaching as *irreformable* and *true*. Since earlier theologians were more interested in the *matter* settled, not the *one* settling it, the doctrine of papal infallibility was an ever present truth although it was not commented upon as such until later centuries.

During these months, Newman repeatedly urged people "not to set themselves against the doctrine," but to make an act of faith in all that the Church teaches. When Anna Whitty, who was the wife of a prominent Liverpool Catholic, wrote to Newman for advice he told her:

> Don't set yourself against the doctrine, then; don't fancy consequences which may never come to pass. I think you should do two things—first make an act of faith "in ALL that the Church

---

127. JHN to David Moriarty, Bishop of Kerry, 1 November 1870, in *LD* 25:222–23. Bracketed translation added.

128. JHN to Lady Simeon, 18 November 1870, in *LD* 25:230–31.

teaches"—and next, when doubts arise against this particular doctrine, put them away, on the ground that *perhaps* the Church teaches this doctrine, and that it is safer therefore *not* to oppose it. I say "perhaps" for considering the great number of religious Catholics who hold it, and how long it has been in the Church there is at least a considerable probability that it is true.[129]

Reflecting in 1872 on his advice about the doctrine of infallibility, Newman wrote to William Monsell: "To any one who has written to me on the subject, I have uniformly answered by advising them to accept the doctrine as an act of the Church."[130]

Finally, Newman counseled people to wait patiently and to have confidence that God was guiding the Church, and to trust that with time this dogma would be better understood and accepted within the teachings of the Church.

> I do not see there is any remedy for the painful state of suspense which I have spoken of, but what is cold comfort, viz. patient waiting. It is often the characteristic trial (in this present *state* of mind) of educated and reasoning minds, to be in doubt. If it is not their fault, they cannot help it; and even though in its origin it was, still they cannot get out of it at will, they cannot break their way out of it, but must wait God's time. He has already done a good deal for you—He will (be sure) do more. Do not disgust Him, but put yourself into His hands as a loving Father. Do not merely say "I will follow the truth," but "I will follow His guidance and will, who is the Truth"—and "I will ask His grace to enable me to do so."[131]

---

129. JHN to Anna Whitty, 31 August 1870, in *LD* 25:200-201. In an eight point letter to Mrs. Beckwith, Newman summarized his position and pastoral practice in this way:
I believe the Pope's Infallibility.
I have strongly opposed to its being defined.
Even tho' an article of faith it need not be *expedient*.
I doubt whether it is yet an article of faith.
Such confusion has been at other times.
Be calm—beware of dangerous steps.
Don't set yourself against the doctrine. Exclude doubts—make an act of faith in all teaching of the Church.
Choose a confessor who will absolve you. Go to communion.
JHN to Mrs. William Beckwith, 21 August 1870, in *LD* 25:189.

130. JHN to William Monsell, 20 January 1871, in *LD* 26:11.

131. JHN to William Gainsford, 27 August 1870, in *LD* 25:196-97.

In the years immediately following the definition, Newman often explained both what the definition said and what it did not say. By sharing his own belief in infallibility, by emphasizing the moderation of the definition, by showing how the early Church functioned as if it were infallible, Newman sought to allay the fears of many people who wrote to him for help on this controversial issue.

Simultaneously, Newman refined his own understanding of infallibility. In 1871 he began to write more about the doctrine of the Church's infallibility, which he had come to see as primarily an inference, grounded on the Church's teaching office. He told Alfred Plummer:

> I have always thought, and think still, that the infallibility of the Church is an *inference* (a necessary inference) from her prerogative that she is the divinely appointed Teacher of her children, and of the world. She cannot fulfill this office *without* divine help—that is, she never can be *permitted to go wrong* in the truths of revelation—this is a negative proposition—the very idea of infallibility is a negative. She teaches by human means, she ascertains the truth by human means—of course assisted by grace, which a Father or a divine, or an inquirer has not—but she has this security, that, in *order* to fulfill her office, her *outcome* is always true in the matter of revelation. She is not inspired—the word has sometimes been used, and in Councils especially—but, properly speaking, inspiration is positive, and infallibility is negative.[132]

Newman continued to think that the definition was inexpedient; his lingering fear was that it placed great powers into the Pope's hands and established the serious precedent that a dogma could be promulgated without special necessity. Newman hoped that God's providence would protect the Church and forestall abuses. Nonetheless, Newman predicted that there would be modifications and safeguards added in the course of time. A new Pope or new Council would provide a proper balance, would "trim the boat."[133] Accordingly, he continued to advise people to be patient. To Lady Simeon he wrote in 1871: "Other definitions are necessary, and were intended, and will be added, if we are patient, to reduce the dogma to its proper proportions and place in the Catholic system."[134]

On the whole, Newman believed that the promulgation of this Definition by the Council was an act of Divine Providence for some good purpose,

---

132. JHN to Alfred Plummer, 3 April 1871, in *LD* 25:309.
133. Ibid., 310.
134. JHN to Lady Simeon, 15 October 1871, in *LD* 25:414–15.

even if that was not clear at the moment. Thus, the duty of Catholics was one of resignation: "Divine Providence has allowed the act of last year for some good purpose, and we must submit to His will."[135]

A summary of his views at this time is found in a letter to Richard Littledale:

> Infallibility is not a *habit* in the Pope, or a state of mind—but, as the decree says, that infallibility which the Church has. The Church when in Council and proceeding by the strictest forms enunciates a definition in faith and morals, which is certainly true. The Church is infallible *then*, *when* she speaks ex cathedra—but he has no habit of infallibility in his intellect, such that his *acts cannot but* proceed from it, *must* be infallible *because* he *imply, involve,* an infallible judgment. He is infallible *pro re nata* (according to the need) *when* he speaks ex cathedra—not except at particular times and on grave questions.
>
> Nay further than this, even on those grave questions the gift is negative. It is not that he has an inspiration of truth, but he is simply guarded from error, circumscribed by a divine superintendence from transgressing, extravagating beyond, the line of truth. And his definitions do not come of a positive divine guidance, but of human means, research, consulting theologians, etc.[136]

In the aftermath of the Council, the more extreme Ultramontanes continued to interpret the dogma as extensively as possible. Manning's Pastoral Letter in 1871, for example, included almost all papal acts under the mantle of infallibility. These maximalist interpretations disturbed Newman as well as many people who wrote asking him to refute such views. Not wishing openly to challenge the Archbishop, Newman waited for the proper moment to speak out. It came in 1874 when Gladstone's *Vatican Decrees in Their Bearing on Civil Allegiance* questioned whether a post-Vatican I Catholic could remain a loyal British citizen. Newman responded in *A Letter to the Duke of Norfolk*, presenting what he saw as the real Catholic interpretation.[137] Advocating a principle of minimizing as necessary for

---

135. JHN to Sir. William Cope, 10 December 1871, in *LD* 25:447.

136. JHN to Richard Littledale, 17 September 1872, in *LD* 26:171. *Pro re nata*, which literally means "for the thing that has been born," usually means "in the particular circumstances" or "according to the specific need."

137. For letters detailing his efforts in drafting his *Letter*, see JHN to Duke of Norfolk, 22 November 1874, in *LD* 27:158–59: "It is the toughest job I ever had, and I have a great anxiety lest after all, when it is done, it should not do its work." Newman wrote Lord Emly on November 23, 1874: "For 5 or 6 weeks I have been hard at it for perhaps 5 or 6 hours a day, and have produced nothing. I have written quires, but not pleased myself and begun again. Gladstone is so rambling and slovenly, it is so difficult to follow

a wise and cautious theology, the *Letter* won many people to a moderate interpretation of the Vatican Decrees by counter-balancing Ultramontane excesses. Bishop Moriarty of Kerry, in gratitude for the *Letter to Norfolk*, wrote to Newman of the effect on the Ultramontanes: "You and Dr. Fessler have shut them up."[138]

Even after his *Letter to the Duke of Norfolk* was published early in January 1875, Newman continued to guide people concerning infallibility. Most of this correspondence consisted in explaining and clarifying for individuals what he had written in the *Letter* as well as reiterating his former beliefs concerning infallibility. As late as 1886, the subject of infallibility continued to find its way into his correspondence. James Bredin had struggled to find religious certitude and when he wrote to Newman for advice he also mentioned that he had heard that Newman was having difficulty with infallibility. In his reply Newman said:

> You describe very vividly the trials you have had in religious inquiry, which have been the experience of so many.
>
> I know but one course to recommend tho' I feel it a difficult one—to resign yourself *patiently* and *unconditionally* to Almighty God, to ask His teaching, and to persevere in waiting for it. It is a tedious, forlorn course. But I believe in its success, when pursued—but few inquiring can be found to place themselves even for a time *unreservedly* into the hands of a superior Power, and few are *constant* in such renunciation of self. As to the reports about myself which you mention, they are utterly unfounded. I never had even the temptation to disbelieve the infallibility of the Pope in matters of faith and doctrine—tho' I did not wish the doctrine to be made a dogma, *necessarily to* be believed by every Catholic. This was what the Catholic popular papers succeeded in getting defined. I believe it to be *true*, but not an article of Christian *faith. Now* I believe it as an article of faith.[139]

---

him with any logical exactness. I can't get a plan. Today I have begun on a new arrangement of matter (for matter I have more than enough) and at present I am satisfied with it—but my great fear is that in two or three days I shall see it won't do." *LD* 27:159. In January 1875, Gladstone wrote a personal response to Newman's letter. He said, "The simple and sole purpose of these lines is to thank you for the genial and gentle manner in which you have treated me and the evident unwillingness you have shown to fasten upon me censures which you not unnaturally think that I deserve." William Gladstone to JHN, 15 January 1875, in *LD* 27:192–93.

138. Joseph Fessler (1813–1872), who was Secretary General of the First Vatican Council, published an interpretation of the Council's teaching about infallibility. Fessler's book was translated into English as *True and False Infallibility of the Popes* (1875) by Ambrose St. John, a member of the Birmingham Oratory.

139. JHN to James Bredin, 10 May 1886, in *LD* 31:137–38.

Much of Newman's direction of others in relation to infallibility involved two dimensions. On the one hand, education played a large role—explaining to various inquirers what exactly was contained in the definition; what it meant and what it did not mean. Second, since many of the letters on this issue came from people who were fearful for the Church or their own belief, Newman's role became one of allaying fears; his advice was to be patient and to have confidence that God was involved in the whole process. As he wrote to Henry Coleridge in 1869: "There is One that is wiser than we are, and has His times and seasons for all things. All of us may securely leave it to Him, to provide against any danger to the Church from her servants as well as her adversaries.

". . . Of course God will, as I have said, provide. Men cannot, not even the Pope, go further than He wills. He has laid down marks from the beginning, which no one can pass."[140]

Two factors were operative in his view of Providence in reference to the Church and infallibility. The first, and more important, was his absolute conviction that the Church is divine and that God will never abandon it. The second factor is a variation of the idea of a "broad truth withstanding small objections." The broad truth, in this case, was the Church under the *enduring* guidance of God, and the small objections were the momentary setbacks the Church suffers. The Definition of 1870, at first seemed like a dreary setback viewed in itself, but if viewed in the context of the past eighteen centuries and of the centuries to come, it was but momentary. Newman had a keen sense of the Church's continual development; growth is not always smooth nor painless. Consequently, his advice to troubled inquirers was to remain patient and trust in Providence.

Sacraments

Newman's personal spiritual life was intimately sacramental; his understanding of the role of the sacraments was closely connected with his understanding of the Church. Because most of his inquirers were Anglicans who asked specific questions about a particular sacrament, his direction of others in this area of the Church's life took the form of education or of clarification concerning specific issues and questions. Accordingly, some sacraments received much more attention than others and he did not treat every aspect of the sacraments.

---

140. JHN to Henry Coleridge, 29 April 1869, in *LD* 24:247.

While Newman pointed out that the sacraments are symbols, as means of grace they are more than symbols.[141] George Edwards wrote to Newman about Caroline Fox, a Quaker who did not understand what Catholics believed about the sacraments. Newman responded: "Her only idea of what we hold about the Sacraments is that they are 'symbols'! Of course, they are symbols . . . but, if we hold them to be nothing more than symbols, we should be like the Jews or Galatians. We believe our Sacraments to be *means of grace*, as well as symbols."[142]

In a letter explaining to Henry Bittleston the importance of the sacraments in the Christian life, Newman pointed out that: "The grace given in a sacrament is two fold—first habitual grace, by which the soul is sanctified and united with God and lives, and secondly the grace just alluded to or the sacramental grace (grace of the sacrament), which is that which is denoted under the outward sign. . . . Hence the matter and form are all that are intrinsically required for the constitution or *confection* [of] a Sacrament, it produces its effect, that is, it confers grace ex opere operato; i.e. by its own vis [power] without depending on the recipient."[143]

Newman hastened to add, however, that the efficacy of a sacrament depends on the dispositions of the recipient: "More or less grace is given, or more effectually given according to the disposition of the recipient.[144]

Since the Eucharist was Newman's major source of strength and consolation, not surprisingly, the sacrament most frequently mentioned by him in his correspondence was the Eucharist. Although he believed as an Anglican in the presence of Christ during the celebration of the Eucharist, he did not believe the doctrine of Transubstantiation until he was a Catholic.[145] After his conversion, much of his correspondence concerning the Eucharist

---

141. In a postscript to Henry Bittleston in a letter on June 29, 1857, Newman described a sacrament. "1. Sacrament, (Lat. Sacramentum etc.) is the received name for the seven special sacred rites of the Catholic Church; . . . 3. Sacraments are distinguished from all other rites, as being both signs and means of grace, instituted by our Lord Himself, whether immediately or through his Apostles. By their being *means* of grace, is meant that they are instruments, through or together with which supernatural grace is given to the recipient; and by their being *signs*, that the visible rite is symbolical (or analogous) of the particular kind or virtue of the grace given." *LD* 18:65.

142. JHN to George Edwards, 8 November 1882, in *LD* 30:146.

143. JHN to Henry Bittleston, 29 June 1857, in *LD* 18:65–66.

144. Ibid.

145. Newman, *Apologia*, 239. "I had no difficulty in believing it, as soon as I believed that the Catholic Roman Church was the oracle of God, and that she had declared this doctrine to be part of the original revelation." In a letter to Henry Wilberforce, dated January 27, 1846, Newman wrote: "And when I was at the early Eucharistic Service at St. Mary's (I thus specify it, because I am appealing to my memory distinctly) I had an absolute and overpowering sense of the Real Presence." *LD* 11:101.

was devoted to explaining Roman Catholic teaching to Anglicans. Newman habitually spent much time in prayer before the tabernacle. During his first year as a Catholic, he shared his devotion to the Real Presence with Henry Wilberforce: "I am writing next room to the chapel—It is such an incomprehensible blessing to have Christ in bodily presence in one's house, within one's walls, as swallows up all other privileges and destroys, or should destroy, every pain. To know that He is close by—to be able again and again through the day to go in to Him; and be sure, My dearest W., when I am thus in His Presence you are not forgotten. It is *the* place for intercession surely, where the Blessed Sacrament is."[146] Twenty years later, in a letter written to Lady Chatterton on Holy Thursday 1866, Newman indicated the importance which eucharistic devotion continued to play in his spiritual life.

> Why, what exercise of devotion is there which equals that of going before the Blessed Sacrament, before our Lord Jesus really present, though unseen? To kneel before Him, to put oneself into His hands, to ask His grace, and to rejoice in the hope of seeing Him in heaven! In the Catholic Church alone is the great gift to be found. You may go the length and breadth of England, and see beautiful prospects enough such as you speak of, the work of the God of nature, but there is no benediction from earth or sky which falls upon us like that which comes to us from the Blessed Sacrament, which is Himself.[147]

Similarly, Newman often advised others to take their problems and troubles to the Lord present in the Eucharist—to find in Him their strength and consolation. After Helen Douglas Forbes, a recent convert, wrote complaining of difficulties she was encountering, Newman replied:

> Pray do not think I do not enter into that solitariness, of which you complain—and of the strange and (so to say) foreign appearance which the Church presents to you. Others have felt this before you, but, O my dear Madam, why do you not speak of the Blessed Sacrament? why have you not found your comfort there? why, in all your troubles, have you not sought His Presence, who is your God before all, and, kneeling before Him, asked Him to be your light and treasure and great reward? I have said, "why have you not" and perhaps you will tell me that you have—but if so, how is it that you mention your solitariness,

---

146. JHN to Henry Wilberforce, 26 February 1846, in *LD* 11:129.
147. JHN to Lady Chatterton, Holy Thursday 1866, in *LD* 22:194.

without speaking of him with whom you are not solitary, who is the stay and delight and Pearl of price to the solitary?[148]

In 1870 Newman wrote to Mrs. Wilson who was experiencing difficulties about the pending definition of Papal Infallibility:

> To myself, with many others, it is the Presence of our Lord in the Blessed Sacrament which is the relief and consolation for all the troubles of ecclesiastical affairs. I wish you could make that your own consolation. What can I do better than call on you to go to Him who is your life and your Strength?—who can do everything for you—who loves you and who desires your love. What can harm you, if you place your hopes, wishes, doubts, difficulties into His hands; if you put your thoughts into His keeping, and beg Him to conform your heart to His heart, and your will to His will. He will make allowances for you, which no man can make—and can give you strength, illumination, and peace, which the world cannot give.
>
> It is but rational in you to put away your doubts, and to trust Him unreservedly.[149]

Newman felt comfortable sharing this part of his spiritual life with others as a way of encouraging and directing them. Reflecting on his own struggles with Church officials, he responded to Lady Simeon who was also struggling to accept the recent definitions of Papal Infallibility.

> For years past my only consolation personally has been in our Lord's Presence in the Tabernacle. I turn from the sternness of external authority to Him who can immeasurably compensate trials which after all are not real, but (to use a fashionable word) sentimental. Never, thank God, have I had a single doubt about the divine origin and grace of the Church, on account of the want of tenderness and largeness of mind of some of its officials or rulers. And I think this will be your experience too. Bear up for a while and all will be right. What you tell me that you have ever held about the Pope's Infallibility is, I am sure, enough now.[150]

---

148. JHN to Helen Forbes, 4 October 1864, in *LD* 21:249.
149. JHN to Mrs. Wilson, 3 July 1870, in *LD* 25:156–57.
150. JHN to Lady Simeon, 18 November 1870, in *LD* 25:231.

Eschatology

Questions from inquirers concerning eternity and salvation provided Newman with another opportunity to direct people according to the Church's teaching. For example, although certainly not the most popular doctrine, Newman stated that personally he had held the doctrine of Eternal Punishment "ever since I was a boy."[151] Moreover, he felt that it was important to preach about eternal punishment in order to be faithful to the complete Christian message. As a Cardinal he wrote in 1879: "I am engaged to preach, not to the world, but to Christians. . . . If so, I must not 'spare to declare to my people the whole counsel of God.' I presuppose faith, I am at eliciting repentance. Is not the doctrine of eternal punishment one of the *most prominent* in Scripture? Am I not giving a most defective view of the motives of repentance, and the attributes of God, if I leave it out?"[152]

Newman felt that this doctrine was not only an important part of Revelation, but also a powerful incentive to grow in the Christian life.

> What's the good of my striving so hard to keep from sin and temptation, if I am not safe when I die, and if my neighbour, who gives himself to the world, the flesh and the devil, and so dies, may, for aught I know, after this life, get to heaven, and I fail of it. . . . It is hard enough to bear the view as at present, of virtue suffering and evil triumphant. Would it not be a second trial, quite as great, nay greater because unexpected, to have to believe that, this weary life passed, the end does not come after all? Such a teaching I have called cruel, unsettling as it is both to faith and hope.[153]

Newman realized many people found this doctrine difficult to accept, even a test of their faith. How could an all loving God permit a person to be eternally lost?

> What is meant by having faith, if you are to have nothing to try it? What does try, what do we feel difficult to accept, but doctrines like this—which do not merely imply miracles . . . but which seem contrarieties in God Himself?
>
> I grant that this doctrine seems to us inconsistent with His infinite love—but we cannot understand any of the divine attributes in their infinitude from the nature of the case—they run into mysteries—they seem to contradict each other. We cannot combine them. We understand enough of them to have ground

---

151. JHN to J. W. Capes, 10 August 1858, in *LD* 18:437.
152. JHN to Henry Bellairs, 27 November 1879, in *LD* 29:205.
153. JHN to Edward Plumptre, 9 August 1871, in *LD* 25:377.

John Henry Newman

for faith, hope, and love towards Him—and we must leave the difficulties which they involve when carried out to their perfection to be solved for us by Himself in a higher state of being.[154]

Because eternal punishment is a difficult doctrine to understand and accept, Newman spent a good deal of time trying to explain the Church's teaching and, perhaps more importantly, what the Church did not teach. He tried to alleviate people's fears; he told Pusey, he was "very eager to soften the difficulty."[155] The crux of the difficulty centered on the meaning of the word "eternity." Since the Church had not spoken conclusively on this topic, Newman felt that many questions remain unanswered.

> Then again, I should say we do not know what is meant by eternity of punishment, except as a negative idea—the lost *never* will see God—but how eternity increases the punishment we do not know. "Torture" need not be everlasting. You recollect the story of the monk and the bird. In the sweetness of the song he lost his sense of time. We do not know that the lost will not lose their sense of time. A million of years may be as one minute. This is no removal of the punishment, for the great punishment is the negative fact, that they never, never will see the face of God. What the positive infliction may be is another thing altogether. Then again, it must be recollected that great divines allow that the punishment may be diminished, as eternity proceeds. Lastly I should say that we have no proper notion while we are here of the malignity of sin, or what may be necessary for setting it right in the eternal kingdom of God.[156]

Similarly, searching for the "positive" element in the word eternity, he honestly stated:

> I am not aware that the word "eternity" has ever been authoritatively explained.
>
> We do not know what positive idea is denoted by the word "eternity," or how far eternity increases the sufferings of the lost. Here on earth duration often shortens the perception or realization of suffering to those who suffer.
>
> Indeed eternity to us is but a word; except in its negative sense; what we can and do understand is the enunciation that the lost *never* go to heaven.

---

154. JHN to Unknown Correspondent, 3 July 1867, in *LD* 23:261.
155. JHN to E. B. Pusey, 26 February 1871, in *LD* 25:292.
156. JHN to Lady Chatterton, 13 June 1873, in *LD* 26:325–26.

> Nor does such a view of the future state explain away the blessedness of "eternal life—" for the blessedness of heaven does not consist strictly in its never ending, but in the sight and fruition of Almighty God, and the certainty and absolute security and peace which the fruition involves.[157]

Newman also helped individuals probe the meaning of "time" and "suffering" in eternity. Several years after his entry into the Catholic Church, J. M. Capes wrote concerning his struggles with this teaching. Newman replied:

> Another consideration is our utter ignorance of what is meant by eternity—it is not infinite time. Time implies a process—it involves the connection and action of one portion upon another—if eternity be an eternal *now*, eternal punishment is the fact that a person is in suffering;—he suffers today and tomorrow and so on for ever—but not in a *continuation*—all is complete in every time—there is no memory, no anticipation, no growth of intensity from succession. I will not say I am right in so considering it, for I have not consulted divines, (and certainly popular views, sermons etc are against me, for in them the growth of pain from succession is expressly insisted on) but if I *be* right, then the question is merely should a soul suffer, should sin be punished, which few will deny.[158]

Elaborating on this same point twenty-two years later in a letter to Pusey, Newman noted:

> As to your question about the *poena sensus* in *inferno*, (sensible pain in hell) I am quite unable to answer it. I am not aware that anything is defined about it, except such vague words as occur in the Athanasian Creed etc. . . . For myself, I do not think that eternal suffering, as such, implies *succession* of ideas, or memory of the past suffering—and, as in the story of the Monk and the bird, the Monk was in ecstasy for 300 years, not being conscious, of any lapse of time. I do not see that continuous pain need involve a consciousness of succession. And it must be a separate revelation, over and above the revelation of "eternal" punishment, if this is so. We do not know what eternity is *positively*, only negatively, that it is that which has *no ending*. That awful idea that the lost are ever asking, "What is o'clock?" shows us

---

157. JHN to Unknown Correspondent, 5 September 1873, in *LD* 26:360–61.
158. JHN to J. M. Capes, 2 December 1849, in *LD* 13:318–19.

that succession implies a *measure of time*—and where there is no sun or moon, there need be no counting.[159]

Moreover, because the Church had not defined the exact nature or meaning of the punishment involved in eternity, Newman speculated on his own interpretation:

> The Catholic Church has not forbidden us to hope, that the punishment of the lost may *diminish* as time (or, if one can so speak, as eternity) proceeds; nor that there may be respites and intervals in it. And again, (though I do not know whether the point has been directly discussed,) how far the sense of *continuance* in suffering, and what measure of *consciousness* of suffering, attaches to the lost, taken one by one, are to me as points still to be determined—and I have no light to determine them;—but these surely are all-important questions in considering the difficulty of the doctrine.[160]

Part of Newman's development of eschatology centered on the meaning of indulgences in relation to temporal punishment. His most complete treatment of indulgences is contained in a response to J. L. Walton: "Having had an argument with a friend, one of the points he brought forward against the Church of Rome, was that she issued 'Indulgences' which he explained as representing to give permission to a man to live with a certain degree of laxity; to allow him to commit a certain number of sins, or rather, to recognize at the 'Confession' certain sins as righteous and just."[161] Newman then explained:

> Indulgences have in principle ever been in the Church of God, though they have had greater efficacy and breadth, since our Lord made atonement for all sin. It is a doctrine which even Protestants admit, that, even when God forgives sin and reconciles the sinner to Himself, He not unfrequently assigns some punishment for what is past. Thus a drunkard may reform and his sins be washed away and he may live and die in the grace of God, yet he may suffer much from disease which is the direct *consequence* of his intemperance, or, what Catholics call, his "temporal *penance*" paena, or punishment.
>
> We differ from Protestants in this, that such temporal penances is [sic] God's *rule*, that it is a great *law*, that punishment follows sin; we differ from Protestants also in considering that,

---

159. JHN to E. B. Pusey, 26 February 1871, in *LD* 25:292–93.
160. JHN to Unknown Correspondent, 3 July 1867, in *LD* 23:261.
161. JHN to J. L. Walton, 9 September 1880, in *LD* 29:298n4.

if not undergone by the repentant sinner in this life, he will have the prospect of it *after* this life, that is, before he is admitted into heaven. As we call it "penance" when undergone by the repentant, reconciled sinner, when undergone in this life, so we call it "purgatory," when undergone after this life.

Penance and purgatory are names for the "temporal" punishment of sin, of *forgiven* sin; "temporal" meaning that punishment which *comes to an end*, and is not eternal.

Penance and Purgatory are the punishment of *forgiven* sinners, *not of unrepentant.*

As all have sinned, all have the prospect of punishment, and the more the repentant sinner suffers here, the less he may trust will be his suffering in purgatory.

The Church has the power of opening another and more certain way, of shortening the suffering in purgatory; she can assign particular works, prayers, etc etc on the performance of which Almighty God shortens that period of suffering which otherwise the repentant sinner would undergo in purgatory. This grant is called an "indulgence."

An indulgence cannot be gained by a man living in sin—nor is it a pardon of *sin*—but it is a remission of *punishment*, for the repentant sinner, whose sins have already been forgiven.[162]

After this explanation, Newman addressed Walton's concerns.

I don't see how such a doctrine can be "giving permission to a man to live with a certain degree of laxity" as you say—on the other hand, to tell him that, though he repents and is forgiven and becomes a child of God, and has a good hope of heaven, still every one of his sins cries for punishment against him, and the less he suffers here, the more he may expect (though he be one of God's elect) to suffer in purgatory, does not seem to me to encourage sin. Nor surely does it encourage sin, to tell him, if he will do certain specified good works, give alms, say certain prayers, etc, he has the prospect of escaping this suffering, which his sins demand.

As to an indulgence "allowing a man to commit a certain (number) of sins, or rather, to recognize at the Confession certain sins as righteous and just," I must ask you to excuse my saying that I cannot understand your words.[163]

In another letter, Newman explained to Dr. Moore that

---

162. Ibid.
163. JHN to J. H. Walton, 9 September 1880, in *LD* 29:299.

pain is not the essential attribute of Purgatory, but imprisonment; the pain, as a general accompaniment of imprisonment, enters into our received teaching, after the way of the early Fathers, Cyprian, Origen, Hilary, Basil, etc. who speak of fire.

That it should *primarily* be a place of punishment can hardly be a difficulty to you, considering that in so many cases, in most cases, of the souls who enter it, it is a substitution of temporal punishment for eternal.

The only point which you would be disposed to contest, is its being a place of painful penance for all who go to it; but this is not held by us *de fide*.

It is the teaching of various Saints that, even those whose first experience of Purgatory is that of a painful penance, and their abode there with a state of calm enjoyment, having that refrigerium (refreshment) and requies (rest), which in our prayers we daily ask for them.[164]

Other aspects of the Church's teaching on purgatory are less formidable. As Newman explained to A. J. Hammer, one of the great advantages to belonging to the Roman Catholic Church is that after death, the whole body of the Church intercedes for the deceased person. "Moreover supposing they are in Purgatory, yet its pains will be shortened and lessened in an indefinitely great measure to those who die in the Church—from the communion of the merits of the Saints, the whole body of the Church exhausts together the temporal punishment, which belongs to it. . . . A Catholic is one of a company, and has a benefit when he dies, which those who do not belong to it have not."[165]

Newman personally held that some persons experience their purgatory in this life; he wrote these encouraging words to his lifelong friend Miss Giberne: "You are, I know, in our Lord's loving hands. You have given yourself to a life of great penance for His sake, and He will not, does not forget it 'When thou shalt pass through the waters, He will be with thee, and when thou shalt walk in the fire, thou shalt not be burnt' for you are one of those who have taken your purgatory in this life, and I rejoice to think that, when God takes you hence, I shall have one to plead for me in heaven."[166]

Ultimately, what can be known about the afterlife is a matter of faith, as he wrote to J. H. Nevins in 1872: "It is difficult to speak on this subject, for the Church has said little—and one has little guide beyond one's own private judgement. The great truth is that death ends our probation, and settles our

---

164. JHN to Dr. Moore, 16 June 1878, in *LD* 28:369.

165. JHN to A. J. Hammer, 16 January 1850, in *LD* 13:388.

166. JHN to Miss M.R. Giberne, 19 December 1884, in *LD* 30:444–45.

state for ever; but there is no passing over the great gulf; that our only happiness is to be with God, and that those who are not with God are without Him."[167] Despite the difficulty in understanding this teaching, Newman still directed people to make an act of faith in the One who revealed it. "I say all this to alleviate, if possible, the awfulness of the doctrine in question; but after all our Lord surely states it in such explicit language, that, difficult or not as it may be to reconcile the mind to it, it is a simple duty to make an act of faith in His words, though it must all through this life be a hard saying to us. Why should we not trust in Him? Shall not the judge of all the earth do right?"[168]

Devotional Life and Practices

Another important area in which Newman directed others was in devotional practices. Personally, he valued devotional exercises as a means of keeping the soul firm in its belief in a personal God. After his conversion, he initially had difficulty in assimilating various Catholic devotions into his own life: "What I did realize was the strangeness of way, habits, religious observance, to which, however, I was urged on to conform without any delicacy towards my feelings."[169] That same year, in a letter to Lady Chatterton, he expressed his difficulty as an Englishman in accepting what he called "Romaic religion": "As an Englishman I do not like a Romaic religion—and I have much to say, not (God forbid) against the Roman Catholic, but against the Romaic Catholic Church. I have no great sympathy with Italian religion, as such—but I do not account myself the worse Catholic for this."[170]

Later, he had the opportunity of directing another recent convert who was experiencing similar difficulties. "The greatest trial a Convert has to sustain, and to women it is often greater than to men, is the strangeness at first sight of every thing in the Catholic Church. . . . Every nation, every body of people, has its own ways—Catholics have their own ways—we may not at first like them—and the question is where is religious *Truth*, where is salvation?—not is this habit, this fashion pleasant to me or not."[171]

---

167. JHN to J. H. Nevins, 4 June 1872, in *LD* 26:105. This letter also contains a good summary of Newman's eschatological teaching in summary form without any elaboration.

168. JHN to Unknown Correspondent, 5 September 1873, in *LD* 26:361.

169. Newman, *Autobiographical Writings*, 255, in his notes on the St. Eusebio Retreat.

170. JHN to Lady Chatterton, 16 June 1863, in *LD* 20:471.

171. JHN to Miss Ellen Fox, 25 January 1868, in *LD* 24:41.

In reading his correspondence, a pattern emerges in the way that Newman directed others in devotional practices. First, he offered an explanation for a particular devotion; second, he shared his own devotional life as a way of encouraging others, but he never "forced" other persons to pattern their devotional lives on his. For example, valuing indulgences himself, he sent a little book of indulgences to Mrs. Bowden with a letter of explanation:

> Indulgences are not very easy to obtain, though at first sight they seem to be so, and their *precise* benefit is not known, or at least defined. The best notion of them, I think, is that the Church wishing to encourage general habits of devotion, etc. among her children, attaches particular rewards to certain actions, and that they do those actions in order to get these rewards, being sure that they are rewards, but without a distinct notion how much they are, or whether they certainly have gained them. Of course a plenary indulgence conveys a very distinct notion, but many indulgences are not plenary.[172]

Newman believed that although doctrines never change, there should be a great deal of personal flexibility in devotions. As he wrote to Mrs. William Froude:

> There is a marked contrast in Catholicity between the views presented to us by doctrine and devotion respectively. Doctrines never change, devotions vary with each individual. Catholics allow each other, accordingly, the greatest license, and are, if I may so speak, utter liberals as regards devotions, whereas they are most sensitive about doctrine. That Mary is the Mother of God is a point of faith—that Mary is to be honored and exalted in this or that way is a point of devotion. The latter is the consequence, indeed, of the former, but a consequence which follows with various intensity, in various degrees and in various modes, in various minds.[173]

This attitude was reflected in the advice he gave to Lady Chatterton in 1863: "While private judgement is forbidden to Catholics in matters of divine revelation, it is fully accorded to them in matters of devotion."[174]

Of greater doctrinal significance was Newman's devotion to the Saints, and in particular to Mary. Extolling the witness value of the saints to the truth of the Catholic Church (as distinguished from the Anglican Church),

---

172. JHN to Mrs. John W. Bowden, 7 March 1864, in *LD* 12:59.
173. JHN to Mrs. William Froude, 2 January 1855, in *LD* 16:341.
174. JHN to Lady Chatterton, 16 June 1863, in *LD* 20:471.

he wrote to Catherine Ward on September 25, 1848: "There is another reason why the Anglican Church cannot take support from the high religious excellence of *individuals* who are found in her. It is that the *direction* of their holy feelings, views, and works is, not *towards* that Church, but *away from it*, and bears testimony, consequently, not to it, but against it; whereas the whole company of Catholic Saints, not only are indefinitely higher in sanctity than the best Anglicans, but are the natural fulfillment of the idea, the due exemplification of the teaching, of the Catholic Church."[175]

Newman emphasized the value of spiritual reading and encouraged people to read the lives of the Saints, who, he felt, reflected the power and grace of God. In a draft of a preface for Faber's *Lives of the Saints*, probably written in the autumn of 1848, Newman underscored the value of the witness given by the Saints:

> The Saints are the glad and complete specimens of the new creation which our Lord brought into the moral world, and as "the heavens declare the glory of God" as Creator, so are the Saints the proper and true evidence of the God of Christianity, and tell out into all lands the power and grace of Him who made Him. What the existence of the Church itself is to the learned and philosophical, such are the Saints to the multitude. They are the popular evidence of Christianity, and the most complete and logical evidence while the most popular . . . in the life of a Saint, we have a microcosm, or whole work of God, a perfect work from beginning to end, yet one which may be bound between two boards, and mastered by the most unlearned. The exhibition of a person, his thoughts, his words, his acts, his trials, his fortunes, his beginnings, his growth, his end, have a charm to every one, and when he is a Saint they have a divine influence and persuasion a power of exercising and eliciting the latent elements of divine grace in individual readers, as no other reading can claim. We consider that the Lives of the Saints are one of the main and special instruments, to which, under God, we may look for the conversion of our countrymen at this time.[176]

However, Newman believed that a person should not blindly read just any life of a saint, but rather be very discriminating in one's choice:

> Where the recorded actions of saints strictly agree with the precepts and counsels of the Gospel, and those of the inspired apostles of Christ, they are then of wonderful force and efficacy

---

175. JHN to Catherine Ward, 25 September 1848, in *LD* 12:273.
176. JHN, Autumn 1848, in *LD* 12:399–400, appendix 5.

in stirring up a hearty desire of embracing a holy life, and of obtaining a heavenly reward. They are then the useful and practical pattern of true sanctity. Where they are otherwise—when they utterly oppose themselves to the natural end and being of man—they are worthy neither of admiration nor imitation, and had far better be consigned to respectful oblivion. They provoke cavil. They give wrong impressions of what true piety really consists in. They reduce religion to an unmeaning course of puerilities. They induce the young enthusiast in religion, and *especially neophytes*, to plunge into austerities and mortifications and practices of devotion, which not only seriously injure their health, but act with perilous effect on their mental powers.[177]

Newman emphasized that the saints belong in a unique way to the family of God and encouraged people to capitalize on their intercessory value: "The intercession of the Blessed Virgin and the saints does not differ from ours for each other, except that it is more perfect than ours, and comes from those whose holy lives have given them a covenanted claim on God's special notice and indulgence."[178] A year later, in 1865, he wrote about the communion of saints in a letter to Edward Berdoe:

> We believe in a family of God, of which the Saints are the heavenly members and we the earthly—yet one family embracing earth and heaven. We believe we have access to the heavenly members, and are at liberty to converse with them—and that we can ask them for benefits and they can gain them for us. We believe at the same time that they are so different from us, and so much above us, that our natural feelings towards them would be awe, fear, and dismay, such as we should have on seeing a ghost, or as Daniel's when he fell down and quaked at the vision of the Angel—these feelings being changed into loving admiration and familiar devotion, by our belief in the communion of saints. Moreover, we believe them present with us as truly as our fellowmen are present.[179]

In his devotion to the saints, Newman gave central place to Mary. His devotion to Mary began as an Anglican; as Newman stated in his *Apologia*: "I had a true devotion to the Blessed Virgin, in whose College I lived, whose Altar I served, and whose Immaculate Purity I had in one of my earliest

---

177. Ibid., 402, appendix 6.
178. JHN to John Perrin, 9 September 1864, in *LD* 15:224.
179. JHn to Edward Berdoe, 2 October 1865, in *LD* 22:64.

sermons made much of."[180] This sermon, preached on the Feast of the Annunciation in 1832, spoke of our Lady's holiness in a way that led people to accuse him of holding the doctrine of the Immaculate Conception.[181]

As an Anglican, Newman possessed a special love for Mary, yet he sought to remain faithful to the twenty-second of the Thirty-Nine Articles

180. Newman, *Apologia*, 239–40, 165.

181. Newman, Sermon 12, in *Parochial and Plain Sermons*, 2:128, 131–32, 135–37; March 25, 1832. As a Roman Catholic, Newman wrote many letters concerning the dogma of the Immaculate Conception, promulgated in 1854. He felt that this belief exemplified his theory of the development of doctrine, and wrote many people on its meaning, origins, and interpretation. See the following letters relating to the Immaculate Conception:
JHN to W. G. Ward, 11 March 1849, in *LD* 13:81–83;
JHN to Mrs. J. W. Bowden, 13 March 1849, in *LD* 13:84–85;
JHN to Bishop Ullathorne, 5 November 1849, in *LD* 13:284;
JHN to Robert Wilberforce, 3 April 1850, in *LD* 13:456;
JHN to J. D. Dalgairns, 8 December 1850, in *LD* 14:161–62;
JHN to J. M. Capes, 28 December 1853, in *LD* 15:513.

On February 2, 1849, Pius IX issued his encyclical *Ubi Primum*, asking the views of the bishops and their people as to the question of defining the doctrine of the Immaculate Conception. Newman felt that the proposed definition was in line with his doctrine of development. See JHN to W. G. Ward, 11 March 1849, in *LD* 13:81n2, 83n3.

The following letters were written after the definition:
JHN to Bishop Ullathorne, 19 October 1854, in *LD* 16:280–81;
JHN to John Flanagan, 13 December 1854, in *LD* 16:317–18;
JHN to Archbishop Cullen, 8 December 1854, in *LD* 16:319;
JHN to F. W. Faber, 30 December 1854, in *LD* 16:338–39;
JHN to A. Lisle Phillips, 3 April 1855, in *LD* 16:435;
JHN to Richard Stanton, 15 August 1855, in *LD* 16:526–27;
JHN to Arthur Alleyne, 30 May 1860, in *LD* 19:346–47;
JHN to Arthur Alleyne, 8 June 1860, in *LD* 19:358–59;
JHN to Arthur Alleyne, 15 June 1860, in *LD* 19:361–70;
JHN to William Wilberforce, 9 December 1860, in *LD* 19:437–38;
JHN to Lady Chatterton, 2 October 1865, in *LD* 22:65–67;
JHN to E. B. Pusey, 3 November 1865, in *LD* 22:93;
JHN to James Hope-Scott, 26 November 1865, in *LD* 22:112–13;
JHN to E. B. Pusey, 19 January 1866, in *LD* 22:133;
JHN to Bishop Ullathorne, 13 February 1866, in *LD* 22:154–55;
JHN to Robert Jenkins, 19 February 1866, in *LD* 22:160–61;
JHN to Sister Mary Imelda Poole, 2 April 1866, in *LD* 22:200;
JHN to M. J. Rhodes, 25 April 1866, in *LD* 22:224–25;
JHN to E. B. Pusey, 31 May 1866, in *LD* 22:243;
JHN to E. B. Pusey, 9 June 1869, in *LD* 24:267;
JHN to E. B. Pusey, 4 July 1869, in *LD* 24:282–84;
JHN to Mrs. Helbert, 10 September 1869, in *LD* 24:328–31;
JHN to Mrs. Helbert, 28 September 1869, in *LD* 24:337–40;

In one letter, Newman explicitly wrote in favor of the Assumption. See JHN to Robert Jenkins, 11 January 1879, in *LD* 29:6.

which maintained that invocation of the saints was against the Scripture teaching of Christ as the sole Mediator. As he explained in a letter to Mrs. George Ryder in 1848, his objections, as an Anglican, against devotions to Mary were twofold: first, it seemed to be absent from the writings of the Fathers, and second, it interfered with the supreme worship of God. "Both," he said, "I have considered, and removed (as I think) in my Essay on Development."[182]

> Newman understood devotion to our Lady as a gift of God. He wrote to the Marquise de Salvo in 1848: "You know perfectly well that devotion to the Most Blessed Mother of God is not imperatively required of all. It is a gift which God gives to those whom He will. I do not see therefore that a person ought to force himself into the use of particular manuals or exercises which do not come natural to him."[183]

As in the case of devotion to the saints, Newman applied the same principles to devotion to our Lady, namely, it should be based on solid doctrine and suitability; people are free to choose those doctrinally authentic devotions best suited for them. In response to a letter from Arthur Alleyne, he commented on the relationship between doctrine and devotion in relation to Mary.

> No one pretends that devotion to the Blessed Virgin is necessary in the sense in which devotion to our Lord is necessary. Devotion to our Lord as God is necessary for salvation; devotion to the Blessed Virgin is not necessary for salvation. It may be dispensed with in *toto* as far as salvation is concerned. In the early Church, if we let history be the measure of fact, many were saved without devotion to her. The *devotion* to her has gradually and slowly extended through the Church; the *doctrine* about her being always the same from the first. But the *gradual* growth of the devotion was a cause why that doctrine, in spite of its having been from the first, should have been but slowly recognized, slowly defined.[184]

Realizing that extravagances occur, Newman emphasized the importance of the guidance of the Church. He counseled Robert Forsaith: "You will see by the pamphlet I sent you that there are extravagances in the devotions practiced by some Catholics to the Blessed Virgin—nay, for what I know, by many—for a popular religion left to itself always runs

---

182. JHN to Mrs. George Ryder, 28 March 1848, in *LD* 12:194–95.
183. JHN to Marquise de Salvo, 11 June 1848, in *LD* 12:217.
184. JHN to Arthur Alleyne, 15 June 1860, in *LD* 19:364.

into excesses and superstitions, and requires the guidance of authority to preserve it inviolate."[185] Simultaneously, Newman encouraged individuals to cultivate more than a minimal devotion to Mary. Several years after his conversion, he advised Catherine Ward: "The de fide doctrine keeps us in the Church, but we are saved by something more than what is just necessary, as by works, so by thoughts, so by devotions. I conceive it is not *safe* to take the least possible sufficient in *itself* for salvation. We should *wish* at least to hold all that is received, though not de fide; devotion to the Blessed Virgin is *the* ordinary way to heaven, and the absence of it is at least a bad symptom of the *state* of our faith."[186]

When some people wrote that devotion to Mary would detract from devotion to her Son, Newman quickly disagreed. In a response to Lady Chatterton he explained:

> And so far from the teaching of the Church concerning the Blessed Virgin being a burden, it seems to me the greatest of privileges and honours to be admitted into the very family of God. So we think on earth, when great people ask us into their most intimate circle. This it is, and nothing short of it, to be allowed to hold intercourse with Mary and Joseph; and, so far from its hindering our communion with our Lord, and our faith in Him, it is all that we should have had without it, and so much more over and over. As He comes near us in His Sacrament of love, so does He bring us near to Him by giving us an introduction (as I may say) to His Mother. In speaking to her, we are honouring Him; as He likes to be petitioned by His chosen ones, so does He especially love the petitions which she offers Him; and in asking her to intercede for us, we are pleasing both her and Him.[187]

With regard to particular devotions, the one most frequently mentioned by Newman in his correspondence was the Rosary. Trying to help George Ryder, a recent convert, grow in his spiritual life through praying the Rosary, Newman counseled:

> I certainly think you *should* get into the Catholic way of devotion by degrees. Perhaps you would feel the Rosary less trying *said with others*. Certainly it would be better if you fixed a *time* for saying it, and kept to it. *How* do you say it? Try it thus, if you don't so use it at present, but perhaps you do;—viz before each mystery, set before you a picture of it, and fix your mind upon

---

185. JHN to Robert Forsaith, 25 December 1876, in *LD* 28:149.
186. JHN to Catherine Ward, 18 November 1848, in *LD* 12:333.
187. JHN to Lady Chatterton, Holy Thursday 1866, in *LD* 22:193–94.

> that picture, (e.g. the Annunciation, the Agony, etc.) *while* you say the Pater and 10 Aves, not thinking of the words, only saying them correctly. Let the exercise be hardly more than a meditation. Perhaps this will overcome any sense of tedium.[188]

In corresponding with two of his closest associates in the Tractarian Movement, Newman delineated his understanding of the intercessory power of Mary. In a letter to John Keble, he explained in theological terms, the efficacy of the intercessory prayer of Mary:

> Our received doctrine is, after St. Justin and St. Irenaeus, as we interpret them, that as Eve had a secondary part in the fall, so had Blessed Mary in the redemption. And interpreting them still, it is our belief, that, whereas all the Saints intercede for us, through the merits and in the grace of Christ, she is the Intercessor or Helper (Advocata, St. Irenaeus)—that this is her distinct part in the economy of human salvation—so that, knowing the Will of our Lord most intimately, she prays according to His will, or thus is the ordained means or channel by which that will is carried out. Therefore "every thing goes through the hands of Mary"—and this is a great reason for our asking her prayers.[189]

Similarly, in answering Pusey's question about Mary, the Queen of Purgatory, Newman wrote: "The Blessed Virgin is the great pattern of prayers, especially intercessory. And in this age especially she (and the Saints too and the Church too) is the *witness* against the prevailing theories, such as Mr. Buckle's that all things go on by fixed laws which cannot be broken; thus introducing a practical atheism.

"If she is the Intercessor, and the effectual intercessor, she is so as regards earth, as regards Purgatory, as regards the whole created Universe."[190]

Because of his belief in intercessory prayer, Newman directed others to avail themselves of Mary's help. As he explained to John Perrin: "The intercession of the Blessed Virgin and the saints does not differ from ours for each other, except that it is more perfect than ours, and comes from those whose holy lives here give them a covenanted claim on God's special notice and indulgence."[191] Similarly, to a recent convert he said: "Our Lady has nothing of her own, that is, nothing, which is not the gift of God to her.

---

188. JHN to George Ryder, 19 September 1848, in *LD* 12:263.
189. JHN to John Keble, 8 October 1865, in *LD* 22:68.
190. JHN to E. B. Pusey, 3 February 1865, in *LD* 21:401–2.
191. JHN to John Perrin, 9 September 1864, in *LD* 21:224–25.

Spiritual Direction and the Roman Catholic Church

When then we ask her for any grace, we are in fact asking her to pray to God for it for us."[192]

Summary

The Church was central in both the Anglican and the Roman Catholic spirituality of John Henry Newman. Although the basic principles of his ecclesiology developed during his Anglican years, it was not until after he became a Roman Catholic that his ecclesiological viewpoint fully matured. Through reading the Church Fathers, he eventually came to believe that the Patristic Church continued on in the Roman Catholic Church. Consequently, his own conversion was primarily an ecclesiological decision which was largely determined by his understanding of apostolicity.

Since the Church was fundamental to his own spiritual life, it also provided the context for much of his spiritual direction. As a convert, Newman desired to share his understanding of the Roman Catholic Church with others. He wanted first of all to help others recognize the Catholic Church as the true Church of Christ, the Teacher of Revelation, the Oracle of God and the Ark of Salvation. By emphasizing the importance of certain "notes" of the Church, he argued persuasively in favor of the Roman Catholic Church, yet without pressuring anyone to join. In directing others towards the Church, Newman made frequent use of these "notes" not in a systematic theological fashion, but in a practical pastoral way. Supporting individuals in their search, he encouraged them to take their time and to convert for the right reasons.

Newman's correspondence emphasized Revelation as the basic priority in the Church. For our salvation, God has revealed himself in various ways but unsurpassingly in Christ. Christ founded a Church to be the inheritor of the Revelation and to be the source of salvation. The Church, as the "ground and pillar of truth" destined to last through time, teaches people in every age the Revelation that saves. For Newman, the Roman Catholic Church today is the continuation of that Church; he "was converted by the manifest and intimate identity of the modern R.C. Church with the Antenicene and Nicene Church."[193]

For Newman, the basis for accepting the Church is that it is trustworthy, because it is the Church of the Apostles, extended into the Nineteenth Century. Once one accepts the Church as Teacher, and consequently as trustworthy authority, one's duty is to accept, as an act of obedience, what the Church teaches. Since the mind will naturally seek for reasons, Newman

---

192. JHN to Miss Ellen Fox, 25 February 1868, in *LD* 24:41.
193. JHN to Francis Wegg-Prosser, 22 February 1852, in *LD* 15:42.

called the duty of acceptance "a trial of our trust and obedience to Him." He told Mrs. William Froude in 1848: "But I will tell you, what I think on the whole, though you do not ask me, in two propositions 1. that it is the *duty* of those who feel themselves called towards the Church to obey it—2. that they must expect trial, when in it, and think it only so much gain when they have it not. This last indeed is nothing more than the inspired warning, 'when thou come to serve the Lord, prepare thy soul for temptation.'"[194]

Even without the infallibility debate at the First Vatican Council, Newman would have discussed infallibility as an important ecclesiological topic. While his correspondence does not offer a complete theological treatise on this issue, it does provide us with considerable insight into the progression of his thought. Newman focused on the "infallibility of the Church" and within that context, encouraged an acceptance of the infallibility of the Pope. Accordingly, he was quick to emphasize that the infallibility of the Pope is not the basis of the Catholic religion, but a doctrine of the Church which the Church teaches along with many other doctrines.

As the controversy on infallibility heightened in the years immediately prior to the First Vatican Council, many people wrote to Newman for clarification. Newman guided people by sharing his own beliefs about the infallibility of the pope, yet without trying to force them on anyone else. While he personally had no difficulty with this doctrine, he opposed a formal definition because he thought such a definition was unnecessary. After the formal promulgation in 1870, Newman's method of direction took many forms depending on the need of the individual. Sometimes he encouraged people to make an act of faith in all that the Church teaches; sometimes he counseled people to wait patiently and to have confidence that God was guiding the Church. In particular, Newman was able to help people understand and accept this doctrine of the Church by his moderate interpretation of the doctrine. In this respect, Newman's approach differed sharply from that of many of his ultramontane contemporaries.

Newman spent a great deal of time writing both Catholics and non-Catholics about particular aspects of Church life. Lengthy letters abound in his correspondence in which he patiently explained the beliefs and teachings of the Church. He helped others by allaying fears and by providing information. In addition, Newman valued devotions as a means of keeping the soul firm in its belief in a personal God. Although he believed that doctrines are nonnegotiable, he felt that there should be a great deal of personal flexibility in devotions. While Newman personally practiced the devotions

---

194. JHN to Mrs. William Froude, 16 June 1848, in *LD* 21:223–24.

that were popular in the nineteenth century, he never forced other persons to pattern their devotional lives on his.

Newman was a product of his age in the sense that the methods he used to help people recognize the Church was conditioned by a nineteenth century theology of the Church. For example, because of his historical understanding of the Church, he was able to argue convincingly from the "notes" of the Church.[195] In his spiritual direction, Newman was answering specific questions within the conventional views of the Church of his time; in contrast, the understanding of the Church is much broader today. On balance, Newman's unique insights into the role and importance of the Church characterize his spiritual life and influenced the way that he directed others.

---

195. From a critical perspective, one can note other models which are employed in speaking about the Church today that were not utilized or emphasized by Newman; for example, see Dulles, *Models of the Church*.

6

Spiritual Direction on Vocation and Religious Life

"And hence it is that those who aim at nothing great, often seem much better, sometimes are better, than those who aim at what is high—they are better, if those who aim at more are bold and fervent without caution—they seem better, because they attempt so much less."[1]

THE QUESTION OF NEWMAN'S vocation within the Catholic Church was complex, involving not only his unique position and talents, but also the lives of other converts. His decision to become an Oratorian was not based on an emotional attraction to a congenial patron saint or his institute. Rather, nothing is more marked in the whole process of his vocation than the deliberate and eminently reasonable nature of his choice. In the process of choosing a suitable way of priestly life for himself and his companions, he reasoned very deliberately on the implications and possible consequences of every option.[2] Wilfrid Ward, for example, characterized the relevant letters as "almost tiresomely fussy from their realization of objections to any plan and their balancing of alternative considerations."[3] In fact, it took him about a year and a half to decide on the Oratory.[4]

---

1. Newman, "Perfection for Oratorians," December 11, 1850, in *Newman the Oratorian*.

2. JHN to Mrs. J. W. Bowden, 13 January 1847, in *LD* 12:12: "My vocation is not yet clear to me."

3. Ward, *Life*, 1:17.

4. Much of Newman's thought concerning religious life and his vocational choice are contained in his Oratory Papers, found in *Newman the Oratorian*, 133–467. These

In his correspondence during the first few years after his entrance into the Roman Catholic Church (1845–47), Newman often spoke as if he were beginning a new life at the end of his days. He first considered joining various religious orders,[5] but realized that his previous life was intended to be the means of future usefulness. To J. D. Dalgairns, a future Oratorian, he wrote: "My name and person are known to a very great many people I do not know—so are my books—and I may have begun a work which I am now to finish."[6] As a religious "no one would know that I was speaking my own words: or was a *continuation*, as it were, of my former self."[7]

His choice of vocation was by a process of examination and elimination. He was not choosing for himself alone; in a sense he was thinking of a group vocation, for his companions as well as for himself.[8] Even after his definite choice he could still sigh: "How much happier for me to have no liabilities (so to speak) but to be a single unfettered convert."[9]

From the beginning, Cardinal Wiseman had favored the Oratory of St. Philip Neri because he believed that in this kind of congregation, Newman could best continue to use his talents.[10] St. Philip had founded the Oratorians in the sixteenth century in Rome, not a new order, but as a group of secular priests, who lived together without taking vows, and with "no bond but that of love."[11] Each house of the Oratory, which lived its own separate democratic life, had to be situated with its church in a town. From there its influence was to radiate, by its services and preaching, teaching, study and learned work.

Oratory Papers are extremely valuable for understanding his thought concerning religious life because most of them are Chapter Addresses given to the Oratorians along with some "Extracts" dealing with specific facets of Oratorian life. For Newman's personal account of his decision to become an Oratorian, see "Memorandum," in *Newman the Oratorian*, June 9, 1848, 434–43.

5. Newman actually considered joining four different communities: the Dominicans, Jesuits, Vincentians, and Redemptorists.

6. JHN to J. D. Dalgairns, 31 December 1846, in *LD* 11:306.

7. Ibid. See also *Autobiographical Writings*, 127: "God still has work for me to do."

8. JHN to Miss Giberne, 22 January 1846, in *LD* 11:96. "As you say 'one step enough for me'—let us hope and believe that the Most Merciful Hand, which has guided us hitherto, will guide us still and that we shall one and all, you as well as I and my Littlemore inmates, may all find our vocation happily. We are called into God's Church for something not for nothing, surely. Let us wait and be cheerful, and be sure that good is destined for us, and that we are to be made useful."

9. JHN to Ambrose St. John, 12 July 1848, in *LD* 12:243.

10 JHN to Bishop Wiseman, 17 January 1847, in *LD* 12:19–20. Newman wrote: "It is curious and very pleasant that, after all the thought we can give the matter, we come round to your Lordship's original idea, and feel we cannot do better than be Oratorians."

11. Dessain, *John Henry Newman*, 92. See also JHN to Lady Georgiana Fullerton, 27 July 1853, in *LD* 31 Supplement:38.

Newman's attraction to St. Philip Neri seems to have been enhanced by his friendship with Keble; as Newman wrote his sister Jemima in 1847: "This great saint (Philip) reminds me in so many ways of Keble, that I can fancy what Keble would have been, if God's will had been that he should have been born in another place or age; he was formed in the same type of extreme hatred of humbug, playfulness, nay oddity, tender love for others, and serenity, which are the lineaments of Keble."[12]

The Oratorians had few rules and had to learn to live together by means of tact, self-knowledge and the knowledge of others. This had been the pattern for Newman and his companions at Littlemore and Old Oscott (Maryvale). He did not intend to reproduce a slavish model of the Italian Oratory, but to realize St. Philip's idea in very different circumstances. Eventually, Newman chose the Oratory for himself and his followers because "the tastes of all of us were very different, the Oratory allowed greater scope for them than any other Institution; again it seemed more adapted than any other for Oxford and Cambridge men."[13]

Spiritual Direction and Vocation

It would be difficult to exaggerate the importance of the Oratory for Newman. It was his chosen vocation; its establishment in England was the first commission he received from Roman Catholic authorities; it was the framework for the rest of his long life and the source of some of his cruelest trials. It was through the Oratory that his understanding of religious life deepened and provided the groundwork for the direction he was to give to others concerning religious life.

Nature of Oratorian Vocation

The "Santa Croce Papers," written by Newman in the autumn of 1847 during his novitiate in Rome, constitute a working plan for the Oratory. Based on his close study of authentic Oratorian documents and his observation of

---

12. JHN to Mrs. John Mozley, 26 January 1847, in *LD* 12:25. Newman also described his attraction to St. Philip Neri in his book *Idea of a University*, 236: "He would be but an ordinary individual priest as others: and his weapons should be but unaffected humility and unpretending love. All he did was to be done by the light, and fervour, and convincing eloquence of his personal character and his easy conversation."

13. Newman, "Memorandum," in *Newman the Oratorian*, 437.

the Roman and Neapolitan Oratories at the time, these papers attempted to define the nature of the Oratory of St. Philip Neri.[14]

Newman, like Philip Neri, emphasized that Oratorians are not a religious body in the canonical sense, but "secular priests" living in community. In his "Santa Croce Papers," he considered the question of whether the Congregation of the Oratory could be called a religious institute. Although Newman felt that the Oratorians were not "religious per se," nevertheless as followers of St. Philip, he wanted the Oratorians to "seek to *imitate the religious* in *perfection*, though they did not imitate them in taking vows."[15] Newman felt the external differences between the Oratorians and a religious order would show themselves in several ways.

> First, there is to be no poverty, and no appearance of it—*habeant, possideant*, (let them have, let them possess) were St. Philip's words, when one of his subjects wished to decree poverty.
>
> They are to have their own rooms, and to make themselves comfortable in them. A remarkable stress is laid upon their rooms as their *nido*, (nest) which would not apply to a monastic house...
>
> There were to be no fastings over and above what the Church prescribed, no other austerities (except discipline)...
>
> Another external difference between his Congregation and Religious was the absence of the appearance of government. At first, there were no Rules or Constitutions at all.
>
> The Superior was to have no show of power. St. Philip only on one occasion used the words "I command." He said that the best means of having power was to command seldom.[16]

Although the Oratory was not a religious institute, but a community of secular priests, nevertheless the obligation to strive for perfection was central to his understanding of the Oratorian vocation. Asking the question, "What is meant by perfection?" he stated in 1856: "To reconcile these opposite statements of the Oratory being a community of secular priests, and a sort of Religion—of its members aiming at perfection, yet not being under vows, we must bear in mind that there are various modes, nay types, or at

---

14. The "Santa Croce Papers" are important for understanding Newman's concept of the Oratorian vocation and religious life. More systematic and documented than anything he wrote or said about the Oratory in later years, these papers are Newman's own body of Oratorian precedents and principles.

15. Newman, "Remarks on the Oratorian Vocation," August 18, 1856, in *Newman the Oratorian*, 315.

16. Newman, "Santa Croce," August-September 1847, in *Newman the Oratorian*, 398-99.

least species, of perfection, and that the perfection of regulars is only one of these. What is meant by perfection?"[17]

Newman's earliest view of perfection is contained in his "Santa Croce Papers," which made a close connection between perfection and community:

> Whatever then is meant by the word "perfection" in its ordinary sense, and that is intelligible enough, such is the characteristic attribute of the Congregation of the Oratory.
>
> But to be more particular (i.e., Proof that the particular perfection of the Oratory is that of yielding one's will to that of the rest):—the nature of the case suggests that what must be the characteristic attribute of the members of any community whatever, viz. their perfection, as members of a community is to act as such or as *parts of a whole*.
>
> Here then is the characteristic and the perfection of the Congregation of the Oratory, that its members act as members, that they do not act in an independent isolated way, but in and for and by and from the body, as having no distinct interest and no private will.
>
> This is a most momentous principle, and must be dwelt upon.
>
> ... A voluntary submission of the will to the Congregation is, as it were, the definition of good membership. In religious, properly so called, it consists in a scrupulous fulfillment of the vows, which includes obedience; but, there being no vows here to protect the life of the Society, to be an Oratorian is directly to consult for that life, to postpone one's own wishes and will to its welfare ...
>
> It is then the fundamental principle of the Oratory, that no one is his own master, no one can live for himself alone. To live and to let live, in this sense of the words, to say "I will not interfere with you and you shall not interfere with me," is the ruin of the congregation—and a person who so speaks has not in him the first element of an Oratorian.[18]

Several years later, when this understanding of perfection and community seemed to be lacking in some Oratorians, Newman shared his concern with his fellow Oratorian, J. D. Dalgairns: "It is this *free and easy* way of going on—this want of recognizing the Congregation as a sacred thing, which makes me more than any thing else anxious about the future. There

---

17. Newman, "Remarks on the Oratorian Vocation," August 18, 1856, in *Newman the Oratorian*, 315.

18. Newman, "Santa Croce," August-September 1847, in *Newman the Oratorian*, 401–3.

seems an enormous tendency in our subjects to act each for himself, as if [he] were in a lodging house, and to be impatient of control."[19]

A second aspect of Newman's understanding of perfection is found in a Chapter Address of 1850 entitled "Perfection for Oratorians."[20] On the occasion of the ordination to the subdiaconate of two members of the Oratory, Stanislas Flanagan and Edward Caswall, Newman emphasized the idea that "if we would aim at perfection, we must perform well the duties of the day."[21]

Newman felt that if all Christians, but especially religious are called to strive for perfection, few actually attain it because it is not only a difficult road to travel but also because it is so unknown and different from what most people experience. When Miss Holmes enthusiastically wrote Newman in 1853 about her recently discovered religious vocation, he pointed out that in the initial years of religious life it is comparatively easy to strive for perfection, but as time progresses it becomes more difficult. "I shall be truly rejoiced and thankful, to feel that God is calling you by His powerful grace—Yet, if so, you will always have a great struggle, and must expect, in the ordinary way of things, much trial. It is comparatively easy in the first moment of conversion to give oneself up to God—but after years have past, and certain habits are formed, and we have learned to serve him in a certain way, though not in perfection, it requires a great Face to rouse and carry on the languid soul to a religious life."[22]

In addressing his Oratorian brothers, Newman used an analogy to stress the point that although we might humanly fear what lies ahead in striving for perfection, nevertheless God's grace is always there to sustain us:

> Watch the bricklayer mounting a high ladder—as he gets up it sways, it is exposed to the wind, He needs to plant it fast at bottom—he needs to be proof against giddiness—he needs to be accustomed to bear his load well, on his head or his shoulder, that he may neither lose it or lose his balance. Watch him—his feet dance up and down—take your hod of bricks or your trencher of mortar on your own shoulder and follow him up the ladder—will you not fear to do so? In like manner, fear much to ascend up the rounds of perfection, fear much, yet shrink not, if you are called to it—fear because you need grace, shrink not for you are promised grace. But without grace, and abundant grace,

---

19. JHN to J. D. Dalgairns, 7 June 1854, in *LD* 16:150.
20. Newman, "Perfection," December 11, 1850, in *Newman the Oratorian*, 232–35.
21. Ibid., 235.
22. JHN to Miss Holmes, 22 April 1853, in *LD* 15:359–60.

ruin is certain—your head, your shoulders, your feet will betray you—you will be precipitated down.[23]

Although Newman believed that we are called to strive for perfection, and that we depend on God's grace to reach any degree of perfection, he was very much aware that along the way were certain traps such as heretical asceticism and illusions of prayer. In order to combat these two obstacles to perfection, Newman would advocate two practices: first, spiritual direction, and second, performing well the duties of the day.[24]

> What then is to be done in these circumstances, in order to guard against a peril so great as to be appalling and discouraging to those who aim at perfection? Masters in the spiritual life, among other important rules, give the following two suggestions, as obvious yet as momentous as is the remark itself in which I suggested the danger when I began. The first is not to act of oneself—not to be one's own director—not to dare to aim at perfection without some definite individual to whom we really and in detail yield obedience. I cannot conceive any more fearful hazard than that to which a soul will be exposed than that of attempting to be a saint on its own capital, as it may be called, by its own management and its own wisdom. We shall float down the stream or drift in any direction, if we have nothing on the shore to steady our course by.
>
> The other remark I would make is, that we need not go too fast. Unless you prune off the luxuriances of plants, they grow bare, thin, and shabby at the roots. The higher your building is the broader must be its base—So it is with sanctity—Acts, words, devotions, which are suitable in saints, are absurd in other men—the second precept then of the religious guides, to whom I have

---

23. Newman, "Perfection," December 11, 1850, in *Newman the Oratorian*, 233. His conclusion is to aim for great things. "And hence it is that those who aim at nothing great, often seem much better, sometimes are better, than those who aim at what is high—they are better, if those who aim at more are bold and fervent without caution—they seem better, because they attempt so much less. When St. Peter said 'Lord I will follow thee to Prison and to death,' and then denied Christ, he aimed at more and in the event sinned more than those who professed nothing—He was right in attempting, but he was wrong in not watching and praying lest he should enter into temptation." Ibid., 234.

24. Ibid. These two ideas that appear here in this Chapter Address are extremely valuable because this is one of the only places where Newman explicitly spoke about the importance of spiritual direction; second, in talking about growth in the Christian life as being a gradual thing, he developed for the first time the corollary idea that "if we would aim at perfection, we must perform well the duties of the day," Ibid., 235. In 1856, he developed these ideas more fully in his "Remarks on the Oratorian Vocation" and "Short Rule to Perfection," in *Newman the Oratorian*, 300 and 359–60, respectively.

alluded, is this:—that, if we would aim at perfection, we must perform well the duties of the day. I do not know anything more difficult, more sobering, so strengthening than the constant aim to go through the ordinary day's work well. To rise at the exact time, to give the due time to prayer, to meditate with devotion, to assist at Mass with attention, to be recollected in conversation, these and similar observances carried duly through the day, make a man, as it is often said, half a saint, or almost a saint. It gives our aspirations too a definite scope. Men often know not what to be at—they have fervent desires to serve God and advance towards heaven, but they choose strange ways of accomplishing them. Here is the true answer to the question—the practical tangible work to be set before the aspirant.[25]

In 1847, when Newman was very new to the Oratorian way of life, he wrote about perfection mostly in relation to community life. In 1850, he viewed perfection as a gradual process more in terms of doing one's duties well each day. Commenting on a fellow Oratorian's dissatisfaction with the spiritual life of the Oratory and his projected departure from the community, Newman commented on striving for perfection as a gradual process. "Its proper effect will be to humble us; make us saints all at once it cannot. We must be content to be despised in (what the Protestant version calls) 'our day of small things.' A shrub must grow before it is a tree—young men in time become old. If we are young, this is a fault which mends—but we can't help ourselves—If Coffin declares we are not Saints, there's no denying it; we can but try to be."[26]

Again in 1856, Newman envisaged striving for perfection as comprised of two elements: obedience to the community and performing one's daily duties well. Since an Oratorian was a secular priest living in community and not a religious with vows, Newman came to believe that striving for perfection was essentially bound up with obedience to the community.

> So far as the Oratory adds anything to the perfection of its subjects, beyond their perfection as secular priests, this perfection does not lie in any counsel of fasting, or of poverty, or of renunciation of the domestic affections, or of external inconveniences: or again of vow. The question follows, after considering what its perfection does not consist in, has it any perfection above that of the secular priest, and if so what.

---

25. Newman, *Newman the Oratorian*, 235.
26. JHN to J. D. Dalgairns, 8 December 1850, in *LD* 14:162.

> The question is this—whereas, as I have said, perfection consists in the exact, ready, pleasant performance of the precepts of the New Law, and the avoidance of known venial sin in performing them; and whereas it is not to be expected that anyone will succeed in this exact fulfillment who aims at nothing more, or can possess the spirit to obey exactly, who has not the spirit to obey heartily and generously, and since such generous obedience is in other words the obedience which embraces counsels as well as precepts, and in this way the observance of some or other counsels are necessary for perfection, and whereas chastity and the vow of it are the great counsels which every priest has embraced, is there any other counsel over and above this, and parallel to this, which the Fathers of the Oratory take upon them on entering the Oratory, as their special instrument of going on to perfection.
>
> Of course there is one, and that both from the nature of the case, and from the express appointment of St. Philip and the declaration of his first disciples, and that is *obedience*, though not the vow of it.
>
> . . . I shall consider then obedience to the Community as our special means of perfection.[27]

In addition to stressing the relationship between striving for perfection and obedience to the community, Newman continued to associate perfection with performing one's daily duties well.

> What is meant by perfection? I suppose it is the power or faculty of doing our duty exactly, naturally, and completely, whatever it is, in opposition to a performance which is partial, slovenly, languid, awkward, clumsy, and with efforts. It is a life of faith, hope, and charity, elicited in successive acts according to the calls of the moment and to the vocation of the individual. It does not consist in any specially heroic deeds; it does not demand any fervour of devotion; but it implies regularity, precision, facility, and perseverance in a given sphere of duties. He is perfect who does the duties of the day perfectly.[28]

---

27. Newman, "Remarks on the Oratorian Vocation: Alternative Version of Letter V," February 28, 1856, in *Newman the Oratorian*, appendix 5, 444–45.

28. These were his words written on August 18, 1856, in his finalized version of "Remarks on the Oratorian Vocation," in *Newman the Oratorian*, 315–16. In his "rough draft" of the same paper, written before this on March 5–9, he wrote: "I define perfection to be a perfect obedience. If this be so, it consists mainly in the performance of our duties, and in the precepts of the New Law, in a life of faith, hope and charity according to the calls of every day and every occupation. He is perfect, in substance, who does the duties of the day perfectly." See "Remarks on the Oratorian Vocation: Rough Draft," March 5–9, 1856, in *Newman the Oratorian*, 300.

Spiritual Direction on Vocation and Religious Life

Finally, Newman's Chapter Address entitled "A Short Rule to Perfection" expressed what striving for perfection meant in the spiritual life.

> It is the saying of holy men that, if we wish to be perfect, we have nothing more to do than to perform the ordinary duties of the day well. <A short rule to perfection. Short, not because easy, but because pertinent and intelligible[.] There are no *short* ways to perfection, but there are *sure* ones.>
>
> I think this is an instruction which may be of great practical use to persons like ourselves who make a profession of aiming at perfection. It is easy to have vague ideas what perfection is, which serve well enough to talk about it, when we do not intend to aim at it—but as soon as a person really desires and sets about seeking it himself, he is dissatisfied with any thing but what is tangible and clear, and constitutes some sort of direction towards the practice of it.
>
> We must bear in mind what is meant by perfection—it does not mean any extraordinary service, anything out of the way, or especially heroic in our obedience (not all have the opportunity of heroic acts, sufferings) but it means what the word perfection ordinarily means. By perfect we mean that which has no flaw in it, that which is complete, that which is consistent, that which is sound. We mean the opposite of imperfect. As we know well what imperfection in religious service means, we know by the contrast what is meant by perfection.
>
> He then is perfect who does the work of the day perfectly—and we need not go beyond this to seek for perfection. (You need not go out of the *round* of the day[.]) We are perfect, if we do perfectly our duties as members of the Oratory.[29]

---

29. Newman, "Short Rule to Perfection," September 27, 1856, in *Newman the Oratorian*, 359–60. Desiring to make this more concrete and applicable to their daily life, he continued: "I insist on this, because I think it will simplify our views, and fix our exertions on a definite aim. If you ask me what you are to do in order to be perfect, I say—first—Do not lie in bed beyond the due time of rising—give your first thoughts to God—make a good meditation—say or hear Mass and communicate with devotion—make a good thanksgiving—say carefully all the prayers which you are bound to say—say Office attentively, do the work of the day, whatever it is, diligently and for God—make a good visit to the Blessed Sacrament. Say the Angelus devoutly—eat and drink to God's glory—say the Rosary well, be recollected—keep out bad thoughts. Make your evening meditation well—examine yourself daily. Go to bed in good time, and you are already perfect." Ibid.

John Henry Newman

Spiritual Direction and Vocational Choice

Newman never formulated a systematic approach to discernment of vocations. Rather, it was through his correspondence with individuals over many years, and specifically in his response to their inquiries, that certain elements of his thinking on vocational matters emerge.

First of all, he felt that an individual had to be called to a particular way of life. In a letter to Miss Munro who was contemplating entering the convent he wrote: "I don't comprehend how a person can go into a convent to try, without having a *call* to try. As a vocation is necessary for the religious life, so a call to try a vocation is necessary for trying it. Now you say that your repugnance to a convent is increased. Then I ask, what is it that makes you think that you should be a nun any more than that your next door neighbour should be one?"[30]

This "call" entailed the effort to discern the will of God, to see if one was genuinely called by God to embrace a particular vocation. Newman did not specify any set procedure for discernment. Nevertheless, several letters suggest some factors that he considered important in trying to discern God's will. First, he considered age an important factor in determining one's vocation especially if the person was thinking of priesthood or religious life. Mrs. J. W. Bowden, the mother of a boy who wanted to join the Dominicans, wrote to Newman asking how she should advise her son. He replied: "Really his apparent vocation does seem very much like a boy's whim—and my reason for saying so is that you may not be afraid of treating it as such. God's inscrutable grace draws the young as well as the matured—and while there was reason to think that Charles was under its influence, one might well be anxious about interfering with it—but I really think you need not be afraid now of putting your own better judgement forward and dealing with him, according to it, as a boy."[31]

Similarly, Newman advised people never to rush their decision. He felt that taking one's time was another way of trying to discern God's will. Robert Froude was eighteen and was thinking of entering the priesthood or religious life because of a retreat that he had just completed. In response to a request for his opinion, Newman replied:

> Almighty God calls the soul in various ways and seasons. It is very seldom that one can know at *once* that one is called. I think that time is generally necessary. This requires patience, and patience is very difficult. I do not see that you can know in three

---

30. JHN to Miss Munro, 20 October 1865, in *LD* 22:80.
31. JHN to Mrs. J. W. Bowden, 24 August 1853, in *LD* 15:411.

days that you have a vocation to the *priesthood*. . . . I trust I never should keep a soul back from God who was called to religion, but I have known so many try and fail, that I am always glad to see a person slow in determining—(a person who tries and fails may do himself great harm) and when ultimately a person waits and does not become a religious, though I know some persons will say "You see he has *lost* his vocation by waiting," it is quite as open to say, and sometimes I *should* say "You see he has *found out* what *is* his real vocation by waiting."[32]

Similarly, Marianne Bowden was considering a vocation to religious life, but was uncertain as to what she should do. After writing Newman for direction, his response incorporated the ideas of waiting in patience and trusting in God:

> You must simply put yourself into God's hands. As I understood F. [Frances Bowden, her sister] you have no call on you to do any thing, or to decide on doing any thing, at this moment. Do you know, though this is of course a trial, yet I have ever felt it a great mercy. One of the greatest of trials is, to have it cast upon one to make up one's mind,—on some grave question, with great consequences spreading into the future,—and to be in doubt what one ought to do. You have not this trial—it is also a trial to wait and do nothing but how great a mercy is it not to have responsibility! Put your self then, my dear Child, into the hands of your loving Father and Redeemer, who knows and loves you better than you know or love yourself. He has appointed every action of your life. He created you, sustains you, and has marked down the very way and hour when He will take you to Himself. He knows all your thoughts, and feels for you in all your sadness more than any creature can feel, and accepts and makes note of your prayers

---

32. JHN to Robert Froude, 24 July 1864, in *LD* 21:161–62. Robert Froude left the Oratory school in June at age 18, but returned for Fr. Suffield's retreat in the middle of July. From his correspondence it is clear that Newman was his spiritual director. After making this retreat Robert became very enthusiastic about following a call to the religious life. This decision prompted a series of seven letters between Newman and Robert and his parents between July 19 and August 8, 1864. These letters comprise some of Newman's most developed thoughts on this vocational issue:

JHN to William Froude, 19 July 1864, in *LD* 21:159;
JHN to Robert Froude, 24 July 1864, in *LD* 21:161–62;
JHN to Mrs. William Froude, 24 July 1864, in *LD* 21:162–63;
JHN to Robert Froude, 28 July 1864, in *LD* 21:170–73;
JHN to William Froude, 28 July 1864, in *LD* 21:173–75;
JHN to Robert Froude, 3 August 1864, in *LD* 21:179–81;
JHN to William Froude, 8 August 1864, in *LD* 21:188–89.

even before you make them. He will never fail you—and He will give you what is best for you. And though he tries you, and seems to withdraw Himself from you, and afflicts you, still trust in Him, for at length you will see how good and gracious He is, and how well he will provide for you. Be courageous and generous, and give Him your heart, and you will never repent of the sacrifice.[33]

Another characteristic in Newman's approach to vocational choices was his willingness to ask advice of others. If he received a letter from someone he did not know inquiring about a vocational matter, he would often ask the opinion of someone else. For example, in 1851, when Charles Harrison (whom Newman did not know) wanted to become an Oratorian, Newman wrote to Richard Stanton for advice.[34]

In addition to these practical considerations, Newman also felt that prayer and penance were important factors in determining one's vocation. To Robert Froude he wrote: "I would not say all this to every one—but I know you are a prudent boy, and I wish you gravely and continually to pray God, that you may be *taught* His Will as regards you. For we must persevere in prayer, if we would learn it."[35] In response to Froude's inquiry about doing penance, Newman replied: "

> I certainly think you *should* have some definite mortification. From my own fault, I daresay, I did not understand your wish for one till now. It is always advisable in such cases as you describe your own to be. The anxiety is to fix on one which is fitting—which may neither be a burden on your conscience nor interfere with your duties to others, and yet answers its purpose.
>
> I do not know how to mention anything at once;—1. because I do not know what you do already. 2. Next because it ought to be something which suits you. I will put down on a separate paper two or three penances, which you might choose from, or use as suggestions for others which I do not happen to mention.[36]

33. JHN to Marianne Bowden, 6 March 1851, in *LD* 22:247–48.

34. JHN to Richard Stanton, 5 June 1866, in *LD* 14:231. Twenty-seven years later, on August 28, 1878, Newman wrote in a similar way to Robert Ornsby, in *LD* 28:399. At times, Newman would also ask an inquirer to seek advice from someone else. For example, see JHN to Miss Munro, 12 December 1851, in *LD* 14:467, where Newman asked her to consult Dr. Whitty about her vocation.

35. JHN to Robert Froude, 3 August 1864, in *LD* 21:181. See also JHN to Edward Bellasis, 6 April 1872, in *LD* 26:56. In this letter, Newman asked Bellasis to pray for Robert's brother Richard, who was also trying to discern which community to join. "Your brother, Richard, will be a great loss to you—You must now pray hard that God would guide him in determining his particular vocation, for it is quite as anxious a thing to decide *where* one is to go as *whether*."

36. JHN to Robert Froude, 3 August 1864, in *LD* 21:180.

Yet, once the preliminary process of discernment was completed, Newman was ready to advise a person to try a vocation. He realized that a director can only give limited advice; eventually, everyone has to take personal responsibility for vocational decisions: "All I can say is that Eddy's inclination is not my doing. No one can answer for a boy's mind—and no one can turn him at his will—No one can control his ultimate intentions. One can but influence him for a time, and *then* he must be his own master, and he must decide for himself whether that influence has succeeded in the interval to determine his decision or not."[37]

Finally, Newman did not feel that those thinking of a religious vocation should be sheltered from the world. He felt that contact with the world was the best thing possible because it made a person more realistic. In response to Edward Bellasis whose son was considering a vocation to the priesthood, Newman wrote:

> I have little belief in true vocations being destroyed by contact with the world—I don't mean, contact with sin and evil—but that contact with the world which consists of such intercourse as is natural or necessary. Many boys seem to have vocations, in whom it is but appearance. They go to school, and the appearance fades away—and then people may say, "They have lost their vocation," when they never had one. In such cases, it is on the other hand, rather, a positive good that they and their parents were not deceived. What I shrink from with dread, as the more likely danger, is not the Church losing priests whom she ought to have had, but gaining priests whom she never should have been burdened with. The thought is awful, that boys should have had no trial of their hearts, till at the end of some 14 years, they go out into the world with the most solemn vows upon them, and then perhaps for the first time learn that the world is not a seminary;—when they exchange the atmosphere of the Church, the lecture room, and the study, the horarium of devotion, work, meals, and recreation, for this most bright, various, and seductive world.[38]

Newman acknowledged that he dreaded "too early separation from the world" because it occasioned "the spirit of formalism." Accordingly, he preferred secular education to seminary education:

> Under then the two opposite difficulties, of depriving our Lord of his priests, and of giving to Him unworthy ones, I myself, if left to myself, should be disposed to act with far greater

---

37. JHN to William Froude, 8 August 1864, in *LD* 21:188.
38. JHN to Edward Bellasis, 5 August 1861, in *LD* 20:21–22.

> sensitiveness of the latter. I think a true vocation in a boy is not lost by secular education—at most it is but merged for a time, and comes up again—whereas a false vocation may be fatally and irreversibly fostered in a seminary. Or at least, it is *more* common in this age for false vocations to be made by an early dedication to the religious or ecclesiastical state, than for true vocations to be lost by early secular education.[39]

Since Newman believed there was a substantial difference in a vocation to priesthood and a vocation to religious life, one of his dominant concerns was that people choose the appropriate vocation. For example, Robert Froude thought he had a vocation to religious life, while Newman thought he had been deliberating about a possible vocation to the priesthood:

> I do not think that you have that certainty about your vocation, to warrant you to go against his (father's) wishes. All this has reference to the *Priesthood*. But you speak of entering religion—this is not what I understood you to say last Monday. I thought you said a vocation to the Priesthood. A vocation to religion is a very different thing. If it would be a difficulty to decide on the Priesthood, much greater is the difficulty to decide on religion. And I confess that your letter has frightened me in this respect. Of course I understand there is a fullness of divine grace which leads the soul to go right in the most unusual courses—but we ought to be sure that we have it. Ordinarily speaking, ordinary means must cooperate with grace. Ordinarily speaking, a greater imprudence could not be committed than for you at your age to decide upon religion. Recollect it is said that as many souls are lost by choosing wrongly as in any other way. A man may be more easily lost by becoming a religious when he is not called, as by not becoming one when he is. And from the difference of what you said to me and write to me, I don't think you have a clear difference between the *religious* and the ecclesiastical state.... I trust I never should keep a soul back from God who was called to religion, but I have known so many try and fail, that I am always glad to see a person slow in determining.[40]

---

39. Ibid.

40. JHN to Robert Froude, 24 July 1864, in *LD* 21:161–62. See also Newman's comments to Robert Froude, August 3, 1864, in *LD* 21:179–81, about the importance of *when* one enters religious life and *where* a person goes. "I think it would be distinctly wrong in you to try your vocation for *religion* at once. You must try it in a particular place and order—and places and orders are *toto caelo* (completely; as different as heaven and earth) different. Nothing is more common among women (who more often try their vocation than men) than to try in a wrong Community, and to get disheartened

Encouragement and Support

With people whom he knew, Newman did not hesitate in taking the initiative in vocational matters. At times he would ask them if they had ever considered a particular vocation: "I have lately wondered why you do not think more of the prospect of embracing the religious life. The reason you used to have, viz, your family, not seeming to tell now, as it did."[41] At other times he would advise a person directly to enter the priesthood or religious life,[42] and if there was a doubt as to which community, he would state his preference in relation to a particular individual.[43] Simultaneously, he wanted people to be realistic about their vocational choice, to know, as well as they could, what their life would be like. Moreover, he was greatly opposed to people acting impetuously and was well aware of the possibility of people wanting to enter religious life for inadequate motives.[44]

---

altogether, and to leave a religious vocation which they might have had, had they tried in the right place. And among men it occurs not infrequently too. Great deliberation then is necessary as regards the place of attempting, lest vocations be quenched.

"Another danger is this, lest a postulant and novice, being young, with warm affections and religious earnestness, should have all the signs of vocation and take the vows, and then after a while fall into a state of tepidity, which *may* indeed only be a fault of natural weakness and a re-action of mind which is to be resisted as a temptation, but on the other hand may quite as easily be the result of that spiritual constitution which God has given him, and such, that, if it had shown itself in him *while* he was a novice, might have made clear that, without any fault of his, he had no vocation for a religious state at all. Certainly, I think I see men who have made serious mistakes in becoming religious suddenly. Of course there are always two ways of explaining the failure—it may be said 'he *fell* from his vocation'—or—'he *never had* a vocation'. As this applies to an ecclesiastical vocation as well as to a religious, I will instance it in the case of Mr. Connelly, an American convert. He separated from his wife; she became a religious, he a Priest. Then he found he had mistaken his vocation—wished to get his wife back—left the Church and is now an Irvingite."

41. JHN to Miss Holmes, 16 January 1852, in *LD* 15:15. See also JHN to Miss Holmes, 8 February 1852, in *LD* 15:33.

42. JHN to Marianne Bowden, 19 July 1852, in *LD* 15:127–28. See also:
JHN to Catherine Bathurst, 16 April 1853, in *LD* 15:352–53;
JHN to F. W. Faber, 8 October 1853, in *LD* 15:462–63;
JHN to George Ryder, 17 August 1854, in *LD* 15:221–22;
JHN to George Ryder, 21 December 1854, in *LD* 16:329;
JHN to Henry Ryder, 24 August 1855, in *LD* 16:531–32;
JHN to Henry Ryder, 25 September 1855, in *LD* 16:548–49;
JHN to Henry Ryder, 13 December 1855, in *LD* 17:89–90;
JHN to James Patterson, 26 June 1858, in *LD* 18:393–95.

43. JHN to Catherine Bathurst, 5 July 1853, in *LD* 15:393. See also:
JHN to Miss Munro, 5 September 1852, in *LD* 15:159;
JHN to Catherine Bathurst, 21 October 1854, in *LD* 16:281.

44. JHN to Mrs. J. W. Bowden, 18 January 1854, in *LD* 16:15–16. Her daughter

With some people, Newman even played the role of "devil's advocate." In a letter to Mrs. Bowden, he told her about the rigors of a community her daughter Marianne was thinking of joining and concluded the letter by saying: "Of course it is my line here to take the office of the Advocatus diaboli, and to urge every thing against any step, which deserves consideration."[45] Several years later, when her sister Emily also wanted to pursue a religious vocation, Newman became concerned over her motivation.

> I had intended not to decide till the Assumption—but my mind is quite clear a month before it. And I have no reason to delay to tell you what I deliberately think.
>
> It is, that you have a vocation to a religious life. You cannot help thinking I have gone to and fro—but I have not. I have wanted to see whether your own thoughts on the subject would undergo a change—and I wanted calmly to reflect on what I already know about you. Now you seem to me precisely where you were—in your last letter you express in a simple natural way just what you expressed months ago. When left to yourself, you seem to me to look one way and one way only.
>
> It comes home to me forcibly, that I know various persons who desire to have a vocation and have not, and would be content indeed to find in themselves those marks of a vocation, which show themselves in you.
>
> My opinion is, that, if you find the right convent, you will never wish to leave it.[46]

In a similar letter, Newman wrote to George Ryder concerning his sister's desire to be a nun. "As to your sister, all depends on how she gets on at Hammersmith—which we shall see—It is not unnatural that she should wish to be settled, and that she should catch at any thing which promises well—but we must take care that this leads her to be precipitate. The convent was not my suggestion—though I think it on the whole a good one. I have put before her very strongly its disadvantageous side."[47]

Emily had attended the religious profession of her sister and then wanted to follow her sister Marianne's example and become a Visitation nun. In this letter to Mrs. Bowden, Newman tries to make her aware of this, and advises her in giving direction to her daughter. Newman wrote a similar letter to Sister Frances Vaughan on January 19, 1854, in LD 16:17–18. Also see Newman's letter on July 22, 1871 to Geraldine Fitzgerald who wanted to run away from her mother and secretly enter a convent, in LD 26:141.

45. JHN to Mrs. J. W. Bowden, 15 September 1851, in LD 14:356.

46. JHN to Emily Bowden, 16 July 1854, in LD 16:197.

47. JHN to George Ryder, 15 December 1848, in LD 12:373. After her conversion, in May 1846, Sophie Ryder wished to become a nun and corresponded at length with Newman on the subject, deciding eventually to enter the Good Shepherd convent at

In general, a characteristic feature of Newman's spiritual direction was his encouragement and support of others in pursuing their vocations. Not only was he sensitive to their trials and difficulties, but he also had a way of helping them understand the action of God in their lives. For example, when Catherine Bathurst entered the convent Newman wrote to her:

> We must be very grateful for so good a beginning—it comes of His infinite mercy who loves you as entirely and wholly as if there were no other souls on earth to love or take care of. You are choosing Him for your portion and your All—and He is your All, and nothing will or can harm you, though your enemy may try to frighten you. And then the Angels will smile at each other and upon you at your fears and troubles—and will say "This poor little soul is in a great taking as if God were leaving her—but He is All faithful, and has loved her—everlastingly, and will preserve her to the end."[48]

However, after a few months, she began to experience difficulties and wondered whether she should enter the novitiate. Newman encouraged her to try:

> You went with a very good heart to Loughborough, and I was thankful to witness it, you felt you could almost volunteer to do so, and I would not for the world damp so promising a purpose. Do not be discouraged and give up, merely because trials come upon you which were sure to come.
> ... But since you have been led there, do not shrink—go on, and go through it. Should you not have a vocation, God will make this known to you—but let it be determined by the event; do not by any act of yours anticipate His decision.[49]

Hammersmith. After Newman's death, she wrote on April 8, 1891, to his successor as Superior of the Oratory, and her own nephew, Henry Ryder, to explain the fate of Newman's letters, and the part he had played in her choice of vocation: "I am very sorry that I have no more letters that I can send you. . . . I had so many before I became a nun and then I was so afraid that I liked them too much that I burnt them. There was a sentence in one I think you would like; it was at the time I was thinking which Order I should enter. I thought when I became a Catholic that I would prefer the Carmelites as I had a very great admiration for Saint Therese. I used to write and ask Father Newman what he thought of the different contemplative Orders, but to my dismay he put doubts and obstacles in my way, so at last I thought I would ask what he thought of the Good Shepherd, devoutly hoping that *he would not think of it*, when to my dismay he wrote me a long letter with nothing but praise and admiration."

48. JHN to Catherine Bathurst, 8 November 1853, in *LD* 15:477.
49. JHN to Catherine Bathurst, 12 February 1854, in *LD* 16:43.

Despite his encouragement she decided to leave and Newman again wrote her a supportive letter.

> Of course I was very sorry to find what disappointment and anxiety you were in, and grieved for the perplexities which still beset your course, but I could not feel any surprise at what you told me, and I have a consolation in thinking that, though you may not see it yourself, the good Hand of Providence is bringing you forward, and by means of your trials bringing you nearer to Him.
> ... Do not be cast down because your Loving Father is bringing you to Heaven in His own way. He sees that way is quite as necessary, as in this world a physician's regimen is for the sick. ... You will see it all clearly enough, please God—hereafter. Now the only question is, what should you do at the moment.[50]

Not only did Newman encourage those persons who were contemplating a religious vocation, but he also supported parents who were distraught by their child's vocational choice. In 1863, he responded to a letter written by the Duchess of Norfolk, whose daughter Minna had decided to become a Carmelite. "It is very kind in you to write to me on a subject so near to your heart. I can well imagine the mixture of feelings, the pain and the joy, with which you have received this intimation of the gracious Will of God. But, though many are able to imagine them, One alone, besides yourself, is able to understand and estimate your sacrifice; and that is He who asks for it. And, while He blesses the child so specially, He will include the Mother in the blessing."[51]

To Lady Henry Kerr, whose daughter Henrietta was about to become a Sacred Heart nun he said:

> You must not think I have been unmindful of you and Lord Henry's letters, though I have not answered them. His news was most surprising and touching. I was extremely pleased to see

---

50. JHN to Catherine Bathurst, 10 March 1854, in *LD* 16:77–78. See also the following letters that portray the encouragement that Newman offered to others:
JHN to Marianne Bowden, 9 July 1851, in *LD* 14:307–8;
JHN to Emily Bowden, 15 July 1854, in *LD* 16:197;
JHN to Mrs. J. W. Bowden, 16 July 1854, in *LD* 16:197–98;
JHN to Miss Giberne, 28 August 1861, in *LD* 20:37–38.
A series of letters to Lavinia Wilson, a convert, who was thinking of entering religious life:
JHN to Lavinia Wilson, 1 December 1864, in *LD* 21:331;
JHN to Lavinia Wilson, 5 January 1865, in *LD* 21:374;
JHN to Lavinia Wilson, 14 January 1865, in *LD* 21:387;
JHN to Lavinia Wilson, 30 January 1865, in *LD* 21:399.

51. JHN to Duchess of Norfolk, 22 February 1863, in *LD* 20:411.

Spiritual Direction on Vocation and Religious Life

your daughter, but how I felt for you and him, when he told me in his letter, that God had claimed her for Himself! . . .

In such a case the real offering is yours rather than hers. She quits a home but for another home and a more sacred. But you make the sacrifice and how vast it must be! But the merit you will have in preparing your daughter for it by the education of years, in your cooperation with it, and in your concurrence of will in it, will gain for you and Lord Henry a Presence under your roof more cheering and more consoling than that dear familiar face which you are losing. Ah how little I thought when I looked on her for that brief minute, that she was passing away from your eyes almost as quickly as she did from mine.[52]

Similarly, Newman consoled Mrs. J. W. Bowden, whose daughter Emily wanted to follow her sister's example and become a Visitation nun: "Your letter and Emily's took me quite by surprise, and startled and distressed me. I cannot doubt that we shall feel quite reconciled to it soon. All along I have felt for you far more than another can know—though far more removed from any one's understanding, except your Lord and Saviour's, is the extent of the trial which is apparently coming on you. He will sustain you, as you know well—and I suppose it is right and safe for you at present to make up your mind that it is to be."[53]

While Newman's letters were supportive, they were also characterized by honesty. For example, when Robert Whitty consulted him about his suitability to be an Oratorian, Newman responded very candidly:

---

52. JHN to Lady Henry Kerr, 18 September 1863, in *LD* 20:524. She wrote back on Christmas Eve to say how much good this letter did her and her husband, when they returned to Scotland, after leaving their daughter in the Sacred Heart Convent at Conflans.

Between January 14, 1852 and July 16, 1854, Newman wrote Mrs. J. W. Bowden seven letters as three of her children, Marianne, Emily, and Charles began thinking of a religious vocation. For these letters see:

JHN to Mrs. J. W. Bowden, 14 January 1852, in *LD* 15:11–12;
JHN to Mrs. J. W. Bowden, 10 July 1852, in *LD* 15:124–25;
JHN to Mrs. J. W. Bowden, 24 August 1853, in *LD* 15:411;
JHN to Mrs. J. W. Bowden, 30 March 1854, in *LD* 16:96;
JHN to Mrs. J. W. Bowden, 15 April 1854, in *LD* 16:112;
JHN to Mrs. J. W. Bowden, 9 July 1854, in *LD* 16:190;
JHN to Mrs. J. W. Bowden, 16 July 1854, in *LD* 16:197–98;
For similar letters supporting and encouraging parents see:
JHN to Lady Henry Kerr, 27 December 1863, in *LD* 20:567;
JHN to Mrs. Edward Bellasis, 21 February 1877, in *LD* 28:168;
JHN to Mrs. Edward Bellasis, 29 March 1875, in *LD* 27:256;
JHN to Lady Henry Kerr, 25 May 1882, in *LD* 30:90.

53. JHN to Mrs. J. W. Bowden, 18 January 1854, in *LD* 26:15–16.

> You may be sure we have none of us any but the kindest feelings towards you, and wish what is best for you and best for us. Do not think it is inconsistent with this profession if I say plainly that every letter you send convinces me more and more that you have not a vocation for the Oratory—for, if it is the deliberate conviction of all of us, as it is surely, our affectionate feelings and our true regard are best shown, not in hiding this conviction, but in telling you of it.
>
> Certainly it would be but insincerity and inconsideration to let you come back here, and cherish a fixed judgement in our hearts, which must come out practically when your first year of probation was ended, and a fresh voting took place for your admission into your second.
>
> You know the very name of the noviceship, in our Rule, is the *probation*—You have been with us since Christmas—and we think we now see, what could we then have seen, there would have been no need of any 'probation' at all, that it will not be for your happiness or for your usefulness, that is, that it is not God's will that you should continue among us ...
>
> It grieves me much to think, that we are losing one so sincerely attached to us, and who has so long taken a personal interest in us, but I am perfectly sure, that I am giving both you and myself and all of us less pain in coming to this decision now, than in protracting what is inevitable. I could say much about your last letter, and how each letter, as it comes, brings home to me with stronger cogency the certainty that God calls you elsewhere.[54]

When Newman perceived that someone was "using" the Oratory or undermining its spirit in any way, it evoked a sharp, immediate response. This was the case with Baron von Schroeter who was causing division in the community. Newman wrote to him:

> All blessings be with you, my dear Baron, wherever you go. I say so the more heartily, because I cannot think of you without sentiments, which it is very painful to me to entertain towards one who has been in the relation towards us which you have held. The Birmingham Oratory received you a year ago, a stranger coming without letters of introduction, with open arms. It has treated you with the frankness and warmth which it shows towards its own subjects. It has consulted for you with the most anxious delicacy and tenderness, and has honored you for the

---

54. JHN to Robert Whitty, 10 August 1849, in *LD* 13:250–51. Whitty was disinclined to leave the Oratory. He felt his vocation was the *London* house, but Faber and the London community disliked him.

Spiritual Direction on Vocation and Religious Life

grace God had given you. It has cherished you in its bosom with the most unsuspicious love.

In recompense, you have availed yourself of the opportunities these gave you to do your utmost to ruin the Institution of St. Philip, to make its subjects despise it, to fill them with suspicions against it and against each other, to prejudice externals against it. I am not simply speaking of the instance of F. Coffin, but of the general action of your presence among us on all who have come near you. One has heard of seducers getting into families, and ruining their peace. You have breathed out from you a sort of moral infection, which nothing could resist, under God's grace, but the antagonist spirit of loyalty towards our great Saint and his institution.

And now I have but one request to make to you; that you will not write to any of us, or hold any communication with us. . . . Not that I fear you; St. Philip has guarded this body and will still; but from charity to the souls of any you may have tempted, I am bound to make this request.[55]

George Ryder, a widower, also wrote to Newman exploring the possibility of dedicating his life in some more definite way. He had thought of undertaking some active work that would have involved mixing with others, rather than keeping to his family and the memories of his wife. With great sensitivity, Newman encouraged him honestly to consider the alternatives and consequences of his desires and whether they would be consistent with his primary vocation in relation to God's will.[56]

The needs of persons thinking about leaving religious life provided another context for insights into Newman's honesty in directing others. When Arthur Hutton told him in 1883 that he had lost all belief in the existence of a personal God, the empathy of Newman is manifested in his response:

> I will not allow that you are, as you say, "irrevocably cut off" from your friends (all that is dear to you),—and since your letter to me came, I have wished to say so. I treasure the words in that letter in which you almost anticipate (may I not use the term?) that the time will come, when you will "make a sincere act of faith in Catholicism." That will be a joyful day, and I assure you of our united prayers that God will hasten its coming. You

---

55. JHN to Baron von Schroeter, 28 November 1850, in *LD* 14:146–47.
56. For a development of this matter see:
JHN to George Ryder, 21 September 1853, in *LD* 15:427;
JHN to George Ryder, 25 September 1853, in *LD* 15:430–31.
JHN to George Ryder, 8 January 1854, in *LD* 16:11–12.

believe more than you think you do, and God loves you better than, in your dishonouring thought of Him, you allow yourself to fancy. He will overcome you in spite of yourself.[57]

On another occasion, in 1861 a controversy arose surrounding the Oratory School. Nicholas Darnell, who had been its headmaster, threatened to resign and leave the Birmingham Oratory. This prompted Newman's response:

> My first thought this morning was to write to you a private line, entreating you for St. Philip's sake to be merciful to yourself and to us. We cannot bear to part with you. You have a place in our hearts, and are rooted both in the Oratory and among our people. Why will you destroy the work of so many years, and leave all our affections lacerated and bleeding?
>
> There is only one thing we prefer above you, and that is our duty to St. Philip. I cannot believe that your good sense will not tell you, that you have been precipitate both in the steps that you have taken towards the Congregation, and in announcing them to the world. But, if your good sense tells you as much as that, why not say so? Is it not unlike your generous disposition to refuse to avow what I venture to say every one feels?
>
> If, however, you still refuse, I will not give up hope. I will hope that time and reflection will effect what our intreaties cannot. Accordingly, I shall propose to the Congregation to put off the consideration of your letter of resignation for six months, giving you leave of absence in the interval.[58]

On the other hand, if Newman felt that a person was changing their vocation for inadequate reasons, he did not hesitate to engage in a long series of letters to help the person clarify the situation. Such was the case with R. A. Coffin who wanted to leave the Oratory because he felt that it had no tradition of spiritual life or spiritual training. However, in reality Coffin had

---

57. JHN to Arthur Hutton, 15 November 1883, in *LD* 30:274–75.

58. JHN to Nicholas Darnell, 11 January 1862, in *LD* 20:119–20. Darnell subsequently resigned the headmastership of the Oratory School and left the Oratory. Three years later, Darnell wrote a letter of apology to Fr. Edward Caswell, who showed it to Newman. Darnell wrote: "I am quite aware that as a member and subject of such a Congregation as that of St. Philip, with such a superior, that my conduct was insufferably violent headstrong and conceited generally to the Congregation, and still more insufferably insolent, ungrateful and ungracious to the Father (Newman), and that anything I have since said by way of acknowledgement of my fault was quite inadequate to the occasion, and could never have been accepted as an apology either by the Father, the Congregation or those externs, alas too many, to whom I must have given scandal." See JHN to Nicholas Darnell, 16 October 1865, in *LD* 22:75n1.

been under the influence of Baron von Schroeter, who was causing dissension in the Oratory. When Newman learned this, he very honestly advised Coffin to leave.

With characteristic perseverance, Newman did not abandon people pursuing their vocational search through doubts and difficulties. Rather, it was not unusual for him to correspond frequently with persons who were attempting to discern God's will. The best example is his correspondence with Miss Maria Giberne; between April 18, 1859 and January 29, 1864, he wrote her twenty-two times concerning her vocation. Through these years she either applied to or entered five different religious communities and throughout this long correspondence Newman's understanding is manifest as he gently encouraged, consoled, questioned, and directed her. Finally his direction bore fruit when she entered the Visitation Convent in Autun in 1863, where she remained for the rest of her life.

Spiritual Direction and Religious Life

"Santa Communita"

Newman constantly emphasized the importance of "Santa Communita" both in his *Oratory Papers* and *Letters*. For him, an Oratorian was not simply a secular priest, but one "living in community." Accordingly, Newman had to work out a doctrine of perfection for a community without religious vows, for the Oratorians were neither "religious" per se, nor simply secular priests.

In his "Oratory Papers," Newman described what he meant by community:

> A community is more than a lodging house—it is more than a number of priests living in one house. It is a home and family; it is a number of priests living as one family; and hence the Superior is, in the Oratory, called simply "Father"—and the rest are called by their Christian names. A community is a whole or unity; it has one spirit, one mind, one view of things, one action; and the obedience which it exacts from its members, in which lies their perfection, is acquiescence, concurrence in this one spirit, view and action, as an act of loyal and dutiful submission.[59]

---

59. Newman, "Remarks on the Oratorian Vocation," February 29, 1856, in *Newman the Oratorian*, 447–48. Later that same year, he resumed reflection on the implications of "community": "Consider what is implied in the word 'community.' To live in community is not to be simply in one house; else the guests in a hotel form a community. Nor is it to live and board together; else a boarding-house is a community. Priests living in a chapel-house or presbytery, with each his own room, and a common table, and common duties

John Henry Newman

Newman's ideas of community life reverted back more to his comfortable Oriel College day, than to his more austere Littlemore experience. One of his earliest Chapter Addresses indicated his preference in unmistakable terms:

> Now I will say in a word what is the nearest approximation in fact to an Oratorian Congregation that I know, and that is, one of the Colleges in the Anglican Universities. Take such a College, destroy the Head's House, annihilate wife and children, and restore him to the body of fellows, change the religion from Protestant to Catholic, and give the Head and Fellows missionary and pastoral work, and you have a Congregation of St. Philip before your eyes. ... An Oratorian has his own rooms, and his own furniture ... they do not form a cell but a nest. He is to have his things about him, his books and little possessions. In a word he is to have what an Englishman expresses by the distinctive word *comfort*. And this characteristic of the Oratorian's private room is but a specimen of every part of an Oratorian establishment.[60]

Almost thirty years later in 1877, Newman reiterated this view in reply to Edward Plumptre, an Anglican, whose correspondence indicated his misunderstanding of the Oratorian vocation. Sensitive to his inquirer's background Newman explained:

> The nearest idea in the Church of England to an Oratory is a College, except that a College is dedicated to various Objects of devotion, the Holy Trinity, Jesus, Corpus Christi, St. Mary, St. Peter, St. John, etc. and an Oratory to one special Saint, St. Philip Neri—also that its few and simple Statutes are the same in all Oratories. Like a College, an Oratory is a local institution, is

in one church and parish, do not therefore live in community. To live in community is to form one *body*, in such sense as to admit of acting and being acted upon as one. . . . An Oratory is an individuality. It has one will and one action, and in that sense it is one community. But it is obvious that such a union of wills and minds and opinions and conduct cannot be attained without considerable concessions of private judgement on the part of every individual so united. It is a conformity, then, not of accident or of nature, but of supernatural purpose and self-mastery. It is the exhibition and the exercise of a great counsel, carrying with it a great sanctification, according to the maxim, which has almost become a proverb in the Oratory: '*Vita communis, mortificatio maxima*,' (community life is the greatest penance). Now I say, this conformity of will and action, based indeed on human affection, limited to place and person, yet rising within its limits to the full dignity of that self-denying religious obedience which is the matter of one of three vows of regulars, while it constitutes the bond of the members of the Oratory with each other, and converts a lodging-house into a community, is also the special index of its vocation and special instrument of its perfection." Newman, "Remarks on the Oratorian Vocation," August 18, 1856, in *Newman the Oratorian*, 333–34.

60. Newman, "Object," January-February 1848, in *Newman the Oratorian*, 192.

Spiritual Direction on Vocation and Religious Life

independent, and has no connexion with any other Oratory. Its members take no vows, may leave when they please, keep their own private property, and are, as a body, self-erecting.[61]

Yet for Newman, the basis of community life was not simply a matter of its collegiate structure; faith must be the basis for charity in community life. Without faith, there is very little chance of stability, and, over a long period of time a person will not persevere. In a Chapter Address to Oratorian novices he stated:

> The Christian life may be comprised in two words, faith and charity, as we all very well know. Faith is the foundation, charity is the building. Faith is the first and chief essential—because no building can stand without something to stand upon. . . . We see instances of this, alas, all around us in this country—instances surely without number of kind warm feelings, benevolent purposes, and pure intentions wasted and lost, because they are not founded and secured on the true faith. . . . This life is *wasted* in the case of so many, because they build their house on no foundation, because they begin with charity, or what seems like charity, when they should begin with faith."[62]

For Newman, the charity which is necessary to unify a community must have its foundation in faith:

> Our great duty we know is charity—that is charity towards each other—a most perfect singleminded openhearted love. . . . And that of course particularly, in the shape of brotherly love, and affectionateness which tends to be like that of kindred. Much do we hear in our rule and the writings of our fathers of former years of this brotherly affection as taking the place of vows, as being the bond between Oratorian and Oratorian, as being the principle of unity and the life of the Congregation. Much is not said about faith—But of course when all this is said about charity, it implies faith as its foundation—and as faith in God is the ground of charity of God, so faith in the Congregation is the ground of charity towards the Congregation—and as we have no security that we shall continue to love God without true faith in Him, so there is no security that affection shall continue towards each other, if we do not start with a firm faith in the Congregation and in each other. We enter the Congregation in faith—we pass on, we take it for granted, and then we go on

---

61. JHN to Edward Plumptre, 6 July 1877, in *LD* 28:219.
62. Newman, "On Faith," in *Newman the Oratorian*, September 27, 1848, 228.

to something higher, to charity—and are enabled to go on to that which is higher on account of that indispensable beginning, which we exercise indeed continually, but which we do not talk about because it is so obvious.[63]

Since Oratorians did not take religious vows, Newman felt that their ability to live in community was a gift from God, "a supernatural grace": "As faith is preceded and sustained by human reasonings, yet is really a divinely imparted assent to the Divine Word, so, were there not a real vocation, the work of a divine influence in the Oratory, its members would not keep together. It is not everyone who has this gift of living with others. Not every holy soul *can* live in community. Perhaps very few can do so."[64]

Although Newman believed that the ability to live in community was ultimately a gift that only God could give, he acknowledged the necessity of natural predispositions. The first of these is human affection. Newman believed that on a human level, it was necessary for the members to have a genuine liking for each other.[65] Human affection is the "animating principle," as well as "the initiative principle and the abiding support" of the Oratorian vocation. "It is this personal feeling which draws us to the Community, and keeps us in it; heightened of course and perfected by that supernatural charity, which enables us to retain and strengthen an affection, year after year, which, if left simply human, would surely die away. Perseverance in that affection is the work of grace."[66]

Consequently, Newman favored small communities; he felt that if they got too large, the members could not truly know one another well and this bond of affection would be lost. As early as 1849, Newman had written to Faber about the importance of small communities.

> Since then mutual carita is the basis of St. Philip's Rule, and love cannot exist among many (in the sense in which it is necessary for the basis of a Rule) *you cannot have a large Oratory*. We are too large for our Oratory. Nothing proves it more than our Recreations. The Rule at Recreation is that conversation

---

63. Ibid., 229–30.

64. Newman, "Remarks on the Oratorian Vocation," August 18, 1856, in *Newman the Oratorian*, 334–36.

65 Whenever he was considering how to recruit members for the Oratory, he stressed this idea of whether prospective candidates liked one another; he favored a slow, extended novitiate in order to observe this. In all of this, he was greatly influenced by his own novitiate, where one of the key questions that was asked of him and his friends was, "Can you all live together?" Newman, "Remarks on the Oratorian Vocation: Alternative Version of Letter V," March 1, 1856, in *Newman the Oratorian*, 448–51.

66. Ibid., 448.

should be general. Is that possible with us? does not every one of necessity talk to his neighbour? Hence Recreation, which is the time for showing and eliciting love, is just the stiffest coldest act of the whole day. For myself, if there is one thing more than another which makes me seem cold, it is our Recreations. No one (certainly not I) can talk confidentially or lovingly to a great number. Where one would unbosom oneself to each person separately, one cannot to all together. So intensely do I feel it myself, that I prophesy I always shall be accused of coldness and reserve, while we are large. What happens to me, will happen in its measure, I do not say in the same measure, to others. . . . If then Recreation *must* be general (as Baronius says,) the Congregation must be small. . . . The Oratory is a family.[67]

Another prerequisite for community life is obedience, which is the backbone of community life. In Newman's understanding of the Oratorian vocation (in contrast to the religious life), obedience is not vowed but voluntary:

In other religious institutions obedience is directed to a Rule or to a vow, and the community is obeyed on that account; here obedience is paid to the community as a first principle; and hence it is both necessary to the Oratory from the nature of the case, and its peculiarity as distinguished from other Congregations. I shall consider then obedience to the Community as our special means of perfection.

Among regulars the vow is the elementary principle of religious society; they obey because they have solemnly promised to do so. It is otherwise with us, we obey for the sake of obedience; we obey because we choose to obey, and for nothing else. Obedience then is our elementary principle, and thus we differ from others who live in community. And again, I say that obedience is not only special to us, but necessary from the nature of the case; for without this obedience for obedience sake, though we lived in one house, we should fall back into the state of secular priests. Thus we are kept out of that state, or rather elevated into something more than that state by the faculty of living together: since we are not obliged to do so, it is a matter of counsel. It is the counsel peculiar to us as members of the Oratory, and the means of our sanctification.[68]

---

67. JHN to F. W. Faber, 17 February 1849, in *LD* 18:55–56.

68. Newman, "Remarks on the Oratorian Vocation: Alternative Version of Letter V," February 28, 1856, in *Newman the Oratorian*, 445.

Oratorian obedience assumed even greater importance when coupled with Newman's understanding of mortification. For him the greatest mortification lay in the demands of community life; *vita communis, mortificatio maxima* ("community life is the greatest penance"): "Perfection involves some mortification, which is of counsel, not of precept. What is that mortification in our case? It is not that of renouncing literature and literary occupations, or the refinement of mind consequent upon them; it is not that of ceasing to be gentlemen and scholars; on the contrary, a certain moral and intellectual standard, higher than is necessary for secular priests in general, is one of the qualifications of the Oratory, as being an institution intended (the English Oratory expressly so) for the service of the upper classes."[69]

Accordingly, Oratorian mortification could not entail abstinence from gentlemanly pursuits. Rather, from his earliest days as an Oratorian, Newman maintained that the greatest mortification was in fact being obedient to each other; of yielding one's will to the others. "*External* mortification, as has been already said, is *not* the work of an Oratorian, but *internal;* or in other words, mortification of his private judgement, and his own will. And the necessity of internal mortification arises out of the simple fact that he lives in a community. For a community, if it be really such, and not a mere lodging or boarding house, if it be really a body or corporation, has a will of its own, to which the wills of individuals must be subordinate."[70]

Another distinctive characteristic of community life for Newman is best described by the Italian word *nido* ("nest"). The Oratory was not merely a place of lodging for ministers; rather, it was their home.

> The Congregation is to be the *home* of the Oratorians. The Italians, I believe, have no word for home—nor is it an idea which readily enters into the mind of a foreigner, at least not so readily as into the mind of an Englishman. It is remarkable then that the Oratorian Fathers should have gone out of their way to express the idea by the metaphorical word *nido* or nest, which is used by them almost technically.... The Congregation, according to St. Philip's institution, is never to be so large that the members do not know each other. They are to be bound together by that bond of love, which daily intercourse creates, and thereby all are to know the ways of each, and feel a reverence for "countenances of familiar friends." Familiar faces, exciting reverence,

---

69. Newman, "Remarks on the Oratorian Vocation," August 18, 1856, in *Newman the Oratorian*, 328–29.

70. Newman, "Santa Croce," August-September 1847, in *Newman the Oratorian*, 403.

daily intercourse, knowledge of each other's ways, mutual love, what is this but a description of home.⁷¹

Interestingly enough, a special place of prominence was given to the Refectory by Newman. Because the nature of Oratorian work throughout the day tended to be mostly personal or isolated, the community meal was one of the few occasions of common meeting each day. He considered it to be one of the chief religious acts of the day: "Our Church belongs to our work, but our Refectory to ourselves. It belongs to us as a Congregation, and has a special recognition in our Rule. It is not too much to say that it has a religious character, and may be called a sort of domestic chapel, and claims, as it is provided with, a ceremonial."⁷²

Building Community

Newman believed that there were three bonds of a community: charity, obedience, and what he called intellectual agreement. These three bonds were the essential factors that made community life endure over a long period of time. In a letter to Anthony Hutchison in 1850, Newman wrote about these three bonds of community, emphasizing the importance of intellectual agreement.

> I am truly rejoiced to hear on all hands so good an account of the London House—I mean internally. That it has a spirit of carita, I know quite well. What I am very anxious it should cultivate, if possible, is another spirit besides—not obedience, for that it has too—but a third. There are three bonds of a community, carita, obedience, and intellectual agreement.... It is astonishing how much men get over who have the same views. It is the way in which good kind of people get on together, and is no mean example of religious principles of love and obedience.⁷³

---

71. Newman, "Object," January-February 1848, in *Newman the Oratorian*, 192. Newman continued: "This is the principle idea conveyed in the word 'nest'; but other things are to be added. An Oratorian has his own rooms, and his own furniture; and according to the traditions of the Chiesa Nuova, without being luxurious, they should be such as to attach him to them. They do not form a cell, but a nest. He is to have these things about him, his books and little possessions. In a word, he is to have what an Englishman expresses by the distinctive word comfort . . . poverty, austerity, forlornness, sternness, are words unknown in an Oratorian house." Ibid. Newman derived this understanding from St. Philip Neri, who, for over thirty years lived in one small room at San Girolamo.

72. Newman, "Refectory," February 1854, in *Newman the Oratorian*, 289–90.

73. JHN to Anthony Hutchison, 18 February 1850, in *LD* 13:425.

In treating charity as a bond of community life, and exhorting others to live it, Newman developed what he termed the "basis of carita." For him, it did not mean that everyone had to agree on everything, but that persons should strive to be amiable and should try to acclimate themselves to each other.

> It is not necessary for carita, even humanly considered, that the objects of it should be strong minded or should agree with us in opinion, but that they should be *amiable*.
>
> However, nothing I have been saying interferes with my acknowledging how much must be done to put the Congregation on a better footing. On this subject I will not write today—but in conclusion I will remind you that all *Acclimation* is painful, and acclimation in a religious body as much as any one. No one but a Jesuit or a Trappist, knows what a Jesuit or Trappist goes thro' in becoming a Jesuit or Trappist—but the vow binds them and they must go thro' it. . . . We have no vows—and there is an urgent temptation to break away from that from which we can break away. We are able to speculate on want of peace and rest, for we have no vow to hinder us. But will our impatience benefit us? What religious order would suit us better than St. Philip's light yoke?[74]

The cumulative value of these three bonds of community for Newman, lay in the fact that he felt these would bring about unity in community life and therefore free individuals to be of service to the Church. As he stated in accepting W. G. Penny's departure from the Oratory, "All things must be subservient to 'santa communità,' and that 'all should accomodate themselves to the good of the community, which rule of conduct includes a treasure of merits,' that the first degree of charity is to the Congregation which is our mother, our nurse, and our guide to heaven; and that 'whoever aspires to sanctity must heartily follow holy community.'"[75]

Newman realized that this level of unity was difficult to attain. In 1850 he wrote to Faber saying, "From the first moment I thought of the Oratory, the natural difficulty that occurred was to secure unity."[76] At the same time it was important for everyone in the community to realize that they were

---

74. JHN to J. D. Dalgairns, 29 December 1851, in *LD* 14:486–88. This long letter was part of a reply to a letter written by Dalgairns in which he expressed his difficulty in living community life. He had written: "You say I take a gloomy view and you talk of a basis of carita. I acknowledge my gloom, and disbelieve in the carita. . . . I am broken in spirit. . . . All this has filled me with temptations to leave the Congregation." See Ibid., 487n1.

75. JHN, 30 January 1851, in *LD* 14:500, appendix 2.

76. JHN to F. W. Faber, 22 July 1850, in *LD* 14:18.

Spiritual Direction on Vocation and Religious Life

striving for this kind of unity together. It could not be brought about by one individual, even if that person be the superior. "A common Superior no more makes united houses, than England and Ireland would be one, with one queen, after the repeal of the Union."[77] Without this common goal, differences of spirit and opinion would arise making persons in the community either good friends or "better strangers."[78]

In his correspondence, much of Newman's direction of others in relation to community emphasized the meaning and value of these three bonds of community and the importance of striving together for unity. For example, during his first few years as a Catholic, he experienced the pains of acclimatization and difficulties encountered in founding two Oratorian houses. Much of his direction of others at this time in relation to community life centered around individual problems occasioned by the division of the Oratory into two communities—one at Birmingham and the other in London.[79] After these initial difficulties, most of his direction dealt with particular aspects of community life.[80]

77. Ibid.
78. Ibid.
79. For a series of letters treating these difficulties, see:
JHN to F. W. Faber, 4 February 1849, in *LD* 13:24–25;
F. W. Faber to JHN, 5 February 1849, in *LD* 13:29–31;
JHN to F. W. Faber, 9 February 1849, in *LD* 13:36;
JHN to F. W. Faber, 10 February 1849, in *LD* 13:38;
JHN to R. A. Coffin, 15 February 1849, in *LD* 13:48–49;
JHN to W. G. Penny, 16 February 1849, in *LD* 13:53;
JHN to F. W. Faber, 17 February 1849, in *LD* 13:55–56;
JHN to F. W. Faber, 20 February 1849, in *LD* 13:61–62;
JHN to R. A. Coffin, 21 February 1849, in *LD* 13:64–65;
JHN to F. W. Faber, 23 February 1849, in *LD* 13:65;
JHN to F. W. Faber, 31 March 1849, in *LD* 13:97–98;
JHN to F. W. Faber, 5 April 1849, in *LD* 13:104;
JHN to F. W. Faber, 21 July 1849, in *LD* 13:234–35.

80. These letters concerning particular aspects of community life are important for an understanding of his notion of "santa communita." See:
Concerning lay brothers and their relationship to the community:
JHN to Edward Caswall, 4 October 1854, in *LD* 16:266–67;
JHN to Ambrose St. John, 16 June 1858, in *LD*: 18:381–82.
On wearing the religious habit:
JHN to F. W. Faber, 16 June 1852, in *LD* 15:101–2;
JHN to Spencer Walpole, 18 June 1852, in *LD* 15:102–3;
JHN to F. W. Faber, 25 June 1852, in *LD* 15:107;
JHN, 17 June 1852, in *LD* 15:523–24, appendix 1. This reference is about leaving off the habit in consequence of the Queen's Proclamation.
On "numbers" in the community and the effect that those who leave have on the community:

At times his direction took the form of fraternal correction. With sensitivity and tact he wrote to J. D. Dalgairns concerning a fault that was affecting the community.

> I think then, Charissime, that you have a great fault, which, if I put it harshly, I should call, contempt of others. This has grown upon me lately, and I have reason to believe that others, independent of me, have the same opinion of you. No one among us speaks against the old Catholic Priests, as you do; no one so laughs at the Bishop as you. You are accustomed to laugh at every way of doing things but your own. At your doubts at table, you have laughed at FF Ambrose, Richard, and perhaps others. Your manner, when you *begin* or *rise* to do a thing, is, "Now I am going to do it." I think I have seen you thrust people aside, and do a thing yourself.
>
> When you came here it was as if *you* were going to do *the* thing and others were "slow." All ways were slow but yours. You never asked my advice from the first in anything. You took up certain youths. . . . You filled the rooms with them, because they were yours; the convenience of others, who had souls or who might care for souls also, being quite out of your thoughts . . . the penitents, the catechumens, the visitors of others might shift for themselves.
>
> Now all this would be defensible, were you simply in your own home, but you were in a community house, and you were one of a Congregation, and the Congregation should be first, and its subjects subordinate. The Congregation should be supreme, it should be the prominent idea in the minds of the people, it endures, its members change, but they are individuals, and only instruments of the whole; whereas, as if to make the Congregation little and *yourself* first, not content with *private* leave takings, you preached a farewell sermon, thus putting yourself (*unintentionally*) above the Congregation.[81]

JHN to Sister Mary Imelda Poole, 21 April 1858, in *LD* 18:325;
JHN to Sister Mary Imelda Poole, 29 April 1858, in *LD* 18:338–39;
On the "spiritual friendship" of Br. Bernard Hennin:
JHN to Ambrose St. John, 30 December 1852, in *LD* 15:232–34;
JHN to Nicholas Darnell, 2 January 1853, in *LD* 15:238–39;
JHN to Nicholas Darnell, 4 January 1853, in *LD* 15:240–41;
JHN to Ambrose St. John, 6 January 1853, in *LD* 15:245;
JHN to Ambrose St. John, 7 January 1853, in *LD* 15:248–49;
JHN to Nicholas Darnell, 11 January 1853, in *LD* 15:256–60;
JHN to Ambrose St. John, 11 January 1853, in *LD* 15:261–62;
JHN to F. W. Faber, 12 February 1853, in *LD* 15:287–98.

81. JHN to J. D. Dalgairns, 26 April 1849, in *LD* 13:130–32. He replied to this

Throughout his correspondence, what emerges is Newman's concern for the individual and that person's growth. He was not in favor of universal rules; he favored personal guidance, as his letters to the novice master, John Flanagan, about the training of the novices indicate: "I like them [rules for the novices] very much, but think you must be very cautious of treating every novice alike. What is too strict for one is not strict enough for another. I don't mind your putting any thing on Harry [Ryder]—but you may break Victor [Duke]. Of course there is such a thing as a vocation or a want of a vocation—but what is a source of life to one is an occasion of scruples to another."[82]

Simultaneously, Newman felt that even though there were problems in community life, a person would grow best in community. For example, when Faber wrote to Newman about Henry Formby wanting to live outside the community, Newman responded: "He should be sure that the *secret motive*, or at least one motive, be not to get free of the restraints of community life. And he should consider whether those restraints are not the very thing he needs both for his moral advancement and his usefulness."[83]

A similar view was expressed in a letter to John Lans:

> The truth is, as you know far better than I can , it does not do for members of a community to live out of community. They lose their interest in the body, and moreover, losing the stimulus which it supplies to progress in the religious life, they become slothful, despondent, and tepid. This seems to have been Mr. Coffin's case, and from his own avowals; and then, finding himself without inward life, he judged of others by himself, and fancied that a disease attached to the body, which was his own. His mind brooded on itself, and at length he coloured the past, as well as the present, with hues derived from his own feelings.[84]

correction two days later. "I thank you again most sincerely for your letter. It has of course given me great pain for many reasons. One element of pain, I suppose, is the same sort of feeling as would come over a person who had thought herself a beauty on being shown her face in a looking-glass after small-pox. I can only now wonder at your forbearance and indulgence in tolerating me at all . . . on the whole I must acknowledge with pain that your picture is too correct." See also the following letters dealing with fraternal correction:

JHN to Ambrose St. John, 8 July 1850, in *LD* 14:7–8;

JHN to Ambrose St. John, 4 April 1856, in *LD* 17:203–4;

JHN to Thomas Godwin, 11 June 1854, in *LD* 16:153–55. To Godwin, Newman said: "Now, my dear Frederic, I judge of you by what I see—and that is, for the most part, by what concerns myself—and I certainly do think there is a great deal whether of indolence or self indulgence, or something or other in you, which, did I know you better, I could give a truer name to, which needs correcting." Ibid., 154.

82. JHN to John Flanagan, 18 February 1857, in *LD* 17:522.

83. JHN to F. W. Faber, 17 October 1848, in *LD* 12:299.

84. JHN to John Lans, 25 December 1850, in *LD* 14:176. To George Ryder, a layman,

On the other hand, he felt that it took effort to build community and that persons ought to encourage each other. When J. D. Dalgairns wrote saying that he was discouraged by several things happening in the community, Newman replied: "You must not droop. I feel this strongly. . . . Your business is to strengthen the bonds, and deepen the feelings, which unite these Fathers to each other. . . . You have everything in your favor—Your only enemy is loss of self confidence."[85] Similarly he wrote to Faber concerning the difficulty of Formby: "Lastly, if he [Henry Formby] is not at all moved, you must not [I think] hesitate to put before him, that he will have a great trial, if he remains with us. He has to overcome *self*. But that in the process he will be cheered by the feeling, that it is a work of all others most pleasing to God; and that we on earth, his brothers, will cheer and help him on as well as we can."[86]

Qualities of an Oratorian

Given the historical background and the development of the special character of the Oratorians, Newman came to emphasize certain qualities as requisites for membership. It is a remarkable fact that one pivotal principle for Oratorian life which Newman brought away with him out of Oxford and Littlemore is the necessity for an Oratorian to be a "gentleman."[87] Basing his beliefs on St. Philip Neri's teaching and early Oratorian life, he conceived

---

he wrote on December 12, 1850: "When men live out of community, there is a great danger of their thinking that community is nothing to them." *LD* 14:168.

85. JHN to J. D. Dalgairns, 17 December 1851, in *LD* 14:472–73.

86. JHN to F. W. Faber, 17 October 1848, in *LD* 12:299.

87. See Newman's well-known "Definition of a Gentleman," in *Idea of a University*, 208–11: "Hence it is that it is almost a definition of a gentleman to say he is one who never inflicts pain. This description is both refined and, as far as it goes, accurate. He is mainly occupied in merely removing the obstacles which hinder the free and unembarrassed action of those about him. . . . The true gentleman in like manner carefully avoids whatever may cause a jar or a jolt in the minds of those with whom he is cast;—all clashing of opinion, or collision of feeling, all restraint, or suspicion, or gloom, or resentment; his great concern being to make every one at their ease and at home. He has his eyes on all his company; he is tender towards the bashful, gentle toward the distant, and merciful towards the absurd; he can recollect to whom he is speaking; he guards against unreasonable allusions, or topics which may irritate; he is seldom prominent in conversation, and never wearisome. He makes light of favours while he does them, and seems to be receiving when he is conferring. He never speaks of himself except when compelled, never defends himself by a mere retort . . . and interprets every thing for the best. He is never mean or little in his disputes. . . . He is patient, forbearing, and resigned, on philosophical principles; he submits to pain, because it is inevitable, to bereavement, because it is irreparable, and to death, because it is his destiny."

this quality to be a help to Christian perfection and essential for their particular apostolate.

In Newman's description, "gentleman-likeness" is the hallmark of a liberal education rather than a badge of social rank. Similarly, although his "Remarks on the Oratorian Vocation," treat "rank" as one of the qualifications of a Father of the Oratory, he posed the question whether the Oratory may have a long wait for recruits, since very few of such rank will be forthcoming. He replied that since St. Philip's time, a whole new class of society has come into being, so that a priest who has the education, if not the ancestry, of a gentleman, could completely exemplify the idea of a gentleman.

To the question "What have gentlemanlike manners and refined feelings to do with religion?", Newman replied:

> We are not here contemplating refinement of mind by itself, but as superadded to a high religious perfection . . . and it does not follow, because refinement is worthless without saintliness, that it is needless and useless with it. It may set off and recommend an interior holiness, just as the gift of eloquence sets off logical argument. . . . The gift of words is necessary to be able to persuade; and so the gift of manners may be necessary to win . . . though Christian excellence is abstractedly most refined, most winning, yet from various circumstances . . . it may not possibly be so. . . . And if this may be true even of saints, so much the more will it be true of a multitude of good men who are not saints, in whom from infirmities of various sorts, from natural temper, from the bad habits of childhood . . . the meek, loving and considerate Spirit of Christ does not flow from the heart to the eyes and the tongue and the other instruments of external communication.[88]

What is more important is the aspect of spirituality that "gentleman-likeness" should include.

There is a far greater tendency to misunderstandings, jealousies, irritation, resentment and contention, when the mind has not been cultivated or what is called enlarged, than where books and the intercourse of society and the knowledge of the world have served to put things in their true light, to guard the mind from exaggeration, to make it patient of differences, and to give it self command amid differences of opinion and conduct. I do not mean to say that these virtues I have mentioned are necessarily Christian—but they are Christian in a Christian— When a Christian mind takes them up into itself they cease to

---

88. Newman, "Object," in *Newman the Oratorian*, January-February, 189–90.

be secular, they are sanctified by their possessor, and become the instruments of spiritual good.[89]

Conversely, the lack of such education can have regrettable results among religious: "We have but to reflect upon the petty quarrels which are apt to divide religious houses, the rivalries, the punctilios and the misconceptions, and then again which exist in such very various and aggravated forms in the world at large to feel the influence of a liberal education and the experience of life in enabling the mind to be at once calm yet observant and versatile."[90]

While Newman wanted the Oratorians to be gentlemen, he also wanted his brothers to relate to each other in fraternal charity. "St. Philip, we know, founded his Congregation in charity—making it the distinguishing mark by which his children were different from regulars, that what regulars did from observance of the sanctity of their vow, the Oratorian was to do from love. Love was to stand in the place of vows."[91] Yet Newman recognized that this is a difficult process. "But it must be confessed such instances are instances of a passion or affection, and we cannot at a moment by willing or by trying bring ourselves into such a state. We cannot have a personal love towards individuals without going through a course of discipline, in order to obtain it, without much care and watchfulness, without knowing them well, without observing many minute rules."[92]

In order to foster this fraternal love in community, its members must see themselves not as isolated individuals who happen to live together but as members of one body. For Newman this implied a willingness to "bear one another's burdens." "What I mean by bearing each other's burdens is simply this: that every one in his place should not only do his own duty, but should try to support and cheer others in theirs. . . . Do not be content with barely doing your duty up to the necessary work, but throw your heart in it—nay more, do the duty of others, and when you help them do it with that delicacy, genialness and good nature that they may feel it, not an encroachment, but a real kindness, and be grateful to you."[93]

In practice, "looking at ourselves as one body" meant "hiding as far as is right the imperfections or deficiencies or mistakes of others, not drawing them into open view, putting them aside from one's mind, and dwelling upon their strong point or amiable points of character."[94] Fraternal behav-

89. Newman, "Stae Apolloniae," in *Newman the Oratorian*, February 9, 1848, 214.
90. Ibid.
91. Newman, "Behaviour towards Each Other," June 30, 1848, 222.
92. Ibid., 223.
93. Ibid.
94. Ibid., 223–24.

ior also means "not to do things grudgingly . . . to avoid any unnecessary criticism (observation), knowing that any one can look on and see faults, but few persons can act without committing a great many: not to say a thing behind a person's back which we would not say to his face."[95] In fraternal life, "as a rule, it would seem best, when we see or think we see any thing going wrong, great or small, not to talk of it, but to mention it privately to the person it concerns, the head of the department or the like."[96]

While the Oratorians were not obliged to share their possessions by a vow of poverty, in a deeper sense, there was "the duty for us to have all things in common."[97]

> Our property, whatever it be, is our own, and there may be duties upon it external to the Congregation. But our persons, if I may so speak, are not our own—our time, our thought, our trouble, our abilities, are not our own. . . . When he became an Oratorian, he gave himself up, and became the property of others. And in like manner, as far as may be, there should be a common mind in the Congregation—each should profit by the advantages of the others—What proceeds from the Congregation of a theological, or literary kind, should be the work of all—I mean, that is one to exhaust what he has of learning or resources on his own name, or should seek the aggrandiziment [sic] of his own name, but should freely give to others, be willing for others to have the credit, of his own labour, knowledge or ability.[98]

Such sharing should effect a simple confidence among the members of the Oratory.

Newman realized that fraternal "behaviour towards each other" was not an easy task. Similarly, acutely aware of the existing divisions among classes in England, Newman wanted the Oratory to be a leaven both in the Church and in society. "There is a very great danger I am persuaded of our body getting (and partly justly) a character of uppishness, flippancy, criticalness and the like, from neglect of mortifying those tendencies which lead to these odious results . . .

"I have already hinted at the divisions in the Catholic body in England—your mission is to lessen them, to destroy them, to bind together in one, good men whom perverse circumstances or rather I suppose our Enemy is keeping separate from one another."[99]

95. Ibid., 224.
96. Ibid.
97. Ibid.
98. Ibid., 224-25.
99. Newman, "Behavior towards Those Who Are Without," in *Newman the*

John Henry Newman

Ministry of the Oratory

"Responsibility for souls," was a pastoral principle indelibly imprinted on Newman from the time of his ordination as a deacon in the Church of England.[100] Both as an Anglican and as a Roman Catholic, Newman had a great dedication to and a capacity for ministry. Although engaged in parish work, it was not specifically characteristic of his care for souls; rather education, considered as pastoral care, was his true field and, in one way or another, occupied most of his life.[101] In 1879, among his replies to Addresses made to him on the occasion of his cardinalate, there is one brief but pregnant response, in reply to the members of the Catholic Poor School Committee, which underlines his lifelong commitment to an intellectual apostolate: "Long before I was a Catholic Priest . . . when I was Public Tutor of my College at Oxford, I maintained, even fiercely, that my employment was distinctly pastoral."[102]

Oratorian, June 17, 1848, 219–20. Newman enumerated certain attitudes that Oratorians should have in relating to people. "It is very difficult to draw the line, and far be it from me to weigh any one's words sentence by sentence—but I urge on you to repress, as far as may be a critical *spirit—be* on your guard against it—do not be fond of finding fault—take everything in the best point of view—and, as far as you can, speak well of people. Not only be humble, but let your humility take such a form that, without your intending it, people may be moved by it. Do not put yourselves forward—do not talk much before others—do not argue much except in private, and when you are sure of people and never dispute and debate, *avoid* argument, when offered and be on your guard against saying strong things, or even sharp things. Meditate on the odiousness of smartness, flippancy, and overbearingness—till you are disgusted with them, and feel the bad taste, not to say the moral impropriety, of such exhibitions. Modesty, gravity, gentleness, cheerfulness, tranquility, these are the tempers suitable for an Oratorian." Ibid. In 1852, many of these qualities became a part of his definition of a gentleman, which he wrote in his *Idea of a University*.

100. Newman, *Autobiographical Writings*, June 13, 1824, 201: "I have the responsibility of souls on me to the day of my death."

101. Newman, *Newman the Oratorian*, 18, 121. Newman saw education as a profoundly religious duty and a mission for which he was destined.

102. Newman, *Addresses*, 184. When he was appointed one of the public tutors of Oriel in 1826, his journal entry on his twenty-fifth birthday expressed his feelings about his tutorship: "And now, O Lord, I am entering with the new year into a fresh course of studies [i.e., the tutorship]. May I engage in them in the strength of Christ, remembering I am a minister of God, and have a commission to preach the Gospel, remembering the worth of souls, and that I shall have to answer for the opportunities given me of benefitting those under my care." Newman, *Autobiographical Writings*, February 21, 1826, 209. After a month's experience of tutoring, he noted: "I think the Tutors see too little of the men, and that there is not enough of direct religious instruction. It is my wish to consider myself as the minister of Christ. May I most seriously reflect, that, *unless* I find that opportunities occur of doing spiritual good to those over whom I am placed, it will become a grave question, whether I *ought* to continue in the Tuition."

Later, as an Oratorian, Newman developed his understanding of Oratorian ministry from a close analysis of the spirit of St. Philip and his early followers. In adapting Oratorian life for England, Newman realized that a slavish interpretation of the Rule was both impossible and undesirable. Rather, he wanted to adapt the spirit of St. Philip to English ways. In a letter to T. F. Knox explaining the difference between Oratorians, Sulpicians, and Jesuits he wrote: "We must throw ourselves into the spirit of that which we are."[103]

Because Oratorian life centered on a particular place, residence became a dominant factor in determining the forms of their ministry.[104] "I consider that any occupation which carries a Father often or for a considerable time from the Oratory, is inconsistent with its spirit but of course some latitude of view is necessary in this matter, and Oratories will differ in their judgement on the point."[105]

In comparing the Oratory to other religious communities in relation to continuous residence, Newman wrote to John Flanagan in 1857: "It seems St. Philip's will that we should depend on our *neighbourhood*—every other

---

Ibid. Newman always considered his office of Tutor as part of his pastoral duties. Ultimately this cost Newman his job, because the Provost, Hawkins, who regarded the Tutor's office as a secular one, objected and refused to assign pupils to him. Dessain, *John Henry Newman*, 12.

103. JHN to T. F. Knox, 10 September 1847, in *LD* 12:112–13. Realizing that the work of the Oratory in England had to be adapted to suit the changing times, he said: "The next subject I shall come to consider is the work of the Oratory. I observe then that every institution gradually forms its objects and duties as it grows, and it would appear that not even St. Philip knew at first what the Oratory was to be. On looking back at its history through several centuries, as far as we have the opportunity of contemplating it, we can see what it has become; and in those traditions of the past we might at first sight have been disposed to rest. But there have been indications at various times of the desire of the Holy See to expand and to accommodate the uses of the Oratory according to circumstances and the change of times, and I think I shall be employing my thoughts usefully, if I lay down some canons or principles upon the subject." Newman, "Remarks on the Oratorian Vocation: Rough Draft," March 5–9, 1856, in *Newman the Oratorian*, 305–6.

104. Newman, "Remarks on the Oratorian Vocation," August 18, 1856, in *Newman the Oratorian*, 329–30. "First of all their vocation is to a *fixed place*, and, I may say, to a particular body. Regulars may consider themselves wanderers upon the face of the earth; such is not a Father of the Oratory . . .

"*Residence* has in consequence ever been enforced as a cardinal point in the Oratory. . . . And this residence, I say, is treated, not simply as a duty, but as a necessary bond of the community in the absence of vows, promoting, as it does, a triple attachment, to the *place and neighbourhood*, to the *Fathers*, and to one's own room."

105. Newman, "Remarks on the Oratorian Vocation: Rough Draft," March 5–9, 1856, in *Newman the Oratorian*, 306. This point was very real for Newman as he was frequently away in Ireland from 1851 to 1858 as rector of the Catholic University. Initially he was not going to accept the position, but finally consented to it after the encouragement of the community and papal approval.

hope seems to break under us. . . . The Oratory is an isolated body, and a local one. If the Jesuits or Redemptorists do not get on well in one country, they can betake themselves to another. But we must found a claim of merit, and exhibit a visible, tangible, serviceableness, in that red brick house which stands upon a triangular island close to the Plough and Harrow. We have yet to find our place, as an Oratory, in the English Church."[106]

Another emphasis in Oratorian ministry was its orientation towards the *ordo honestior* ("upper classes").[107] Although this emphasis eventually proved to be a serious source of tension in the development of the English Oratory,[108] it is one of the major reasons why Newman wanted the Oratorians to be a learned body, pursuing science, the arts and literary endeavors.[109]

Following St. Philip, Newman believed that his own role as well as that of the Oratory was to be one of personal influence. It was primarily through the ministry of education that this influence could be exerted. Newman was able to realize his ideas to some degree by accepting the Rectorship of the Catholic University in Ireland (1851–1858). Subsequently, the Birmingham Oratory opened a school for boys. In spite of delays, disappointments, and the prospect of failure, the school "while remaining small, proved a real success, and its example and competition raised the standard of the other Catholic schools."[110]

In addition to educational work, Oratories commonly had a parish attached to them; within the general parish structure, particular emphasis was given to both preaching and hearing confessions.[111] Finally, and per-

---

106. JHN to John Flanagan, 31 October 1857, in *LD* 18:158–59.

107. This important phrase is found in the official Brief of Pius IX authorizing Newman to establish the Oratory in England. "We highly approve of the intention of Newman and his companions, who, while performing all the functions of the sacred ministry in England, have at the same time this especially in mind, to aim at doing whatever they think will best promote the cause of religion in the higher cities, and among the more educated." Pius IX, "Papal Brief," in *Newman the Oratorian*, November 26, 1847, 426.

108. For a discussion of the disagreement between Newman and Faber in relation to ordo honestior, see Newman, *Newman the Oratorian*, 95–104.

109. Newman, "Remarks on the Oratorian Vocation," August 18, 1856, in *Newman the Oratorian*, 323. "It is indeed its very characteristic, on the contrary, to admit distinctly and freely of the cultivation of art, learning, and science, in those members whose gifts lead that way, provided of course that that cultivation be directed solely to the glory of God and the salvation of souls, which are the ends of the Christian ministry. . . . I say, that learned studies and literary pursuits and fine arts, far from being proscribed in the Oratory, have had a distinct place there from the first."

110. Dessain, *John Henry Newman*, 110.

111. When Newman returned from Ireland in November 1858, he had to consider whether he should devote his time and energy to routine confessions; Newman,

haps surprisingly, Newman felt it important for Oratorians to minister at the Union Workhouse and the prison:

> The Union Workhouse comes next to be mentioned: and the care of it is just one of those works, which, historically belong to the Oratory. Not only did St. Philip send the Brothers of the Oratory, to the hospitals, as their distinct work on feast days; but Baronius, when a priest and as a priest, attended them. The Blessed Sebastian is said to have preached, among other places, in poor houses, prisons, and hospitals . . .
> The care of the prison is another of those works; we may trust that, as time goes on, we may be able to do more there [than] the law of the land allows us at present.[112]

"Counsels"

Although Oratorians as secular priests living in community did not take vows, the counsels of poverty, chastity and obedience were important aspects of Newman's idea of religious life, and one of the principal areas in which he directed others. In contrast to the religious life where poverty is vowed, the Oratorian vocation did not entail the obligation of poverty. As Newman observed, "Our perfection, as we well know, does not consist in the counsel of *poverty*. '*Habeant possideant*', (let them own, let them possess) were the words of St. Philip, when some persons were anxious to introduce it into his Congregation."[113] Since the Oratorian vocation did not include in the counsel of poverty, Newman rarely wrote about it. Occasionally, he connected poverty with mortification, especially mortifying one's own self-will, in what can be called poverty of spirit.[114]

"Return," 1857–1858, in *Newman the Oratorian*, 377–79. Deciding to resume his duties as regular confessor, Newman often spent long hours in the confessional; JHN to John Flanagan, 31 May 1858, in *LD* 28:261–62. In fact, one of his reproaches against Fr. Dalgairns, who eventually left the Birmingham Oratory for the London Oratory, had been his complaints of "the uninterestingness of routine confessions in the Church." Newman, "Chapter Address: Father Bernard Dalgairns," August 31, 1856, in *Newman the Oratorian*, 356.

112. Newman, "Remarks on the Oratorian Vocation: Rough Draft," March 5–9, 1856, in *Newman the Oratorian*, 312.

113. Newman, "Remarks on the Oratorian Vocation," August 18, 1856 in *Newman the Oratorian*.

114. There are only three letters in Newman's correspondence that deal precisely and explicitly with poverty; first, in writing to F. W. Faber on May 31, 1849, Newman deals with the proposed division of the Oratory and what individuals would have to

Second, in regard to celibacy,[115] Newman, early in life felt called to live a single life; he described this call in a well-known passage of the *Apologia*:

> I am obliged to mention, though I do it with great reluctance, another deep imagination, which at this time, the autumn of 1816, took possession of me,—there can be no mistake about the fact; viz. that it would be the will of God that I should lead a single life. This anticipation, which has held its ground almost continuously ever since,—with the break of a month now and a month then, up to 1829, and, after that date, without any break at all,—was more or less connected in my mind with the notion, that my calling in life would require such a sacrifice as celibacy involved; as, for instance, missionary work among the heathen, to which I had a great drawing for some years. It also strengthened my feeling of separation from the visible world, of which I have spoken above.[116]

Although he wrote in February 1829, that he had the "continuous will and resolution, with divine aid, to live and die single," still he admitted that at times he felt the need of the interest and sympathy that only a wife can

---

give up when they joined either house, in *LD* 13:165–66. In a second letter to F. W. Faber on June 12, 1849, he considered the situation of one person ministering to the rich and another ministering to the poor, in *LD* 13:170. A third letter to Sir Frederic Rogers on January 23, 1868, discussed the evils of accumulating wealth, in *LD* 24:14–15.

115. Newman preferred the terms "single life," "celibacy," and "virginity" which he seemed to use without distinction; the word "chastity" occurred once in a letter to Ambrose St. John on October 15, 1854, in *LD* 26:280. For example, in praising his friend Hurrell Froude Newman noted in *Apologia*, 32: "He had a high severe idea of the intrinsic excellency of Virginity." In February 1829, Newman wrote that he had "the continuous will and resolution, with divine aid, to live and die single;" eleven years later he stated: "All my habits for years, my tendencies, are towards celibacy." Newman, *Autobiographical Writings*, 137. His "Address on Virginity," January 12, 1854, in *Newman the Oratorian*, 176–77, which is his most thorough treatment on this subject, spoke about celibacy and virginity in consecutive paragraphs.

116. Newman, *Apologia*, 19. In the original draft of the *Apologia*, there is a passage written by Newman, but never sent to the printer; after the initial sentence of the passage just quoted, the manuscript continues: "This anticipation has held its ground almost continuously ever since, and it has been closely connected with that feeling of dissociation from scenes about me, of which I have already spoken. I had a strong persuasion that offences against the rule of purity were each of them visited sharply and surely from above: I have still extant prayers and memoranda of the years 1816 and 1821, showing my distress at the thought of going to dances or to the theater.

"This imagination arose from my feeling of separation from the visible world, and it was connected with a notion that my mission in life would require such a sacrifice as it involved. When I was first on the Oriel foundation it was associated in my mind with Missionary employment, or with duties at Oxford." See Manuscript of Apologia, Oratory Archives A., 36, as cited by Bouyer, *Newman*, 28.

give: "Shall I ever have in my old age spiritual children who will take an interest such as a wife does?"[117]

Newman did not flaunt his personal choice of celibacy in the Anglican Church where clerical marriage was normal. In fact, he had few Anglican precedents for his ideal of celibacy; his theological sources are patristic, not Anglican.[118] Although he had an unequivocal devotion to Our Lady as an Anglican,[119] his thought on Christian virginity is centered more on Christ than on Mary. His *Essay on the Development of Christian Doctrine*, speaking of the "Virgin Life" in the early Church as an anticipation of its future growth throughout the history of the Church, linked virginity directly with Christ: "Tertullian speaks of being 'married to Christ . . .' Origen speaks of 'devoting one's body to God' and St. Cyprian 'of Christ's Virgin, dedicated to Him and destined for His sanctity.'"[120]

As a Roman Catholic, Newman delivered an almost lyrical address on virginity on the occasion of the religious profession of Marianne Bowden, the daughter of one of his earliest friends. He linked virginity with, rather than opposed it to, the fulfillment of human love in marriage; human affection is not sacrificed, but transferred to Christ himself. "The Virginity of the Christian soul is a marriage with Christ. . . . And this it is to be married to Jesus. It is to have Him ours wholly, henceforth, and for ever—it is to be united to Him by an indissoluble tie—it is to be His, while He is ours."[121] For Newman, it was a positive choice that fundamentally oriented his life in a certain way, yet also a choice that entailed sacrifice. Celibacy is not an end in itself, not a "state of independence or isolation, or dreary pride, or barren indolence, or crushed affections." Rather, "man is made for sympathy, for the interchange of love, for self-denial for the sake of another dearer to him than himself."[122]

Manifesting his understanding of the pain and struggle that a celibate lifestyle can cause, Newman wrote to Thomas Godwin in 1854 because it seemed that Godwin's life was becoming more and more self-centered: "You have one yoke upon you, and far from me be it to say that it is not in its nature to all of us a severe one. God's grace does all things for us, as He has promised; and those whom He calls to a single life, He enables (blessed be

---

117. Newman, *Autobiographical Writings*, March 25, 1840, 138.

118. Newman, "Address on Virginity," January 12, 1844, in *Newman the Oratorian*, 271–78.

119. Newman, *Apologia*, 33.

120. Newman, *Development*, 409.

121. Newman, "Address on Virginity," January 12, 1854, in *Newman the Oratorian*, 277.

122. Ibid.

His Name) to lead it in all purity and honesty."[123] However, most of Newman's spiritual direction in his *Letters* concerning celibacy dealt with very concrete problems in the community.[124] The incident which occasioned the most letters by Newman occurred in 1852, when Bernard Hennin, a lay brother, entertained a kind of "spiritual love" for Mrs. Wootten. He sought occasions for speaking with her alone, and on one occasion attempted to kiss her. In July 1852, he came to her sitting room and spoke about "spiritual love" in a way that alarmed her. Since she did not want to be the cause of his dismissal, she spoke to Nicholas Darnell about it. Eventually, the news reached Newman, who wrote a series of eight letters within a period of a month and a half.[125]

Third, since Newman wanted to develop a doctrine of perfection in a community without religious vows, a constituent principle of the Oratorian vocation was needed as a point of practical spirituality. For him, the whole question hinged on obedience as the backbone of community life: where there are no vows, there must still be obedience if the back of the body is not to be broken.[126] He wanted an obedience which was the immediate result of a free,

---

123. JHN to Thomas Godwin, 11 June 1854, in *LD* 16:153–54.

124. For Newman's concerns, see: JHN to F. W. Faber, 23 June 1849, in *LD* 13:189; JHN to Ambrose St. John, 12 October 1854, in *LD* 16:278–79. In this letter, Newman wrote: "I am exceedingly displeased to find that Frederic has actually made a proposal to a young woman, *being in our house and having our habit on*." (Brother Frederic, Thomas Godwin, left the Oratory in 1854.) For other letters concerning celibacy, see JHN to F. W. Faber, 17 October 1849, in *LD* 13:271–72, where Newman wrote about how the Bishop had made a comment to one of the Oratorians about their conduct towards female penitents: "The Bishop . . . turned round and said (of course in love) he had heard a report that we were so familiar with our female penitents that they said they could marry us next morning—and that I was so reserved and had such notions about the line of delicacy, that he did not know how to come here and judge for himself of the reports circulated against us." See also a series of letters to T. F. Knox who had written to Newman about a nun who seemed to be mentally ill and had made a number of accusations against some priests:
JHN to T. F. Knox, 5 January 1851, in *LD* 14:189–92;
JHN to T. F. Knox, 7 January 1851, in *LD* 14:193;
JHN to T. F. Knox, 9 January 1851, in *LD* 14:193;
JHN to T. F. Knox, 20 February 1851, in *LD* 14:216.

125. JHN to Ambrose St. John, 30 December 1852, in *LD* 15:232–34;
JHN to Nicholas Darnell, 2 January 1853, in *LD* 15:238–39;
JHN to Nicholas Darnell, 4 January 1853, in *LD* 15:240–41;
JHN to Ambrose St. John, 6 January 1853, in *LD* 15:245;
JHN to Ambrose St. John, 7 January 1853, in *LD* 15:248–49;
JHN to Nicholas Darnell, 11 January 1853, in *LD* 15:256–60;
JHN to Ambrose St. John, 11 January 1853, in *LD* 15:261–62;
JHN to F. W. Faber, 12 February 1853, in *LD* 15:297–98.

126. Newman, *Newman the Oratorian*, 113.

spontaneous charity. Following St. Philip, he encouraged voluntary obedience based on love and not on a vow. In fact; the precise point of contrast between Oratorians and both religious or seculars is their willing submission to the ascesis of community life as the great means of perfection. "I should prefer to treat the subject of obedience, which is the counsel of perfection incumbent on us, more as a matter of loving conformity to the will of the Congregation, to considering it as a necessary duty to be paid to Rule and to Superiors. And in this higher, more comprehensive, and more generous way of viewing it, it has sometimes been compared to that voluntary and loving obedience which the Eternal Son rendered to the Father in our flesh, when He came to do His will."[127] In sum, Newman's understanding of obedience was three dimensional; obedience to the community, to the Rule, and to Superiors—an obedience patterned on Christ as the exemplar.

Voluntary obedience to the community was *the* special means of perfection for an Oratorian. "In other religious institutions obedience is directed to a Rule or to a vow, and the community is obeyed on that account; here obedience is paid to the community as a first principle; and hence it is both necessary to the Oratory from the nature of the case, and its peculiarity as distinguished from other Congregations. I shall consider then obedience to the Community as our special means of perfection."[128] To postpone one's own desires, to mortify one's private judgement and will in deference to the community was essential to Newman's way of thinking. "As *mortification of selfwill* is the vital principle of the Oratory, so *obedience* is the essential and necessary means by which it is exercised. We are to mortify ourselves by obedience, that is, by submitting our own will to that of another."[129]

Newman stressed this "unreserved obedience" to the community in a letter to Faber in 1850: "How can you trust a man's *perseverance*, who is confessed not to have the *principle* of obedience in him? Till he gives up his will, till he relinquishes that nasty unphilippine jansenistic notion of 'yielding an *Oratorian* obedience,' (unreserved obedience to his community) I cannot trust him."[130] This "unreserved obedience" included both an internal and external dimension, what he called "an obedience of heart, spirit, and the razionale [sic], as well as of external conduct."[131] For this reason, he felt

127. Newman, "Remarks on Oratorian Vocation", August 18, 1856, in *Newman the Oratorian*, 337.

128. Newman, "Remarks on the Oratorian Vocation: Alternative Version of Letter V," February 28, 1856, in *Newman the Oratorian*, appendix 5, 445.

129. Newman, "Santa Croce", August-September 1847, in *Newman the Oratorian*, 338.

130. JHN to F. W. Faber, 8 January 1850, in *LD* 13:374.

131. JHN to F. W. Faber, 11 February 1849, in *LD* 13:40.

that it was essential that a community have a superior. In corresponding with Richard Stanton he stated: "And I am sure you require a head—then he will have the responsibility, and you the bond of obedience. You cannot be a real community without a resident head—and you are a real community all but it. At present you are neither one thing or the other."[132]

Newman believed that obedience was the most difficult vow. In a letter to Mrs. J. W. Bowden, whose daughter Marianne was thinking of entering religious life, he explained: "The vow of obedience is the difficult vow. It is very complex—it is not merely obedience to one Superior, but to a state of things, resignation to companions she may not like, etc. etc."[133]

Since St. Philip Neri "did not write a Rule, as St. Ignatius might write one,"[134] but left what he had laid down for the experiment and judgment of the future, after his death, other decrees were gradually added. It was a collection of these decrees which tried to capture the genius, character, and customs of the Congregation which finally received papal approval. Because St. Philip "was most averse to rigid forms and burdensome externals," and because "the Congregation has not been established upon the Rule, but the Rule established by the Congregation," Newman felt "that what had been made since the Founder's time could equitably be unmade."[135] Accordingly, with papal permission, Newman adapted the Rule and Oratorian life to contemporary English life. And although the Rule did not bind under sin, nevertheless a voluntary obedience to it was essential for each member.

In speaking of those to whom obedience is to be shown, Newman listed first of all "the Congregation itself . . . in its legislative capacity" as the highest law-making Body.[136] Second, Newman wanted his fellow Oratorians to show a prompt obedience to all superiors in the Congregation as well as to each other in community and to do this "with the greatest cheerfulness."[137]

Newman's understanding of obedience was strongly influenced by Cardinal Tarugi's book *The Lives of the Companions of St. Philip Neri*. In a letter to F. W. Faber, he quoted from the book:

> As to your questions I think Tarugi's instance is sufficient—
> "Know, holy Father," he said to St. Philip, "that I am always and

---

132. JHN to Richard Stanton, 30 September 1850, in *LD* 14:83.

133. JHN to Mrs. J. W. Bowden, 9 July 1851, in *LD* 14:307.

134. Newman, "Remarks on the Oratorian Vocation," August 18, 1856, in *Newman the Oratorian*, 338.

135. Ibid., 339.

136. Newman, "Remarks on the Oratorian Vocation," August 18, 1856, in *Newman the Oratorian*, 342.

137. Ibid.

in all things entirely yours, and in this submission with your counsel and blessing I desire to live and die. I ask not to live either in Naples or in Rome, but I ask to live wherever you command me, even in a distant country if you should send me there."
"All the respect and subjection shown towards our holy Father Philip, must now be transferred to the new Father Superior, in whose person we must be careful to recognize the representative of the Almighty."[138]

As Superior of the Oratory, Newman did not always feel comfortable in his position of authority. In a postscript to a letter written to Faber in 1849 Newman said: "It is true there are persons who can by their manner and bearing claim to be loved and obeyed; and so would solve the problem at once, I feel deeply that I have not that gift, and so far, am unfitted (as also in many other ways) to be a Superior."[139] Later that same year, in writing about some difficulties in the community in terms of obedience and authority he said: "I can't command people about like so many soldiers or pieces of wood."[140]

Newman felt that the will of God was manifest through his superiors; in 1865 writing to Mary Porter he said:

> As you well know, a Catholic cannot expect to be prospered in any line of action which is not done under obedience.
>
> Since I have been a Catholic, I have ever wished to follow the call of God, and considered that He calls us through those whom He puts over us . . .
>
> When Dr. Wiseman the Vicar Apostolic in whose district Oxford lay, called me to Oscott on my conversion, I gave up Littlemore and went. When he sent me to Rome, I went. When he placed me in Birmingham, I obeyed him. Some years afterwards, when the Holy Father wished me to bring into existence the Catholic University of Ireland, I did that work diligently. Later still, when the Synod of Oscott, placed in my hands the charge of making a new translation of Scripture, I undertook it without a word.
>
> Last summer my Bishop gave me the Mission of Oxford, and I complied with his wish at once, and began without any delay to buy ground and collect subscriptions for a Church there. There was no work which could promise better than this for the fulfillment of that object to which you would call me; but

---

138. JHN to F. W. Faber, 10 January 1850, in *LD* 13:379.
139. JHN to F. W. Faber, 4 January 1849, in *LD* 13:25.
140. JHN to F. W. Faber, 9 December 1849, in *LD* 13:336.

the will of Providence was otherwise. The plan was stopped by persons who did not wish it done, if I was to be the doer of it.

I am old now; but, did Providence open a way for any important work, which I felt I could prudently pursue, I hope I should not shrink from it.[141]

Newman realized that people who have problems with authority can disrupt a community and make the superior's task more difficult. "They cannot bear, or at least some of them, the slightest exertion of authority,"[142] he wrote to J. D. Dalgairns in 1854. Nevertheless, Newman realized the value of consultation and of collegiality. Frequently he would ask the opinions of others[143] and after extensive dialogue, votes would be taken among the general Congregation on specific issues. He encouraged others to be involved in the decision-making process.[144]

Prayer

Newman's teaching about prayer, which is primarily developed in his sermons, emerges as an important theme in his personal correspondence. It was a topic he wrote about often in his correspondence with both religious and laity.

---

141. JHN to Mary Porter, 19 March 1865, in *LD* 21:430–31. See the comments of J. M. Capes about Newman's obedience in "Queen's Government and the University," *Rambler*, September 4, 1854, 189–209, as quoted in *LD* 16:201n1 (20 July 1854): "We believe it would be impossible to name any person, of whatever station, who has in practice, and in the most difficult of circumstances, more consistently acted upon his professions, and personally made every submission which authority could possibly require of him, without grudging, without ostentation, and without reserve. Obedience to authority, spiritual or secular, elevated or humble, has been a doctrine which he has uniformly taught, and which he has uniformly practised."

142. JHN to J. D. Dalgairns, 28 February 1854, in *LD* 16:63.

143. JHN to F. W. Faber, 20 June 1849, in *LD* 13:181. On one occasion when Faber seemed not to believe that his opinion mattered very much after Newman had consulted him, Newman wrote: "What in the world should I ask your opinion for, but to let it influence me? Else I might have acted without asking."

144 In a postscript to a letter Newman made an interesting distinction between seeking testimony and opinion in the consultation process. "I cannot help being amused at you, the more I think. I asked of you all two things—a testimony and opinion—an opinion whether it was *desirable for* the Oratory to serve St. W's [St. Wilfrid's Church, Colton, Staffordshire: the original location of the community founded by Faber], a testimony whether you in London *could*. I have taken your testimony, and rejected your opinion. *I have not given up my views* to yours, but I have carried it out in that way which, according to your testimony, was alone possible." Ibid., 182.

Although Newman did not have to unlearn anything concerning prayer in his conversion from Anglicanism to Roman Catholicism, he did sense an expansion of possibilities in his new religion:

> Again the effect of Catholic teaching concerning intention in prayer is so momentous, as to make a broad separation between the two religions. e.g. the Catholic believes that he can offer prayers which he does not hear, or which he does not understand, because He unites his intention with that of the person offering them. He says the Ave Maria with a certain intention, or he applies the virtue of it to the benefit of a certain person, perhaps departed. The difference is manifest externally. The Catholic Priest says his Mass as quickly as possible: The Protestant clergyman is slow and distinct, perhaps pompous or mouthing.[145]

Newman was convinced of the efficacy of the prayer of intercession, even though "we do not know how it is that prayer receives an answer from God at all."[146] As an acknowledgement of one's creaturehood in relationship to God is the foundation of this prayer of petition and at the same time answers the objection that a person is unworthy of such favors. In 1868, Newman wrote to Henry Wilberforce:

> God has given His friends a privilege—that of gaining favours from Him. A father says to his child going to school, "Now mind you write to me once a week." And he rewards him in various ways, if he is obedient in this respect. We are God's children—we are not grown men—Saints would worship God solely because He is God—"we all much love Him for Himself, but considering what we are, it is merciful that He has made hope, as well as faith and love, a theological virtue." But this is but a poor and scanty exposure of a wonderful paradox.[147]

The mysterious paradox and privilege of intercessory prayer was an essential part of Newman's spirituality and ministry. Parallel to his recommendation of praying for one another was Newman's belief that we are being prayed for by the Communion of Saints. His sense of the unseen world and the reality of the intercession of the Saints was an important factor in his teaching on prayer. He wrote to Mrs. William Froude in 1848: "To know too that you are in the Communion of Saints—to know that you have cast your lot among all the Blessed Saints of God who are the choice fruit of His

---

145. JHN to E. J. Phipps, 3 July 1848, in *LD* 12:235.

146. Newman, Sermon 19, in *Parochial and Plain Sermons*, 1:250; December 20, 1829.

147. JHN to Henry Wilberforce, 27 July 1868, in *LD* 24:107.

Passion—that you have their intercession on high—that you may address them—and above all the Glorious Mother of God, what thoughts can be greater than these."[148]

Immediately after his becoming a Roman Catholic, Newman began, and he advised other converts, to pray for the enlightenment of mutual friends. He urged Miss Giberne: "And now, My dear Miss G., that you have the power, pray, begin your intercessions very earnestly (though I need not say it) for those dear friends of mine, or ours, who are still held back, or rather imprisoned in their old error, and that by their own good feelings and amiable affections."[149] In a similar vein, he encouraged Ambrose St. John to pray for more conversions: "I think we shall have a haul of conversions *after Lent*, but do not repeat it. I would suggest the propriety of our having some prayers through Lent on the subject."[150] He likewise urged prospective converts to pray God "gravely and continually . . . [to] be *taught* His Will."[151]

The Oratorians maintained a private prayer list to which Newman added intentions as different needs came to his attention. He promised prayers and ask others to pray for those who were sick, and sometimes saw a connection between prayer and improved health. Concerning the pleurisy of Henry Bittleston, he wrote: "I think he is kept alive by prayers, and that, when the hands of Moses get tired and fall then he relapses."[152] He wrote to J. D. Dalgairns about F. W. Faber's sickness in 1861: "I am quite sure that his illness has been supported, and his recovery brought about, by means of the many prayers which he has earned from those to whose souls he has been of service."[153]

Yet Newman was prepared to accept the fact that sometimes restored health is not the will of God; and, with peaceful resignation, he encouraged others to a similar acceptance. When his close friend James Hope-Scott lay gravely ill, Newman wrote to the Duke of Norfolk: "I am writing as if I gave up hope—but of course we go on praying for a respite, nay a recovery—but how can we know what is best for him and for his? He is in better hands than

---

148. JHN to Mrs. William Froude, 16 June 1848, in *LD* 22:224. Linking prayer and the Communion of Saints together in 1837, Newman had said: "When we pray in private, we are not solitary; others 'are gathered together' with us 'in Christ's Name', though we see them not, with Christ in the midst of them." Sermon 11, in *Parochial and Plain Sermons*, 4:177; May 14, 1837.

149. JHN to Miss Giberne, 21 December 1845, in *LD* 11:74. Newman added: "You have all the saints of heaven to add [aid] you now, and especially that first and most glorious of Saints whose name you bear."

150. JHN to Ambrose St. John, 15 February 1846, in *LD* 11:115.

151. JHN to Robert Froude, 3 August 1864, in *LD* 21:181.

152. JHN to T. W. Allies, 12 March 1858, in *LD* 18:292.

153. JHN to J. D. Dalgairns, 3 December 1861, in *LD* 20:74.

ours. He who made him what he is, loves him more than we can love him. And as He cares for him, so He cares for all his also."[154] Similarly, during the fatal illness of his beloved fellow Oratorian Ambrose St. John, Newman confided to Mrs. Henry Wilberforce: "I can only say, 'Lord, he whom thou lovest, is sick' (John 11:3) and leave the event to him. I seem as if grief would kill me—but I cannot get beyond leaving the event to God. He knows what I wish, but why should I make any petition, when He knows what is good for us all? . . . Yet God will be good to us, and all things will turn out well, if we do but go right forward."[155] Subsequently after the death of Ambrose St. John, a letter to Mother Mary Imelda Poole provides eloquent testimony to Newman's grateful acceptance of Divine Providence: "I thank God for having given him to me for so long. I thank Him for taking him away, when there was a chance for him of a living death. I thank Him for having given me this warning to make haste and prepare myself for His coming."[156]

Anything of serious consequence in his own life and ministry was presented to God by Newman in his prayer.[157] When he was first trying to discern his vocation, he requested the prayers of Mother Makrena in Rome.[158] When the question arose of how to divide the membership between the two Oratories at Birmingham and at London, Newman asked for prayers for the gift of discernment. He commended his involvement in the Catholic University in Dublin to the prayers of his friends and acquaintances. He prayed and advised others to pray during the ordeal of the Achilli trial. In founding

---

154. JHN to Duke of Norfolk, 27 October 1872, in *LD* 26:190.

155. JHN to Mrs. Henry Wilberforce, 9 May 1875, in *LD* 17:294.

156. JHN to Mother Mary Imelda Poole, 5 June 1875, in *LD* 27:314.

157. Newman's ministry of prayer is evident in his notebooks which contained various intentions for which he prayed, usually before his morning Mass. These prayers were composed in Latin, Italian, and English, and he seemed to be particularly conscious of the indulgences attached to some particular prayers. Each day of the week had its particular intentions and people listed under a general heading: Sunday—the Oratory; Monday—the Household of the Faith; Tuesday and Wednesday—Catholic friends; Thursday—Protestant friends; Friday—General objects; Saturday—Occasional objects and persons. Under "General Objects" in the listing dated February 28, 1853, were: "Increase of Priests. Sanctification of Priests and People. Spread of Religion. Conversion of the Nations. All who befriend or help us. All who ask my prayers. All who attend our chapel. All who are in our schools. All I have forgotten. All who helped me in the Achilli matter. All in our mission. All in Birmingham. All in my land—the Queen. Catholic Education." Newman also prayed for the Faithful Departed, benefactors, and his opponents and enemies; listed under the last category were Brownson, J. Mozley, and Golightly. Ivory, "Doctrine," 197–98.

158. JHN to J. D. Dalgairns, 10 January 1847, in *LD* 12:9. Mother Makrena had a certain reputation for obtaining favors by her prayers.

and directing the Oratory school and in his efforts to establish an Oratory at Oxford, he likewise depended on the strength gained from prayer.

Newman did not hesitate to ask his friends to pray for his personal needs. There are numerous references in his correspondence requesting prayers for spiritual gifts, such as wisdom and peace, as well as physical gifts, such as good health and strength. When Mrs. Wilson wrote that she was not going to pray for him any longer, Newman replied: "One thing in your letter, however, I cannot bear at all—and that is your saying that you cannot and will not pray for me. I value your prayers very much, and I will not allow you, without my making a strong protest, to take such a despairing tone. I know God loves you, and wishes you to avail yourself of His love—and you must co-operate with Him in His merciful and great purpose on your behalf."[159]

This relationship between prayer and life was addressed directly in 1850 when Faber wrote to Newman, complaining of Dalgairn's unwillingness to be "called upon for community sympathies. Why is it, Padre mio, that men get more selfish the more they pray? Is it a stage like irritability in fasting?"[160] With unusual insight Newman replied: "As to prayer, it has two effects an acquired habit, and grace; and the acquired habit is often the stronger. The tendency of any one habit is to oppose others, or certainly contrary ones. Thus prayer as an acquired habit, becomes selfish, there's a great decision! It falls in with your parallel about irritability."[161]

There seems to be only one recorded instance when Newman refused to accept the prayers of another, and that was because he considered them misdirected in their motivation.[162]

For his part, Newman was always grateful for his benefactors and those who responded to him in his need. For example, he wrote to Eleanor Bretherton: "May all the kind thoughts, which you have for me, return upon your own head and into your own heart abundantly—and be a sort of stock of blessing for you all through life, in all trials and troubles, which you cannot now anticipate, and I shall never see."[163]

---

159. JHN to Mrs. Wilson, 21 February 1875, in *LD* 27:229.

160. F. W. Faber to JHN, 13 February 1850, in *LD* 13:425n1.

161. JHN to F. W. Faber, 18 February 1850, in *LD* 13:425.

162. JHN to Archdeacon Allen, 10 October 1876, in *LD* 28:121. "It is very kind of you to think of me, and I pray God that He may return your prayers into your own bosom. Not that I do not need prayer, but I cannot think that the particular prayer you make for me is pleasing to God. . . . My dear Sir, I have stood where you stand, and understand you—you have never stood where I stand and cannot understand me—but God bless you for your good intentions."

163. JHN to Eleanor Bretherton, 21 February 1866, in *LD* 22:161.

Spiritual Direction on Vocation and Religious Life

Newman also manifested in his correspondence his belief in the fact that God answers persevering prayer. The answer may not always be in conformity with the petitioner's expectations, but the answer will ultimately be for the person's good.

> It is no want of faith in you to put yourself simply into the hands of our dear Lord, that He may do with you what He will. He must not be supposed to turn a deaf ear to prayer, because he answers it in His own way. It is impossible that a blessing should not come to you in consequence of so many prayers made for you—and if He does not give the very favour asked for, it is because He has it in purpose to give you a greater. Any how, you are His—and prayer will make you more fully His.[164]

When Mrs. Lockhart told Newman that some of her relatives had recently been accepted into the Catholic Church, he counseled her to be thankful to God for answering her persevering prayer. "It is indeed a great instance, for which we cannot be too thankful, how God answers persevering prayer."[165] Even when the person was mistaken in the intended object of his prayer, Newman was confident that God would answer such kind prayers "by a true interpretation of them."[166]

Finally, although Newman prayed a great deal, preached about prayer and directed others in prayer, he rarely wrote about the "way" he prayed or the "method" he used in meditation. However, there is one letter, written in 1865, to Miss M. R. Giberne (by then Sister M. Pia) in response to a question she had asked concerning meditation. In this letter Newman shared his own personal struggle along with his realization of the need for adapting one's prayer to changing age.

> If I have not written in answer to any question of yours about yourself, it was because I did not observe it, because I fancied you had sufficient advice where you are, and because I am so little fitted to give it. What you say of your own difficulty in meditation, is quite what I should say of myself, if that is any comfort to you. I think the mind is weakened as one gets old, and cannot hold an idea any more than the muscles can hold

---

164. JHN to Marianne Bowden, 29 May 1867, in *LD* 23:242–43.
165. JHN to Mrs. Lockhart, 7 July 1850, in *LD* 14:5.
166. JHN to Robert Whitty, 26 January 1884, in *LD* 30:301. "It is difficult for others to know one's trials and their kindness often mistakes where the sharpness of them really lies. We certainly have some great anxieties, but they are not easy to guess; and as to the one to which you seem to refer, what to the many friends would seem the trial is to me the greatest relief and compensation of it. But God who knows all secrets answers their kind prayers for us, by a true interpretation of them."

a heavy weight. And then again, as the eyes get dim and the hearing dull, so in like manner the affections do not act in sensible emotions as they do when people are young. All this is very painful, and unsatisfactory—but I trust it is not a sign of falling back. What I try to do is to live more in the sight of God, and to try to be acting to His glory. But you must pray for me that I may not get into a bad way—and that I may not do anything that may mislead you.[167]

Penance

Another area of the spiritual life in which Newman directed others was that of penance. As an Oratorian, Newman was greatly influenced by St. Philip Neri, who maintained that mortification of the *razionale* was what mattered most—the submission of our own opinions to the will of God. Physical discipline of any kind should be a means to mental discipline.[168]

Specifically, Newman believed that the greatest mortification was to do well the ordinary duties of the day.[169] When George Ryder, a layman, wrote to Newman asking his advice as to whether he should do some penance, Newman replied: "I would not have you go to any mortifications. I will tell you what is the greatest—viz. to do well the ordinary duties of the day. De-

---

167. JHN to Miss M. R. Giberne, end of May 1865, in *LD* 21:480.

168. For a treatment of St. Philip's influence on Newman's thinking about penance, see "Santa Croce," August-September 1847, 403–4. In reflecting "On Mortification of Self," Newman distinguished between external and internal mortification: "*External* mortification, as has been already said, is not the mark of an Oratorian, but *internal*; or in other words, mortification of his private judgement, and his own will." By *razionale* is meant "every superfluous or undue exercise of the intellect, and not to aim to be wise and rational in every matter, since perfection consists in bringing one's own will into captivity." On August 30, 1855, Newman, writing to Catherine Bathurst concerning what he termed "mortifications of intellect," listed eight points:

"Not to ask for reasons why
Not to say, 'I hope it will turn out well' (with the Vicar of Wakefield)
Not to say 'I told you so.'
Not to desire to hear the news
To be willing to be ignorant of many branches of knowledge, etc.
Not to be eager about history
Not to be eager for the explanation of Scripture difficulties, or difficulties and mysteries of faith

In a conflict of opinions and judgements, instinctively to feel you are less likely to be right than another." *LD* 16:533–34.

169. Newman, "Short Rule to Perfection," September 27, 1856, in *Newman the Oratorian*, 359–60.

termine to rise at a certain hour—to go through certain devotions—to give certain hours to your boys—Don't oppress yourself with them, but *keep* to your rules—and you will find it a sufficient trial."[170]

Newman found ample opportunity for mortification in fulfilling the duties within his community. For example, reflecting on the anxiety occasioned by the Oratory School, he wrote Robert Ornsby: "For ourselves here, of course the School is a perpetual anxiety, though we have been abundantly blessed in our endeavours—but it is a hair shirt, and nothing short of it—and one which you can never put off. May we be able to offer it up to God worthily, and gain merit from it."[171]

Similarly, in 1869, Newman characterized his brief tenure as editor of the *Rambler* as a mortification that he only accepted because he thought it was God's will. Sharing his feelings with his friend Henry Wilberforce, he wrote: "I have the extreme mortification of being Editor of *The Rambler*. I have never had in my life (in its time) so great a one. It is like a bad dream, and oppresses me at times inconceivably."[172]

Newman believed in the value of fasting as a means of spiritual growth yet always emphasized the importance of prudence. If a person was able and felt called to fasting or abstinence, and if this did not interfere with their other primary responsibilities in life, Newman would accede to their desire. To Mrs. Peter Bretherton he wrote:

> As to your fasting, I fear it will interfere with your keeping your Rule. You will feel tired, and unable to go to Mass, or to attend when hearing it. Again, you have so much to sadden and depress you—and fasting may prevent your bearing up against such trials, and having the physical strength to go through them. But these two conditions being clearly kept in view, I mean, that fasting does not weaken your *observance of your Rule* and your *care of your husband*, I do not mind your trying it. But you must be quite honest, watch the effect—and use the full liberty which the Church allows you.[173]

Sometimes people wrote to him wanting to fast, but because of their age, health, travel, or other labors, he felt it would be better if they did not; at other times, he would suggest that they do some other kind of penance. With people who tended to want to do too much, he would gently advise them to be good to themselves. To W. J. Copeland he said: "Now, you are not

---

170. JHN to George Ryder, 2 December 1850, in *LD* 14:153.
171. JHN to Robert Ornsby, 27 December 1863, in *LD* 20:569.
172. JHN to Henry Wilberforce, 31 March 1859, in *LD* 19:96.
173. JHN to Mrs. Peter Bretherton, 17 February 1860, in *LD* 19:305.

indeed as old as I am, but you are old enough, not to be able to keep a strict Lent—and, since such fellows as you judge for yourselves, and not by good advice, I am tempted to preach to you, and beg you to be very gentle with yourself—for I want you to live many years, and never, never again to be so cruel to me as you were for near 17 long years."[174]

Since taking the discipline was part of the Oratorian rule, Newman originally pressed for its implementation for Oratorians in England over the objections of Faber.[175] Yet Newman realized that it was not a helpful practice for everyone; again prudence ought to be the practical guide. For other religious, he thought that they should follow the tradition of their community with regard to this practice, and for laymen he did not press it.

Summary

Throughout his Catholic years, Newman had many opportunities for directing people on matters relating to vocation and religious life. His direction of others was to a great extent colored by his Anglican background, his own vocational search culminating in his decision to be an Oratorian, and his emphasis on personal responsibility in the spiritual life.

Foundational to his concept of spiritual direction was "striving for perfection." His understanding, both theological and practical, of this "striving" was developed in his Oratorian addresses, and subsequently manifested in his correspondence. His letters "translated" what "striving for perfection" should mean for people in different vocational situations. His letters were practical not theoretical: their aim was to encourage people to strive for perfection (whether they were "religious" or not) in their daily life. Although a clear method of discernment does not emerge from his correspondence, Newman did mention such factors as never rushing one's process of discernment and decision and asking the advice of others, as well as prayer and penance. Favoring personal responsibility rather than universal rules,

---

174. JHN to W. J. Copeland, 23 January 1863, in *LD* 20:399. In a similar letter to Miss Giberne on December 25,1854, Newman wrote: "I have been very anxious to hear about where you were. I should like to put you under obedience to make yourself comfortable.... You must feed well.... It does not answer letting the spirits sink—and living by yourself must try you—so, please, do indulge a bit in the pleasures of the table." *LD* 16:336.

175. When Newman established the Oratory in England and wished to introduce the taking of the discipline three times a week in accordance with the Rule, Faber objected and sent to Newman at Maryvale a paper saying that it would deter people from joining the Oratory, and that it represented "the ascetic genius" which he thought contrary to St. Philip's spirit. For these letters, see: JHN to F. W. Faber, 12 December 1850, in *LD* 14:165–66; JHN to F. W. Faber, 18 December 1850, in *LD* 14:171.

Newman helped many people to discern God's will in choosing a vocation or in living out the implications of their vocation.

Newman's chapter addresses and correspondence indicates his belief that an English Oratory should be very much like an Oxford college whose members are "English gentlemen." Through personal influence, he wanted the Oratory to be an effective instrument of faith within society. While not neglecting to serve the poor, the primary ministerial emphasis was to the upper class. In order to minister to their needs, Newman encouraged the Oratorians in their scientific, artistic and literary endeavors.

In regard to the Oratory as "santa communita," Newman believed that faith must be the basis for the charity necessary to live in community. While this ability is a supernatural gift, human affection is the underlying principle, while voluntary obedience cements community. Since he believed that personal qualities would greatly influence their ministry, he exhorted the Oratorians to develop affection and obedience as essential in living their way of life. Accordingly, Newman favored small communities comprised of a select group of people, whose basis was not simply personal liking or ministerial compatibility, but rather charity, obedience and intellectual agreement.

Although Oratorians were not religious in the strict sense, Newman frequently directed others to follow the evangelical counsels. Because the Oratorian vocation did not entail the obligation of poverty, Newman rarely wrote about it. Second, although he felt a call early in his life to live celibately, he came to see that it was a positive choice that fundamentally oriented his life in a certain way, as well as a choice that involved sacrifice. Because he believed that people were made for an "interchange of love," celibacy was not an end in itself, but rather the transferring of human love to Christ. Third, he coupled obedience with mortification, seeing obedience as the backbone of community life. However, in his desire to delineate a spirituality for secular priests living in community without vows, he seemed to establish a false dichotomy between "vowed" and "voluntary" obedience. Last but not least, two particularly important aspects of the spiritual life for Newman are prayer and penance. However, his approach in these areas was more pastoral than theological; he desired to help correspondents understand the importance of prayer and penance in their spiritual lives.

7

Spiritual Direction and Friendship

*"Blessings of friends which to my door,
Unasked, unhoped, have come."*[1]

JOHN HENRY NEWMAN WAS a mixture of contrasting qualities. He manifested a certain detachment from the world and from things, yet he was never alone, never isolated from his friends. He had the gift of inspiring affection as well as reverence in those who came under his influence. He was preeminently a man who did not follow others, but whom others followed, at Oriel, at Littlemore, at Edgbaston—he became the center of a group of men for the most part younger than himself, who admired him and took him for their guide. To these disciples, he was always a hero, a person quite apart, yet both attractive and attracting.

A person's uniqueness is very often discovered through correspondence. Letters, whose purpose is so different from a book or sermon, enable us to catch a glimpse of the inner workings of a person. This was certainly true of Newman. Emerging from his *Letters* are certain qualities that tend to go unnoticed in his other literary works. The dominant quality that surfaces in Newman's correspondence with his friends is his humanness. With them he felt an interior freedom that enabled him to talk about himself. With them he could "let his guard down" and be comfortable, sincerely manifesting what was on his mind and in his heart. It is in his *Letters* to his friends that he spoke about his real feelings, his needs, his struggles, his joys.

---

1. Newman, *Apologia*, 25. Newman wrote: "It was not I who sought friends, but friends who sought me. Never man had kinder or more indulgent friends than I have had.... They have gone; they came to my great joy, they went to my great grief. He who gave took away."

Spiritual Direction and Friendship

Yet Newman had the need not simply to be admired, but to have persons with whom he could share his life—to have friends. In a very unique way, his personal correspondence portrays him not as a writer nor as a religious leader, but simply as a person who lived with others, who was loved by them and loved them in return. Since the experience of friendship is very significant in a person's development and spiritual life, this chapter investigates Newman's friendships in relation to his spiritual direction.

Newman's Conversion and His Friends

Prior to his reception into the Roman Catholic Church, Newman was living at Littlemore and struggling with his decision about the future. His own family lacked sympathy for and understanding of his crisis of confidence. When he began telling his family and friends that he intended to give up his Fellowship at Oriel, his sister Jemima protested, "What can be worse than this? It is like hearing that some dear friend must die. I cannot shut my eyes to this overpowering event that threatens any longer."[2] In a letter on Palm Sunday 1845, he described his anguish to his sister Jemima:

> At my time of life men love ease. I love ease myself. I am giving up a maintenance involving no duties and adequate to all my wants. What in the world am I doing this for (I ask *myself* this) except I think I am called to do so? I am making a large income by my sermons. I am, to say the very least, risking this; the chance is that my sermons will have no further sale at all. I have a good name with many; I am deliberately sacrificing it. I have a bad name with more; I am fulfilling all their worst wishes, and giving them their most coveted triumph. I am distressing all I love, unsettling all I have instructed or aided. I am going to those I do not know, and of whom I expect very little. Oh, what can it be but a stern necessity which causes this?
>
> Pity me, my dear Jemima. What have I done thus to be deserted, thus to be left to take the wrong course, if it is wrong . . .?
>
> Continually do I pray that He would discover to me if I am under a delusion; what can I do more? What hope have I but

---

2. Trevor, *Newman: The Pillar*, 349. Newman had written to Jemima that her letters "would have brought one to many tears unless I had so hard a heart. You must take what I do in faith . . . my circumstances are not of my making. One's duty is to act under circumstances. Is it a light thing to give up Littlemore? Am I not providing dreariness for myself? If others, whom I am pierced to think about, because I cannot help them, suffer, shall I not suffer in my own way?" Graef, *God and Myself*, 96.

in Him? . . . All is against me—may He not add Himself as an adversary . . . !

Who has a right to judge me but my judge?

. . . He may have purposes so merciful as they are beyond us. Let us do our best and leave the event to Him; He will give us strength to bear. Surely I have to bear most; and if I do not shrink from bearing it, others must not shrink. May I do my best; am I not trying to do my best?—may we not trust it will turn to the best?[3]

Similarly, his conversion caused a great reaction among his friends and significantly influenced his understanding of the meaning and importance of friendship both in his own life and for others. In 1863, he wrote to Charles Robins that the loss of his Oxford friends was "the greatest trial of my change of religion."[4] A week after his entrance into the Roman Catholic Church, his great friend and collaborator, Edward Pusey published a favorable reaction in a letter in the *English Churchman*:

> He (Newman) is gone unconscious (as all great instruments of God are) what he himself is. He has gone as a simple act of duty with no view for himself, placing himself entirely in God's hands. And such are they whom God employs. He seems to me not so much gone from us, as transplanted into another part of the Vineyard, where the full energies of his powerful mind can be employed, which here they were not. And who knows what in the mysterious purposes of God's good Providence may be the effect of such a person among them? . . . It is perhaps the greatest event which has happened since the Communion of the Churches has been interrupted, that such a one, so formed in our Church, and the work of God's Spirit as dwelling within her, should be transplanted to theirs.[5]

Such tolerance was the exception, however, and even Newman's relationship with Pusey became quite strained.[6] Moreover, Newman's brother-

---

3. Bouyer, *Newman*, 241–42.
4. JHN to Charles Robins, 20 May 1863, in *LD* 20:449.
5. Liddon, *Life*, 2:461.

6 See Newman's letter to Pusey, February 21, 1846, in *LD* 11:123–24: "How rightly I judged that it was best at present that we should not meet! This has been the reason of my keeping away from you. Since I saw you on Wednesday, I have heard that you thought my manner, on the only time I called, at the beginning of December, sharp. Such misunderstanding must be just now. . . . Would that I could say something which would sound less cold than this, but really I dare not. I could not without saying something which would seem rude. Alas! I have no alternative between silence and saying

in-law, James Mozley, publically questioned Newman's motives in an article in the *Christian Remembrance*.[7] The loss of old friends was keenly felt by Newman, as a letter to Miss Giberne revealed:

> Can you point to any one who has lost more in the way of friendship, whether by death or alienation, than I have? . . . So many dead, so many separated. My mother gone; my sisters nothing to me, or rather foreign to me; of my greatest friends Froude, Wood, Bowden taken away, all of whom would now be, or be coming, on my side. Other dear friends who *are* preserved in life *not* moving with me; Pusey strongly bent on an opposite course, Williams protesting against my conduct as rationalistic, and dying—Rogers and J. Mozley viewing it with utter repugnance. Of my friends of a dozen years ago who have I now? and what did I know of my present friends a dozen years ago?[8]

Although Newman had anticipated the price he would have to pay in the loss of friends, the impact was more than he expected. In 1854, he wrote to Robert Wilberforce: "In my own case, the separation from friends was the one thing which weighed on me for two years before I became a Catholic—and it affected my health most seriously."[9] For him, this was a special sacrifice that he offered to God. Seven years later, he described to Isaac Williams, what a trial this had been: "There is no pleasure of this world which to me would be so great in itself, as to see you and other of my old friends. Before I became what I am, the loss of them was the great trouble which lay before me, and it has not ceased to be, up to this hour, the special sacrifice which I offer up to my Lord and Saviour out of my deep unworthiness as a plea in my behalf when He comes to me in judgement."[10] Similarly, in a response to a writer in the *Literary Churchman*, Newman wrote: "No one knows as I do, what a piercing sorrow it was to me to part from my dear friends twenty years ago, and no one knows as I do how imperative was my duty, and how great has been the reward."[11]

---

what would pain me. May the day come, when it will not be so. Then old times will come again, and happier."

7 Trevor, *Newman: The Pillar*, 371–72.

8 JHN to Miss Giberne, 28 January 1846, in *LD* 11:101–2. See also, over thirty years later, JHN to R. W. Church, 9 December 1889, in *LD* 31:280.

9 JHN to Robert Wilberforce, 1 September 1854, in *LD* 16:242.

10 JHN to Isaac Williams, 21 October 1861, in *LD* 20:59–60.

11 JHN, 28 February 1864, in *LD* 21:65. The *Literary Churchman* was published by former Tractarians from 1855 until 1892. High Church in outlook, it aimed at being literary rather than controversial. Newman's response was to an article that had appeared in the *Literary Churchman* 10, February 27, 1864, 83–84, concerning his pamphlet "Mr.

John Henry Newman

After a separation of eighteen years, Newman, Keble and Pusey met again. In a letter to Keble on August 15, 1863, Newman expressed the depth of his friendship along with his love of God:

> Never have I doubted for one moment your affection for me—never have I been hurt at your silence. I interpreted it easily—it was not the silence of men, nor the forgetfulness of men, who can recollect about me and talk about me enough, when there is something to be said to my disparagement. You are always with me a thought of reverence and love—and there is nothing I love better than you, and Isaac, and Copeland and many others I could name, except Him whom I ought to love the best of all and supremely. May He Himself, who is the over abundant compensation for all losses, give me His own Presence—and then I shall want nothing and desiderate nothing—*but* none but He, *can* make up for the losses of those old familiar faces which haunt me continually.[12]

Newman's own loss of friends at his conversion became an avenue for his spiritual direction of others. Knowing how difficult his own loss of friends had been, he encouraged others to write about their fears of the possible loss of friendship over their pending conversion. Frequently, Newman shared his own struggle so that others might have some encouragement. Lady Chatterton had written to him concerning the unsettlement and skepticism her friends were experiencing when a person converted to the Church of Rome. Newman responded:

> I entirely sympathize in what you say about the force of the argument against a member of the Protestant Church leaving it for Catholicism, on the ground of the unsettlement and skepticism which it tends to produce in friends who do not feel the evidence for Catholicism as he may do. I felt it most forcefully myself. It made me miserable to think, that many and many a friend, whom I had been instrumental in bringing on a certain way towards the recognition of a dogmatic and organic Church, could not be brought further than what is called Puseyism, and, instead of going on with myself, would relapse into indifference or doubt. It was one of the principle sorrows I had to endure as I made up my mind to be a Catholic, and the prospect of it made me very slow and cautious before I finally decided on becoming one.
>
> But then I felt, the question was one of personal duty in the most solemn of matters—and that, if I saw that there was

---

Kingsley and Dr. Newman."

12. JHN to John Keble, 15 August 1863, in *LD* 20:503.

one Church to which the promises were made, and that I as yet was not in it, I must join it, and leave to the Providence of God to overrule all consequences, and must act on faith that He who called me could order things better than I could, with a higher wisdom and in unknown ways—and, sad as it has been for me to see that my anticipations have been fulfilled, I never have for an instant repented of the step which gave occasion to them.[13]

When the Marquise de Salvo was concerned that her conversion would pain her relatives, Newman counseled her to trust in God:

> You say you have to pain relations by your step—that is the trial which *all* have to go through. You hardly can be called on to inflict such pain as has been the duty of some of my friends—nay perhaps such, as has been my own duty to inflict. But God will support you under every trial He puts upon you—and you will have the strength of the whole Church of all saints who ever lived. You will be one of a body who have gone through far more than any of us are called to undergo—and their prayers and their sanctity will operate in you, and raise you above yourself. I am not speaking necessarily of *sensible* comfort, but of real power which will be yours in God's presence.[14]

Similarly, when Miss Giberne expressed her loneliness over the loss of her friends at her conversion, Newman understood how she felt and advised her to believe that God's mercy would more than compensate for her loss.

> Your feelings at present must indeed be very much tried, and I sincerely thank you for letting me share them. Take your present trial as you do, as a gracious means of bringing you under the more intimate protection of your true friends, those Saints and Angels unseen, who can do so much more for you with God, and in the course of life, than any mere child of man, however dear and excellent. . . . But even as regards friends of this world I have found that Divine Mercy wonderfully makes up my losses, as if "instead of thy fathers thou shalt have children" were fulfilled in individuals as well as to the Church. . . . I am very happy with them, (his new Catholic friends) and can truly say with St. Paul "I have all and abound"—and moreover, I have with them, what I never can have had with others, Catholic hopes and beliefs—Catholic objects. And so in your own case, depend on it,

---

13. JHN to Lady Chatterton, 19 July 1863, in *LD* 20:495.
14. JHN to Marquise de Salvo, 18 December 1845, in *LD* 11:71.

God's Mercy will make up to you all you lose, and you will be blessed, not indeed in the same way, but in a higher.[15]

Although Newman was denied the pleasure of personal contact with his family and friends for many years, he did not neglect to remember them in prayer. Each Thursday he prayed for a long list of his Protestant friends. To his sister Jemima he wrote in 1865: "You have let your children grow up, and I not know them (sic). They have ever been in my prayers."[16]

Friendship as Gift

Newman realized that one could not force friendship; he considered friendship a gift of God, based on many human qualities. Acknowledging a compliment paid to him by his lifelong friend Mrs. William Froude, he wrote: "This only I know, that all through my life God has mercifully given me good friends, and that I never know how to be grateful enough to Him for so precious a gift."[17] Before Newman became a Catholic, he subscribed to the Tractarian notion "that mutual love must have as its basis mutual reverence,"[18] so that basic to his understanding of friendship as gift was the sacredness of the other person.[19] Coupled with this, was his emphasis on the uniqueness and individuality of the person. When Henry Ryder discovered that his father did not want him to join the Oratory, he wrote to Newman for direction. After attempting to allay his fears, Newman said: "We love you for your own sake, and St. Philip will provide."[20]

Considering friendship a gift, Newman believed that it should not be taken lightly. He wrote to H. A. Woodgate in 1865: "I can only say, friendships are not put on, put off, put on again, like a glove."[21] Through the years, as his

---

15. JHN to Miss Giberne, 28 January 1846, in *LD* 11:101–2.

16. JHN to Mrs. John Mozley, 31 October 1865, in *LD* 22:86. See also JHN to H. A. Woodgate, 29 October 1872, in *LD* 26:193. However, in one interesting sentence in a letter written to Mrs. Bowden, Newman stated that he felt that many of the friends he had lost at the time of his conversion had returned. "As in Job's case, the friends lost by me becoming a Catholic, are now nearly made up to me in full tale—and they themselves are constantly coming over." JHN to J. W. Bowden, 13 September 1856, in *LD* 17:378.

17. JHN to Mrs. William Froude, 9 July 1876, in *LD* 28:86.

18. Tristram, *Newman and His Friends*, vii.

19. In discussing with Faber how to treat the boys attending their school, Newman told him, "I think their persons should be sacred." JHN to F. W. Faber, 6 February 1849, in *LD* 13:27.

20. JHN to Henry Ryder, 4 September 1865, in *LD* 17:372.

21. JHN to H. A. Woodgate, 16 December 1865, in *LD* 22:121.

Spiritual Direction and Friendship

friendships matured through some difficult experiences, he came to see that if they were to endure, then they had to be based on honesty. In a relationship he felt that it was important that the other person truly know him and not simply some "idea" of him. Reflecting on this with his friend Sister Mary du Boulay, he advised her to have a more realistic understanding of who he was. "And am I not wise, not to lessen the sort of imagination you have of me—so kind, yet so unreal, by showing myself in propria persona? I always feel like a hypocrite who can be detected by holy eyes, just as an accomplished thief or thimble rigger is at once recognized by a police officer. But at a distance I look like a great man, without any hang dog look which I can't throw off, do what I will, when I am in places where brass will not go for gold."[22]

Even before Newman published his *Letter* in response to the *Irenicon* that his friend Edward Pusey had written in 1865, Newman wrote to him personally explaining as honestly as he could how he intended to reply.

> You must not be made anxious that I am going to publish a Letter on your Irenicon. I wish to accept it as such, and shall write in that spirit. And I write, if not to hinder, for that is not in my power, but to balance and neutralize other things which may be written upon it. It will not be any great length. If I shall say anything which is in the way of remonstrance, it will be, because, unless I were perfectly honest, I should not only do no good, but carry no one with me—but I am taking the greatest possible pains not to say a word which I should be sorry for afterwards.[23]

In 1831, he preached a sermon on the Feast of St. John the Evangelist on the subject of "Love of Relations and Friends."[24] Commenting on Christ's special friendship for John, "the beloved disciple," Newman affirmed

> that there is nothing contrary to the spirit of the Gospel, nothing inconsistent with the fullness of Christian love, in having our affections directed in a special way . . . towards those whom the circumstances of our past life, or some peculiarities of character, have endeared to us. There have been men before now, who have supposed Christian love was so diffusive as not to admit of concentration upon individuals; so that we ought to love all men equally. . . . Now I shall here maintain . . . that the best preparation for loving the world at large, and loving it duly and wisely, is to cultivate an intimate friendship and affection towards those

---

22. JHN to Sister Mary Gabriel du Boulay, 7 April 1863, in *LD* 20:317.
23. JHN to E. B. Pusey, 8 December 1865, in *LD* 22:119.
24. Newman, Sermon 5, in *Parochial and Plain Sermons*, 2:51–60; December 27, 1831.

who are immediately about us.... We are to begin with loving our friends about us, and gradually to enlarge the circle of our affections, till it reaches all Christians, and then all men. Besides, it is obviously impossible to love all men in any strict and true sense. What is meant by loving all men, is to be ready to assist them.[25]

Both the continuity and development of his thought was manifested in a letter written eighteen years later to Faber concerning "particular friendship" in community life. Rather than simply reiterating his former belief, he added a new dimension by stating that it is normal for people to feel differently towards individuals; what makes the difference is the way that one shows it or acts upon it. "As to particular friendships, I have much wished a *definition* of what is meant. St. James and St. John had a sort of particular friendship among the Apostles—so must brothers in a Congregation ever—i.e. there *must* be feelings between them which are not between others. The point, I conceive, is that they should not show it,—should not *act* upon it. . . . Again what is more striking, think of Our Lord's love for St. John."[26] Speaking of his own friendship with Ambrose St. John, he went on to say: "For if from circumstances I *have* been brought closer to F. Ambrose than to others, let me *hide* the fact as I will, I can do nothing to undo it, unless I actually did cease to love him as well as I do. All I can do is to try to love others *as well*—which if I omit to try to do is certainly a fault."[27]

Soon after his conversion, Newman went to Rome to study for the priesthood. From there he wrote a letter to Henry Wilberforce reflecting on the value of long friendship.

> I am tempted to write to you again . . . the more because it is pleasant to think of an old friend in a far country. Nothing can exceed the kindness of the people with whom I am . . . but after all there is nothing like an old friend. New friends cannot love one, if they would; they know nothing of one—but to one who has known another for twenty years his face and his name is a history; a long series of associations is bound up with every word or deed which comes from him, which has a meaning and an interpretation in those associations. And thus I feel that no one here can sympathize with me daily—for even those who think highly of me have the vaguest, most shadowy, fantastic

---

25. Ibid. Newman went on to emphasize the fact that it is by a person loving their friends that their hearts are rooted in charity.

26. JHN to F. W. Faber, 7 February 1849, in *LD* 13:30.

27. Ibid., 30–31. See also JHN to F. W. Faber, 9 February 1849, in *LD* 13:34–35.

notions attached to their idea of me—feel a respect, not for me but for some imagination of their own which bears my name.[28]

Newman understood friendship not only as a gift but as a source of healing. He felt that in our human condition, one of the ways that God brought us comfort and healing was through our friends. To Catherine Bathurst in 1863, he wrote: "While then I sympathize with you, it is a sort of comfort to me to know I am not alone in this kind of suffering—would I could feel and believe that you allowed yourself so to take interest in the similar sufferings of others, as to feel the comfort I speak of yourself!"[29] Nonetheless, Newman had no illusions about friendship and realized that it was not always possible for a friend to know one's trials, as he wrote late in his life: "It is difficult for others to know one's trials, and their kindness often mistakes where the sharpness of them really lies. We certainly have some great anxieties, but they are not easy to guess; and, as to the one to which you seem to refer, what to the many friends would seem the trial is to me the greatest relief and compensation of it. But God who knows all secrets answers their kind prayers for us by a true interpretation of them."[30]

Comfort of Friends

During his Roman Catholic years, Newman did not hesitate to write to his friends concerning the various trials and difficulties he experienced. When he felt disappointed or discouraged, when he was physically ill or in mental turmoil, he not only sought comfort and healing from God, but he also looked to his friends. When his good friend, Mrs. William Froude wrote to him concerning his health, Newman replied:

> As to health, I never was better or so well—the only disposition is that I am always tired—but that I think is merely owing to the growth of years. As time goes on too, one's features grow more heavy—At least I feel it an effort to brighten up. Or rather, I believe those sad long years of anxiety have stamped

---

28. JHN to Henry Wilberforce, 13 December 1846, in *LD* 11:294. Newman continued to speak about how the lack of presence of his friend helped him to turn more to God. "Both what people here can do for me, and what they cannot, carries off the mind to Him, who 'has fed me all my life long unto this day—' whom I find protecting me most wonderfully under such new circumstances, just as He ever has before, and who can give me that sympathy which man cannot give."
29. JHN to Catherine Bathurst, 21 January 1863, in *LD* 20:398.
30. JHN to Robert Whitty, 26 January 1884, in *LD* 30:301.

themselves on my face—and now that they are at an end, yet I cannot change what has become a physical effect.

And now you know all about me, as far as I am able, or can get myself, to talk of myself, I will but add that the Hand of God is most wonderfully over me, that I am full of blessings and privileges . . .

O that I were near to you, and could have a talk with you!—but then I should need great grace to know what to say to you—this is one thing that keeps me silent—it is, dear friends, because I don't know what to say to you. If I had more faith, I should doubtless know well enough; I should then say "Come to the Church, *and you will find all you seek.*" I *have myself* found all I seek.[31]

Several weeks later, when he was not feeling well and taking medicine, he wrote to Ambrose St. John: "It (the medicine) makes me languid and drowsy, and then I can't do my duties, and people think me reserved etc. when I don't mean to be.

"At times the sense of weight (of responsibility) and desolateness has come on me so strongly, that I could fancy it might grow equal to any pain . . . . It is useless to tell you on paper all the little trials which constitute all this—and it is ungrateful in me not to be more cheered with the improvement of things in some quarters."[32]

The most problematic period in Newman's life were the years 1850–1862. Within these dozen years, a number of events had a tremendous impact on him: the division of the two Oratories, the Achilli trial, the Catholic University in Dublin, the Scripture translation project, the *Rambler* incident, and the Oratory school foundation. As one might expect, the inner anguish and turmoil of these events are clearly manifest in his correspondence, which exemplify his human struggle and the important role that friends played in his life during these years.

Because of the difficulties connected with the division of the two Oratories in 1850 and of the ordeal of the Achilli trial which culminated on June 25, 1852, Newman became extremely tired. The events of these past years had drained him physically and mentally. Almost immediately he began to write to his friends expressing his feelings, looking for understanding and consolation. For example, a month after his trial was completed, he wrote to J. D. Dalgairns about how he was feeling and his desire to be with his friends. "I am very much tried, as you may think. . . . What tries me most, is, at my age, the difficulty of keeping up the *steam*. Nothing but grace can do

---

31. JHN to Mrs. William Froude, 16 June 1848, in *LD* 12:223.
32. JHN to Ambrose St. John, 12 July 1848, in *LD* 12:243.

it for me. I want a holiday so bad, and have not had one for two years; not a week of uninterrupted rest. . . . How I should like a quiet week, with some of you at Sydenham!"³³

Two letters to Sister Mary Imelda Poole within a week of each other indicate both his physical and mental strain. "It is now above a year that my medical adviser told me, my life almost ultimately depended on my laying by for a while, and this year has been the most exhausting I ever have had."³⁴ Nine days later he continued: "He (the doctor) now tells me distinctly I shall have a premature old age, and an early death—because the only thing which can save me is a simple lying by. He says my brain and nerves cannot bear it. . . . He says I have nothing the matter with me at present, but that my vital powers are so low that mischief might take place at any time—and that nothing can keep me up but tonics."³⁵ Meanwhile, in November 1851, before the Achilli trial had been completed, Newman accepted the offer to be the first rector of a Catholic university in Ireland. Until he resigned in 1857, this also was to be a constant source of tension.³⁶

Another very human dimension sometimes emerged when people put pressure on Newman to accomplish things. He was feeling this in 1853 when he wrote to his friend, Mrs. Bowden: "People *won't* believe me. Because I seem to do things easy, they say, 'O, Dr. Newman writes so easily—it gives him no trouble—he writes things off—he can sit up and write a sermon for next morning—he merely talks, he does not exert himself'—and they simply discredit me. I can't get Cardinal, Bishop, or any one else to believe me—and I am tried

---

33. JHN to J. D. Dalgairns, 23 July 1852, in *LD* 15:133.

34. JHN to Sister Mary Imelda Poole, 13 October 1852, in *LD* 15:181. At this time, Newman was also in the process of writing his *University Discourses* which put him under added pressure; he commented on how difficult he found it to write: "The first book I wrote, my 'Arians' I was almost fainting daily, when I was finishing it—and (except my *Parochial Sermons*) every book I have written, before and since I was a Catholic, has been a sort of *operation*, the distress has been so great." JHN to Sister Mary Imelda Poole, 22 October 1852, in *LD* 15:183.

35. Ibid.

36. See the following letters concerning some of the problems that caused anxiety for Newman as rector of the university:
JHN to Henry Wilberforce, 30 December 1853, in *LD* 14:517–18;
JHN to Richard Stanton, 28 February 1854, in *LD* 16:64–65;
JHN to Archbishop Cullen, 18 June 1854, in *LD* 16:166–67;
JHN to William Monsell, 21 August 1855, in *LD* 16:530;
JHN to Patrick Leahy, Archbishop of Cashel, 31 July 1857, in *LD* 18:108;
JHN to James Hope-Scott, 5 August 1857, in *LD* 18:111;
JHN to Robert Ornsby, 21 December 1857, in *LD* 18:211–12;
JHN to Robert Ornsby, 5 January 1858, in *LD* 18:219–22;
JHN to John O'Hagan, 11 October 1858, in *LD* 18:483.

day by day by earnest requests, I would come only here, or only there—and though I do refuse, yet people think me ungracious and unaccommodating."[37]

Whenever he became frustrated because he could not explain something adequately, he felt comfortable sharing that frustration with a friend. Highlighting some recent difficulties in 1856, he told Ambrose St. John:

> One hears tales of men who cannot speak and are bound, and taken to and fro at the will of others. . . . I go to Rome to be snubbed. I come to Dublin to be repelled by Dr. McHale and worn away by Dr. Cullen. The Cardinal taunts me with his Dedications, and Fr. Faber insults me with his letters. I would be let alone, but I have no means of defending myself more than if my hands and tongue were tied I cannot explain any thing to friend or foe intelligibly. Ryder strikes me, for I can call it nothing else. When I drop a word to H. W. [Henry Wilberforce] he talks of "sensitiveness, which is the penalty of great ability." . . . What enormous irritation Job must have felt, when his friends came and prosed to him.[38]

Moreover, Newman believed at this time that the anxieties he was going through actually affected his preaching. Patrick Leahy, Archbishop-elect of Cashel wrote to Newman asking him to preach at his consecration and Newman replied: "And I am as eager that you should not think me ungrateful in asking you to let me answer it in the negative. I really am obliged to do so;—not only have I not the gift of preaching, but I have not power just now to turn my mind to any duty which will require so much thought and effort to discharge it suitably. I am oppressed with cares and anxieties both here and in Dublin, and have too much on my hands even to fulfill the responsibilities of each day as it comes."[39]

During the course of the problems with Darnell over the management of the Oratory school, Newman again was able to express his feelings to a friend at the beginning of 1860:

---

37. JHN to Mrs. J. W. Bowden, 9 December 1853, in *LD* 15:494.

38. JHN to Ambrose St. John, 30 October 1856, in *LD* 17:426. Sometimes part of the healing process for Newman occurred not only when he could verbalize his feelings, but also when he received his friend's response. To the above letter, Ambrose encouraged Newman not to take matters so seriously. "In spite of your troubles though it is a shame to say so, your last letter amused me considerably. I don't care for you when you have got your tail up, because it shows you are not anxious about the result, but see light thro' the cloud. I cared for you (though you don't believe it) when you were in the anxieties of the A. [Achilli] trial much more than I did when we were drinking the judges' health in the Queen's Bench." Ibid., 427n1. See also JHN to Ambrose St. John, 26 October 1856, in *LD* 17:420.

39. JHN to Patrick Leahy, 17 June 1857, in *LD* 18:57.

Spiritual Direction and Friendship

> You must not think that several things I have said to you lately, came of low spirits, which I fancy you have done, and taken them as a proof I was out of health—It is not this—It is good for me to have trials—and I am in a state of chronic trial, which only those who come very close to me know. This has been the way with me for many years, the clouds of one kind or another returning after the rain, or, as I have before now expressed it, a shower of meteoric stones falling about me, as those which fall down from heaven, in a regular return, in the month of November. I might almost say that a pleasant event has not happened to me for more than I can count.[40]

Newman needed the understanding and concern of his friends and often it was their words that enabled him to feel comfortable in pouring out his heart to them. For example, his good friend Sister Mary Gabriel du Boulay wrote him a very consoling and encouraging letter which meant a great deal to him.

> We are so very sorry to hear of continued weakness and shaken health, and shall pray most earnestly that sufficient strength may be given you to work on, yet many years in the service of your Lord and Love...
>
> Earth is indeed full of desolateness as far as anything belonging to it is concerned, and the greater the soul the more it must suffer from its keen vision of the hollowness and corruption of all things merely human.—The love and labour and the tender sympathy it pours out on every soul with which it comes in contact, must widen the circle of its suffering—and help to wear out the bodily frame. But each suffering brings forth its own child of benediction which will not die because it is not of nature but of grace. There are thousands of such springing up from you very dear Father in hidden places, where

---

40. JHN to William Froude, 28 February 1860, in *LD* 19:313. After Darnell's resignation, Newman was able to run the school as he wished and his health began to improve. The doctor ordered him to take a vacation and simply rest, which he did with two of his friends. Soon after he left for his vacation, Edward Bellasis wrote expressing his concern over his health and Newman replied: "On Friday next I go to London for final advice and directions—meanwhile, I have had a very able opinion in London, and am assured in the strongest terms that there is nothing at all seriously the matter with me—but that sorrows (for though not great ones, they have been various and continual) of thirty years have at last told upon my nerves—and that I want rest." JHN to Edward Bellasis, 5 August 1861, in *LD* 20:21. See also:
  JHN to Ambrose St. John, 6 July 1861, in *LD* 20:8–9;
  JHN to Sir John Acton, 21 August 1861, in *LD* 20:35–36;
  JHN to Marianne Bowden, 11 September 1861, in *LD* 20:43.

> you do not suspect them:—hearts that love you as their guide into the Faith—hearts that you have reconciled—that you have comforted, that you have guided to the bridal chamber of their Spouse.—Those many voices of childlike love and gratitude all blend in one persevering prayer that you may be rewarded with Life, Eternal Life, for all the good things that you have done to them. They will be with you through old age, in death and after death, and you will let them cheer you, though they come from the least and lowest.
>
> It would seem such an impertinence writing all this to you, only that you know so well, that the deepest expression of reverence is the uttermost confidence—It is just because you are so great, and I am so little that I have ever felt my heart might speak out all it felt to you.[41]

Her letter enabled Newman to recount the things that were troubling him.

> Your letter was a great consolation to me. . . . I am much better—but what has been so long coming on, will not easily go off.
>
> I have not the faith, patience, and resignation which I ought to have—but this is another matter. My ailment is a physical effect, I may call it, on my mind. It is said that in a naval engagement, while the vessels near, and the men are standing quite still, the knees of the bravest shake. It is so bad to be simply passive in suffering. When we act as well as suffer, the effort alleviates the pain; in that case men are troubled without knowing it; but it is otherwise when you are hit, without hitting. It would have been better with me humanly and naturally, had I given as good as I took.
>
> Now excuse my folly in speaking. Thirty years have passed since I have been a sort of target for a shot, when any one wished to try his hand, and had nothing better to do. I used as a Protestant, to say, that no one, except O'Connell was so well abused as I was. I have very seldom *replied*; if so, for the sake of others, or of our cause. . . . Gross misrepresentations remain of me to this day, and even now they bring up what I did 20 years ago, knowing that *they* can speak, and I cannot.[42]

After mentioning several things that people brought up, he continued: "These are little and ridiculous things taken separately, but they form an atmosphere of *flies*—one can't enjoy a walk without this finger on the nerves of the mind. They are nothing in the eye of reason, but they weary.

41. Sister Mary Gabriel du Boulay to JHN, Mid August 1861, in *LD* 20:28–29.
42. JHN to Sister Mary Gabriel du Boulay, 18 August 1861, in *LD* 20:29.

"For myself, I don't think I have called any one a bad name, or been ill natured. I never charged any one with any crime or fault except Achilli, and I suffered for that pretty considerably."[43]

Newman began to speak of his sense of failure.

> Then I have tried to do works for God year after year, and for thirty years, so far forth as they were *works*, they have all failed. My first sermon as an Anglican, was on the text "Man goes forth to his work and to his labour until the evening"; and now the evening is come and I have done nothing. I think of Keble's lines "In disappointment thou canst bless etc."—and I know that it is better for me to seem to have done nothing—but still it is most difficult to go on working in the face of thirty years disappointment. And so it is—every thing seems to crumble under my hands, as if one were making ropes of sand.[44]

Newman concluded this letter by indicating that we are all fragile vessels, which, in spite of their weakness, hold a treasure:

> And so one man's skin endures a hair shirt better than another's—so it is with the effect of these trials on different minds respectively. For myself, I know I am deeply deficient in that higher life which lasts and grows in spite of the ills of mortality—but had I ever so much of supernatural love and devotion, I could not be in any different state from the Apostle, who in the most beautiful of his inspired epistles speaks with such touching and consoling vividness of those troubles, in the midst of which these earthen vessels of ours hold the treasure of grace and truth.[45]

Several months later, Newman wrote to his faithful friend Ambrose St. John and enumerated some of his difficulties by outlining his life in ten-year segments:

> I then said that, as, when I was 20 I was cut off from the rising talent of the University by my failure in the Schools, as, when 30, I was cut off from distinction in the governing body by being

---

43. Ibid., 30.
44. Ibid., 30–31.
45. Ibid., 31. Two days later, August 20, 1861, Newman wrote a similar letter to Edward Bellasis: "But I cannot in a few words express to you what the matter is with what I may call the *physical* texture of my soul. It is not a matter of reason, nor of grace—but, just as the body wearies under continual toil, so does the mind. . . . I think I never have been praised for any thing I did, except once, for my lectures on Catholicism in England by the Bishop and Catholics of Birmingham." *LD* 20:34. See another letter eight days later to his friend Miss Giberne: JHN to Miss M. R. Giberne, 28 August 1861, in *LD* 20:37–38.

deprived of my Tutorship, as, when 40, I was virtually cast out of the Church of England, by the affair of Number 90, as when 50 I was cast out of what may be called society by the disgrace of the Achilli sentence, so, when I should arrive at 60 years, I should be cast out of the good books of Catholics, and especially of ecclesiastical authorities. This appalls me in this way—viz what is to happen, if I live to be seventy? Am I to lose all of you and to be left desolate? Or is our house to be burned to the ground? Or am I to be smitten with some afflicting disorder?

These are the questions which come before me, and don't be angry with me for mentioning them—for it is a great relief to me to speak, and a pain to be silent. Well, I suppose it is all intended to keep me from being too happy. How happy should I be, if let alone—how fond of living! On the other hand, certainly I have been carried marvelously thro' all those troubles which have come on me hitherto, and so I believe I shall be to the end.[46]

By the end of 1862, Newman's health had improved, and he was involved with running the Oratory school. Letters to friends indicate that he now possessed more energy and was concerned that "perhaps I am hiding my talent in a napkin."[47] Reflecting on past years, he wrote: "We have had, as you seem to know, great trials—though no one can know them, as we know them—but we have been, and are, wonderfully prospered under and through them."[48]

Friendship, Encouragement, and Support

Another important value of friendship relates to Newman's understanding of the Christian life: friends are given to each other for encouragement and support. Often he would write to friends encouraging them in some way and they would reciprocate. For example, to Sir John Simeon he wrote in 1867: "I do not know in what terms to thank you enough for your letter so full of hearty affectionate feeling for me. It is the great compensation for such small trials as come upon me, to have such expressions of true friendship.

"The mercy of God gives me only just so much to endure, as suffices to serve for an occasion of bringing to me so much to take pleasure and rejoice

---

46. JHN to Ambrose St. John, 25 October 1862, in *LD* 20:328–29.

47. JHN to Emily Bowles, 29 May 1863, in *LD* 20:454.

48. JHN to A. J. Hammer, 25 December 1862, in *LD* 20:373. See also JHN to Mrs. Henry Bowden, 31 December 1862, in *LD* 20:380–81.

in—for can there be a greater blessing here below than to have good friends who sympathize both with the good and evil that befalls one?"[49]

After the division of the Oratory, T. F. Knox joined the London Oratory but soon wrote to Newman expressing his gratitude for his friendship by saying: "As this is the first time I have written to you since the Separation, I cannot let pass the opportunity of expressing to you my sorrow that we are parted, and also to thank you from the bottom of my heart for all the love and forbearance you have shown me. The more I think over the past the more deeply I feel how miserably in every way I have acted towards you in the last fifteen months."[50]

Similarly, in 1857, John Flanagan told Newman that "you are the tenderest and gentlest of men,"[51] while Robert Whitty said, "I hope you will sometimes remember one who has not lost one particle of his veneration and affection for you."[52] Late in his life, Newman responded to T. W. Allies' expression of gratitude by writing: "I thank you for your affectionate letter. Of course I am not worthy of all you say, but if you had not a love of me, it would not come into your mind to speak of me as you do, and it is a token, which comforts me, that you do not forget me in your prayers."[53]

When Mrs. William Froude was trying to discern whether she should join the Catholic Church, it meant a great deal to her to have Newman as a friend who could help her in her religious quest. "I am almost ashamed to trouble you with these questions, as I daresay I could find them in books, though I don't exactly know where to look for them—also to have the opinion and support of a kind friend is a great comfort."[54] Similarly, when Newman's name was unjustly being maligned in the extremely anti-Catholic *Standard*, his friend Bishop Ullathorne defended him: "I will take the liberty of saying that I know of no dignitary in the Catholic Church whom I consider more sound in orthodoxy, more solidly formed in the ecclesiastical and Christian virtues, or more deferential to church authority than Dr. Newman. I love him as one of my dearest friends; I have often consulted his judgement, and admired his prudence; and I have nothing either in my

---

49. JHN to Sir John Simeon, 10 April 1867, in *LD* 23:140.

50. T. F. Knox to JHN, 29 April 1849, in *LD* 13:139n1. Newman replied: "Thank you for your affectionate remarks about myself. I do trust things are progressing well now, under God's blessing and with the powerful intercession of our Lady and St. Philip, for a permanent arrangement of all those difficulties which have hitherto tried us." JHN to T. F. Knox, 5 May 1849, in *LD* 13:139.

51. John Flanagan to JHN, 21 February 1857, in *LD* 17:529n2.

52. Robert Whitty to JHN, 11 April 1857, in *LD* 18:44n2.

53. JHN to T. W. Allies, 24 February 1884, in *LD* 30:313.

54. Mrs. William Froude to JHN, 20 May 1856, in *LD* 17:243n2.

mind, or my heart, that I could have the slightest wish to conceal from his knowledge."[55] Along the same lines, Robert Ornsby, who had worked with Newman at the Catholic University in Dublin spoke of his personal loss at Newman's resignation. "Now for three years or more, I have had the continual advantage of your friendship and counsel, besides the great trust of working with you in one of the most important vocations of your life."[56]

Although Mother Margaret Hallahan hardly ever saw Newman, nevertheless it meant a great deal to her to have him as her friend. More than once she personally expressed her appreciation; responding to a letter he had written to her in 1865, she said: "Your handwriting always gives me a thrill of delight it is so kind and condescending of you to write to me. True friends, and true friendships are such rare things that I hope and pray that what has ever been felt by this Community and by their worthless mother towards you and all that concerns you may ever be the same."[57] Sister Mary Gabriel du Boulay also wrote of the pleasure Newman's letter gave Mother Margaret, "As years pass on, there seems to grow a feeling of confidence and freedom of heart, which is strange considering she never sees you."[58]

The following year Mother Margaret became ill, and Newman wrote to her telling her that he would offer Mass for her once a week. Sister Imelda Poole replied for her: "Our dear Mother is deeply grateful to you for your most kind letter and still kinder promise of prayers. She cannot express all she feels in words—all she can say is, and she bids me tell you so—that she always was *fond of you* and now shall be *fonder of you* than ever, and she is afraid she shall live and die with an *irregular affection* for you—these are her own words."[59] After her superior's death in 1868, Sister Imelda Poole wrote about Mother Margaret Hallahan's "special" regard for Newman: "She instinctively felt that you understood her, and as many did not understand her—she felt a freedom of soul with those who did—and could show her genuine self to them. You were one of those for whom she most constantly prayed and she took the most lively interest as you know in all that concerned her."[60]

However, it was not always the friends who were closest to him who expressed their feelings toward Newman. Sometimes it was an estranged friend or someone who disagreed with him. James Hope and Newman had

55. Bishop Ullathorne to JHN, 4 October 1851, in *LD* 14:382n1.
56. Robert Ornsby to JHN, 8 January 1858, in *LD* 18:225n2.
57. Mother Margaret Hallahan to JHN, 12 May 1865, in *LD* 21:465n1.
58. Ibid.
59. Sister Imelda Poole to JHN, 1 February 1866, in *LD* 22:145n2.
60. Sister Imelda Poole to JHN, 31 December 1868, in *LD* 24:196n2. Newman responded by saying: "It is as great, as it is an unmerited and unexpected mercy to me, that your dear Mother should have thought of me with such affection." Ibid.

not corresponded for several years, and after Newman took the initiative to write, Hope answered:

> It [your letter] renews a correspondence which I value very highly and which my own stupidity had interrupted—Offence I had never taken, but causes such as you describe much better than I could have done, were the occasion of my silence. You may now find that you have brought some trouble on yourself, for there are many things on which I should like to ask you questions. . . . However at present my chief object is to assure you how very glad I am again to write to you as the friend whom I almost feared I had thrown away.
>
> Whatever occurs do not let us again be estranged. It is not easy as one gets older to form new friendships of any kind and least of all such as I have always considered yours.[61]

Although Isaac Williams disagreed with Newman over religious issues, he still wrote to him, expressing his friendship and affection, whenever he learned of Newman's troubles.

> I can no longer forbear writing to you a few lines to express my deep sympathy and affection for you in your troubles—How can I forbear to do so when the mere thought of you fills my eyes as it has so often done with tears? Of your trials I mean first and chiefly the loss of your sister Harriet, knowing what she once was to you and that you have so little remaining to fill up such a place in your mind.
>
> Your other troubles [Newman has written above the line "(Achilli)"] of another kind must be very harassing to you I am sure, and I cannot but hope that at such a time a line from an old friend may be not unacceptable to you. And indeed, my dear Newman, I do earnestly hope that we have a place in each others' prayers—other offices of friendship have long ceased between us— . . . Although of course there are many things which you think and do with which I cannot agree—yet they are not such as can impair that glad hope and confidence which one must always entertain for you.[62]

Even some members of his religious community, who disagreed with him concerning certain things, expressed their true feelings to him. Richard

---

61. James Hope to JHN, 27 November 1850, in *LD* 14:147n4.
62. Isaac Williams to JHN, 17 December 1852, in *LD* 15:226–27n4. Newman began his response to Williams, "I received your affectionate letter here last night, and thank you for it with all my heart." Ibid.

Stanton, who opposed Newman's position on the division of the Oratory, wrote to him in 1856 stating:

> My immediate object is only to secure an expression or two of kindness for myself, a consolation of which I feel great need—I have during my life entertained great love and friendship for various persons (though now I hardly know whether I have a friend) but towards yourself my feelings have always been something quite peculiar, for regard and attachment. Since I have been parted from you, the rare occasions on which I have met you, have been of the pleasantest hours of the whole year, and the few lines you have from time to time written been among my greatest treasures.[63]

Even Nicholas Darnell, who was at the center of the Oratory boys' school controversy, wrote to Newman saying: "Need I say that in spite of your infatuation, and my own coldness and pride, I love you from my heart and shall always love you from my heart and shall always love you, better if possible, than my own Father."[64]

Not only did Newman receive expressions of love and friendship from others, he also expressed his feelings to others.[65] Realizing the importance of encouraging and supporting others, he often expressed how he felt about someone either to that person or to someone else. Writing to R. A. Coffin in 1849, he said: "I long to see you, my dear F. Rector, and to have some quiet talk with you and others who are so much in my heart."[66] Years later, when Newman learned that John Keble's wife was dying, he struggled to find words that expressed his feelings.

> What am I to say to your most touching letter? I can do no more than think of you and her. I cannot write except to tell you that I am so thinking.
>
> You are under the severest trial which man can suffer; and I earnestly pray that you and she may be supplied in all your need, day by day, and have every grace necessary to bring you

---

63. Richard Stanton to JHN, 21 February 1856, in *LD* 17:160.

64. Nicholas Darnell to JHN, 28 December 1861, in *LD* 20:93n2. Newman answered: "Your letter was an extreme consolation to me. I return your affection with all my heart." Ibid.

65. Newman has been criticized for being cold and unemotional: his *Letters* certainly do not support this position. While at times he tended to be somewhat reserved, he was a man who felt things very personally himself, and one who could feel and express his feelings for others.

66. JHN to R. A. Coffin, 25 April 1849, in *LD* 13:124.

both to heaven. When I think how ill you have been lately, I am full of anxiety.

I can do no more than think of you and love you. I wish I could do more—but there is only One who can will and do.[67]

The following month he wrote to R. F. Wilson about his friendship for Keble. "He is, and ever has been, '*pars animae*' ["part of my soul"] in so special a sense, though I have but once seen him in twenty years and more, that I can't tell how I shall feel when he is taken away."[68]

When Catherine Bowden asked Newman to be present at the Mass in which she began her novitiate with the Dominican nuns, he responded: "I congratulate you most sincerely on your approaching clothing. If any thing would carry me away from my '*nido*' (nest) here, it would be the claim which you and yours have on me for every [sic] the most affectionate manifestation of my interest in you and for your welfare; but the greatest thing I can do is to say Mass for you."[69]

Joseph Gordon, after a year as a novice in Newman's community, wrote to him complaining of being "let alone," and of an absence of friendliness on the part of the community, and that Newman did not seem to want his love. Reassuring him of his love, Newman responded: "And now what can I say in return but what with all my heart I love you? As you would see, if you could look into it."[70]

However, Newman was also sensitive to the fact that some individuals had a difficult time manifesting their love or friendship for others. With Philip Gordon, Joseph's brother, Newman took the initiative in writing; sensing Gordon's difficulty, Newman wrote, using the words of a song: "Many is the time I have stood over the fire at breakfast or looked at you at Recreation, hunting for something to talk about. The song says that 'Love cannot live on flowers;' not so; yet it requires material, if not for sustenance, at least for display."[71] In turn, Gordon was able to express his own feelings: "It was very kind of you to write to me. I have never doubted that you loved me as one of your children although the most unworthy of all. I have ever

---

67. JHN to John Keble, 7 February 1866, in *LD* 22:147–48.

68. JHN to R. F. Wilson, 28 March 1866, in *LD* 22:193. For expressions of friendship to Newman from John Keble, see the following letters: John Keble to JHN, 28 June 1864, in *LD* 21:143n1; John Keble to JHN, 3 February 1866, in *LD* 22:147n3. Bracketed translation added.

69. JHN to Catherine Bowden, 25 November 1868, in *LD* 24:175.

70. JHN to Joseph Gordon, 7 February 1849, in *LD* 13:31–32.

71. JHN to Philip Gordon, 7 February 1849, in *LD* 13:32. He was the brother of Joseph Gordon; both Philip and Joseph joined the Oratory on February 24, 1848.

had the greatest difficulty in manifesting my affections and this in proportion to their depth, it almost pains me to have to profess my love."[72]

At times Newman would express his feelings to another person; for example, writing to H. A. Woodgate about his friend Hope-Scott, Newman said: "He is a man I love with my whole heart, and his loss to me is very grievous [sic]."[73] In the same way, he wrote to Lady Herbert of Lea concerning his friend Isy Froude: "It is pleasant to hear you talk so warmly of Isy Froude—I love her so much."[74]

"Speaking the Truth in Love"

Although people were able to express their feelings for Newman and he for them, because he believed friendship had to be based on honesty, he was honest with people even though it meant communicating difficult matters or perhaps risking the loss of their friendship. In 1849, after Newman had backed Faber in a controversy concerning the *Lives of the Saints*, it seemed that Faber was still provoking certain groups of people. So Newman wrote to him:

> This is what has fidgeted me and more than fidgeted, about the whole matter. I have been trying all along to put you on your true footing in the eyes of certain old Catholics—I identified myself wholly with you last Autumn—and now you seem to wish to show the world that after all there is something unmanageable in you, that you can't be relied on, that you are fickle, take up schemes, give them up, insult benefactors, are heartless and willful. Now though such an accusation is of course absurd, yet I do think you have given countenance to it—I don't wonder if people so think;—"a clever man, but you can't depend upon him." I am sure this is said. It has provoked me very much.[75]

Two years later Faber was sent to the continent to rest for six months, but word got back to Newman that he was preaching and teaching and finally returned to England early. This occasioned a rebuke from Newman:

> I am going to write you a very ungracious letter, that is, to express my *sorrow* at your return.
>
> The truth is, I have been fuming ever since you went, at the way you have been going on . . .

---

72. Philip Gordon to JHN, 8 February 1849, in *LD* 13:32n3.
73. JHN to H. A. Woodgate, 29 October 1872, in *LD* 26:193.
74. JHN to Lady Herbert of Lea, 7 February 1873, in *LD* 26:246.
75. JHN to F. W. Faber, 22 May 1849, in *LD* 13:160–61.

> St. Philip used to obey his physician. Have you taken one of the few opportunities a Father Superior has for obedience? I saw his letter—he prescribed six months for you.
>
> You are *not* recovered—the very impatience with which you have come back shows it. As far as I can see, you are still bound to obey your medical advisor... Your life is precious.
>
> This, I know is very ungracious but I am bound to say it.[76]

When J. D. Dalgairns, who was acting as occasional confessor to Mother Hallahan's nuns, began to act as a censor and reformer, Newman corrected him: "I spoke severely to you in the Congregation, because I thought you gave evidence of that deep self conceit (for I know you wish me to speak plainly) which you sometimes show. It would have been better, if you had come *directly after* the meeting to me, and I would have explained it to you, instead of waiting till now."[77]

In 1846, Newman felt that a member of his community, J. B. Morris, was living in a very selfish way. This situation prompted the following letter which Newman re-wrote several times. He began by encouraging Morris to see this as an opportunity to learn something about himself for his own growth.

> One is so seldom able in the common course of things to hear from others what concerns oneself, that I cannot bring myself to let slip the opportunity which now offers of begging you to hear me say about you what will be painful to me as well as to you, yet acceptable to you, I am sure notwithstanding. Nay I feel confident, that, even though you should not see the justice of some things I am going to say, you will on the whole thank me still, from the chance of your learning something or other about yourself amid whatever I may say irrelevant or erroneous. Angel visits are said to be "few and far between": and speaking as I wish to do in Christian charity, I know, my dear Morris, you will pay me back that charity, and consider my words, in spite of their infirmity, as almost an Angel's, and a blessing.
>
> Nor am I unmindful, as I do trust, of what may be the beam in my own eye while I venture to speak of the mote in another's; nor again do I forget the weakness of your general health, which may seem to account for some points which I am to notice. And here I am brought at once to my subject.

76. JHN to F. W. Faber, 30 December 1851, in *LD* 14:490.

77. JHN to J. D. Dalgairns, 22 January 1855, in *LD* 16:357–58. Dalgairns replied to Newman, "I am often conscious of the fault you mention. In the midst of so much to dishearten one, it is not encouraging to know that at the age of six and thirty, such a fault is still so little subdued as to be visible. However it is better that it should be out than in; and I beg of you to let me know whenever you perceive it." Ibid., 358n1.

> Weak health certainly has a tendency to make us selfish, unless we are watchful; and though I dare not use so hard a word of so good a person as you, yet I do think it has made you your own center, more than is expedient, to the disparagement of the Scripture exhortations of yielding to one another, consulting for each other, and bearing one another's burdens.[78]

Newman then detailed a number of instances in community life where this self-centeredness had been manifested, before concluding:

> These are illustrations, my dear Morris, of what I mean to point out to you; and it distresses me to pursue the tokens of a similar habit of mind into other matters. I am reluctantly led to think that you like your way, more than you ought, generally. You have before now done serious things which ever seemed to me to be marks of something faulty in you, and for which I have not been able to account. . . . You are apt too, without knowing it, to set up your own views as a standard, in different matters, so as even to smile on those who measure things differently. You would be surprised to be made aware how frequent the word "I" is in your mouth. E.g., your first remark on a book being mentioned is, "This is a book I have never read," though it is nihil ad rem (nothing pertinent) to say so, or "I have read part of that book," or "That is a book I don't think much of." And as perhaps one remembers best, what has been personal to oneself, I will add my feeling, that you have been bent, more than you are aware of, on forcing your own judgement on me in my matters.
>
> And now, My dear Morris, I beg your pardon if I have not written this as kindly as I might have done. I have been anxious to do it well, and have written it more than once over; but I know well that had I more of the spirit of love, I should have written it better.[79]

In his relationship with others, Newman tried to be sensitive and understanding, even while disagreeing on specific issues. Moreover, if he felt that he had been insensitive or wrong, he did not hesitate to apologize and asked forgiveness. To his lifelong friend, Henry Wilberforce, he wrote:

> I wish very much to write to you, though I have very little to say. But somehow I was left with a painful impression on my mind after seeing you that I had, not knowing how very much depressed you were, been in a former letter inconsiderate towards

---

78. JHN to J. B. Morris, 8 May 1846, in *LD* 11:156–57.
79. Ibid., 158–59.

you. In writing as I did in an apparent offhand manner, I acted as I thought rightly—because I did not wish to say what I had to say seriously—but, when I saw you, I fully saw that you were too sad to be able to bear what would at other times have been the natural tone for me to write to you in—so forgive me.[80]

During the controversy about the nature of the Oratorian, numerous letters were exchanged between the two Oratories; misunderstandings occurred and false rumors were publicized; these caused both Newman and Faber as well as others a great deal of pain. In 1853, in two successive letters, Newman apologized to Faber for any unkindness he might have shown to him. "This alone I will say that the thought of the pain I was giving to all of you has afflicted me, and will afflict me, in a way which you cannot believe.

"At present I will only ask your pardon, my dear F. Wilfrid, for every unkindness or want of consideration I may have shown you in the business—and beg you to suggest to me any thing I can do to show you the perfect love and gratitude which I feel to you and all of you."[81] In a letter the next day, Newman wrote about the pain this situation caused.

> You say that I must bear with all of you, if you are sad. How little you know or can estimate what I have felt in this matter! Part of my pain, indeed, which has been great and continued, has been about myself,—because nothing I could do, as I ought and wished to do—but mixed the most miserable rudeness and inconsiderateness in every thing I did. But a very great portion of it has arisen from the vivid perception of the pain of yourselves; which, though I have not made it lighter by bearing, indeed I have borne . . .
>
> One thing I will add to the many things I have to say, though it is hateful to me to say it. Never, for an instant, I solemnly declare, did I mean to accuse you of treachery. Never did I accuse you of any deliberate act of unkindness. Never did I doubt your love of me, nor impute any thing to you inconsistent with the substance and reality of that love.[82]

In the same way, he apologized to T. F. Knox:

> I thank you most warmly for your affectionate letter. Be assured that you are all of you always in my thoughts, and that I wish your welfare just as I do those with whom I happen to live . . .

---

80. JHN to Henry Wilberforce, 24 September 1846, in *LD* 11:251–52.
81. JHN to F. W. Faber, 4 October 1853, in *LD* 15:448–49.
82. JHN to F. W. Faber, 5 October 1853, in *LD* 15:451–52.

> As to yourself in particular, My dear F. Francis. It is always a subject of regret to me, that I show to you so little the love I really bear you. And the more so, because I think I have been sometimes unjust to you. Forgive me for every rash thought or word I have had about you, and believe me.[83]

After a disagreement with his friend and fellow Oratorian, Edward Caswell, Newman apologized:

> You may think how much I was touched by your affectionateness last night—but it was impossible I could at a moment, and at that moment, say what you wished me.
>
> I will say it now. I have not for an instance thought, that by your letter you meant to hurt me; nor to be inconsiderate to me in any way I think you meant to exercise the virtue of obedience, and to do just what I wished. Indeed, I know perfectly well that you love me, as I love you . . .
>
> Having said all this, I have said all I have to say on the subject—I feel most grateful to you for your affection, as shown to me last night, and I am much distressed that I should have been obliged so much to pain you.
>
> But I have more to say—I wish to pass it all over and to think no more about it, for the following reason, which weighs very much with me. My dearest Edward, I have long had it on my conscience, that from time to time I have behaved very rudely to you in conversation—and it certainly is not for me to complain of any real or supposed inconsiderateness of you to me. So begging you to forgive me for what I have so often done amiss, and begging God to give me grace to forgive you as a first step to my being forgiven.[84]

Once, when Newman's friends, the Wilberforces, visited him, he thought he had been unconversational in the evening after supper. Sensing that the evening had not been a pleasant one for them, he wrote to Mrs. Wilberforce:

> Ever since you were here, I have been intending to write to you to express my great annoyance at having been so very unconversational in the evening. You know my infirmity, but, in spite of that, it was a great trouble to me that I should have used so ill the opportunity of seeing you which your dining here gave me. The immediate cause was that I had been walking about and talking all day, and being very tired, became (alas) very drowsy.

---

83. JHN to T. F. Knox, 30 September 1853, in *LD* 15:441.
84. JHN to Edward Caswell, 22 March 1854, in *LD* 16:94.

Spiritual Direction and Friendship

> The provoking thing is that I am generally much better than I used to be—and have not been in so wretched a condition once since I have been here except on that unlucky evening, and only twice at all tired.
>
> I wish I could promise myself the prospect of making my apology to you in person—but in one way or other my time is taken up—and I have not been absent from Birmingham many days running.[85]

In 1860, when Mrs. Ward came to visit him, Newman guided the conversation in his own direction rather than allowing her to speak freely. Realizing later what he had done, he apologized and asked her as "the truest act of friendship" to tell him anything she could think of about himself that annoyed her.

> I felt some perplexity that, when you called on me the other morning so kindly, "in order to say something" to me, yet you said nothing—and the more, because you were not the first person who has thus balked me. Since then, I have found that you really had something to say. Forgive me, if, by myself beginning the conversation and going off to questions of my own or in any other way, I have been the cause of your not fulfilling your intention.
>
> Now you must be so good in writing to fulfill your intention.
>
> It is impossible you can hurt me for many reasons. As to yourself, I shall account it the truest act of friendship, and shall be very grateful to you for getting yourself to do what you do not like to do, for my sake and for the sake of the Oratory.[86]

Because Newman trusted her, he encouraged her to confide in him:

> You know well that for many, many years I have been the object of innumerable idle reports, and it is impossible you can pain me, if what you have to say is of that nature. There are things which I could deny or explain at once. There are things, which, from circumstances of duty, I should have to be silent about—leaving it to time, which so often has been God's instrument in clearing me, to clear me now. There may be definite things about myself or others, which I might be able to correct. Or there may be definite and serious charges which I should find it a duty to refute. Of all that you had to say, might be of that light and unsubstantial kind, which is the sure attendant of anyone who attempts to do a work, and which, as I have said, has been my lot all through life, things

---

85. JHN to Mrs. Henry Wilberforce, 4 December 1861, in *LD* 20:75.
86. JHN to F. R. Ward, 13 September 1860, in *LD* 19:403–4.

said in the air and carried about by the winds, and if annihilated today, sure to be brought into being again tomorrow—but, whatever it is, I can never, I am sure, feel anything but gratitude to you for having the courage to tell me of them.[87]

Seeking Advice and Expressing Concern

Another characteristic of Newman's friendships was that he sought the advice and opinion of his friends whenever he was uncertain. During the Achilli trial, whenever Newman's lawyer wanted to work for a lighter verdict by retraction, saying that Newman did not speak about Achilli on personal knowledge, but rather on knowledge based on an article in the *Dublin Review*, Newman wrote to James Hope for his advice:

> Will you give me your *wise* judgement?
>
> The Judges are against me and there is a Protestant feeling over Westminster Hall altogether, tho' this must not be said. Lewin, my lawyer, called the Judges prejudiced. It is impossible I can escape before a Jury—what I can do is to lighten the judgement [verdict] and to blacken Achilli.
>
> Lewin wishes me to admit (if the opposite side will let me)—i.e., I suppose say I did not speak on personal knowledge, but on the Dublin Review etc.
>
> Now there are two questions I wish you to consider for me.
>
> 1. how it will look in *me*? Of course I could do nothing inconsistent with truth and honor. I could not withdraw the charges in such sense as to imply I did not believe them, or was sorry for saying them. Still what shall I think of the whole matter, how shall I wish to have acted, *ten years hence*? I want a *broad* judgement.
>
> 2. its effect on the Catholic body—it is *giving them up* as (apparently) liars and slanderers . . .
>
> Write to me soon in Birmingham—give me your prayers—and may you be guided to give me a good, honest, and sound opinion on the point.[88]

---

87. Ibid., 404. For others letters where Newman apologized to someone, see his letters to Stephen Flanagan, 26 December 1856, in *LD* 17:487, and to Ignatius Grant, 23 December 1882, in *LD* 30:165.

88. JHN to James Hope, 21 November 1851, in *LD* 14:431–32. On November 24, Hope replied that although Achilli might be glad to let the matter drop, his supporters would only do so in return for an acknowledgment that he had been traduced. "My opinion then is—1. that you cannot avoid fighting except by retracting. 2. that

Spiritual Direction and Friendship

In his literary endeavors, Newman often asked for advice and criticism from others as he did in the following letter to Robert Ornsby. "At last I find a quarter of an hour to begin to write. Your criticisms on my Composition Paper are very valuable—and please always give me your remarks, whether I always take them or not—for they are always a guide to me, even when I do not literally act upon them."[89]

Correspondingly, Newman's care for his friends was manifest. No situation seemed unimportant to him. When he learned that a friend was in need, he either tried to help that individual personally, or, if that wasn't possible, he never hesitated to ask someone else to help his friends. When Eleanor Bretherton seemed to be experiencing difficulties because of her engagement, Newman noticed it and wrote of his concern to her mother.

> I should not forgive myself, if I did not write to you about dear Eleanor. I never saw her as she was yesterday. All her playfulness was gone; she was very serious; and her manner, though she was not conscious of it, was nervous, and had the appearance of a mind anxious and uneasy . . .
>
> I seemed to myself to see the day when dear Eleanor's face was pale, and her manner habitually subdued and sad . . .
>
> These are the reasons which lead me to urge on you if possible to come to some understanding with his parents. Eleanor is too precious to trifle with. They must take the case up in earnest. Else, the affair will linger, languish on—nothing settled—every thing in prospect—hope—disappointment—hope again—to and fro, and no end of it.[90]

Moreover, when the opportunity presented itself, Newman was quick to praise his friends. He praised the goodness of his friend, Hope-Scott, in a letter to Emily Bowles: "It is rare to find a man of the world so deeply

---

a complete legal victory is not essential to the cause of the Church or to your own justification—But I do not forget the two points which personally affect you—expense and punishment. As to the former of these we ought all to help you, and I for one am ready. As to the second I cannot see that, short of retraction, you can hope in any way to escape so lightly as by proving all you can against Achilli . . . and if you can prove him a fornicator or an adulterer I doubt much whether an English jury will consider his theology." Ibid., 432n1.

89. JHN to Robert Ornsby, 19 July 1854, in *LD* 16:198. For similar letters where Newman asked advice from others, see JHN to Edward Badeley, 14 April 1853, in *LD* 15:345–46; JHN to Richard Simpson, 14 March 1859, in *LD* 19:79–80.

90. JHN to Mrs. Peter Bretherton, 17 May 1865, in *LD* 21:468–69. With his non-Catholic friends, Newman maintained a vital interest in their faith and looked for ways in which he might interest them in Catholicism. See also JHN to H. P. Liddon, 31 March 1878, in *LD* 18:337, when Newman learned that his friend Pusey was dying.

religious, so holy in the inner man. A man may have many good points, yet have no interior: Hope-Scott speaks for himself."[91]

Maria Giberne, a close friend of Newman, entered a convent at Autun, a city which was bombarded by the Garibaldians in 1870. Newman, learning that she had developed some kind of nervous symptoms during the battle, feared for her health and safety. Immediately he wrote to the Bishop of Marseilles for help.

> I write to you in great anxiety about a friend of your Lordship and myself, who is in great trouble, at Autun—Sister Pia, Miss Giberne. A letter has come to me from her this morning dated the 22nd of November, which is such that I doubt whether, if the Bishop of Autun or her Mother Superior proposed to her to leave for England, she would not gladly accept the proposition.
>
> I know well in what great anxieties you are yourself—and I had thought [of] writing to the Cardinal Archbishop of Besancon about her, not to your Lordship ...
>
> ... I write to say that if you will decide what to do in her behalf, I will bear the expense whatever it is. Perhaps it will be best for her (1) to remain at Autun, and be supplied with money by some messenger, or, (2) if it be possible, supplied by his Lordship the Bishop of Autun—or (3) for some messenger to go to fetch her, either to Marseilles, and from whence she may proceed to England by sea, or (4) to Geneva hence she might go round by the Rhine to England; whatever you think best for her, pray be kind enough to do, without regard to the expense.[92]

Newman also helped his friends to find employment. In 1851, he wrote a letter to Archbishop Cullen in Ireland about employing T. W. Allies and Henry Wilberforce to teach at the Catholic University.[93] At the same time, he took a sincere interest in the financial difficulties of several friends and actively sought help for them; for example, in 1857, Newman wrote to William Leigh about a mutual acquaintance:

---

91. JHN to Emily Bowles, 13 April 1882, in *LD* 30:77. Likewise, when Maria Trench was preparing for publication of Keble's *Occasional Papers and Reviews*, she asked Newman for an evaluation and criticism of Keble and his literary works, which once again gave Newman the chance to praise his friend. For this letter, see JHN to Maria Trench, 29 October 1875, in *LD* 27:370–73.

92. JHN to Charles Place, Bishop of Marseilles, 5 December 1870, in *LD* 25:239–40. At the beginning of December, the Mother Superior at Autun sent Miss Giberne to the Visitation Convent at Fribourg in Switzerland. Mgr. Place, who received Newman's letter on December 16, wrote on December 17, to tell Newman that Miss Giberne had left Autun.

93. JHN to Archbishop Cullen, 28 April 1851, in *LD* 14:268.

> I take the liberty of writing to you on the subject of a lady, with whom members of your Family were, I believe, at one time intimate, and had opportunities of knowing and valuing more than I can have had. Yet, as I have heard of her several times lately, and you probably have not, I seem to have a reason for introducing her name to you—I mean Miss Holmes.
>
> She is at Boulogne, and I fear in some pecuniary embarrassment—to what extent I do not know—I suppose not much. The anxiety seems to have affected her health—a fresh letter has just come to me from her—and she speaks of having been confined to her room for a month, but now getting about . . .
>
> No one regrets more than I can, to find her so often change her plans. I have never attempted to offer her any advice on the subject, when she has happened to write to me, as knowing literally nothing, and having no means of judging, about the circumstances which influenced her—but I have been grieved to see that, as years go on, she is as uncertain about the future, and as destitute of means of meeting it, as ever.
>
> I am writing to you, as I have written to a friend elsewhere who knows her, from the interest I take in her, and my own utter incapacity to give advice—and, while I have reason to believe that you take interest in her also, I am quite sure that you are far more able than I to make suggestions which may be of service to her in her present difficulties.
>
> She has no notion whatever that I am writing to any one about her.[94]

Another friend of his, Miss Bowles, had written a text book for use in Irish schools, but had to wait until her work could be revised and published before she could be paid. However, because she needed the money badly, Newman wrote to another friend, William Monsell, asking if he could advance her half the money.

> Miss Bowles has done her work—and writes to know when she shall get her money. I was surprised to find she was literally unable to pay for her lodgings—it was simple news to me that she was in distress—though I knew she had lost her patrimony.
>
> I answered that it was necessary that her work should pass revision and be published, before she had paid, and she

---

94. JHN to William Leigh, 7 October 1857, in *LD* 18:138. Mr. Leigh agreed to help as a letter from Newman on October 10 indicated: "I am very much pleased to receive so kind a letter from you. And I also thank you and Mrs. Leigh very much, for showing me so promptly that I judged rightly in believing that you took a warm interest in Miss Holmes." *LD* 18:141.

> wrote back acquiescing. However, if you thought you could conscientiously advance half the money, it would I know be a great kindness. Her brother here has lent her some pounds for the moment. It is, I know, on your part, a question of justice, since it is trust money.[95]

Friendship and Trials

Every person is vulnerable to sickness and death, as well as personal trials, which need to be accepted as part of maturity and life. To be supported and encouraged at such times by an understanding person is a special privilege and to receive a letter from Newman in a moment of trial was a great consolation. During his Roman Catholic years, his personal correspondence is filled with letters to friends—consoling, encouraging, supporting, and directing them amid the vicissitudes of life. His desire was to be present with them, to support them in their times of trial.

Because the sufferings and trials of individuals are so unique, Newman found himself directing and encouraging persons who experienced many different kinds of spiritual trials. When Miss Giberne (Sister Pia) wrote to him about feeling less pleasing to God, Newman responded:

> I don't think seriously of what you tell me except as it is a trial to you. It is no proof that you are less pleasing to God; perhaps you are more so. One may fairly argue that it is indeed that it is a special honour to you that you are thus tried. It is easy to serve God, when consolations abound. Think of the lives of the Saints; consider what desolations weighed upon them for years. Do you think that none of them, though it is not mentioned in their history, had the very same cause of unsettlement of mind and desolation which you have? . . . Who says that it is easy to love those who ill-treat us? I should never be surprised if your trial was long, but it would be, long or short, a sign of God's special love towards you.[96]

Because Newman had experienced the anguish of being separated from friends due to his conversion, he could understand his friend, Robert

---

95. JHN to William Monsell, 22 December 1857, in *LD* 18:212.

96. JHN to Miss Giberne, 5 December 1880, in *LD* 29:324. Sixteen years earlier, Newman had encouraged her on December 26, 1864: "I do trust those sad trials of mind, which you spoke of, are not what they were; and that, in place of such desolation, you have begun to reap the fruits of your generous and singular Sacrifice of yourself to our dear Lord." *LD* 21:356.

Wilberforce, who spoke of broken friendships as "rending the heart." By sharing his own struggle, Newman hoped to give him strength.

> I have been saying Mass for you this morning, and have just received your letter, which you may be sure I read with great interest. Of course I can enter into your special pain, better than anyone else except Manning. In my own case the separation from friends was the one thing which weighed on me for two years before I became a Catholic—and it affected my health most seriously. It is the price we pay for a great good. Every one has to give his best—There are few things, besides, which either you or I had to give; for I don't suppose that either of us cared much for any thing else.[97]

Similarly, after Mrs. William Clark, whose husband was the Vicar of St. Mary Magdalen Church in Taunton, became a Catholic in October 1877, she began to experience puzzling difficulties. In one of three different letters supporting and encouraging her, Newman said:

> I am grieved to hear from Mrs. Pereira that you are too much overcome by your great trial to be able to come with her here. Few indeed have so heavy a cross laid upon their shoulders—but I am sure grace and strength will be given to you according to your day, and that on looking back on this sad time you will be able to thank Him who so afflicted you, both for the affliction and for His Presence all through it.
>
> It is such trials as yours which makes one feel what it was that the early martyrs suffered. I have not forgotten you in my prayers, and I earnestly hope and trust and am sure that a portion of that special comfort from the Paraclete which was given to them will be given to you—"To him that overcometh," is the inscription which our Lord has written on His banner, let us pray Him for the gift of perseverance—and, towards the attaining it, for a real and vivid sense of the shortness of this life and the length of Eternity Ah, how short this life will seem, when it is gone.[98]

Trials in religious life as well as ecclesiastical difficulties also received his attention. For example, Newman gently guided T. F. Knox, an Oratorian

---

97. JHN to Robert Wilberforce, 1 September 1854, in *LD* 16:242. Wilberforce became a Roman Catholic on November 1.

98. JHN to Mrs. William Clark, 14 March 1878, in *LD* 28:329. Newman wrote two more letters to Mrs. Clark: on December 7, 1877, in *LD* 28:276, and on December 30, 1878, in *LD* 28:437. For similar letters concerning the spiritual trials of converts, see his letters to Louisa Simeon on April 29, 1869, in *LD* 24:248, and to Miss Rowe on June 21, 1874, in *LD* 27:81.

friend, who was upset because of a misunderstanding: "Meanwhile be sure that no one can feel more affectionately minded to you than myself. It is little indeed to say, but what you ask leads me to assure you, that you are constantly in my remembrance at sacred times. And I trust you will find a home with us, and that we all may have the comfort, for we all need it in our various ways, of each other's love."[99]

Trials in family life found Newman supporting his friends. Briefly comparing married life with religious life, Newman told T. W. Allies that his responsibility was to care for his family. "Your trial is one of the severest which can befall a man, but be sure that all who take the step we have taken, in some way or other have to pay for it to the world. The world asks a price to let us go. Your trial is *care*, which is a most exceedingly great one, but those who are unmarried have their own. They are solitary and thrown among strangers more intimately and intensely than married people can be. You have a home. We have not had one."[100]

In 1851, William Dodsworth, a married man with a large family, wrote to Newman saying that he wanted to become a Catholic but was hesitant because of his family. Supporting his decision, Newman replied: "Indeed I do not undervalue the great sacrifices you are making from obeying the divine call made to you, and it has long seemed to me that these were as great as have been exacted of any one, if not greater. But He who has put on you the burden, will enable you to bear it, and will repay you sevenfold for all you do for Him."[101]

Whenever Lady Simeon became discouraged over the direction the lives of her boys were taking, Newman wrote her an encouraging letter. "All the blessings of this sacred season be upon you—and they will be, since you so courageously do the work which God gives you to do, amid that weight of suffering and that deep despondency which, after so great a trial, you cannot escape. I trust, and I believe, that even here you will be rewarded by seeing the good fruit which must come of your anxious care of the boys."[102] Similarly, when W. J. Daunt wrote an anxious letter to Newman because his son would not listen to his advice, he advised his friend to be patient. "I am sorry to hear the anxiety you are in about your son. Personal trial is often the only way in which young men learn wisdom, which they might have gained cheaply and

---

99. JHN to T. F. Knox, 13 January 1846, in *LD* 11:92–93.

100. JHN to T. W. Allies, 7 April 1851, in *LD* 14:248.

101. JHN to William Dodsworth, 1 January 1851, in *LD* 14:187–88.

102. JHN to Lady Simeon, 5 January 1872, in *LD* 26:6–7. Several months later, one son married outside the Church; thirteen years later, when the second son was also planning to do the same thing, Newman again wrote her a supportive letter on July 22, 1885, in *LD* 31:75.

at once if they would only profit by the experience of others. But generally the trial and the wisdom comes sooner to them then we think—and I trust it will not be long before your son learns at least so much as this, that those who love him well are better guides for him than himself."[103]

On several occasions, Newman had the opportunity to support a friend who was upset at the decision of a family member to follow a religious vocation. When Emily Bowden wanted to become a nun, Newman knew it would be difficult for her mother, and so he immediately wrote to Mrs. Bowden:

> It took me quite by surprise to hear from dear Emily. You must indeed be very much tried just now—Yet still, how joyful it is, and what an honor to you, that you should be allowed thus to give up to your Lord those He has given you!—and what a wonderful contrast to the uncertainties, risks and darkness of the future, to which a mother generally surrenders her children, and thinks herself happy in the surrender, what a contrast to this will be your parting with these dear girls, whom I cannot look at without wishing to weep, as a relief to me.[104]

Likewise, Agnes Wilberforce found it difficult to accept that her sister Caroline wanted to be a Franciscan nun. Anticipating her struggle, Newman took the initiative in writing.

> This is a sad Christmas for you and Mama, I am sending you all my best Christmas greetings—and hope you will not forget me in your prayers—and I don't forget on my part how you too need the prayers of all friends in what is so like the loss of a sister and a daughter. She indeed has left you for a better home—and she therefore can bear the separation better. She has her career visible and clear before her—to serve God in His Temple and to go to heaven—but that it should happen at Christmas, the special festival of our earthly home, perhaps makes the Will of God more trying for you. However, He does all things well.[105]

After Lady Simeon's daughter's vocation ran into difficulties, Newman was quick to support her.

> Though I had not felt C's [Cecilia] vocation to be otherwise than uncertain as yet, the failure of it has, on your account, given me very great pain. It is not by any means a common blow, and I

---

103. JHN to W. J. Daunt, 29 August 1868, in *LD* 24:134–35.
104. JHN to Mrs. J. W. Bowden, 19 July 1852, in *LD* 15:127.
105. JHN to Agnes Wilberforce, 24 December 1873, in *LD* 26:398.

> grieve for it with all my heart. You have nobly and with great self-denial and silent suffering taken on you a very difficult office and work for the sake of most dear and ever present memories, and it seemed as if your reward had come, and the day of peace had come for you.... I am saying more perhaps than you will yourself allow—but it is the way I view it for you, though I know full well you will be strengthened and cheered and prospered to do whatever is God's will in respect to you.
>
> May God bless you and guide you and lift up His countenance upon you, and give you peace.[106]

In addition to the trials experienced by his friends in their spiritual lives or in their families, Newman also dealt with the personal sorrows of those he loved. Because he had experienced failure in his own life, he was able to help others understand theirs. In 1830, after he had to resign his tutorship at Oriel College because of a disagreement with the Provost over the duties of a tutor, Newman wrote to his friend, Hurrell Froude. "All my plans fail. When did I ever succeed in any exertion for others?"[107] Many years later as a Roman Catholic, Newman shared his own sense of failure with John Flanagan as a way of helping him.

> Don't be cast down—all will turn out well. Recollect, and let me myself recollect, that from the first it has been my fortune to be ever failing, yet after all not to fail. From the first I have had bad strokes of fortune—yet on the whole I have made way. Hardly had I begun life, when misfortunes happened to my family—then I failed in the Schools; then I was put out of office at College; then came Number 90—and later the Achilli matter. You talk of "brilliant success" as not our portion—it is not. ... When I was a boy, I was taken beyond any thing in Homer, with Ulysses seeming "like a fool or an idiot," when he began to speak—and yet somehow doing more than others, as St. Paul with his weakness and foolishness. I think this was from some presentiment of what was to happen to me. Depend upon it, we shall be happier and more blessed and more successful in my way than in any other.[108]

---

106. JHN to Lady Simeon, 21 March 1882, in *LD* 30:70.

107. Trevor, *Newman's Journey*, 42. However, out of the ruin of his hopes at this time, he composed Sermon 9, "Jeremiah, a Lesson for the Disappointed," in *Parochial and Plain Sermons*, 8:124–40, September 12, 1830, in which he meditated on a recurring theme, that Christians must expect disappointment in this world: to the world, Christ was a failure.

108. JHN to John Flanagan, 24 February 1858, in *LD* 18:271.

Spiritual Direction and Friendship

In his letters, Newman did not explicitly write a great deal about mental problems or sufferings. Nevertheless, he certainly felt emotionally drained, especially through the 1850s and early 1860s.[109] To a great extent, the source of his sufferings during these years was the anxiety produced by his apparent failures. Consequently, he was very sensitive to the anxieties that other people experienced. Writing to Lady Henry Kerr in 1857, he said: "I think suspense and the anxiety connected with it one of the greatest of mental troubles."[110] One time, in a reflective letter to his friend, Ambrose St. John, Newman shared a passage from a book he happened to be reading: "I am reading Ellen Middleton for the first time, and have been struck with the following passage: 'I have often wondered whether the sensation of moral suffering is as surely allied to physical pain in every one else as in myself. The expression of an aching heart has always appeared to me to have a literal as well as a figurative sense; there is a sort of positive pain which accompanies certain kinds of mental sufferings, different in its nature from the feeling of grief, even in its highest degree.'"[111]

Without literally stating whether he agreed with the passage or not, he concluded his letter by saying: "I have just finished Ellen Middleton—It is far superior to Grantley Manor—But I hardly know whether I ought to have read it—it has distressed me so. I wish people would not write sad things—they only make one's head ache; there are sad things enough in the world."[112]

Four years after his conversion, in a letter to Mrs. Bowden, Newman spoke of the trials of advancing years and the feeling of loneliness that accompanied them: "It is this day 27 years that I was elected Fellow of Oriel—what a changed state of things I find myself in! One of the trials of advancing years is, that one has no one to recollect those earlier days, and to whom one can converse about them. This day was quite a turning point in my life—and, humanly speaking, I should never have been a Catholic but for God's Providence to me upon it."[113] The following year, William Maskell wrote to Newman about his feelings of loneliness that accompanied his position of responsibility. Although Newman could certainly identify with this kind of loneliness, at the same time he realized how unique this experience was for each person. Since he was not satisfied with a facile answer, he encouraged Maskell to turn to the Lord. "Every one thinks his own trial worst, else I do

---

109. Trevor, *Newman's Journey*, 202, remarked: "Newman certainly came near to a nervous breakdown in these years."

110. JHN to Lady Henry Kerr, 8 December 1857, in *LD* 18:197.

111. JHN to Ambrose St. John, 4 August 1852, in *LD* 15:141.

112. Ibid. Lady Georgiana Fullerton (1812–1885), a convert to Roman Catholicism in 1846, was the author of novels *Ellen Middleton* (1844) and *Grantley Manor* (1847).

113. JHN to J. W. Bowden, 12 April 1849, in *LD* 13:108.

not know why you should not allow I can feel sympathy in yours from my own experience. I feel sympathy so fully that I will not attempt to do for you what is beyond me. You *must* in your circumstances stand by yourself. He alone can bring you through your trial, *who will*. I have always felt responsibility to be one of the heaviest of sorrows, an over whelming oppression. Doubtless it was one of the causes of the Agony, the weight of a whole world. Loneliness is its very condition."[114]

Sickness and Death

Newman, who had been seriously ill several times in his life, realized that sickness can be a great trial, not only to those who are ill but also to those who are close to the sick. Very often he wrote to his friends empathizing with them and assuring them of his prayers. At times these letters would try explicitly to help people accept their illness as part of God's providential will; at other times his intention seemed to be more of an attempt to show that he cared about the person who was ill. For example, wondering how his own recent conversion would affect his relationship with someone who was ill, Newman wrote to Francis Demainbray expressing his concern. "I was told last night how ill you were—and you will believe without my saying it how deeply it concerned me. Though I am now in another communion, do not refuse to let me express to you my deep sympathy in your trial."[115]

Feeling that the illness of his friend, Miss Munro, was at least partially caused by anxiety, he tried to reassure her. "I am very sorry to hear you speak of being unwell—as I cannot help fearing it is in good measure owing to anxiety of mind from not being settled. When you get here, I am sanguine that your way will be clear before you, for we have every prospect of success."[116]

His love for his friend and fellow Oratorian, John Flanagan, was manifest in a long letter responding to a report that Flanagan had sent from his doctor in London concerning his lungs. Because Newman was concerned that he be given the best possible care, he encouraged Flanagan to seek a second opinion as to the best course of treatment. After discussing the entire matter with all the Oratorians, he delineated six possible ways to proceed.[117] However, with his own sister, Newman took a very common sense approach in directing her in her illness. "I am sorry to hear your account

---

114. JHN to William Maskell, 6 April 1850, in *LD* 13:459.

115. JHN to Francis Demainbray, 30 October 1845, in *LD* 11:21–22. Newman was received into the Roman Catholic Church three weeks earlier.

116. JHN to Miss Munro, 9 November 1849, in *LD* 13:289.

117. JHN to John Flanagan, 21 February 1858, in *LD* 18:264–66.

Spiritual Direction and Friendship

of yourself on the whole—but I am sure every one who knows you would say that the best restorative is *rest*, if you can take it, but you ought to take it now. Especially, what is most difficult and hardly in your power, rest, in the sense of sleep; for you never used to sleep hours enough, and that habit of getting up so early or lying awake, I am certain, is very bad for you."[118]

When his friend, Marianne Bowden, whom he had known from birth, wrote on July 14 that "I get worse by steady degrees, though with no marked symptoms",[119] Newman responded the very next day.

> Your letter of this morning brought tears into my eyes—first because you spoke so affectionately of me, and said, that, wherever you are, you will not forget me. When God brings you to His Blessed Presence, then at length you will know how weak I am, though so old, and how I need your prayers, and what good you can do me by them. You are one of my most faithful friends—I have ever said Mass for you under that title—and you will not cease to be faithful to me, though God calls you to Himself. Meanwhile, if He gives me grace, I will try to do what I can to merit your remembrance of me, by keeping you and your present necessities in mind.
>
> You are one of those to whom God has been most good—He has shielded you from evil all your life long—He has brought you into His Holy Church, and then made you one of His own elect children and spouses and now if it is His blessed will to take you hence, it is in order to bring you to Himself for all eternity . . . May our Lord Jesus and His dear Mother and St. Joseph be with you, when ever that solemn change comes.[120]

The illness or death of a friend affected Newman a great deal. He came to realize the value of writing to his friends at these times; simultaneously, he understood how someone else could feel when one of his family members or friends was ill, and so he would often write an encouraging or consoling letter. For example, to Mrs. Bretherton, whose daughter Eleanor was ill, he promised to say Mass for her:

> I am deeply concerned at what you say about dear Eleanor, but do trust that your own natural anxiety makes you fear more than you have need to fear . . .

---

118. JHN to Mrs. John Mozley, 14 October 1861, in *LD* 20:56.
119. Marianne Bowden to JHN, 14 July 1867, in *LD* 23:267n2.
120. JHN to Marianne Bowden, 15 July 1867, in *LD* 23:267–68.

I trust to say Mass for her for the next three days—but before then I hope you will write me word that all anxiety is over.[121]

Learning that Fr. Gordon's mother was seriously ill, Newman quickly wrote to console him. "I . . . said Mass this morning for your dear mother. . . . You and your sister have long expected it, but that does not make the trial less, when at last it comes. Please say every thing kind from me to her."[122]

The reality of death offered Newman a unique way to manifest his love for his friends. Frequently, at the death of a friend, Newman wrote down how he felt about a person. In this way, his capacity for friendship is reflected over the many years of his long life since he survived most of his friends. Reflecting once on our lack of knowledge in general as to the time of one's death, he wrote: "One of the most awful aspects of our ignorance here, is ignorance of the time of death. To what different kinds of work should one give oneself, if one knew that life was to be continued for one, two, or three years, or on the other hand for 20! Such is the trial of a person at my age—I may be entering on a long course of years, or closing my reckoning."[123]

In any case, the death of his close friends had a deep impact on him which is clearly reflected in his correspondence. When he received word of a death, he would often write to a number of other people, reminiscing about the friend who had just died. Writing about his feelings was apparently a part of the healing process enabling him to cope with his sense of loss. Similarly, he wrote numerous letters of consolation or encouragement to a friend who had lost someone by death.[124] In both situations, the sheer volume of letters indicates Newman's great sensitivity to the feelings of people, as well as his personal concern for each individual.

Before his conversion, Newman keenly felt the death of his friend Richard Hurrell Froude. When the letter arrived with the news, "Newman opened the letter in my room," Tom Mozley wrote to his sister, "and could only put it into my hand with no remark."[125] Later, Newman wrote to Bowden: "He was so very dear to me that it is an effort to me to reflect on my thoughts about him. I can never have a greater loss; for he was to me, and was likely to be ever, in the same degree of familiarity which I enjoyed

---

121. JHN to Mrs. Peter Bretherton, 3 July 1865, in *LD* 22:6.

122. JHN to William Gordon, 29 May 1872, in *LD* 26:101.

123. JHN to Bishop Ullathorne, 27 February 1857, in *LD* 17:534. Newman lived for another thirty-three years.

124. One of Newman's methods of encouragement and consolation at the time of death was to urge his friend to see the mystery of death as part of God's Providence.

125. Trevor, *Newman's Journey*, 70.

with yourself in our Undergraduate days.... Everything was so bright and beautiful about him, that to think of him must always be a comfort."[126]

To Miss Giberne he wrote: "As to dear Froude, I cannot speak of him consistently with my own deep feelings about him, though they are all right and pleasant.... I love to think and muse upon one who had the most angelic mind of any person I ever fell in with—the most unearthly, the most gifted. I have no painful thoughts in speaking of him (though I cannot trust myself to speak of him to many) but I feel the longer I live, the more I shall miss him."[127]

After his conversion and as he grew older, Newman began to reflect more in his personal correspondence on the reality of death. He was shocked to receive word of his sister Harriet's sudden death and wrote immediately to his friend, Mrs. J. W. Bowden: "It is to me *most* unexpected—and indeed the whole matter is a most painful mystery."[128] In 1873, when he learned of the death of his good friend, Edward Bellasis, he quickly wrote a consoling letter to his wife:

> I have just got your letter, so very sad, yet so very joyful. For is it not joyful to know that a soul so dear to God is at length in His glorious Presence and His Eternal Embrace? He has now the reward of his long faithfulness to God's service, and assuredly not one of his many good deeds, not any day of his life long devotion, not any one of the many services he has done to religion, not any part of his care for his family, of his kindness to his friends, of his dutifulness to the Church, of his zeal for the faith, no aspect of his bright and beautiful example, but is now having its full reward.
>
> I know my pain is nothing to yours and those about you—but I feel deeply I have lost one of my best, my most constant, dearest friends—still it is a great consolation beyond words to think that I have such a friend with God, who I am sure still loves me, although he is now cleansed from all sin and infirmity and I am still encompassed by both, that I have such an intimate friend so near to my Saviour and my Judge. You, my dear Mrs. Bellasis, must feel the bitter and the sweet, a hundred times more intensely than I—you have an irreparable loss, but you have an inestimable gain. You have a memory which will cheer and support you through life, and will gladden you in that hour, whenever it shall be, when Divine Mercy shall call you hence. As

---

126. Ibid.

127. Ibid. At the back of his diary, in 1837, when he was preparing Froude's *Remains* for publication, are the scribbled lines: "Farewell most loved, so much missed, until that Day which shall make you, known to so few, manifest to all as you were." Ibid.

128. JHN to Mrs. J. W. Bowden, 18 July 1852, in *LD* 15:126.

for me, I can only trust and pray that, when my own time comes, I may be found as ready to leave the world as he has been.[129]

Only three months later, his good friend, Henry Wilberforce, died and on the day of his death, Newman, greatly affected, penned these words to his son:

> There never was a man more humble than your dear father—never one so intimately realized what it was to die—and how little we know, and how much we have to know about it. Now he knows all: he knows all that we do not know. He has the reward of all his prayers; there is an end of all his fears. He has served God with a single aim all through his life, and he now understands how good it has been to have done so. I have known him most intimately for forty-seven years and he has always been the same. . . .
>
> May God sustain your dear Mother and all of you—but I don't doubt they will have abundant strength and consolation in their trial.[130]

The occasion of the death of his fellow Oratorian, Edward Caswell, in 1878, allowed Newman to reflect on how the loss of many of his friends affected him: "Thank you for your kind words about dear Fr. Edward. We have so long expected his death that we are in a way prepared for it—but there is a sorrow for the loss of friends which grows with years, because (to use

---

129. JHN to Mrs. Edward Bellasis, 27 January 1873, in *LD* 26:240. Several days later, on February 11, 1873, Newman wrote to H. P. Liddon about the death of Bellasis: "I have, through God's mercy, had many friends, but never a truer than he." *LD* 26:250.

130. JHN to Wilfrid Wilberforce, 23 April 1873, in *LD* 26:296. The *Weekly Register*, May 10, 1873, 295, gave the following account of Newman's presence at the funeral. "At the end of Mass, Father Bertrand Arthur Wilberforce said something to Dr. Newman, and after a little whispering, the venerable man was conducted to the pulpit. For some minutes, however, he was utterly incapable of speaking, and stood, his face covered with his hands, making vain efforts to master his emotion. I was quite afraid he would have to give it up. At last, however, after two or three attempts, he managed to steady his voice and to tell us 'that he knew him so intimately and loved him so much that it was almost impossible for him to command himself sufficiently to do what he had so unexpectedly been asked to do—viz., to bid his dear friend farewell. He had known him for fifty years, and though no doubt there were some there who knew his goodness better than he did, yet it seemed to him that no one could mourn him more than he did.' Then he drew a little outline of his life—of the position of comfort, and all 'that this world calls good,' in which he found himself, and of the prospects of advancement, 'if he had been an ambitious man.' 'When the word of the Lord came to him as it did to Abraham of old, to go forth from that pleasant home and from his friends, and all he held dear, and become'—here he fairly broke down again, but, at last, lifting up his head again, finished his sentence—'a fool for Christ's sake.' Then he said that he now committed him to the hands of his Saviour." See *LD* 26:300n1; see also Newman's letter to Lady Herbert of Lea about Wilberforce's death, 3 May 1873, in *LD* 26:303.

Spiritual Direction and Friendship

the hacked phrase) they become '*conspicuous* by their absence.'"[131] Similarly, fifty-four years after his sister Mary's death in 1828, Newman manifested his continued love for her on the anniversary of her death. "This is the anniversary of my dear Mary's death in 1828, an age ago; but she is as fresh in my memory and as dear to my heart, as if it were yesterday; and often I cannot mention her name without tears coming into my eyes."[132]

Not only did the death of a friend affect Newman personally, but he was keenly aware of friends who had lost someone through death. Numerous letters manifest his sensitivity to the feelings of people, along with his desire to comfort and support them in their loss. Frequently, these were not long letters; rather they indicated his wish to be present with the bereaved in their sorrow.

For Newman, the loss of one's mother was one of the greatest trials. Consequently, whenever he learned that a friend's mother had died, he wrote immediately. For example, to Sir John Acton, he wrote: "Not supposing that any human words whatever could aid you in so great a suffering. A mother

---

131. JHN to Mrs. F. R. Ward, 13 January 1878, in *LD* 28:301. See also JHN to Miss Caswall, 2 January 1878, in *LD* 28:292. He wrote to Caswall's sister on the day of his death: "He was one of my dearest friends, and is a great loss to us all, for he was loved far and wide round about the Oratory. That God may comfort you and your sister under this great grief is the sincere prayer of
Yours most truly John H. Newman."

132. JHN to Miss M. R. Giberne, 5 January 1882, in *LD* 30:48. For similar letters where death provided Newman the opportunity to express his love for his friends, see:
On the death of Fr. Joseph Gordon, an Oratorian:

JHN to William Gordon, 14 February 1853, in *LD* 15:299–300;
JHN to J. Spencer Northcote, 14 February 1853, in *LD* 15:300–301;
JHN to Bishop Ullathorne, 14 February 1853, in *LD* 15:301–2;
JHN to Nicholas Darnell, 18 February 1853, in *LD* 15:304;
JHN to Henry Wilberforce, 23 February 1853, in *LD* 15:309.

On the death of Robert Wilberforce: JHN to Mrs. John Mozley, 20 February 1857, in *LD* 17:527–28.

On the death of Faber: JHN to W. J. Copeland, 27 September 1863, in *LD* 20:529;
JHN to J. D. Dalgairns, 27 September 1863, in *LD* 20:30;
JHN to Miss Holmes, 20 November 1863, in *LD* 20:559–60.

On the death of Marianne Bowden: JHN to Mother Margaret Weld, 12 October 1867, in *LD* 23:352; JHN to Mrs. J. W. Bowden, 13 October 1867, in *LD* 23:352.

On the death of Sister Agnes Philip (Moore): JHN to Mother Mary Imelda Poole, 26 April 1872, in *LD* 26:74.

On the death of Miss Holmes: JHN to Mrs. Brackenbury, 2 October 1878, in *LD* 28:402.

On the death of Mother Mary Imelda Poole: JHN to Sister Mary Gabriel du Boulay, 15 October 1881, in *LD* 30:8–9; JHN to Augusta Drance, 16 October 1881, in *LD* 29:9.

On the death of Maria Giberne: JHN to the Superior of the Visitation Convent at Autun, 15 December 1885, in *LD* 31:102.

can be lost but once. And the trial is unlike any trial before or after it."[133] To William Leigh he said: "I have said Mass for the soul of your dead Mother this morning. No trial is greater than that of losing a mother, and in your case, it is more than usual because it is the final of many losses."[134] Newman encouraged Charlotte Wood, who had cared for her sick mother for years:

> I have said Mass for your dear Mother this morning. I could not be surprised. The end *must* have come soon, the wonder is, it has not come sooner. In spite of your present grief, you have happy memories to cheer you, as you move out of the cloud which at first must over shadow you. You have been allowed many years of affectionate service to her whom you have lost. God has accepted all you have done for her in return for what she once did for you; and now your anxious service is at length ended.—You must bless God and rejoice.[135]

Similarly, when John Hardman's father died, Newman's letter concentrated on his father's goodness as a way of consoling him.

> I said Mass for the soul of your dear Father, as soon as I heard he was taken from us. . . .
> Of course I have little right to speak about him to you, who knew him so well—but still the witness of one who saw him as I saw him has a value of its own, and therefore I will say to you that I don't think I ever met with any one who came up more exactly to my idea of a good Christian—a God-fearing, honest, straightforward, single-minded man—a man of clear simple robust faith, and of large charity. It is pleasant to think of such, for they are the salt of the earth. He was ever most friendly to the Oratory and me—and has done us many a service—and we now mourn over his death, as a personal sorrow as well as a public loss. May we live his life, and die his death.[136]

133. JHN to Sir John Acton, 19 March 1860, in *LD* 19:316.

134. JHN to William Leigh, 20 October 1878, in *LD* 28:411. He was also a widower.

135. JHN to Charlotte Wood, 16 December 1873, in *LD* 26:396. For similar letters where Newman wrote to friends whose mothers had died, see:

JHN to J. D. Dalgairns, 12 September 1852, in *LD* 15:163;
JHN to Miss Holmes, 10 August 1858, in *LD* 18:438;
JHN to William Monsell, 5 January 1859, in *LD* 19:8;
JHN to Charles Devaux, 2 August 1870, in *LD* 25:170;
JHN to Mrs. John Kenyon, 13 February 1884, in *LD* 30:309.

136. JHN to John Hardman, Junior, 1 June 1867, in *LD* 23:244. For other letters to friends whose fathers had died see:

JHN to Richard Westmacott, 5 September 1856, in *LD* 17:374;
JHN to Mrs. Frederick Lee, 17 September 1870, in *LD* 25:207–8;

Spiritual Direction and Friendship

Persons who had lost a member of their family received the most attention from Newman. Parents whose son or daughter had died were always remembered; for example to Mrs. Ward, whose son had died of diphtheria, he wrote:

> Your letter is most touching and long to be remembered. May we all be as ready for death, when out time comes, as that dear boy was. He could never be more fit to die than now, and so God took him. And for what, my dear Mrs. Ward, was he given to you, what was your mission in cherishing and rearing him up so carefully, except to bring him to heaven? That was your very work,—not to gain him a long life and a happy one, but to educate him for his God. That was your work, and through God's grace you have done it. You have carried it home. What can you want more? Your loving Lord has fulfilled all your largest prayers—and now your dear boy will pay them back to you a hundred fold by praying for you and for all who are so dear to him. And one of his first prayers, be sure, will be that his Mother may be able to bear her loss well.[137]

Similarly, he counseled his friend, Mrs. J. W. Bowden, to have patience with herself—that with time she would be able to integrate the loss of her son into her life.

> I know there is only One who can comfort you in your present great suffering. All those mercies which you have had shown you more than other Mothers, that you have had so much of his company up to the very last, and spent a life with him, and that you have for so many years had him in charge and lived for him, and your recollections of him at so many different ages, and that sweet sereneness and peace which his dear Father used to talk to me of, when he was an Eton boy, and the picture of him which you must bear about with you in your mind, all these mercies now only make the trial greater. But in a little time they will come to you as mercies again, when you are able to bear them. And they will enable you almost to touch that heaven, to which so innocent and blameless a life has, one cannot doubt, already carried him.

JHN to Hugh Blount, 3 May 1881, in *LD* 29:369;
JHN to A son of Sir Henry Cole, 20 April 1882, in *LD* 30:80;
JHN to James Wheble, 29 January 1884, in *LD* 30:302;
JHN to Joseph Monteith, 31 March 1884, in *LD* 30:339;
JHN to Lady Wolseley, 19 June 1885, in *LD* 31:73.
137. JHN to Mrs. F. R. Ward, 22 September 1866, in *LD* 22:92.

> What can you desire more than to have given a soul to God?[138]

Again, having learned that Sir Rowland and Lady Blennerhassett's second son died at the age of nine months, Newman tried to comfort them by saying:

> I write a line to say, what you cannot doubt, that I was very much concerned that you and Lady Blennerhassett should have so trying an affliction.
>
> None but yourselves can understand how great it is but any one may be able to foretell, that in proportion to the pain of your loss now, will be the comfort, as time goes on to know that one so dear and precious to you is safe lodged in heaven—And you feel already something of this consolation.[139]

Comparing his friend, Mrs. William Froude, to the Blessed Virgin under the cross at the death of her son, he said: "This is a sorrowful Easter day for you—yet a joyful one too. Through the past week you have been like the Blessed Virgin under the Cross. What a great mercy it was he should die at home, and not in some foreign place among strangers. This is what makes a time of mourning so bright. You have landed him safe on the eternal shore—What could you wish better?"[140]

---

138. JHN to J. W. Bowden, 14 December 1874, in *LD* 27:172.

139. JHN to Sir Rowland Blennerhassett, 24 September 1878, in *LD* 28:400–401.

140. JHN to Mrs. William Froude, Easter Day, 1868, in *LD* 24:61; her son Arthur died at Chelston Cross, Torquay, at the age of twenty-four. He was in the Royal Navy and had become a Catholic at seventeen. Reflecting on the importance of Newman's friendship with her family, Mrs. Froude wrote on February 20: "I thank God every year more and more, that we have had you for a friend. It is curious to me to see that—although my children are all so different, yet there is something in your writings which fits into their minds in a way that no other serious reading does. I read your books over and over again to Arthur, now that he is ill, and he is never tired of hearing them. . . . I cannot help feeling that . . . this quiet time at home, for thought and attention to his religious duties, will have been of great advantage to him." Ibid., n3. For other letters where Newman wrote to a parent who had lost a son, see:

JHN to Henry Wilberforce, 10 March 1847, in *LD* 12:61;
JHN to The Marchioness of Lothian, 26 January 1855, in *LD* 16:365;
JHN to John Pollen, 24 January 1858, in *LD* 18:238–39;
JHN to Mrs. Gordon, 24 February 1858, in *LD* 18:253;
JHN to Lord Charles Thyme, 9 February 1881, in *LD* 29:337;
JHN to Richard Lamb, 17 April 1881, in *LD* 31:96–97 Supplement.
For letters to parents who had lost a daughter see:
JHN to John Hardman, 1 November 1861, in *LD* 20:62;
JHN to James Hope-Scott, 9 June 1862, in *LD* 20:204–5;
JHN to John Sparrow, 13 March 1865, in *LD* 21:429;
JHN to Mrs. Buckle, 19 June 1869, in *LD* 24:272;
JHN to George Ryder, 15 August 1877, in *LD* 28:231;

Spiritual Direction and Friendship

In the same way, he would often write to a friend whose brother or sister had died. Sensing that the death of the sister of his lifelong friend, Miss Giberne, would be difficult for her, Newman wrote: "By this time you must have heard of your dear Sister's death. Tho', as having given yourself to your Lord, you have died to the world, still it must pain you deeply, for invisible ties connect us with the earth while we are in it. To me of course, it is very touching as throwing me back to the thought of her husband, and snapping remembrances while it re-kindles them.

"I hope that you are well . . . and that you are supported by the full consolations of the Almighty Paraclete."[141]

In 1872, Tom Mozley died; his father had bequeathed his house in Derby to him, but he had sold it on his mother's death with the result that his unmarried sisters had to leave their home. Knowing of the family reconciliation before his death, Newman wrote these words of consolation to his sister Anne:

> It is very kind of you to write to me. I supposed you would form a large party, and rejoice indeed at what you tell me about Tom. You have had, I can feel, a very great loss, which cannot be made up—and of which perhaps you will be more sensible as time goes on—but it still will be a great consolation to you always to look back on yesterday—as a time, when the last sad duties and offices towards one you loved so much, in themselves so soothing as well as so powerful, were sealed and consecrated by a reconciliation.[142]

The death of a spouse provided Newman with another opportunity to manifest his friendship. Sir John Simeon's death in Switzerland prompted Newman to share his reflections on the gifts of this friend with his widow:

> Our good God has visited you with a dreadful blow, and has put upon you a very heavy burden—but He will enable you to sustain both.
>
> He never will forsake you or afflict you overmuch, He will ever be with you—Already, I am sure, He has made you feel how strong His strength is.

JHN to Henry Ellacombe, 1 January 1885, in *LD* 31 Supplement:51.

141. JHN to Miss M. R. Giberne, 21 July 1865, in *LD* 22:17. In 1824, Sarah Giberne married Walter Mayers, who died in 1828. A master at Ealing School, Mayers in 1816 was "the human means" of Newman's first conversion. Mayers was appointed Rector of Over Worton, near Banbury, in the church there Newman preached his first sermon on June 23, 1824.

142. JHN to Anne Mozley, 29 October 1872, in *LD* 26:192.

He has given you a brave spirit, and He will both try it and reward it.

It is a most dear and pleasant thought, as to him whom we have lost, to think how much he has gained by our losing him—There is now an end with him of all distress, anxiety, heaviness, perplexity, and end for ever.

No one can know as you know, how honest and true were all his thoughts, and how beautiful his inward self. God gave him many gifts. He gave him uprightness and religiousness of mind—and amid severe trials, has led him forward, and at length brought him through and out of this scene of confusion and infirmity into that state of being which is true and eternal. Shadows have departed for him, and he is with his God. Those who have gone from us, have, so far, a blessing which the best and holiest of men cannot have here. He is beyond sin, trial, fear and uncertainty. If we had the power of bringing him back by wishing, we could not bring ourselves to wish it.[143]

Besides writing to friends who had lost relatives through death, it is evident from his correspondence that Newman also wrote to his friends who had suffered the loss of cherished acquaintances. Richard Jelf, a close friend of Pusey, died in 1871, and Newman immediately wrote: "I am grieved indeed to hear of the great loss you have had in dear Jelf's death. To you it must be a very severe trial—when even to me it is really felt as a great loss—for I have always calculated on the chance of seeing him again, having never lost the affection for him which so affectionate heart as his created in his friends. But he has been to you from the time he was at Eton an intimate companion—and for many years a confidential adviser and associate."[144]

Fidelity and Friendship

One final characteristic of friendship embedded in Newman's correspondence is fidelity. To be faithful to one's friends was the desired goal; although some events in his life, such as his conversion, at times made fidelity difficult, nevertheless it was for him an important value. Newman was a realist and realized that in every friendship there would be joy and sorrow, as well as the need for reconciliation. At the same time, his own lasting relationships with people attest to the importance of fidelity.

---

143. JHN to Lady Simeon, 30 May 1870, in *LD* 25:136–37.
144. JHN to E. B. Pusey, 20 September 1871, in *LD* 25:404–5.

Spiritual Direction and Friendship

In 1862, Newman wrote to Miss Holmes about the value of having "unchanging friends" in a changing world. "In this world of change, it is a great thing to have unchanging friends—and you are one of those who have been most faithful to me amid all vicissitudes."[145] Three years later, briefly reminiscing about his life, Newman thanked Isaac Williams for his faithfulness as a friend in contrast to others who had abandoned him on his conversion. "I don't forget, but remember with much gratitude, how for twenty years you are perhaps the only one of my old friends who has never lost sight of me—but by letters, or messages, or inquiries, have ever kept up the memory of past and happy days. How mysterious it is that the holiest ties are snapped and cast to the winds by the holiest promptings—and that they who would fain live together in a covenant of gospel peace, hear each of them a voice and a contrary voice, calling on them to break it!"[146]

Ten years later, Newman expressed to Miss Giberne his thankfulness to God for his many faithful friends who had supported him throughout the years. He began by noting the fidelity of Ambrose St. John in 1875:

> What a faithful friend he has been to me for 32 years! yet there are others as faithful. What a wonderful mercy it is to me that God has given me so many faithful friends! He has never left me without support at trying times. How much you did for me in the Achilli trial, (and at other times), and I have never thanked you, as I ought to have done. This sometimes oppresses me, as if I was very ungrateful. You truly say that you have been [seen?] my beginning, middle, and end. Since his death, I have been reproaching myself for not expressing to *him* how much I felt *his* love—and I write this lest I should feel the same about you, should it be God's will that I should outlive you. I have above mentioned the Achilli matter, but that is only one specimen of the devotion, which by word and deed and prayer, you have been continually showing towards me most unworthy.[147]

---

145. JHN to Miss Holmes, 2 April 1862, in *LD* 20:180. Similarly, in 1867 he asked Sir John Simeon: "Can there be a greater blessing here below than to have good friends who sympathize both with the good and evil that befalls one?" JHN to Sir John Simeon, 10 April 1867, in *LD* 23:140.

146. JHN to Isaac Williams, 31 March 1865, in *LD* 21:441–42.

147. JHN to Miss M. R. Giberne, 4 June 1875, in *LD* 27:311. See also a letter on December 31, 1883, to Mrs. Borlase who, in 1883, sent Newman a Christmas turkey which his good friend, Mr. Copeland, had sent for the past twenty years. Commenting on Copeland's faithfulness, Newman wrote: "My dear friend [Copeland] has sent it to us for at least twenty years past, and it has been a record year by year, and a symbol, of that loyalty to friends, which was one of his characteristic traits. I have had, through a kind of Providence, many friends, but few can be put in comparison of him for faithfulness." *LD* 30:284. For an example of Newman's fidelity in friendship, see his correspondence

Through the years, Newman was reconciled with many friends who had found his conversion difficult to accept. In 1856, he wrote about the general situation, noting: "As in Job's case, the friends lost by my becoming a Catholic, are now nearly made up to me in full tale—and they themselves are constantly coming over."[148] Although Newman had corresponded with both Pusey and Keble, he had not seen either of them for almost twenty years—not until 1865. In a letter to Ambrose St. John, Newman wrote a long description of their re-union at Keble's home. Arriving for supper, Newman wrote of Keble: "Keble was at the door, he did not know me, nor I him. How mysterious that first sight of friends is! For when I came to contemplate him, it was the old face and manner, but the first effect and impression was different."[149] Continuing, he spoke of Pusey:

> Indeed, the alteration in him shocked me . . . it pained and grieved me. I should have known him any where—his face is not changed, but it is as if you looked at him through a prodigious magnifier. I recollect him short and small—with a round head—smallish features—flaxen curly hair—huddled up together from his shoulders downward—and walking fast. This was a young man—but comparing him even when last I saw him [in 1846], when he was slow in his motions and staid in his figure, still there is a wonderful change. His head and his features are half as large again—his chest is very broad—and he has, I think, a

---

with Mark Pattison in 1883. Newman, then in his eighties, had known Pattison for over forty years. Pattison, who had been a Catholic, but no longer practiced his faith, was in his last illness, and it was thought that only Newman could have a good effect upon him. Newman wrote to him asking him if there was any way in which he could serve him, along with asking if he could come and see him at Oxford. Even though Pattison refused at first, eventually Newman was able to make the trip. The journey was a very difficult one for Newman at his age. Nevertheless, because of their friendship and because of Newman's hope of being able to reconcile Pattison with the Church, he went. Although he was unsuccessful in terms of reconciling him to the Church, it meant a great deal to Pattison. For their correspondence, see the following letters:

JHN to Mark Pattison, 25 December 1883, in *LD* 30:282;
JHN to Mark Pattison, 27 December 1883, in *LD* 30:283;
Mark Pattison to JHN, 28 December 1883, in *LD* 30:284;
JHN to Mark Pattison, 2 January 1884, in *LD* 30:287–88;
JHN to Mark Pattison, 4 January 1884, in *LD* 30:288–89;
Mark Pattison to JHN, 5 January 1884, in *LD* 30:290;
JHN to Anne Mozley, 7 January 1884, in *LD* 30:291;
JHN to Mark Pattison, 8 January 1884, in *LD* 30:292–93.

148. JHN to Mrs. J. W. Bowden, 13 September 1856, in *LD* 17:378.
149. JHN to Ambrose St. John, 13 September 1865, in *LD* 22:52.

paunch. His voice is the same—were my eyes shut, I should not have been sensible of any lapse of time.[150]

Yet Newman knew that somehow the wounds of broken friendships could be very deep even after reconciliation. In a letter to William Froude in 1860, he wrote: "When I became a Catholic, I think I wrote to Rogers to beg his forgiveness if in any thing I had acted unkindly to him. My severance from him and others is a wound which will never heal. This is no inconsistency to say so, though I feel myself in possession of supernatural truth and consolation. The natural heart has wounds as well as the body."[151]

In Newman's correspondence, there are literally hundreds of letters to friends in which he promised to offer Mass or to pray for them. For example, he regularly offered Mass for several women whom he called his "faithful friends"—it was "the greatest thing" he could do for them.[152] In 1864, he wrote to one of these women, Marianne Bowden, who became a nun in 1852:

> Now I have said Mass for your two holy sisters departed, and for your Anniversary—ten years! what a time! It is well to think and trust that we are so much nearer to our Eternal House. God grant it may be so. How pleasant it is to think of those who have gone and are secure. Your account of your Sisters was very interesting. I say Mass for you continually. There are eight ladies, you make a 9th, whom I call my faithful friends—and for whom I say Mass at short intervals. . . . And there are certain days besides, on which I always say Mass for you.[153]

Three years later, she became very ill and wrote to Newman expressing her gratitude for his friendship:

> I get worse by steady degrees, though with no marked symptoms. Thank God I feel very calm and peaceful, and though I have no idea whatever what I shall find in Eternity, still I feel most happy to go, for I know that God loves me. And what you have so often said, He now enables me to feel very strongly, that as He has always been so good to me, He will continue to be as good hereafter. I wish I had more ardent desires for heaven, but really I can only say that I have been very happy to live and shall be still more happy to die whenever our Lord pleases. . . . I need

---

150. Ibid.

151. JHN to William Froude, 2 January 1860, in *LD* 19:273.

152. JHN to Catherine Bowden, Sister Mary Alban, 25 November 1868, in *LD* 24:175.

153. JHN to Marianne Bowden, 14 January 1864, in *LD* 21:16–17.

not say dear Father that wherever I am I can never forget you, and if God shows me mercy as I trust, I hope you will feel the effects of my prayers.[154]

Newman responded the very next day, calling her one of his most faithful friends: "Your letter of this morning brought tears into my eyes—first because you spoke so affectionately of me, and said, that, wherever you are, you will not forget me. When God brings you to His Blessed presence, then at length you will know how weak I am, though so old, and how I need your prayers, and what good you can do me by them. You are one of my most faithful friends—I have ever said Mass for you under that title—and you will not cease to be faithful to me, though God calls you to Himself."[155]

Newman understood that friendship is permeated with both joy and sorrow. The manner in which a person reacts to these experiences determines whether or not the friendship will grow and deepen. Newman wanted to share his own joys with his friends. Although he did not do this to any great extent, scattered letters indicate that at certain times and in his own quiet way, he wrote to others about some joyful event in his own life.

In 1877, Samuel Wayte, president of Trinity College, Oxford, wrote to Newman inviting him to become the first Honorary Fellow of the College.[156] Reflecting on whether he should accept or not, he quickly wrote to Bishop Ullathorne: "I have just received a very great compliment, perhaps the greatest I ever received and I don't like not to tell you of it one of the first."[157] Deciding to accept several days later, he replied to Samuel Wayte, saying: "It has been a singular gratification to me to receive your letter, informing me of the proposal of your Society to make me an Honorary Fellow of Trinity, it being the first instance of their exercising the power given them of making such an appointment, and I accept with a full heart an honour which is as great a surprise to me as it is a pleasure.

"It is indeed a most strange good fortune, after a long sixty years and more, to become again a freshman of my first and dear College."[158]

---

154. Marianne Bowden to JHN, 14 July 1867, in *LD* 23:267n2.

155. JHN to Marianne Bowden, 15 July 1867, in *LD* 23:267. See also Newman's letter to Sister Mary Gabriel du Boulay on December 27, 1870: "I was glad to have your affectionate note. You are one of those whom I emphatically call my 'Faithful women' for whom I have said 52 Masses this year." *LD* 25:256.

156. In his letter to Newman on December 14, 1877, Samuel Wayte noted: "I may mention that if you should do so, you will be the first person in whose case the College will have exercised the power which was given to it in 1857, and that at present it is not contemplated to elect another Honorary Fellow." *LD* 28:279n4.

157. JHN to Bishop Ullathorne, 18 December 1877, in *LD* 28:283.

158. JHN to Samuel Wayte, 20 December 1877, in *LD* 28:285.

Spiritual Direction and Friendship

In a letter to his lifelong friend, Mrs. William Froude, two days before Christmas, one can sense Newman's joy about receiving the honorary fellowship: "I have a piece of news to tell you, which William will be glad to hear—the Trinity President and Fellows, my old Undergraduate College, have made me an Honorary Fellow of their Society. I have always cherished a great love for the College—greater than for any thing in Oxford—and it is a great gratification to me. It is only two or three days since this gracious act was done—and you are one of the first I have thought of telling, knowing your affectionate thoughts of me."[159]

Another occasion which provided Newman the opportunity of sharing his joy was the offer of Leo XIII to raise Newman to the Cardinalate. Initially, thinking that he should decline the offer, he wrote to Bishop Ullathorne:

> I trust that his Holiness and the most eminent Cardinal Nina will not think me a thoroughly discourteous and unfeeling man, who is not touched by the commendation, or a sense of gratitude or the splendour of dignity, when I say to you, my Bishop, who knows me so well, that I regard as altogether above me the great honour which the Holy Father proposes with wonderful kindness to confer on one so insignificant, an honour quite transcendent and unparalleled, than which his Holiness has none greater to bestow.
>
> For I am, indeed, old and distrustful of myself; I have lived now thirty years "in my little nest" in my much loved Oratory, sheltered and happy, and would therefore entreat his Holiness not to take me from St. Philip, my Father and Patron.
>
> By the love and reverence with which a long succession of Popes have regarded and trusted my St. Philip, I pray and entreat his Holiness in compassion of my diffidence of mind, in consideration of my feeble health, my nearly eighty years, the retired course of my life from my youth, my ignorance of foreign languages, and my lack of experience in business, to let me die where I have so long lived. Since I know now and henceforth that his Holiness thinks kindly of me, what more can I desire?[160]

However, at the urging of Bishop Ullathorne and other friends[161] and after further reflection, Newman decided to accept. Writing to Bishop

---

159. JHN to Mrs. William Froude, 23 December 1877, in *LD* 28:288.

160. JHN to Bishop Ullathorne, 2 February 1879, in *LD* 29:18–19. Newman was advised by his brother Francis to decline the invitation in a letter dated February 27, 1879, in *LD* 29:44n1.

161. Soon after the accession of Leo XIII, there were rumors that Newman was to be made a Cardinal. When Cardinal Howard arrived in London in July 1878, his cousin,

Ullathorne in gratitude, Newman said: "You may fancy how I am overcome by the Pope's goodness. And it is only the crown of the kindness and affectionateness of so many. And specifically of yourself, for whom I shall always give thanks and pray as one of my benefactors."[162] In the same way, he shared his happiness with Anne Mozley explaining why he had accepted the invitation of the Pope:

> I have this very day learned that the offer of a Cardinal's Hat is to be made to me with the privilege of living still here as before. So great a kindness, made with so personal a feeling towards me by the Pope I could not resist, and I shall accept it.
>
> It puts an end to all those reports that my teaching is not Catholic or my books trustworthy, which has been so great a trial to me so long.
>
> Refusal too would have created a suspicion that it was true that I was but half and half Catholic, who dared not commit himself to a close union with the Church of Rome, and who wished to be independent.
>
> It would have unsettled some Catholics, and would have thrown back inquirers.
>
> It would [have] disheartened so many zealous well-wishers, who had so rejoiced or so laboured personally, that my fair name should be vindicated, and who felt that a refusal would be most ungracious to the Pope, nay, as it was expressed to me, "a snub and no mistake to him," and would be shrinking from aiding him in my place when he was pursuing the very line of policy which for so many years I had desiderated at Rome.[163]

At other times, Newman would write to his friends as they celebrated joyful occasions in their lives. He often used these events, such as wedding anniversaries, a person's reception into the Church or birthdays, as opportunities to encourage them in some way as well as promising them his prayers. For example, he wrote in 1878 to Helen and Mary Church, who were twins, on the occasion of their twentieth birthday saying: "How shall I best show kindness to you on your birthday? It is by wishing and praying that year by year you may grow more and more in God's favour and in inward peace,—in an equanimity and cheerfulness under all circumstances which is the fruit of faith, and a devotion which finds no duties difficult, for

---

the Duke of Norfolk, asked him what the possibilities were, and then with Lord Ripon made an approach to Manning. For these letters, see *LD* 29:423–26, appendix 1.

162. JHN to Bishop Ullathorne, 1 March 1879, in *LD* 29:51.
163. JHN to Anne Mozley, 1 March 1879, in *LD* 29:50.

it is inspired by love. This I do with all my heart, and am, my dear children very affectionately yours."[164]

Newman realized that at times difficulties would arise between friends, that disagreement and misunderstandings would cause pain and sorrow. In fact, some of his own greatest suffering occurred because of the reaction of some of his friends at the time of his conversion. In time he came to realize that some of the events of life that affected his friendships could not be changed. These he tried to accept without bitterness and to offer to God.[165]

Yet he also realized that time was a great healing factor; he remained open to the possibility of reconciliation with former friends and appropriately pursued this reconciliation. In his later years, Newman was reconciled with many Anglicans who had once been his friends.

Newman understood disagreements among friends not as lessening or destroying friendship, but rather as an opportunity for growth. With some of his closest friends Newman disagreed the most. Writing to Lady Acland in 1882 about his good friend, Pusey, who was now dying, Newman said: "I said Mass for him this morning. I have known him for sixty years; and he has ever been the same, subduing me by his many high virtues, and, amid severe trials of friendship, the most faithful of friends."[166] The challenge in friendship, in relation to disagreements, was to remain open to the other person. The temptation for most people, he felt, was to close off the other person.

Although he felt the immense pain of separation from his friends at the time of his conversion, he tried to understand their objections to his move.[167] Waiting patiently, he believed that with time reconciliation would occur; he also believed that the separation of friends because of conversion, might also be the trial necessary to bring others into the Church. For example, several months after his own conversion he wrote to Henry Wilberforce: "And as doubt long continued may be the fiery process by which one person is brought into the Church, so the loss or alienation of friends by their conversion may be the divinely sent trial of others. It may be the gradual operation by which God prepares their own souls for the truth."[168]

---

164. JHN to Helen and Mary Church, 21 February 1878, in *LD* 28:315–16;

165. JHN to Mrs. John Mozley, 28 September 1850, in *LD* 14:78–79. In this letter, Newman spoke of his sorrow because of his sister Jemima's lack of openness to the Catholic faith.

166. JHN to Lady Acland, 15 September 1882, in *LD* 30:126.

167. JHN to Mrs. William Froude, 3 July 1848, in *LD* 12:232–33. In 1858, Newman said: "The thing I do feel is the falling off of friends." JHN to John Flanagan, 31 May 1858, in *LD* 18:361.

168. JHN to Henry Wilberforce, 29 May 1846, in *LD* 11:166–67. In this letter, he went on to speak of his joy at his first Catholic godson.

With friends who disagreed about religious beliefs, Newman manifested a great tolerance and a continual willingness to dialogue. For example, his skeptic friend, William Froude, wrote him a long letter in 1859 elaborating his position.[169] Newman answered several days later, saying he was thankful that Froude wrote explaining how he felt: "Your letter of this morning has been a very great comfort to me. The greatest of evils in the intercourse of friends is ignorance about each other's feelings."[170]

At times disagreements or misunderstandings strain a friendship. This was the situation with Newman's friend of many years, George Ryder. In 1855, Ryder apparently felt that Newman was in some way coming between him and his son, Harry, who was attending the Catholic University in Dublin. Newman decided to write to Ryder's brother-in-law, Henry Wilberforce.

> One of my great trials is about poor George Ryder. Last June year, as if thundering out of a clear sky, he *suddenly* accused me of something like *lying*. Within the last fortnight on my having occasion to notice this to him, he did not deny it—and, since I wrote to you, he has sent me a letter beginning "Revd Sir," ending "Your obt Servant," and in the course of it saying "You treated me a greater insult than ever I sustained. I demand of you, as you will answer for it hereafter, not to take my son Harry as a novice." Is he mad? I am conscious of nothing but great affection and active kindness towards him—and I really don't know what his charge is. As far as I can make out, it is that I have tried to make his sons like me more than him—but there is something he has said to Harry, which he has not said to me. You may conceive what a dreadful trial this is at the moment for dearest Harry.[171]

Division or separation was another area of life that caused pain for Newman in relation to his friends. When the Oratory was divided and some members were assigned to the London foundation, Newman felt the separation very keenly. Speaking of the separation from Dalgairns, he wrote in 1849: "Your loss to me, my dearest F. Bernard, is in many ways very great indeed. I have the tenderest recollections of you, and shall always love you;

---

169. William Froude to JHN, 29 December 1859, in *LD* 19:270. Newman continued in dialogue with Froude concerning certainty in faith for over twenty years.

170. JHN to William Froude, 2 January 1860, in *LD* 19:272.

171. JHN to Henry Wilberforce, 25 October 1856, in *LD* 17:418. For other letters where a misunderstanding or disagreement occurred, see the following letters: JHN to Henry Wilberforce, 18 January 1859, in *LD* 19:21–22; JHN to J. R. Bloxam, 8 March 1877, in *LD* 28:174.

Spiritual Direction and Friendship

and I hope and know you will always give me your prayers, nor shall I be so far off as not to have still the comfort of your intimacy and your counsel."[172]

Similarly, after Newman had gone to Ireland to assume the rectorship of the Catholic University, he wrote back to his fellow Oratorian, Edward Caswell, saying how difficult it was to leave his friends and community. "No one knows but myself the desolateness I sustain in leaving Birmingham, and being thrown among strangers—I trust it will be taken as my penance, and be of eternal good to me—but it has been my lot through life, to make friends and to be sent away from them."[173] When Newman accepted this position in Ireland, he had hoped that his friend, Henry Wilberforce, would come and be one of the professors. Wilberforce kept vacillating, and Newman's disappointment is obvious in the following letter.

> I have certainly thought you were trifling with the University for some time, and I have said to people "O he will never take part in it." . . .
>
> And now you still are going on your shilly shally way. I have offered you a *Professorship* and you won't say whether you will take it or not . . .
>
> From the first you have taken up the whole matter in quite a different way from Thompson or Stewart. *They* have thrown themselves into it with enthusiasm. But I have long said to Ambrose, "H. W. never comes into any of my plans, much as he loves me." . . . I *don't wish* you to do so, merely *because* I ask you;—unless you do it with love, I don't want you to do it at all.[174]

Newman's Genius for Friendship

Newman had a genius for friendship. When one visits his room at the Birmingham Oratory, one is struck by the fact that the wall above the alcove, where his little altar is located, is lined with photographs of his friends. As he offered Mass, he remembered them. When, in October 1845, he was received into the Roman Catholic Church, what pained him was the separation of friends. He felt it physically—as a pain about the heart. The loneliness was intense. "It was like going on the open sea." However, he was now consoled by the real presence in the Blessed Sacrament. "This is what swallows up every

---

172. JHN to J. D. Dalgairns, 26 April 1849, in *LD* 13:131.
173. JHN to Edward Caswell, 25 February 1854, in *LD* 16:58.
174. JHN to Henry Wilberforce, 13 June 1854, in *LD* 16:159–60.

pain," he wrote to his close friend, Henry Wilberforce. "When I am thus in his presence you are not forgotten. It is *the* place for intercession."[175]

Newman never forgot that people are social beings, that they do not live in a vacuum, and that only by cultivating natural love and friendship, will they learn to love supernaturally. How deeply he felt the need for friendship and intimacy emerges from an entry in his diary for March 25, 1840. After a detailed description of his illness in Sicily, he asked himself why he was writing all this:

> For myself, I may look at it once or twice in my whole life, and what sympathy is there in *my* looking at it? Whom have I, whom can I have, who would take interest in it? . . . This is the sort of interest which a wife takes and none but she—it is a woman's interest—and that interest, so be it, shall never be taken in me. All my habits for years, my tendencies, are towards celibacy. I could not take that interest in this world which marriage requires. . . . And therefore, I willingly give up the possession of that sympathy, which I feel is not, cannot be, granted to me. Yet, not the less do I feel the need of it. Who will care to be told such details as I have put down above? Shall I ever have in my old age spiritual children who will take an interest such as a wife does? . . . What a dream is life. I used to regret festival days going quick. They are come and they are gone; but, so it is, time is nothing except as the seed of eternity.[176]

Newman's capacity for friendship and love can be measured by the love he inspired in others, because no one is loved who is not lovable, and no one is lovable who is not loving. However, love can diminish with age if a person becomes circumscribed, even totally imprisoned in his own habits and wishes. Yet, in spite of his shyness and the difficult gift of self-awareness, Newman's love and sympathy for others did not narrow as he grew older, but increased and included quite different types of people. Newman seems to have acquired this openness by the way he passed through the successive crises of his personal development. In his youth, Newman experienced the temptation of intellectualism and self-will. Later in life, he experienced repeated rejection. However, he not only survived these crises but each time emerged with a greater capacity to feel for others.

When Newman became a Roman Catholic and had to choose a form of life to follow, it was natural that he did not choose a "regimented" religious life, but something more informal, not a rule, but a fellowship—what he was

---

175. JHN to Henry Wilberforce, 26 February 1846, in *LD* 11:129.
176. Newman, *Autobiographical Writings*, 137–38.

to call a "weapon-less condition." He believed that a religious congregation could be established upon those uncoerced relationships which characterize a good family. If a family is to survive, it must strive for some kind of homogeneity of spirit, not by means of an imposed rule, but by the exercise of the wise diplomacy of love. Each member had to understand the minds of the rest and consult them, to consult them, to take their hints and to try and please them. Tact, not obedience to the rule, is the rule of the family. It is informed by the patient spirit of an active charity. Such were the virtues of many of the middle class families of Victorian England: these virtues were Newman's own and he believed that a religious congregation could rest upon such foundations, in which friendship could substitute for vows.

Newman's qualities were evident in the way he dealt with his academic colleagues at the Catholic University. He was firm without being assertive. The challenge of his job was to bring together and work with many different kinds of persons—to utilize talents while minimizing limitations and to inspire diverse personalities to work together for a common good. His professor of fine arts, John Pollen has described their association:

"What a time it was! Reading, thinking, writing, working, walking with him in times of recreation over the pleasant fields, parks and gardens of the Phoenix; listening to talk that was never didactic and never dull.... He shed cheerfulness as a sunbeam sheds lights, even when many difficulties were pressing. He encouraged you to put your conclusions into terms; to see what they looked like from various sides ... but all this under the form of easy conversation."[177]

Newman had an ability to make friends easily—especially among the laity. In turn, they were attracted to him because he was "natural, energetic, humorous and practical." He likewise fostered a spirituality which may be better understood by laymen than by clergy. Many of his most famous and profound generalizations about the spiritual life arise from a prolonged and detailed examination of some friend or correspondent. He was certainly a master of the spiritual life as lay-people understood it, and he kept this balance to the very end. In 1879, referring to Newman's Biglietto speech when he received the Cardinal's hat, his friend Pusey remarked: "The great day of John Henry Newman has come and gone, and his grand speech has been made. It was a beautiful speech, quite the old John Henry Newman speaking out the truth, yet not wounding a single heart."[178]

---

177. Letter from J. H. Pollen, 13 May 1855, in McGrath, *Newman's University*, 359.

178. *LD* 29, 144n1. His remark was contained in a letter by Dr. Pusey to the Rev. Belaney, at Christ Church, Oxford, May 20, 1879. It was reproduced in the *Guardian*, June 4, 1879, 766, and published by the *Weekly Register*, May 24, 1879, 330–31.

John Henry Newman

Summary

Since friendship is significant in the development of a person's spiritual life, Newman's personal concern for his friends was an important aspect of his spiritual direction. Newman possessed the rare gift of inspiring affection as well as reverence in those who came to know him intimately. For many people, he was a leader whom they admired and looked to for guidance. But there was another dimension of his personality that emerges from his correspondence. It was his humanness. In his letters to his friends, he felt comfortable speaking about his real feelings, his fears, his struggles, his needs, and his joys.

Newman's conversion to the Roman Catholic Church caused an adverse reaction among his family and friends, which significantly influenced his understanding of the meaning and importance of friendship. His loss of friends because of his conversion became a vehicle for his spiritual direction of others. As they sensed how difficult his conversion had been for him in regard to severed friendships, they felt comfortable seeking his advice in their struggles.

Newman came to understand friendship as a gift of God, yet a gift based on many human qualities. Basic to his understanding of friendship as gift was the sacredness, uniqueness and individuality of other persons. He understood friendship as one of the ways God manifests comfort and healing power in our world. When he felt disappointed or discouraged, he not only sought comfort and healing from God, but he also looked to his friends. In addition, he believed that friends were given to each other for encouragement and support. In fidelity to his friends, he would often write to encourage them and expected them to do the same. Honesty was an important quality in Newman's understanding of friendship. He always desired to "speak the truth in love," even at the risk of losing a person's friendship. However, if he felt that he had been insensitive or wrong, he did not hesitate to ask forgiveness. During his Roman Catholic years, his correspondence is filled with letters to friends consoling, encouraging, supporting, and directing them in the trials of life. His own sufferings and struggles caused him to be sensitive and empathetic to the anxieties and trials of others.

One notable characteristic of friendship embedded in Newman's correspondence is fidelity. Realizing that in every friendship there would be joy and sorrow, as well as the need for reconciliation, his *Letters* attest to his lasting relationships with people. Thus, he understood difficulties or disagreements among friends as an opportunity for growth rather than occasions for diminishing or destroying friendship.

Newman has sometimes been criticized for being cold and unemotional. However, his *Letters* certainly do not verify this charge. Emerging

Spiritual Direction and Friendship

from his correspondence, is the portrait of a man who at times tended to be reserved yet was sensitive to others, a person who could feel and express his feelings for others. He was a man who had the ability to make friends easily and who felt the need for friendship and intimacy. While possessing a great sensitivity to others, he nevertheless remained a man of principle.

Summarizing his own way of looking at life and friendship, Newman wrote in 1880:

> Looking beyond this life, my first prayer, aim, and hope is that I may see God. The thought of being blest with the sight of earthly friends pales before that thought. I believe that I shall never die; this awful prospect would crush me, were it not that I trusted and prayed that it would be an eternity in God's Presence. How is eternity a boon, unless He goes with it?
>
> And, for others dear to me, my one prayer is that they may see God.
>
> It is the thought of God, His Presence, His strength which makes up, which repairs all bereavements.
>
> "Give what Thou wilt, without Thee we are poor,
> "And with Thee rich, take what Thou wilt away."
>
> I prayed that it might be so, when I lost so many friends 35 years ago; what else could I look to?[179]

A press notice, which appeared in the *Athenaeum* shortly after Newman's death in 1890, summarized the effect that Newman had on others: "It seems almost a paradox to say of the author of fifty volumes that his true sphere was in action, not thought or literature, yet it is a paradox that contains more than the usual fraction of truth. He was born to lead men; the very modesty that caused him at times to deny this concealed his dissatisfaction even with the enormous mastery he wielded over men's souls and fates for so many years. It was by personal intercourse he sought to move the world and *did* move it."[180]

---

179. JHN to John Mozley, 26 February 1880, in *LD* 29:241.
180. Hodge, "Was Newman a Saint?" 12.

John Henry Newman

Conclusion

THE LIFE OF JOHN Henry Newman intersected the lives of many of the leading ecclesiastical and political figures of the nineteenth century: Pius IX, Leo XIII, Wiseman, Ullathorne, Manning, Faber, Ward, Gladstone, Acton, Dölinger, Montalembert, among others Newman was in contact not only with the leaders of his age, but also with people from all walks of life. Through an enormous correspondence in the midst of many other duties, Newman generally wrote with an apostolic purpose in mind. In particular, he wrote, as he preached, for lay people whose duty it was to live and work in the world. Newman recognized the importance of the laity for the renewal of the Church. He frequently corresponded with lay people who desired to grow in the Christian life.

With empathetic understanding, cogent explanation, and patient waiting, Newman encouraged others to strive for holiness. For example, he urged people to perform well the ordinary duties of the day as "a short rule to perfection." Similarly, his teaching on the sacraments, his approach to penance, his devotion to the Blessed Sacrament and to Mary indicate his balanced approach to the spiritual life. His correspondence shows him to have been both a theologian and a spiritual director, although he explicitly denied that he was either—at least in the technical sense. There are several reasons why Newman claimed that he was not a theologian: first, because he was not conversant with neo-scholastic theology nor was he a specialist in any particular field of theology; in addition, he believed that he was more of a controversialist, responding to particular needs and questions as they arose. He also recognized that any claim to be a theologian might place him in jeopardy with ecclesiastical authorities.

Similarly, Newman did not consider himself a spiritual director because he felt that he did not possess the knowledge, training, experience, and patience required of a director. While his spirituality was an expression of his theology, his approach to the spiritual life and spiritual direction was grounded on scriptural and patristic study, a consciousness of the unseen world, and his personal experiences. His belief in and explanation of the centrality of Christ and the indwelling of the Holy Spirit, as well as his dogmatic, sacramental, and ecclesial principles gave his understanding of the spiritual life a strong theological framework. In a century that tended to separate theology and piety, Newman's letters reveal that he consistently sought to keep them united. Accordingly, his spiritual direction flowed from and expressed his personal theology. His correspondence frequently provided him with the occasion to work out his theology and spirituality. In particular, the questions of both old friends and new critics often challenged Newman's concept of faith and provided the vehicle for his understanding of faith to develop. In retrospect, it can be seen that his correspondence was especially important during the years when he was not writing publicly, since his letters discussed a number of topics which later appeared in his books. In effect, his correspondence provided Newman with the opportunity of deepening his theological understanding and spiritual awareness.

The hefty volumes of *Letters* from his Roman Catholic years make it clear that there are two major bases for his spiritual direction—theology and experience. At times, Newman's spiritual direction was a reflection of a particular theological position; this is especially the case in the development in his understanding of faith and church which were, in turn, reflected in the spiritual direction he gave to others. At other times, his own experience greatly affected his direction, as was the case particularly with his advice on vocation, religious life and friendship. Sometimes both theology and experience were operative sources in his guidance as was the case with his emphasis on the Providence of God. The specific determinant of Newman's advice was usually that aspect of the Christian life which was most relevant to his correspondent's situation.

Not only did Newman's spiritual direction possess a strong theological basis, he also believed that some type of devotional life was a necessary support for faith. Accordingly, he encouraged individuals to nurture an active devotional life based on sound Roman Catholic doctrine. Correspondingly, while he wanted people to be free to choose those devotions best suited for them, he did not favor "tangential" spiritualities, or expressions of devotions that were on the fringes of the Church's life.

A second fundamental principle on which Newman based his spiritual direction was experience. His correspondence shows how his guidance of others was often influenced by his own experience. As an Anglican, his family life, his first conversion experience, the death of his sister, and his illness in Sicily, as well as his contacts with a variety of people—all contributed to the formation of his own spiritual life and continually found expression in his letters. Similarly, as a Roman Catholic, Newman experienced various purifying events, such as the Oratory dispute, the Achilli trial, the Catholic University difficulty, the Scripture translation problem, the *Rambler* incident, the *Apologia* challenge, and the Oxford Oratory setback. All of these experiences further contributed to shaping his life, his thinking, his spirituality and consequently his direction of others.[1] For example, his experience of God's Providence provided a constant backdrop from which to direct others, particularly in times of trial; his experience of Oratorian life influenced his understanding of vocation and religious life; his experience with friends helped him to value friendship as a dimension of the spiritual life.

Newman's *Letters* do not provide a precise method or technique for spiritual direction. Rather, his approach is similar to the rhetorical style he employed in many of his other works. Accordingly, when he was seeking to convince a correspondent of a particular point, Newman would argue masterfully along certain lines of thought. For example, in trying to guide people into the Church, Newman directed others to look for apostolicity; thus, his correspondence focused on the "notes" of the Church. Similarly, in directing others in their concerns about the doctrine of infallibility, his approach was to help people understand the infallibility of the Church and only then to consider the infallibility of the Pope as one of the Church's teachings. In this sense, there is a general pattern or style to his direction. Nonetheless, the needs of each individual appear to have been the primary factor in molding his responses. Consequently, what emerges from his correspondence is not so much a method or technique of spiritual direction, but the personality of Newman. In addition to his theological acumen and experience, Newman's *Letters* implicitly show the unique importance of the personality of the spiritual director. His correspondence highlights the belief that one of the means that God uses to manifest His grace, love and presence in the process of direction is the person of the director. By implication, the director is truly a divine instrument in spiritual direction.

Newman believed that his own role was one of personal influence. His correspondence shows that his spiritual direction was characterized by several features: first, he respected the dignity of the individual. His letters had a way of making people feel accepted, important, and unique; for example, he patiently responded to their inquiries, sometimes writing at length, at other times corresponding over a period of many years. In addition, Newman possessed a genuine concern for every person. For instance, his correspondence encouraged and supported people in their search for truth and

---

1. Appropriating the Pauline theme of the Christian life as a sharing in the Paschal Mystery, Newman believed that he was participating in Christ's death-resurrection process through the purifying events of his life, and his correspondence encouraged others to do the same.

faith, in the quest for finding their vocation, in guiding them in personal trials. Newman also had the kind of personality that could challenge people while still allowing them to be free. Without being overbearing, his desire was "to speak the truth in love," to be honest with people even at the risk of personal sacrifice; yet, when he realized that he had been insensitive or wrong, he did not hesitate to apologize. Finally, his correspondence shows that Newman was extremely sensitive to others. People constantly wrote to him about almost every facet of life, presumably because they believed he would understand. He had a way of eliciting from others what was really on their minds and in their hearts. Because of his own personal struggle in coming to the Roman Catholic Church, Newman understood the hesitation of others; because of his own experience of sickness and death, Newman could appreciate what others were experiencing; because he had personally known failure and misunderstanding, he could be empathetic with others. He was a man of great sensitivity.

Newman, whose personality was many sided, resembled the Fathers of the Church, whose works he cherished and studied; like them, he was a preacher, spiritual director, theologian all in one. Nonetheless, the more one studies his correspondence, the more human Newman becomes; his strengths and limitations are more clearly appreciated as integral to his unique personality. Because the purpose of letters is so different from that of books or sermons, correspondence enables us to catch a glimpse of the inner workings of a person. Emerging from Newman's *Letters* are certain qualities that tend to go unnoticed in his other literary works. The dominant quality which surfaces in Newman's correspondence is his humanness. With his friends, Newman felt he could be free, sincerely manifesting what was on his mind and in his heart. In his letters to his friends, he spoke about his real feelings, his needs, his struggles, his joys.

Finally, Newman's *Letters* offer the opportunity to experience a wealth of information on how Newman understood the spiritual; life and how he directed others to grow in their life of faith.

Appendix

Achilli, Giovanni (1803–1860), born in Italy; ordained Dominican priest in 1825; married in 1849; after the libel trial, he came to America.

Acland, Lady, wife of Sir Thomas Acland. Both were close to Pusey; Sir Thomas was guardian of Pusey's children.

Acton, Sir John (1834–1902), born in Italy, a pupil of Döllinger; Member of Parliament and proprietor of *The Rambler* in 1858; strongly opposed to the definition of "papal infallibility."

Allen, John (1810–1886), scholar of Trinity College, Cambridge; friend of Fitzgerald, Thackeray, and Tennyson; first corresponded with Newman in 1839.

Alleyne, Arthur, joined the Roman Catholic Church at 16; left the Church to become a deacon in the Anglican Church; wrote to Newman about his difficulties in 1860.

Allies, Mrs. T. (1822–1902), Eliza Newman, married T. W. Allies in 1840, became a Roman Catholic in 1850, four months before her husband.

Allies, Thomas (1813–1903), greatly influenced by Newman, joined the a Roman Catholic Church in 1850; became a lecturer at the Catholic University in Dublin in 1855.

Anstice, Elizabeth (1807–1889), widow of Joseph Anstice who was a friend of Gladstone. She became a Catholic in 1845.

Argyll, Duchess of (1801–1874), Anne Cuninghame, married the seventh Duke of Argyll in 1831; became a Catholic in 1851 and was a benefactor of the Oratorians.

Appendix

Arnold, Thomas (1795–1842) the "Elder," a fellow of Oriel but an opponent of the Tractarian Movement, was headmaster of Rugby.

Arnold, Thomas (1823–1900) the "Younger," received into Roman Catholic Church in 1856; professor at Catholic University in Dublin; left the Church and later returned.

Arundel, Countess of (1820–1886), Augusta Catherine, married the Earl of Arundel, the fourteenth Duke of Norfolk in 1839; became a Roman Catholic in 1850; generous to charities.

Banner, H. W. (1783–1865), Liverpool merchant and philanthropist.

Bathurst, Catherine (1825–1907), became a Roman Catholic in 1850; began a school for girls and later an orphanage for boys; tried her vocation in two religious communities; depended on Newman for guidance and friendship.

Bellairs, Henry, Anglican priest; professor at University of Bombay; wrote to Newman for advice in preaching on the subject of eternal punishment.

Bellasis, Edward (1800–1873), distinguished parliamentary lawyer; became life-long friends with Newman in 1839; became a Roman Catholic in 1850. His family was devoted to Newman; two of his sons joined the Birmingham Oratory.

Bellasis, Monica (1855–1918), daughter of Edward Bellasis; entered the Society of the Holy Child in 1879.

Bellasis, Mrs. Edward (1815–1898), Eliza Jane, married Edward Bellasis in 1835; mother of ten children; became a Roman Catholic in 1851.

Berdoe, Edward, London chemist; became interested in Catholicism through reading the *Apologia*; received into the Roman Catholic Church in 1866.

Beveridge, William (1637–1708), went to St. John's College, Cambridge; ordained in 1661; his *Private Thoughts* revealed the awe with which he entered into his ministerial duties.

Bittleston, Henry (1818–1886), was received into the Roman Catholic Church by Newman in 1849; joined the Birmingham Oratory in 1850 but left in 1879; went to Rome in 1867 with Ambrose St. John to vindicate Newman.

Blachford, Lord, see Rogers, Sir Frederic.

Blennerhassett, Sir Roland (1839-1909), a liberal Roman Catholic and lifelong friend of Döllinger and Sir John Acton; Member of Parliament.

Bloxam, John R. (1807-1891), Newman's curate at Littlemore; regular visitor at the Birmingham Oratory though he never became a Roman Catholic.

Bourne, Henry (1826-1870), became a Roman Catholic in 1845; his son Francis (1861-1935) became Archbishop of Westminster (1903) and a cardinal (1911).

Bowden, Catherine (1844-1940), Sister Mary Alban, third daughter of Henry Bowden; in 1868 became a Dominican nun at Stone, the convent where Mother Margaret Mary Hallahan was superior.

Bowden, Emily (1832-1909), younger daughter of Mrs. J. W. Bowden.

Bowden, Henry (1804-1869), younger brother of J. W. Bowden; he and his family became Roman Catholics in 1852.

Bowden, John (1829-1874), elder son of Mrs. J. W. Bowden; became a Roman Catholic in 1848; joined the English Oratory in 1850; Faber's biographer.

Bowden, Marianne (1831-1867), elder daughter of Mrs. J. W. Bowden; entered the Visitation Convent in 1852.

Bowden, Mrs. Henry (1806-1864), Marianne Burgoyne, second wife of Henry Bowden; received into the Roman Catholic Church in 1852.

Bowden, Mrs. J. W. (1804-1896), Elizabeth Swinburne, youngest daughter of Sir John Swinburne; married Newman's great friend J. W. Bowden in 1828; became a Roman Catholic in 1846.

Bowles, Emily (1818-1904), first met Newman in 1840; became a Roman Catholic in 1843; joined the Society of the Holy Child Jesus, which Cornelia Connolly (1809-1879) founded in 1846.

Bredin, James (1864-?), corresponded with Newman and became a Roman Catholic in 1888; after trying his vocation at the Birmingham Oratory, he became a priest in the Birmingham diocese.

Bretherton, Eleanor (1845-1887), Mrs. F. J. Watt, had Newman as her confessor from childhood. Newman officiated at her wedding in 1866 and was always concerned for the welfare of her family.

Appendix

Bretherton, Mrs. Peter, mother of Eleanor, was a frequent correspondent with Newman.

Brown, Thomas (1798–1880), Benedictine of Downside; first bishop of Newport in 1850; delated Newman's *Rambler* article to Rome in 1859 but later wanted Newman as his theologian at Vatican I.

Brownlow, William (1830–1901), Anglican priest who became a Roman Catholic in 1863, a diocesan priest in 1866 and Bishop of Clifton in 1894.

Buchanan, Emily, became a Roman Catholic against the wishes of her family and friends after she read Newman's a *Letter to the Duke of Norfolk*.

Burnand, Francis. (1836–1917), became a Roman Catholic in 1858. A lawyer and writer of plays, he later became the editor of *Punch* in 1880.

Butler, Joseph (1692–1752), graduated from Cambridge; ordained an Anglican priest in 1718; appointed Anglican Bishop of Bristol (1738–1750) and Durham (1750–1752), influenced Newman through his *Analogy of Religion, Natural and Revealed* (1736).

Campbell, Robert (1814–1868), born in Scotland; studied law at Edinburgh; friend of Wegg-Prosser. After corresponding with Newman, he became a Roman Catholic in 1852. He devoted much time to the education of the poor.

Capes, John Moore (1812 –1889) an Anglican priest who became a Roman Catholic in 1845; founded the *Rambler* in 1848; returned to the Church of England in 1870, but rejoined the Roman Catholic Church in 1882.

Caswall, Edward (1814–1878), attributed his conversion to Newman and his *Development of Christian Doctrine*; after his wife's death in 1849, he joined the Birmingham Oratory; famous as a writer and translator of hymns.

Chatterton, Lady Henrietta (1806–1876), Georgina Lascelles, a writer who married Sir William Chatterton in 1824 and, after his death, Edward Dering in 1859; received into the Roman Church by Newman in 1865. She wrote Newman about her religious difficulties.

Christie, Lydia, became a Roman Catholic in 1879 after consulting Newman; she attended his funeral; her son later became an Oratorian.

Appendix

Church, Helen (1858–1900), twin daughter (with Mary) of R. W. Church; married Francis Paget, who became Bishop of Oxford in 1901.

Church, Mary (1858–1954), twin daughter (with Helen) of R. W. Church and author of *Life and Letters of Dean Church*.

Clark, Mrs. William, wrote to Newman in 1873. Although she was drawn to the Roman Catholic Church, she feared the reaction of her husband. Newman wrote to him; she became a Roman Catholic in 1877.

Clifford, William (1823–1893), served Newman's first Mass in 1847; ordained priest in 1850; bishop of Clifton in 1857; Scripture scholar and staunch friend of Newman, he preached the sermon at Newman's funeral.

Coffin, Robert (1819–1885), received into the Roman Catholic Church in 1845; entered the Oratorian novitiate at Rome in 1847, where he was ordained a priest; chosen to go to the London Oratory, he joined the Redemptorists in 1850. Later, he opposed Newman.

Coleridge, Henry (1822–1893), brother of John (Lord) Coleridge; Fellow of Oriel in 1845, he was received into the Roman Catholic Church in 1852; ordained a priest in 1856 and entered the Jesuits; he was a close friend and frequent correspondent of Newman.

Coleridge, Lord (1820–1894), John, brother of Henry; appointed Lord Chief Justice in 1873. He had known Newman at Oxford; after the *Apologia*, he became an admirer and close friend.

Cope, Sir William (1811–1883), Anglican priest and follower of the Tractarians, who collected all of Newman's works; two of his children became Roman Catholics.

Copeland, William (1804–1885), close friend of Newman; curate at Littlemore in 1840; instrumental in bringing Keble, Rogers and Church into contact with Newman again. Copeland served as the editor of the republication of Newman's *Parochial and Plain Sermons* in 1869.

Crawley, Charles (1788–1871), high Churchman and an admirer of Newman; when Newman left Littlemore, Crawley bought his land.

Cullen, Archbishop Paul (1803–1878), became Archbishop of Armagh in 1850 and Archbishop of Dublin in 1852; invited Newman to found the Catholic University in Dublin; Cullen, though

Appendix

friendly, was difficult to work with; he was the first Irish bishop to be named a cardinal.

Dalgairns, John (1818–1876), a young Tractarian who became a Roman Catholic in 1845; ordained a priest in 1846; he made his Oratorian novitiate with Newman in Rome in 1847; Dalgairns succeeded Faber as superior of the London Oratory.

Darnell, Nicholas (1817–1892), lawyer; became a Catholic in 1847; joined the Birmingham Oratory in 1848; ordained a priest in 1849, he was appointed the first headmaster of the Oratory school in 1859 but resigned in 1861 due to a conflict with Newman.

Daunt, William (1807–1894), an ardent Irish nationalist who became a Roman Catholic in 1827; helped inaugurate the movement which led to the disestablishment of the Church of Ireland.

Demainbray, Francis (1795–1846), friend of the Tractarians; in 1844 he was inquiring whether Newman still went to Church.

Dering, Edward (1827–1892), second husband of Lady Chatterton in 1859; both were received into the Roman Catholic Church by Newman in 1865.

Doddridge, Philip (1702–1751), nonconformist divine; ordained Anglican priest in 1730. His most noted work is *On the Rise and Progress of Religion in the Soul*.

Dodsworth, William (1798–1861), friend of Newman in 1838; helped Pusey to found the first Anglican sisterhood in 1845; friend of Allies and Manning; became a Roman Catholic in 1850; wrote Catholic apologetic books.

Du Boulay, Sister Mary Gabriel (1826–1906), niece of Catherine Ward; received into the Roman Catholic Church by Newman in 1850; entered the convent at Clifton under Mother Margaret Hallahan.

Dunn, Margaret, young penitent of Newman; thought of becoming a nun, but felt obliged to care for her parents. Newman encouraged her in her lonely life.

Dunne, David (1828–1892), appointed lecturer in Logic at the Catholic University in 1854; devoted to Newman throughout his life.

Edwards, George, was secretary of the London Evangelization Society.

Emly, Lord (1812–1894), see Monsell, William.

Appendix

Faber, William (1814–1863), author and poet; met Newman in 1837; became a Roman Catholic in 1845; founder of a community known as Brothers of the Will of God who joined the Oratory in 1848; Newman made Faber the superior of the London Oratory in 1849.

Fielding, Lord (1823–1892), Rudolph Basil, was received into the Roman Catholic Church in 1850 along with his wife; became the eighth Earl of Denbigh in 1865.

Forbes, George (1821–1875), founded a press which issued theological pamphlets and liturgical books.

Forbes, Helen, became a Roman Catholic in 1846; wrote to Newman because she had neither comfort nor peace in the Church.

Forsaith, Robert, was a Congregationalist minister at Hertford.

Fortey, Emily, wrote to Newman as a teenager about her desire to become a Roman Catholic. She was received into the Church in 1884 and visited Newman in 1887.

Fourdrinier, Jemima, Newman's mother, of a Huguenot family driven from France after the revocation of the Edict of Nantes (1685); a practicing member of the Church of England; John Henry was the eldest of six children.

Fox, Ellen, a convert, who was received into the Roman Catholic Church in 1868.

Fräulein M. wrote to Newman in 1883 for direction concerning her doubts of faith. Newman asked her to find a priest to direct her and to trust in God's love for her.

Frederic (Brother), see Goodwin, Thomas.

Froude, Isy (1840–1931), Eliza, eldest daughter of William Froude; became a Roman Catholic in 1859; faithful friend of Newman.

Froude, James (1818–1894), historian, younger brother of Richard Hurrell and William Froude.

Froude, Mrs. William (1809–1878), frequent correspondent and close friend of Newman; married William Froude in 1839; became a Roman Catholic in 1857.

Froude, Richard Hurrell (1803–1836), close friend of Newman and fellow of Oriel. Along with Newman and Keble, he was one of the principal founders of the Oxford Movement.

Appendix

Froude, Robert (1846–1924), third son of William Froude; received into the Roman Catholic Church by Newman in 1863.

Froude, William (1810–1879), fourth son of Archdeacon Froude; railway engineer and later naval architect; agnostic friend of Newman; his wife and children became Roman Catholics.

Fullerton, Lady Georgiana (1812–1884), writer and novelist; daughter of the ambassador to France; became a Roman Catholic in 1846; after her son's death, she gave herself to works of charity.

Gainsford, William (1842–1926), lost his belief in the authority of the Church; came to visit Newman and corresponded with him; returned to Roman Catholicism by the early nineties.

Giberne, Maria (1802–1885), Sister Pia, lifelong friend and correspondent of Newman; in 1828, Newman became her spiritual director; she became a Roman Catholic in 1845 and a Visitation nun in 1863.

Gladstone, William (1809–1898), educated at Oxford; drawn to Tractarianism; elected a Member of Parliament in 1832; Prime Minister of England four times; friends with Cardinal Manning; wrote polemical pamphlets against Vatican I; prompted Newman's *Letter to the Duke of Norfolk*.

Godwin, Thomas, (Brother Frederic), was Faber's servant and followed him to the Oratory as a lay brother; in 1854, he left and married.

Goodwin, William, solicitor; a Methodist, who wrote to Newman in 1884, seeking certitude in religious belief.

Gordon, John (1811–1853), brother of William; became a Roman Catholic in 1847; joined the Oratory in 1848; went to Italy to collect witnesses for Achilli trial in 1852; died the following year; Newman dedicated *The Dream of Gerontius* to him.

Gordon, William (1827–1900), brother of John; became a Roman Catholic in 1847; joined the Oratory with his brother in 1848; went to London Oratory in 1849, and was ordained the following year.

Hallahan, Mother Margaret (1802–1868), born in London; met Newman at Bishop Ullathorne's consecration and remained a faithful friend throughout her life. In 1859 she began a congregation of Dominican nuns.

Appendix

Hammer, Anthony (1817–1907), became a Roman Catholic in 1849 after corresponding with Newman; briefly joined the London Oratory; always supported Newman, especially in his Oxford plans.

Hampden, Renn (1793–1868), Broad Churchman who opposed the Tractarians; became Regius professor of divinity in 1836; later, despite much opposition, became a bishop in the Anglican Church.

Hardman, John (1812–1867), leading Birmingham Roman Catholic; owner of ecclesiastical metal works; prominent in collecting money for Newman during the Achilli trial.

Harrison, Charles, came from Cheshire; converted to Roman Catholic Church before Newman; considered joining the Oratory, but decided against it.

Haweis, Thomas (1734–1820), graduated from Christ Church, Oxford; ordained an Anglican priest in 1757; author of about forty works; his *Communicant's Spiritual Companion* enjoyed considerable popularity.

Hawkins, Edward (1789–1882), Provost of Oriel College; staunch opponent of both the Oxford Movement and the efforts of Newman and Froude to raise the standards at Oriel by tutoring.

Helbert, Magdalene, a married woman with four children; corresponded with Newman about joining the Church in 1869; became a Roman Catholic in 1874.

Herbert of Lea, Lady (1822–1911), called on Newman in Rome in 1847. Manning was her spiritual director from the time of her marriage in 1846 and received her into the Roman Catholic Church in 1865.

Heywood, Lady Margaret, married her first cousin Sir Thomas Heywood in 1846 and became a Roman Catholic in 1876.

Holmes, Mary (1815–1878), spent her life as a governess; one of Newman's major correspondents; she met him in 1842 and he was her director until she became a Roman Catholic in 1844.

Hope, James (1812–1873), began a friendship with Newman in 1837. One of the chief legal advisors of the Tractarians; married Charlotte Lockhart in 1847, the grand-daughter of Sir Walter Scott; inherited Abbotsford and changed his name to Hope-Scott; became a Catholic in 1851; Newman often sought advice from him.

Appendix

Hope-Scott, James (1812–1873), see Hope, James.

Hope-Scott, Mary (1852–1920), only surviving child of James Hope-Scott by his first marriage; married in 1874; wrote various Catholic biographies and always remained in close touch with Newman.

Houldsworth, Mrs., wrote to Newman about her desire to join the Church and also visited him. With his encouragement, she became a Roman Catholic in 1872.

Howard, Philip (1801–1883), Catholic Member of Parliament who was a zealous defender of Catholic causes.

Hutchison, William (1822–1863), was received into the Roman Catholic Church in 1845; ordained in 1847; joined the Oratory in 1848 with Faber and went with him to start the London Oratory in 1849.

Hutton, Arthur (1848–1912), became a Roman Catholic in 1876, joined the Oratory and was ordained in 1879. He left and married in 1884; after Newman's death, he published surprisingly bitter reminiscences about him.

Hutton, Richard (1826–1897), editor of several magazines; intervened decisively for Newman in the controversy with Kingsley; reviewed *A Grammar of Assent* sympathetically; published one of the first and best biographies of Newman in 1891.

Jenkins, Robert (1815–1896), went to Trinity College, Cambridge and took Orders in 1841; he wrote extensively on historical and ecclesiastical subjects.

Keble, John (1792–1866), fellow of Oriel, author of *The Christian Year* (1827), and became vicar of Hursley, Hampshire; though absent from Oxford, he remained a powerful spiritual force in the High Church Movement, especially after Newman left in 1845.

Kenrick, Francis (1796–1863), born in Dublin; ordained in Rome in 1821; came to America and taught theology at St. Thomas Seminary in Bardstown, Kentucky. In 1830, he became Bishop of Philadelphia; in 1851, Archbishop of Baltimore. He was a scholar who translated the Bible and wrote on Scripture and theology.

Keon, Mrs. Anne, was the widow of Miles Keon whom she married in 1846 and who died in 1875.

Kerr, Lady Henry (1811–1884), Louisa, sister of James Hope-Scott; married in 1832; became a Roman Catholic shortly after her husband in 1852.

Kingsley, Charles (1819–1875), studied at Cambridge and reacted strongly against the Oxford Movement. He accidentally gave Newman the opportunity of vindicating his career in 1864 when he wrote in *Macmillan's Magazine* that "truth for its own sake, had never been a virtue with the Roman Catholic Clergy," and attributed this opinion to Newman who replied with his *Apologia Pro Vita Sua*.

Knox, Thomas (1822–1882), went to Trinity College, Cambridge; he and Faber were received into the Roman Catholic Church together in 1845; joined the Oratory in 1848 and went to London; ordained in 1849; was known as an historian of English Catholics.

Köller, Baroness von, wrote to Newman in 1864, having been abandoned by her husband. She wondered whether she would be supported by Catholic sources if she became a convert.

Law, William (1686–1761), graduated from Emmanuel College, Cambridge; ordained an Anglican priest in 1711; published his *Serious Call* in 1828. He lived a disciplined and ascetical life.

Leahy, Patrick (1806–1875), studied for priesthood at Maynooth; became president of St. Patrick's College; appointed Archbishop of Cashel in 1857 and was always sympathetic with Newman.

Leigh, William (1802–1873), son of a wealthy Liverpool merchant, followed the Tractarian Movement and became a Roman Catholic in 1844.

Leo XIII (1810–1903), ordained in 1837; archbishop in 1843; cardinal in 1853 who voted with the majority at Vatican I; Pope in 1878 whose pontificate lasted over twenty-five years; one of the most significant Popes in recent times because of his teachings, initiative, and exceptional prestige.

Lilly, William (1840–1919), studied at Cambridge; became a Roman Catholic about 1869; wrote many articles on religion and history.

Littledale, Richard (1833–1890), went to Trinity College, Dublin; became a leading Anglo-Catholic controversialist.

Appendix

Lockhart, Martha (1798–1872), second wife of Alexander Lockhart who died in 1831; became a Roman Catholic in 1846; devoted her life to writing and promoting popular Catholic literature.

Makrena, Mother, a Basilian nun who went to Rome in 1846 where Gregory XVI and Pius IX visited her because of her reputation for sanctity.

Manning, Henry (1808–1892), went to Balliol College in 1827; took Anglican Orders in 1832; married Caroline Sargent in 1833; became a Roman Catholic in 1851 and ordained ten weeks later; became Archbishop of Westminster in 1865 and a Cardinal in 1875.

Maria Pia (Sister), see Giberne, Maria.

Mary Alban (Sister), see Bowden, Catherine.

Mary Edward (Sister), see Bellasis, Monica.

Maskell, William (1814–1890), liturgist and medievalist; matriculated at University College, Oxford in 1832; was greatly influenced by the Tractarians; took Orders in 1837; became a Roman Catholic in 1850. He was opposed to a definition of papal infallibility and had a public controversy with Manning in 1870.

Mayers, Walter (1790–1828), experienced an evangelical conversion in 1814; influenced Newman at Ealing School during the summer holidays of 1816; was curate of the church in which Newman preached his first sermon in 1824; married Maria Giberne's sister, Sarah.

Milner, Joseph (1744–1795), an ardent disciple of the rising evangelical school in 1770; his *History of the Church of Christ* emphasized the bright side of Church history.

Monsell, William (1812–1894), was received into the Roman Catholic Church in 1850; became one of Newman's close friends and correspondents; created Lord Emly in 1874 and held various offices in government.

Monteith, Robert (1812–1884), friend of the poet Tennyson; called on Newman at Littlemore in 1844; two years later he became a Roman Catholic.

Moore, John (1807–1856), Anglican priest in charge of St. Chad's Cathedral in Birmingham from 1840–1848 and President of Oscott College from 1848–1853.

Appendix

Moriarty, David (1814–1877), President of All Hallows College, Dublin; became Bishop of Kerry in 1856; friend of Newman and an opportunist at Vatican Council I.

Morris, John (1812–1880), a patristic scholar, an extremist, and an eccentric who embarrassed the Tractarians by his extravagant sermons. He became a Roman Catholic in 1846; joined Newman's community at Maryvale; was the first to leave; ordained in 1849.

Mozley, Anne (1809–1891), was the sister-in-law of Newman's sisters. Newman asked her to edit the letters of his Anglican period; she completed this a few weeks before his death.

Mozley, James (1813–1878), went to Oriel College in 1830; became very attached to Newman and was his curate at St. Mary's in 1838. He became coeditor of the *Christian Remembrances* in 1844; was one of the chief theologians of the High Church party.

Mozley, John (1805–1872), printer and publisher at Derby; brother of Thomas and James; married Newman's sister Jemima in 1836.

Mozley, Mrs. John (1808–1879), Jemima, younger of Newman's surviving sisters; married John Mozley in 1836; although she did not approve of Newman's conversion, they corresponded regularly.

Mozley, Thomas (1806–1893), Newman's pupil at Oriel College in 1825; married Newman's sister Harriett; an ardent Tractarian; succeeded Newman as editor of the *British Critic* in 1841; his *Reminiscences, Chiefly of Oriel College and Oxford Movement* (1882) was severely criticized by Newman; became a Roman Catholic in 1845.

Munro, Miss (?–1913), received into the Roman Catholic Church in 1845; Newman was her spiritual director; his last known letter to her was written in 1882.

Neville, William (1824–1905), was received into the Roman Catholic Church by Newman in 1851; joined the Oratory a week later; became Newman's secretary in later years; after Newman's death, he collected and copied Newman's letters and papers.

Nevins, J. H., became a Roman Catholic in 1868; left the Church over papal infallibility; became an Anglican deacon; married; after corresponding with Newman, he returned to the Roman Catholic Church in 1873 but returned to the Church of England in 1886.

Appendix

Newdigate, Mrs. Alfred, was married in 1860; she, her husband and children became Roman Catholics in 1875.

Newman, Francis (1805–1897), younger brother of John Henry; eventually became a Unitarian; espoused various eccentric causes; he and Newman drifted apart very early, but always kept in touch and met periodically.

Newman, Jemima (1808–1879), see Mozley, Mrs. John.

Newman, John (1767–1824), banker, who married Jemima Fourdrinier in 1799; father of John Henry Newman.

Newton, Thomas (1704–1782), graduated from Trinity College, Cambridge; ordained an Anglican priest in 1730; consecrated bishop in 1761; composed his *Dissertations on the Prophecies* in 1754.

Norfolk, Duchess of (1854–1887), Lady Flora Hastings, became a Roman Catholic in 1875; married the Duke of Norfolk in 1877.

Norfolk, Fifteenth Duke of (Henry Howard, 1847–1917), went to the Birmingham Oratory school until 1864; devout layman; supporter of Catholic schools and churches; engaged in numerous public and political activities. Newman addressed his *Letter to the Duke of Norfolk* to him in 1875; the Duke played a chief role in obtaining the cardinalate for Newman.

Northcote, James (1821–1907), greatly influenced by Newman; close friend of Pusey; became a Roman Catholic in 1846; editor of *The Rambler*, 1852–1854; President of Oscott 1860–1876.

O'Brien, Dominic (1798–1873), studied at Propaganda; ordained at Rome in 1821; Bishop of Waterford and Lismore from 1855 until his death.

Ornsby, Robert (1820–1889), married Dalgairns' sister in 1846; became a Roman Catholic in 1847; Newman appointed him professor of Greek and Latin at the Catholic University in 1854.

Pearson, Fanny, became a Roman Catholic about 1871 and then a nun of the Sacred Heart.

Penny, William (1815–1885), became a Roman Catholic in 1844; went to Rome to enter the Oratorian novitiate and was ordained in 1847; left the Oratory in 1851; always remained a friend of Newman.

Appendix

Perrin, John, was an Anglican clergyman living in Dublin; wrote to Newman in 1864 inquiring about the Catholic Church; became a Roman Catholic in 1865.

Phillipps, Ambrose (1809–1878), became a Roman Catholic at the age of fifteen; met Newman at Oxford in 1842; constantly worked for union between the Anglican and Roman Catholic Church; used his wealth and position for the restoration of the Roman Catholic Church in England.

Phipps, Edward (1806–1884), entered Exeter College in 1824; Rector of Devizes 1833–1853; Rector of Stansfield in Norfolk.

Pius IX, (1792–1878), was ordained in 1819; created archbishop 1827; cardinal 1840; Pope in 1846; his pontificate of thirty-two years is the longest on record.

Place, Charles (1814–1893), Paris lawyer; became secretary to the French ambassador to Pius IX in 1849; Maria Giberne met him at this time; Bishop of Marseilles in 1866 and a Cardinal in 1886; an inopportunist at the Vatican Council.

Plummer, Alfred (1841–1926), translated several of Döllinger's works and wrote commentaries on Scripture and books on English Church history; served as an intermediary between Döllinger and Newman.

Plumptre, Edward (1821–1891), a scholar at University College, Oxford; wrote a number of Scripture commentaries.

Pollen, John (1820–1902), an Anglican priest who became a Roman Catholic in 1852; he went to Dublin in 1855 as Newman's professor of Fine Arts and built the University Church. He was one of Newman's most devoted and faithful friends.

Poole, Sister Mary Imelda (1815–1881), Maria Ruscombe, was greatly influenced by the *Tracts* and Newman's sermons; she and her sister Lucy entered St. Catherine's Convent in 1849; she was a devoted friend of Newman.

Pope, William (1825–1905), nephew of Richard Whately; Anglican priest; became a Roman Catholic in 1853; sent Newman the copy of *Macmillan's Magazine* with Kingsley's attack which led to the *Apologia*.

Porter, Mary, wrote to Newman in 1865 praising him for the effect that he had on others.

Appendix

Pusey, Edward (1800–1882), close friend of Newman; one of the leaders of the Oxford Movement; although they only met two or three times after Newman left Oxford, they corresponded frequently.

Radford, Daniel, broker in Liverpool; an Anglo-Catholic whom Newman thought to be a "clever young Puseyite."

Renouf, Peter (1822–1897), was greatly influenced by Newman's sermons; became a Roman Catholic in 1842; went to Dublin in 1854 to become Professor of Ancient History and Geography at the Catholic University; had great interest in the controversies over infallibility.

Robins, Charles (1827–1882), matriculated at Oriel College, Oxford in 1844; Anglican priest who was in charge of Clare Market Mission, one of the poorest and worst parts of London. He thanked Newman for his parochial sermons which had helped him in his difficult ministry.

Rogers, Sir Frederic (1811–1889), a pupil of Newman's at Oriel College; was Newman's most intimate friend until religious differences divided them; in 1863, Rogers visited Newman and their friendship was restored; he was created Lord Blachford in 1871.

Romaine, William (1714–1795), Anglican divine and author, of the extreme Calvinist wing.

Rowe, Miss, an isolated and ill-instructed convert, who first consulted Newman by letter in 1873; she met him some time after 1874.

Ryder, George (1810–1880), brother-in-law of Henry Wilberforce, had Newman for a tutor at Oriel College; became an Anglican priest, converted to Roman Catholicism in 1846; Newman was his spiritual director until 1855.

Ryder, Henry (1837–1907), eldest son of George Ryder; joined the Birmingham Oratory taking the name Ignatius.

Ryder, Mrs. George (1814–1850), youngest daughter of Rev. John Sargent; in 1834 she married George Ryder and her sister married Henry Wilberforce.

Ryder, Sophie (1817–1901), sister of George Ryder; became a Roman Catholic in 1846 and a Good Shepherd nun in 1849.

Rymer, Frederick, President of St. Edmund's College, Ware from 1868–1870; he was removed by Manning on account of his inopportunist views concerning the definition of papal infallibility.

Salvo, Marquise de (1813–1892), Lucy Claxton, cousin of Manning; became a Catholic in 1846; lifelong friend of Lady Georgiana Fullerton; known for her piety and good works.

Schroeter, Baron von (1802–1866), Heinrich von Gottlieb, was born in Germany; became a Catholic in Rome; joined the Oratory in 1849 but caused trouble and left in 1850.

Scott, Thomas (1747–1821), was ordained an Anglican priest in 1773; published *The Force of Truth* which is a narrative of his religious conversion in 1773; wrote his *Commentary on the Bible* between 1788 and 1792.

Seccombe, John (1835–1895), doctor and writer who became a bishop in the Church of England in 1867.

Shiel, S. S. (1803–1871), Sir Justin, educated at Stonyhurst; joined the Indian Army and became a Major-General in 1859.

Simeon, Lady (?–1904), Catherine Dorothea, became a Roman Catholic when she married Sir John Simeon as his second wife in 1861.

Simeon, Louisa (1843–1895), eldest daughter of Sir John Simeon; tried her vocation as a Benedictine nun; consulted Newman in 1869 about her religious difficulties; married Richard Ward, only surviving son of F. R. Ward, in 1872.

Simeon, Sir John (1815–1870), became a Roman Catholic in 1851; became a friend of Newman and turned to him for advice; supported the Oratory School and Newman's efforts to found an Oratory at Oxford.

Simmons, Gilbert (1846–1919), became a Roman Catholic in 1868; went to Canada; taught at Fordham University; entered the Paulists in 1879; ordained in 1882; taught Philosophy and Theology and was master of novices.

Simpson, Richard (1820–1876), became a Roman Catholic in 1846; linguist; Shakespearean scholar; involved in *The Rambler* and the *Home and Foreign Review*; a devout and "liberal" Roman Catholic, whose extravagances Newman tried to moderate.

Smith, Albert, a civil servant and High Churchman who became a Roman Catholic about 1869.

Appendix

Smith, Alice, a prospective convert in 1870, she heard that Newman was returning to the Church of England and wrote to him for an answer and for personal counsel.

St. John, Ambrose (1815–1875), classical scholar; orientalist; began his close association with Newman in 1843; until his death, he was the constant companion and friend of Newman.

Stanton, Richard (1820–1901), joined Newman at Littlemore in 1845; received into Roman Catholic Church with him; one of the original members of the English Oratory.

Stephen, Sir James (1789–1859), strong Evangelical; possessed a great deal of political influence; showed sympathy toward Catholic heroes in his *Essays*.

Talbot, George (1816–1886), received into the Catholic Roman Church by Wiseman in 1843; ordained in 1846; refused admission into the Oratory in 1847; appointed Papal Chamberlain and played an important part in English affairs while in Rome.

Tennant, Elizabeth, a Roman Catholic who was troubled in her faith; wrote to Newman and visited him in 1878.

Thompson, Edward (1813–1891), became a Roman Catholic in 1846 under Newman's influence; devoted himself to religious, literary and translation work; he was an uncle of Francis Thompson.

Thynne, Lord Charles (1813–1894), became an Anglican priest in 1837; a Roman Catholic with his wife in 1852; after her death he was ordained a priest at Rome in 1886 by Cardinal Manning.

Ullathorne, Bishop William (1806–1889), organized the Church in Australia; consecrated Vicar Apostolic in 1846; became the first Bishop of Birmingham in 1850.

Vaughan, Herbert (1832–1903), ordained in 1854; founded the Mill Hill Missionaries and worked closely with Manning; in 1872, he became Bishop of Salford; succeeded Manning as Archbishop of Westminster in 1892; made a Cardinal in 1893.

Wackerbarth, Francis (1813–1884), Anglican clergyman who converted to the Roman Catholic Church in 1841; professor at Oscott College; went to live in Sweden in 1851.

Appendix

Walford, Edward (1823–1897), an Anglican priest who became a Roman Catholic in 1851; returned to the Church of England in 1860; became a Roman Catholic again almost at once; an Anglican once more before his death.

Walker, John of Scarborough (1800–1873), educated at Ushaw and was ordained there in 1826; became one of Newman's major correspondents.

Walton, John (1852–1908), lawyer and politician; son of a Wesleyan minister; Member of Parliament from 1892–1908.

Ward, Catherine (1813–1897), began to read Newman's sermons in 1839; Pusey became her spiritual director in 1845; became a Roman Catholic in 1849; married George Tyler in 1857.

Ward, Mrs. F. R. (1811–1889), Eliza Welsford, became a Roman Catholic with her husband in 1851; one of Newman's close friends.

Ward, William (1812–1882), an extremist Tractarian; he and his wife became Roman Catholics in 1845; from 1863–1878 he edited the *Dublin Review* and made it the organ of extreme ultramontanism.

Watt, Mrs. F. J. see Bretherton, Eleanor.

Wayte, Samuel (1819–1898), scholar of Trinity College, Oxford from 1838–1842; President 1866–1878; on December 14, 1877, he wrote to Newman inviting him to become the first Honorary Fellow of Trinity.

Wegg-Prosser, Francis (1824–1911), Member of Parliamen, 1847–1852; resigned when he was received into the Roman Catholic Church; began to correspond with Newman in 1851.

Whately, Richard (1787–1863), went to Oriel College in 1805; Principal of Alban Hall, Oxford; became Archbishop of Dublin in 1831; at Oriel, he was one of the leading Noetics; his views on logic and the Church greatly influenced Newman as he explained in the *Apologia*.

Whitty, Anna, a convert and the wife of a Liverpool journalist who founded the *Liverpool Daily Post* in 1855.

Whitty, Robert (1817–1895), met Newman in 1845; became an Oratorian but left in 1850; always remained attached to Newman; entered the Jesuits in 1857.

Wilberforce, Agnes (1845–1890), eldest surviving daughter of Henry Wilberforce; married Richard Froude as his second wife in 1881.

Appendix

Wilberforce, Henry (1807–1873), brother-in-law of George Ryder; Newman's pupil in 1826 and a lifelong friend; took Anglican Orders in 1834; became a Roman Catholic in 1850; later, he became editor of the *Catholic Standard*; Newman preached at his funeral.

Wilberforce, Mrs. Henry (1811–1878), Mary Sargent, daughter of Rev. John Sargent; sister-in-law of Manning, George Ryder and Samuel Wilberforce; married Henry Wilberforce in 1834; became a Roman Catholic in 1850.

Wilberforce, Robert (1802–1857), became a Fellow at Oriel College in 1828; a tutor there with R. H. Froude and Newman; the leading Tractarian theologian; became Manning's confidant; entered the Roman Catholic Church in 1854.

Wilberforce, Wilfrid (1850–1910), son of Henry Wilberforce; attended the Oratory School from 1859–1863; on the staff of the British Museum.

Williams, Isaac (1802–1865), Newman's curate at St. Mary's and Littlemore; after Newman's conversion, they corresponded occasionally; they met again when Newman went to see him as he was dying; Newman dedicated his *Church of the Fathers* to him.

Wilson, Margaret, a convert who complained that she had been received too soon and who was troubled by the definition of papal infallibility.

Wilson, Robert (1809–1888), had Newman for his tutor at Oriel College; took Anglican Orders in 1834; became John Keble's curate because of Newman's recommendation; he edited Keble's spiritual letters.

Wiseman, Nicholas (1802–1865), Rector of the English College in Rome, 1828–1840; Wiseman's article in the *Dublin Review* on the Monophysites was among the "blows" that upset Newman. Wiseman followed the Tractarian Movement closely; in 1850 he was made the first Archbishop of Westminster and a Cardinal.

Wood, Charlotte (1789–1873), a disciple of Newman; she and her daughter were received together and they always remained close friends of Newman.

Woodgate, Henry (1801–1874), became friends with Newman in 1825; he and Isaac Williams were with Newman in 1828 when Newman's sister Mary became ill; in 1839, he dedicated his Bampton lectures to Newman, who was godfather to his eldest daughter.

Author's Bio

PETER C. WILCOX, STD, has been a psychotherapist and spiritual director for over thirty years. He holds a doctorate in theology from the Catholic University of America and has taught at the Washington Theological Union, Loyola University Maryland, and St. Bonaventure University. He has directed retreats and conducted seminars on personality development and spiritual growth for many years.

Dr. Wilcox lives in Millersville, Maryland, with his wife and daughter.

Synopsis

JOHN HENRY NEWMAN (1801–1890) was a man who sought to integrate life and holiness. He believed that the spiritual life needed to be lived in an active and dynamic way, touching a person's fundamental attitudes and actions.

Although Newman rejected the title of spiritual director as such, it is obvious from his correspondence that directing others through various facets of the Christian life was one of his dominant concerns. Surprisingly, comparatively little has been written about Newman's idea of spiritual direction. This book investigates Newman's understanding of spiritual direction during his life as a Roman Catholic, 1845–1890. It examines the major areas in which Newman gave spiritual direction through an analysis of the correspondence from his Catholic years. It also explicitates those principles of Newman's own spiritual life that found expression in his direction of others.

Newman had a mammoth "apostolate of correspondence." His *Letters and Diaries* have been edited and published in a series of thirty-two volumes, embracing more than twenty thousand letters. The first ten volumes deal with Newman's Anglican period; the remaining twenty-two volumes cover his Catholic period and are the primary source for this book. These volumes have been studied chronologically in order to determine and extract the major areas in which Newman gave spiritual direction to others, and to investigate the stages of development in his spiritual advice.

Bibliography

Abbott, Walter. *The Documents of Vatican II.* New York: Guild, 1966.
Aquino, Frederick D. *Communities of Informed Judgment: Newman's Illative Sense and Accounts of Rationality.* Washingotn, DC: Catholic University of America Press, 2004.
Beaumont, Keith. *Blessed John Henry Newman: Theologian and Spiritual Guide for Our Times.* Fort Collins, CO: Ignatius, 2010.
Beveridge, William. *Private Thoughts.* 8th ed. London: printed for Knapton et al., 1735.
———. *Theological Works.* 12 vols. Library of Anglo-Catholic Theology. Oxford: Parker, 1842–48.
Blehl, Vincent. "The Holiness of John Henry Newman." *Month* 19 (1958) 325–34.
———. *Pilgrim Journey: John Henry Newman 1801–1845.* New York: Paulist, 2001.
———. *The White Stone: The Spiritual Theology of John Henry Newman.* Petersham, MA: St. Bede's, 1993.
Bouyer, Louis. *Newman: His Life and Spirituality.* Translated by J. Lewis May. London: Burns & Oates, 1958.
Butler, Cuthbert. *The Life and Times of Bishop Ullathorne.* 2 vols. London: Burns, Oates & Washbourne, 1926.
Butler, Joseph. *The Analogy of Religion.* New ed. London: Macmillan, 1900.
———. *The Works of Bishop Butler.* 2 vols. New ed. London: Macmillan, 1900.
Capes, J. M. "Four Years' Experience of the Catholic Religion." *Rambler* 4 (1849) 161–71.
Carney, E. J. "Theology of Providence of God." In *New Catholic Encyclopedia*, edited by the Catholic University of America, 184–86. New York: McGraw-Hill, 1967.
Connolly, John R. *John Henry Newman: A View of Catholic Faith for the New Millennium.* Lanham, MD: Rowan & Littlefield, 2004.
Cunningham, Lawrence S. *John Henry Newman: Heart Speaks to Heart; Selected Spiritual Writings.* Hyde Park, NY: New City, 2004.
Dessain, Charles S. *John Henry Newman.* London: Nelson, 1966.
———. *The Mind of Cardinal Newman.* London: Catholic Truth Society, 1974.
———. "Newman's First Conversion." In *Newman Studien*, vol. 3, edited by Heinrich Fries, 37–53. Nüremberg: Glock & Lutz, 1957.
———. *Newman's Spiritual Themes.* Dublin: Veritas, 1977.
———. "Newman's Spirituality. Its Value Today." In *English Spiritual Writers*, edited by Charles Davis, 136–60. London: Burns & Oates, 1961.
———. *Why Pray? A Defence of Prayer.* Langley, UK: St. Paul, 1969.

Bibliography

Doddridge, Philip. *The Rise and Progress of Religion in the Soul*. New ed. Leeds: Binns, 1795.

Dulles, Avery. *Newman*. Outstanding Christian Thinkers. London: Continuum, 2002.

Elwood, J. Murray. *Kindly Light: The Spiritual Vision of John Henry Newman*. Notre Dame, IN: Ave Maria, 1979.

Faber, Geoffrey. *Oxford Apostles*. London: Faber & Faber, 1933.

Fey, William. *Faith and Doubt: The Unfolding of Newman's Thought on Certainty*. Shepherdstown, WV: Patmos, 1976.

Ford, John T. *John Henry Newman: Spiritual Writings*. Modern Spiritual Masters Series. Maryknoll, NY: Orbis, 2012.

Fullerton, Lady Georgiana. *Ellen Middleton: A Tale*. 3 vols. London: E. Moxon, 1844.

———. *Grantley Manor: A Tale*. London: Moxon, 1847.

Graef, Hilda C. *God and Myself: The Spirituality of John Henry Newman*. New York: Hawthorn, 1968.

Guitton, Jean. *The Church and the Laity: From Newman to Vatican II*. Translated by Malachy Carroll. Montreal: Palm, 1964.

Harrold, Charles. *John Henry Newman: An Expository and Critical Study of His Mind, Thought and Art*. New York: Longmans, Green, 1945.

Haweis, Thomas. *The Communicant's Spiritual Companion*. London: Killy, 1763.

Hodge, Robert. "Was Newman a Saint?" *Clergy Review* 62 (1977) 9–18.

Honoré, Jean. *The Spiritual Journey of Newman*. New York: Alba, 1992.

Ivory, Thomas. "The Doctrine of Prayer in John Henry Newman." STD diss., Catholic University of Louvain, 1974.

Keble, John. *The Christian Year: Thoughts in Verse for the Sundays and Holy Days throughout the Year*. 2 vols. Oxford: Parker, 1827.

Kelly, Edward. "Newman, Vatican I and II, and the Church Today." *Catholic World* 202 (1966) 293.

Ker, Ian. *Healing the Wound of Humanity: The Spirituality of John Henry Newman*. London: Darton, Longman & Todd, 1993.

———. *John Henry Newman: A Biography*. Oxford: Clarendon, 1988.

Ker, Ian, and Terrence Merrigan. *The Cambridge Companion to John Henry Newman*. Cambridge Companions to Religion. Cambridge: Cambridge University Press, 2010.

———. *Newman and Faith*. Louvain Theological and Pastoral Monographs 31. Grand Rapids: Eerdmans, 2004.

Law, William. *A Serious Call to a Devout and Holy Life*. Edited by J. H. Overton. New ed. London: English Theological Library, 1898.

Liddon, H. P. *Life of Edward Bouverie Pusey*. 2 vols. London: Longmans, Green, 1894.

Linnan, John. "The Evangelical Background of John Henry Newman 1816–1826." STD diss., Catholic University of Louvain, 1965.

Martin, Brian. *John Henry Newman: His Life and Work*. New York: Continuum, 2000.

May, J. Lewis. *Cardinal Newman: A Study*. London: Centenary, 1945.

McGrath, Fergal. *Newman's University, Idea and Reality*. London: Longmans, Green, 1951.

Milner, Joseph. *History of the Church of Christ*. New ed. London: Cadell & Davies, 1819.

Mozley, Anne. *Letters and Correspondence of John Henry Newman during His Life in the English Church*. 2 vols. London: Longmans, Green, 1891.

Bibliography

Mozley, Thomas, *Reminiscences: Chiefly of Oriel College and the Oxford Movement*. 2 vols. London: Longmans, Green, 1882.

Nédoncelle, Maurice. Introduction to *Apologia Pro Vita Sua*, by John Henry Newman. Translated by L. Michelin-Delimoges. Paris: Bloud et Gay, 1939.

Newman, John Henry. *Addresses to Cardinal Newman with His Replies*. New ed. London: Longmans, Green, 1905.

———. *Apologia Pro Vita Sua*. Edited by David J. DeLaura. New York: Norton, 1968.

———. *The Arians of the Fourth Century*. London: Longmans, Green, 1901.

———. *Autobiographical Writings*. Edited by Henry Tristram. New York: Sheed & Ward, 1957.

———. *Certain Difficulties Felt by Anglicans in Catholic Teaching Considered: In a Letter Addressed to the Rev. E. B. Pusey, D.D.* 2 vols. London: Longmans, Green, 1891.

———. *Correspondence of John Henry Newman with John Keble and Others, 1839–1845*. Edited at the Birmingham Oratory. London: Longmans, Green, 1917.

———. *Discourses Addressed to Mixed Congregations*. London: Longmans, Green, 1906.

———. *An Essay in Aid of a Grammar of Assent*. New ed. London: Longmans, Green, 1895.

———. *An Essay on the Development of Christian Doctrine*. 6th ed. London: Longmans, Green, 1890.

———. *Essays Critical and Historical*. 2 vols. 9th ed. London: Longmans, Green, 1890.

———. *Fifteen Sermons Preached before the University of Oxford*. 3rd ed. London: Longmans, Green, 1896.

———. *Historical Sketches*. 3 vols. 5th ed. London: Longmans, Green, 1885.

———. *The Idea of a University*. London: Longmans, Green, 1902.

———. *John Henry Newman: Sermons, 1824–1843*. Edited from previously unpublished manuscripts by Placid Murray. Oxford: Clarendon, 1991.

———. *Lectures on the Doctrine of Justification*. London: Longmans, Green, 1874.

———. *Lectures on the Present Position of Catholics in England*. New ed. London: Longmans, Green, 1913.

———. *The Letters and Diaries of John Henry Newman*. 32 vols. Edited by Charles Dessain et al. London: Nelson, 1961.

———. *Letters of John Henry Newman: A Selection*. Edited by Derek Stanford and Muriel Spark. London: Owen, 1957.

———. *Loss and Gain: The Story of a Convert*. London: Longmans, Green, 1906.

———. *Newman the Oratorian*. Edited by Placid Murray. Dublin: Gill & Macmillan, 1969.

———. *On Consulting the Faithful in Matters of Doctrine*. Edited by John Coulson. New York: Sheed & Ward, 1961.

———. *Parochial and Plain Sermons*. 8 vols. London: Longmans, Green, 1902.

———. *The Philosophical Notebook of John Henry Newman*. Edited by Edward Sillem and A. J. Boekraad. 2 vols. Leuven: Nauwelaerts, 1970.

———. *Select Treatises of St. Athanasius*. 2 vols. 6th ed. London: Longmans, Green, 1895.

———. *Sermons Bearing on Subjects of the Day*. London: Longmans, Green, 1902.

———. *Sermons Preached on Various Occasions*. London: Burns & Lambert, 1857.

———. *The Theological Papers of John Henry Newman on Faith and Certainty*. Edited by Hugo M. de Achaval and J. Derek Holmes. Oxford: Clarendon, 1976.

———. *Tracts for the Times*. 6 vols. New ed. London: Rivington, 1839.
———. *Verses on Various Occasions*. New ed. London: Longmans, Green, 1890.
Newton, Thomas. *Dissertations on the Prophecies*. 2 vols. New ed. London: Sharpe, 1820.
O'Connell, Marvin R. *The Oxford Conspirators: A History of the Oxford Movement, 1833–45*. New York: Macmillan, 1969.
Page, John. *What Will Dr. Newman Do? John Henry Newman and Papal Infallibility, 1865–1875*. Collegeville, MN: Liturgical, 1994.
Purcell, Edmund. *Life of Cardinal Manning, Archbishop of Westminster*. 2 vols. 4th ed. London: Macmillan, 1896.
Sarolea, Charles. *Cardinal Newman and His Influence on Religious Life and Thought*. Edinburgh: Clarke, 1980.
Scott, Thomas. *Essays on the Most Important Subjects in Religion*. 9th ed. London: Seeley, 1822.
———. *Force of Truth*. 4th ed. London: Seeley, 1817.
Swanston, Hamish. "Newman Praying." *Mount Carmel* 14 (1966) 133–36.
Tarugi, Francesco. *The Lives of the Companions of St. Philip Neri*. London: Richardson, 1847.
Teresa of Avila. *The Complete Works of Teresa of Jesus*. Translated by Edgar Allison Peers. 2 vols. New York: Sheed & Ward, 1946.
Trevor, Meriol. *Newman: Light in Winter*. Garden City, NY: Doubleday, 1963.
———. *Newman: The Pillar of the Cloud*. Garden City, NY: Doubleday, 1962.
———. *Newman's Journey*. Glasgow: Collins, 1974.
Tristram, Henry. *Newman and His Friends*. London: Lane, 1933.
Turner, Frank. *John Henry Newman: The Challenge to Evangelical Religion*. New Haven: Yale University Press, 2002.
Velocci, Giovanni. "Perception and Theology of Providence." Paper presented at the Cardinal Newman Academic Symposium, Rome, April 3–8, 1975.
Walgrave, Jan H. *Newman the Theologian*. Translated by A. V. Littledale. New York: Sheed & Ward, 1960.
Ward, Maisie. *Young Mr. Newman*. London: Sheed & Ward, 1948.
Ward, Wilfrid. *The Life and Times of Cardinal Wiseman*. 2 vols. 2nd ed. London: Longmans, Green, 1897.
———. *The Life of John Henry Cardinal Newman*. 2 vols. London: Longmans, Green, 1912.
Willey, Basil. Introduction to *Apologia Pro Vita Sua*, by John Henry Newman. London: Oxford University Press, 1964.
Zeno, Father. *John Henry Newman: His Inner Life*. 3 vols. Hilversum, Netherlands: Brand, 1960.

www.ingramcontent.com/pod-product-compliance
Lightning Source LLC
Chambersburg PA
CBHW071144300426
44113CB00009B/1077